AFTER EFFECTS 5.5 MAGIC

Nathan Moody, Mark Christiansen, Dan Ablan, Eric Chauvin, Michael "Syd" Garon, Terry Green, Eric Henry, Sherry Hitch, Kory Jones, Fred Lewis, Patrick Siemer, Ben Stokes, and Nori-zso Tolson

201 West 103rd Street, Indianapolis, Indiana 46290

After Effects 5.5 Magic

International Standard Book Number: 0-7357-1144-5

Library of Congress Catalog Card Number: 2001088392

Printed in the United States of America

First Printing: March 2002

06 05 04 03 02 7 6 5 4 3 2 1

Interpretation of the printing code: The rightmost double-digit number is the year of the book's printing; the rightmost single-digit number is the number of the book's printing. For example, the printing code 02-1 shows that the first printing of the book occurred in 2002.

Trademarks

All terms mentioned in this book that are known to be trademarks or service marks have been appropriately capitalized. New Riders Publishing cannot attest to the accuracy of this information. Use of a term in this book should not be regarded as affecting the validity of any trademark or service mark.

Warning and Disclaimer

Every effort has been made to make this book as complete and as accurate as possible, but no warranty of fitness is implied. The information provided is on an "as is" basis. The authors and the publisher shall have neither liability nor responsibility to any person or entity with respect to any loss or damages arising from the information contained in this book or from the use of the CD or programs accompanying it.

Publisher
David Dwyer

Associate Publisher
Stephanie Wall

Executive Editor
Steve Weiss

Production Manager
Gina Kanouse

Managing Editor
Sarah Kearns

Acquisitions Editors
Jody Kennen
Leah Williams

Project Editor
Jake McFarland

Copy Editor
Amy Lepore

Product Marketing Manager
Kathy Malmloff

Publicity Manager
Susan Nixon

Manufacturing Coordinator
Jim Conway

Cover Designer and Project Opener Images
Aren Howell

Interior Designer
Steve Gifford

Compositor
Kim Scott

Proofreader
Sarah Cisco

Indexer
Angie Bess

Media Developer
Jay Payne

CONTENTS AT A GLANCE

Appendixes on the CD-ROM

About the Authors

Nathan Moody is a web designer, illustrator, motion media designer, imaging expert, digital video editor, and electronic musician. He is a creative director at Fluid, Inc. (**www.fluid.com**) and works independently as the creative dictator of Atomick Industries (**www.atomick.net**). Nathan has produced innumerable projects for the web, video, film, and print. Nathan has worked on projects for AllBusiness.com, AT&T, EA Games, the Leakey Foundation, Network Associates, New Line Cinema, Random House Children's Books, Reuters/TIBCO Finance, and Sun Microsystems. A music video he created is being distributed by AtomFilms/Shockwave.com and has been shown on SciFi.com, BBC Channel 4, and the Signcast network. He has also worked on projects that have been showcased at the FlashForward and Macromedia User Conferences, and has appeared as a guest speaker at the Seybold Seminars and the Adobe Dynamic Media User Conference.

His other writing credits include *Photoshop Channel Chops* (co-authored with David Biedny and Bert Monroy, also for New Riders Publishing), a tutorial chapter for the *Adobe After Effects Classroom in a Book* (version 3 and version 4, also with David Biedny), and several white papers for Adobe Systems on Photoshop and After Effects. He has written for *MacUser* and *New Media* magazines, as well as Photoshop Central (**www.photoshopcentral.com**). He was also the series editor and lead animator for the *Photoshop Inside and Out* video learning series (**www.photoshopio.com**).

Mark Christiansen, creative director, storyteller, and technological conceptualizer, is always interested in blazing new trails (when and where appropriate). After brief stints as an actor/singer and production assistant at places like Disney and ILM, Mark had a five-year tenure at LucasArts Entertainment in Marin County, California, working in the art department. There he developed a wide range of computer graphics skills. His proudest achievement there was as lead artist of the critically acclaimed (but alas little heard of) *Star Wars: Behind the Magic*, which *Entertainment Weekly* named #1 of 1998. While at LucasArts, he led the video-compositing efforts on *Rebel Assault II*, the company's first foray into live action, using After Effects version 2; he also produced a number of trailers for 35mm film and broadcast. Mark is also a contributing editor for *DV Magazine*, a CMP publication. He has spoken at NAB and the Computer Game Developer's Conference, among others, and has been interviewed in *How Magazine* and on *E! Entertainment News*. This is his first book. Mark can be located at **www.christiansen.com**.

Dan Ablan has been animating for 10 years. He has created animations for broadcast television, numerous videos, and print media. Dan is a graduate of Valparaiso University with a degree in broadcast journalism and a minor in photojournalism. Dan's animation company, AGA Digital Studios, Inc., is located in the Chicago area and produces 3D animation for broadcast media, architectural visualization, corporate clients, and advertising agencies. Dan has written articles for the past seven years in magazines such as *LightWave Pro*, *Video Toaster User*, *3D Design*, and *3D World Magazine*. He also teaches LightWave 3D on a regular basis through AGA Digital Studios, Inc., an authorized NewTek LightWave training facility. Look for Dan's books from New Riders: *LightWave Power Guide*, *Inside LightWave 3D*, *Inside LightWave [6]*, *LightWave 6.5 Magic*, and *Inside LightWave 7*.

Eric Chauvin received his master's degree in drawing and painting from California State University Fullerton. He began his career at Industrial Light & Magic (ILM) in Marin County, California, as an assistant matte painter on Steven Spielberg's movie *Hook*. While there, he also did matte painting work on *Memoir's of an Invisible Man* and *Star Trek VI*.

Eric was part of an innovative technology in special effects known as digital matte painting. In 1993, he earned an Emmy for his work on George Lucas's television series, *The Young Indiana Jones Chronicles*. He was also nominated in 1995 and 1996 for his continued work on this series. Eric has continued to do digital matte paintings for commercials and features at ILM and work freelance on other feature film and television projects.

Michael "Syd" Garon and **Eric Henry** co-directed and animated DJ QBert's *Wave Twisters*, a hip-hop featurette that premiered at last year's Sundance film festival. "Syd" Garon is an old skool punk-rock DIY filmmaker turned computer animator. He has done everything from live visuals for bands to music videos, commercials, album covers, and even short films. Once he even had a job covering swimming pools with insulating bubble wrap stuff to keep them warm at night. Co-directing and animating *Wave Twisters the Movie* was without a doubt the best job he will ever have. Really. Except maybe for when he was in *Frosty* and went on tour and met chicks and played bass and drank too much. But that wasn't really a job, so he would have to say that definitely, on reflection, *Wave Twisters* was his most fun gig. You can email him at **suckerdjamateur@yahoo.com**. Eric Henry is a San Francisco–based computer artist and teacher. He has been making experimental digital motion pictures since 1991. Eric's work has enjoyed international success, screening at the Institute of Contemporary Art in London, the Metropolitan Museum of Art in New York City, the Museum of Contemporary Art in Chicago, and elsewhere in the United States, Europe, and Japan. Eric's computer-animated short, *Wood Technology in the Design of Structures (or, How to Live Happily Ever After)*, was named Best Experimental Video at the 1998 Atlanta International Film and Video Festival and was awarded the Festival Director's Special Citation at the 1997 Cinematexas Film, Video, and New Media Festival in Austin.

Terry Green and **Nori-zso Tolson** are the design-partners of twenty2product, a motion graphics and interactive production company in downtown San Francisco. Terry Green received a BA in graphic design/corporate identity from Rutgers in 1985 and an MFA in computer graphics from the Academy of Art in 1987. Nori-zso Tolson learned her craft within a family of television directors at Tolson Visuals, New York. She continued developing her skills as an artist at San Francisco animation house Colossal Pictures and then later as a 3D animator at Synthetic Video, where she and Terry met and decided to go into business as twenty2product in 1988. 22p's internationally recognized client work appears as title design, broadcast identity, motion graphics for commercials, and prototyping for WWW sites. 22p mostly serves a technology-, sports-, and entertainment-based clientele, including Nike, NEC, Applied Materials, IBM, Levi Strauss & Company, MTV, America Online, Yahoo!, Apple Computer, Sony, and Hewlett-Packard.

Sherry Hitch started out with an interest in visual effects while majoring in TV/film at Ball State University in Muncie, Indiana, working with Cubicomp graphic computers in 1988. Currently the supervising visual effects compositor, Sherry has been with Foundation Imaging since 1993. During her time at Foundation, Sherry has won numerous awards and has been nominated for two Emmy Awards and has won a third. Instrumental in the visually groundbreaking effects in *Babylon 5*, the first television series to utilize feature quality effects, she was one of the few Foundation animators who received a Sci-Fi Universe Award. After honing her skills as an animator and visual effects artist, she turned her sights to compositing. Her past television projects include *Babylon 5*, *Deep Space 9*, *Star Trek: Voyager*, *Mystic Knights of Tir Na Nog*, *Hypernauts*, and *Dawson's Creek*, and she has worked on feature films such as *The Jackal* and *Men in Black*. She is also working on compositing a restoration of Robert Wise's *Star Trek: The Motion Picture* for a special-edition DVD.

Kory Jones attended college at the University of Illinois before moving to Southern California in 1987, where he worked as a graphic designer and airbrush illustrator for a typesetting studio. He then started his first company, K.C. Jones & Associates, at the age of 22, creating graphics and package design on the Macintosh. In 1991, Kory closed his business to design and direct a series of children's CD-ROM games as well as numerous 3D game prototypes at GTE, including the Journeyman Project. After the two years spent completing the Journeyman Project, Kory took a position with Fox Sports designing broadcast graphics for such events as the Stanley Cup, the World Series, and Superbowl XXXI. Kory started Reality Check in 1997 with partners Andrew Heimbold and Steven Heimbold.

Fred Lewis has been designing and creating animation, with or without computers, since the early 1980s. Fred and his wife, Thalia Georgopoulos, are co-owners of a computer animation company in San Francisco called Moving Media. Since 1989, they've been designing and creating 2D and 3D computer animations for a variety of uses, including broadcast (TV commercials and shows), computer games, and interactive presentations (kiosks, CD-ROMs, the web, and so on). Fred also has a variety of experiences in related industries and has a film animation degree from San Francisco State University.

In 1990, **Patrick Siemer** was promoted from floor sweeper to animator at H-Gun Labs, a music video production company in Chicago. Desktop video had not been invented yet, so he and the artists at H-Gun labs used every method available to get pictures to move, including tearing up photos and burning them. Laborious frame-by-frame Photoshop techniques were happily abandoned when AE 1.0 was introduced. Over the next seven years, he worked his way up from animation director to commercial director, teaching and learning about After Effects within the band of artists at H-Gun. In 1997, he became a partner of H-Gun and pioneered the move of animators to H-Gun West in San Francisco, where he continued to direct broadcast design and commercials. In 2001, he formed his own company, Tape and Glue. Patrick has lectured about desktop animation techniques at numerous conferences, including ResFest and the Broadcast Design Awards. His credits from a wide array of clients include MTV, Cartoon Network, Nickelodeon, Turner Classic Movies, Pillsbury, Kraft, and Hasbro. He recently worked on the opening animated title sequence for the Disney-Pixar film, *Monsters, Inc*.

Ben Stokes co-founded H-Gun Labs in 1989 in Chicago. H-Gun, a production company, went on to do broadcast design, TV commercials, and more than 100 music videos. Stokes has directed music videos for Nine Inch Nails, Public Enemy, De La Soul, The Orb, Meat Beat Manifesto, and many more. Stokes has, all the while, been a composer of music and has started a record label with fellow music collaborator Jack Dangers (also known as Meat Beat Manifesto). Ben's own music project, Dimensional Holofonic Sound, incorporates video in a live setting. H-gun has used After Effects since version 1.0 when it fit on a single floppy disk!

About the Tech Editors

Beth Roy is a freelance motion graphics designer and visual effects artist based in Santa Monica, CA. Beth began her career at CoSA (the Company of Science and Art) as the first version of After Effects was developed. After several years at Adobe as the After Effects marketing project manager, she then followed artistic pursuits, including a passion for typography that also lead her to teaching After Effects all over the U.S. Recently she has developed a niche as a technical editor/writer for After Effects training materials. In addition, she designs broadcast graphics for television and works as a visual effects compositor.

Gary Reisman was an original member of NBC2000 back in 1994. NBC2000 was the first non-linear to broadcast department of NBC On-Air Promo, and it was one of the first departments to put After Effects to broadcast production on a daily basis. In 1998 he joined NBC Magic, the graphics department of NBC On-Air Promo. Based in Los Angeles, Gary now works as a freelance 2D/3D compositor and animator for clients such as Reality Check Studios and Access Hollywood.

Dedications

Nathan Moody: *For their patience, guidance, and support over the years, Nathan gratefully dedicates his efforts on this book to David Biedny and Krista Fechner.*

Mark Christiansen: *To my wife, Amy, for her patience (and when she runs out of that, her love and support), and to Chloë, our little peanut, who came into our family while this book was in progress.*

Acknowledgments

Nathan Moody

I would like first to thank my co-lead author, Mark Christiansen, for his insight, humor, and expertise. Extra-special thanks go out to all of our ultra-talented contributors. Special thanks also go out to Roger and Audrey Moody; Chris Nelson, Leah Williams, Katie Pendergast, David Dwyer, and the rest of the crew at New Riders Publishing; Andrew Sirontik and all of Fluid, Inc.; Ed Apodaca and Lisa Berghout at l.inc design; Stuart Sharpe; Mike Levine at Pileated Pictures; Beth Roy; Alex Lindsay; Kevin Archibald at Dystopian Records; Josh, Sharon, and Jonathan of Gun Music; and Frank Colin at Gulture Enterprises. A shout of gratitude also goes out to the original crew from Atom Films.

Mark Christiansen

The first thank you goes to Nathan Moody for pulling me into this project; it's been a true honor to collaborate with you on this. Huge thanks to Michael Natkin at Adobe for his timely, sharp feedback on my forays into expressions and to Stu Maschwitz at The Orphanage for inspiring early experiments and helping improve later ones. My metaphorical hat goes off to the Adobe After Effects development team: Dave S., Dan, Dave H., Erica, and Steve, and to the whole development team for creating such a consistently awesome product all these years. Thank you to all of the authors who said yes to contributing. Thanks to Chris Nelson and Katie Pendergast at New Riders, and good luck to Leah Williams in her next adventure as a nonfiction writer. Thanks to Jim Feeley, Dominic Milano, Kim Reed, and all the people at *DV Magazine* who have broadened my knowledge over the years (don't be mad that we did this book for New Riders—they asked!). Thanks to Jim Thill at Toolfarm and Jon Wells at RES for networking. Thanks to Nathan Moody for pulling me into this whole adventure, and to Fluid for laying me off and giving me more time to work on this book and be with my new daughter. And thanks to all of you innovative, independent creators of digital media out there who inspire us all to keep trying new things and send some of the inspiration back.

A Message from New Riders

As the reader of this book, you are our most important critic and commentator. We value your opinion and want to know what we're doing right, what we could do better, in what areas you'd like to see us publish, and any other words of wisdom you're willing to pass our way.

As Executive Editor at New Riders, I welcome your comments. You can fax, email, or write me directly to let me know what you did or didn't like about this book—as well as what we can do to make our books better. When you write, please be sure to include this book's title, ISBN, and author, as well as your name and phone or fax number. I will carefully review your comments and share them with the authors and editors who worked on the book.

Please note that I cannot help you with technical problems related to the topic of this book, and that due to the high volume of email I receive, I might not be able to reply to every message. Thanks.

Fax: 317-581-4663

Email: steve.weiss@newriders.com

Mail: Steve Weiss
Executive Editor
New Riders Publishing
201 West 103rd Street
Indianapolis, IN 46290 USA

Visit Our Web Site: www.newriders.com

On our web site, you'll find information about our other books, the authors we partner with, book updates and file downloads, promotions, discussion boards for online interaction with other users and with technology experts, and a calendar of trade shows and other professional events with which we'll be involved. We hope to see you around.

Email Us from Our Web Site

Go to www.newriders.com and click on the Contact Us link if you

- Have comments or questions about this book.
- Want to report errors that you have found in this book.
- Have a book proposal or are interested in writing for New Riders.
- Would like us to send you one of our author kits.
- Are an expert in a computer topic or technology and are interested in being a reviewer or technical editor.
- Want to find a distributor for our titles in your area.
- Are an educator/instructor who wants to preview New Riders books for classroom use. In the body/comments area, include your name, school, department, address, phone number, office days/hours, text currently in use, and enrollment in your department, along with your request for either desk/examination copies or additional information.

Foreword

When I was asked to write the foreword to the book you're holding, I thought it would be a good idea to take a look at what other people had written for technology books. Even though I've had one of my own books, the original *Adobe Photoshop Handbook*, with a foreword written by John Warnock (I never did get to thank him for that wonderful gesture) to use as a reference for what I was going to do, something just didn't seem right. In fact, I might be wrong, but I'm not sure that Mr. Warnock even really *wrote* that foreword.

So I searched for other introductions and forewords, and not just from books on computer stuff. I turned to science fiction books—Isaac Asimov could make you absolutely burst out with laughter at the self-deprecating humor he employed when introducing the work of a friendly peer. I looked at design books, art books, you name it (I have *a lot* of books, as my friends, including Nathan Moody, will confirm).

The trend with software books seems to be as follows: someone, usually from the software's publisher, injects healthy doses of marketing hype and prosaic praise into a few paragraphs that could have been culled from any press release issued by said company, with an obligatory mention of how the authors, experts in their field, will clarify, astound, and maybe even amuse you with the nuggets of knowledge offered therein. Most of the time, it seems that the authors' names are almost included as an afterthought.

I'm not going to tell you how revolutionary and amazing Adobe After Effects is—if you're reading this, you already know that. You've already likely spent countless hours of your life wishing you owned a separate monitor for the Timeline window, or for just a few more cool filters (regardless of how many you already have). You are doubtlessly aware of how After Effects has leveled the playing field for people who want to be animators, but who feel that the tens of thousands of dollars needed to purchase high-end compositing systems might be better spent as a down payment on a house.

Well, in my quest to be a different kind of guy in just about every way possible, I want to tell you a couple of stories about Nathan Moody. You see, even though I know Mark (I met him years ago at a Photoshop class I was teaching in San Francisco), it's Nathan who I spent over six years of my life working with, living with, exploring software with, hunting for rare Opal Wappaziods with... Oh, we're not supposed to talk about Wappaziods with humans from Earth. Sorry.

I first met Nathan while I was teaching at the long-gone Kodak Center for Creative Imaging (CCI), a wonderful and unfortunately short-lived experiment in technological training. Years later, Nathan worked as my trusted right-hand man, a full-fledged creative collaborator in every sense of the word, and we had our hands in all sorts of weird, fun projects. Nathan showed me an After Effects animation he was working on. I marveled at the slick, densely layered visuals, and all of a sudden I realized that there was no color; everything was black, white, and gray. Thinking that this was part of some dark Goth vision, I asked him about it. He replied, "Well, all my imported graphics are eight-bit grayscale anyway, and there's a 2 GB file size limit for QuickTime files [at the time he did this project]. Rendering my compositions as grayscale makes the output a third of the size it would be for RGB color visuals. I'm rendering it all on one machine, so I need to be efficient with my resources." Very smart, indeed.

This kind of critical, creative thinking is something practiced by all of the contributors to this book. The contributors will guide you through some of the best and brightest work being done with After Effects today, with real examples of real work done for real clients, from ultra-polished compositing to underground animation. I'll warn you now: their skill and enthusiasm is contagious.

This is not a book by writers—it's a book written by a host of talented motion artists who have helped to revolutionize broadcast design. They are musicians, actors, and artists in their own right. They're crazy, passionate, incredibly intelligent, and dedicated to their discipline. They've helped change the look of contemporary motion graphics, and want to help you to do the same.

In other words, it's a book by our own kind. Read, learn, and enjoy.

David Biedny
Winter, 2001

INTRODUCTION

Adobe After Effects has been called by its competition the "900-pound gorilla" of desktop compositing, and at least one world-renowned visual effects artist (who will remain nameless) has called it "the best compositing application on any platform." It is more than a motion graphics design and effects tool, however; it is software that is so well designed that you can problem-solve complex video or film questions by working them out in the software. You can *think* in this software.

This book uses version 5.5 of Adobe After Effects, and features specific only to version 5.5 have been incorporated into the majority of its tutorials. Every tutorial is annotated for users of After Effects 5.0, but not earlier versions. If for some reason you find yourself with a copy of this book and no copy of After Effects, by all means download the fully functional demo from **www.adobe.com** and then get yourself a copy!

Who We Are

Nathan Moody and Mark Christiansen are both experienced creators of computer graphics, as well as seasoned writers of books and journal articles about digital production. We are big proponents of desktop tools and diverse skill sets.

This book features the efforts of a number of the world's most experienced After Effects users. Most of these people have been using After Effects for several years, and a few make their living predominantly from using After Effects all day (the lucky bums).

Who You Are

We decided to target this book to intermediate and more advanced After Effects users, and we offer tutorials on some of the most advanced material we could find that would fit into a single chapter or two. Although we're thorough about leading you step by step through the material, a background in After Effects, or at least a solid understanding of digital video, will help you get the most out of this book.

Therefore, you are a skilled effects or motion graphics artist who wants to be inspired and enlightened by real-world tutorials from some very advanced users of After Effects.

What's in This Book

This book covers pure design, pure effects, and a range of material in between the two. We made a list of features in After Effects 5.5 that readers would most want to know more about and made sure these were covered. For example, After Effects users are intrigued (but often mystified) by expressions in version 5.5, so there are a full five chapters that deal only with expressions techniques, starting simple and building up to very advanced. We also cover 3D, parenting, blue-screen/green-screen effects, working with 3D renders from other applications, character animation, and a host of other current topics.

The CD

The CD accompanying this book includes the source files and project files needed to complete the exercises, as well as examples of the completed projects. We've also found a little space for links to third-party goodies and other resources.

Our Assumptions as We Wrote This Book

Overall, we assume that if you use After Effects, you're a pretty smart cookie. You not only know your way around the After Effects interface, you understand what compositing is all about and why After Effects can help you solve visual problems that can't be resolved in a video editing, 3D, or paint package.

For the expressions chapters, we assumed that you are a visual person with little or no experience using lines of code to create animations. Most of the resistance to expressions from users comes not from being underqualified to understand them, but simply from being put off by deciphering lines of text. The author of these chapters had the same problem before he tackled them, and so they (and Appendix D, "Expressions Explained") are written from the point of view of a visual person with no patience for programming.

Conventions Used in This Book

This book is way more visually oriented than most. We hope you've picked it up because you were inspired by what you saw in the pictures. The book itself is also laid out with visual people in mind, as follows:

The left column contains step-by-step instructions for completing each tutorial, along with notes and explanations of what is going on.

Corresponding to the steps on the left are screen captures, which further illustrate the steps, along with captions.

At the end of each chapter are suggested modifications or other ways of adapting the material of the tutorial for use in the real world.

CEL-STYLE ANIMATION TRICKS

"We judge ourselves by what we feel capable of doing, while others judge us by what we have already done."

—HENRY WADSWORTH LONGFELLOW, "KAVANAGH: A TALE"

Digital Ink and Paint

Traditional cel animation is a complicated process requiring massive amounts of time and labor. Pencil testing, scanning, inking, and painting are some of the steps usually handled by different departments in large animation studios. Even with the latest digital techniques, cartoon-style cel animation still involves so many steps that it can seem impossible for someone working alone. This project covers the basics of manipulating masks and using the Stroke filter to streamline the process so you can get the job done on your own without losing too much sleep.

Project 1

Cel-Style Animation Tricks

by Patrick Siemer

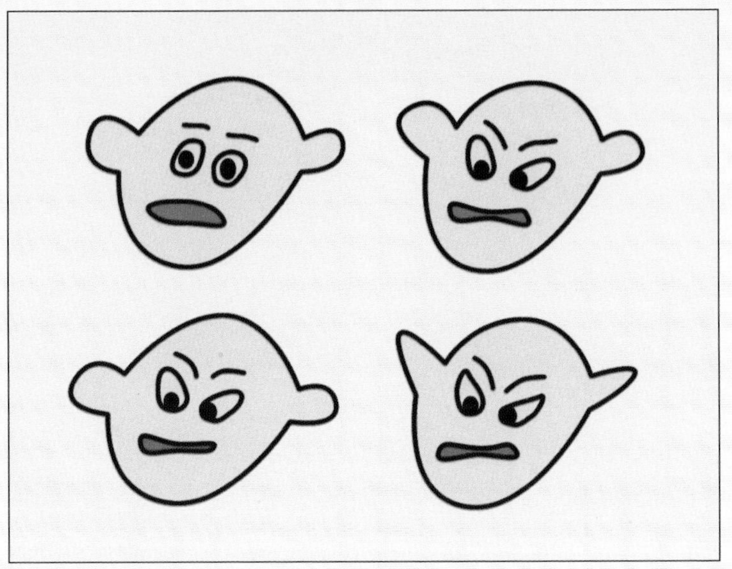

How It Works

This simple but powerful process begins with a sketch. There are four major steps: converting your line drawing to editable paths, stroking the paths, manipulating the paths, and coloring the paths. These four steps are the basis for cel-style animations, but they are useful in many situations such as for tracing over existing footage or altering the shape of any layer. The lessons in this project will give you a good foundation of techniques that can be modified to fit a wide range of styles, but they might not be perfect for every project. Simple animations can require so many layers that even an expert can get overwhelmed. When you first use these tricks in your own work, my best advice is to keep it simple.

Getting Started

Although After Effects is a powerful program, it will not draw for you, so it is important for your idea to be well thought out. Creating storyboards (or at least starting with rough sketches of your idea) is the most important step because you will need to refer to them often. Before you begin, you should be familiar with the Pen tool in After Effects. For this lesson, you will need the **worry.pct** file located on the accompanying CD-ROM; a simple little sketch made in Photoshop. The worry sketch is for those of you who don't feel like drawing. Feel free to use your own picture, but for the purposes of this tutorial, remember to keep it as simple as worry.pct.

Note: Check out the finished project, **worryface.aep**, on the accompanying CD-ROM. Also check out the finished movie, **cel_trick.mov**. There is another movie called **smellfoot.mov** on the CD-ROM that shows the technique in a real commercial.

Converting Your Drawing to Paths

In this section, you will import your cartoon drawing and use it as a template to make clean cartoon lines.

Note: You can copy line art from Illustrator and paste it directly into a layer in After Effects.

1. Import the **worry.pct** file from the accompanying CD-ROM. Drag worry.pct in the Project window to the bottom of the window and drop it onto the New Composition icon, located to the left of the Trash icon.
2. To create a light background on which to work, select Composition > Background Color [Cmd+Shift/Ctrl+Shift + B] and change the background color to 87% gray. Click OK. A new composition will appear.
3. Save the project as **Worry_Project.aep**.

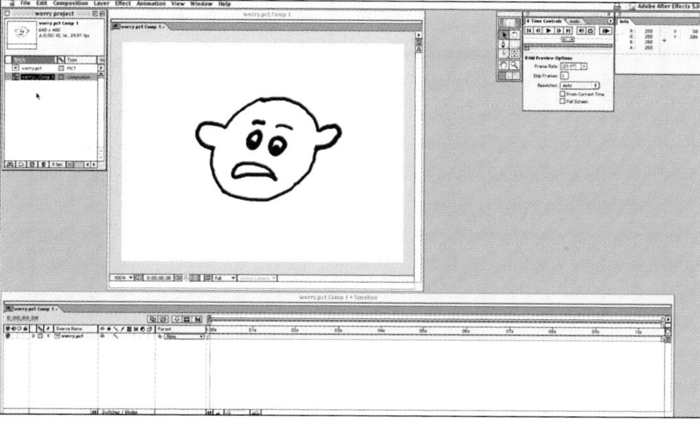

A new Composition window and a new Timeline window will appear.

4. Highlight worry.pct Comp 1 in the Project window and select Composition Settings from the Composition menu.
5. Make sure your composition Frame Rate is 15 (to ensure real-time previewing) and that its Duration is 10 seconds. The composition should have inherited the rest of the parameters of the worry.pct file (640×480 pixel dimensions, square pixel aspect ratio). Click OK.

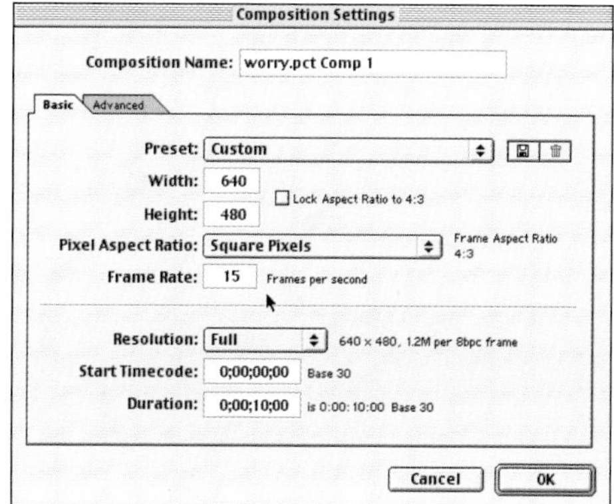

Change the settings for the Composition window.

Now you will start to make the paths.

6 Double-click worry.pct in the Timeline window.

This brings up the Layer window.

Note: You can make and manipulate paths in the Composition window, but it can be faster to manipulate paths in the Layer window because you'll avoid rendering unwanted layers. If you want to work in the Layer window, select the worry.pct layer in the Timeline and press the Enter key. You can also close the Composition window by Option/Alt + clicking on its Close button; this will still keep the Timeline window open.

7 Select the Pen tool in the Tool palette [the G key]. This is the tool you use to create paths.

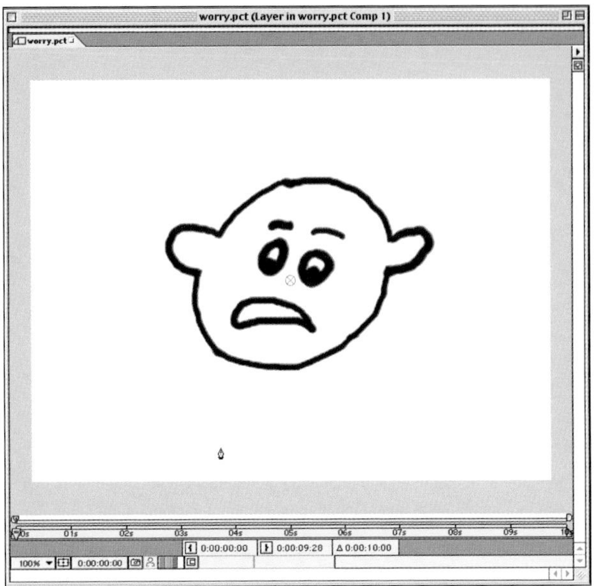

The Layer window.

8 Using the sketch lines as a template, drag and click a path around the outline of the head.

Don't worry if you are not directly on the lines; they can be adjusted later. The most important thing is to use as few points as possible as you make the path.

Note: If you can't see your masks, make sure your layer controls are visible. You can check this by going to the View menu. If there is an item called Show Layer Controls, your controls and layer masks are currently hidden. This can be toggled from the keyboard using Cmd+Shift/Ctrl+Shift + H. You can also choose View > View Options [Cmd+Option/Ctrl+Alt + U] and make sure the Masks option is checked.

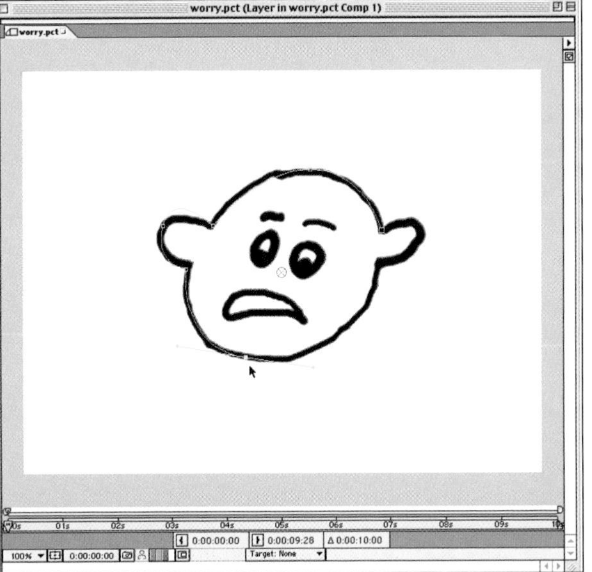

Clicking and dragging around the lines with the Pen tool.

9 Continue dragging around the head until you reach the first point; click on the first point and it will close the path.

Notice the change in the Composition window. If you have a closed path, you can fill it with any color later.

Note: You can start with a clean path by using the **worryPathproject.aep** file on the accompanying CD-ROM. The paths are already made for you, so you can continue with the lesson.

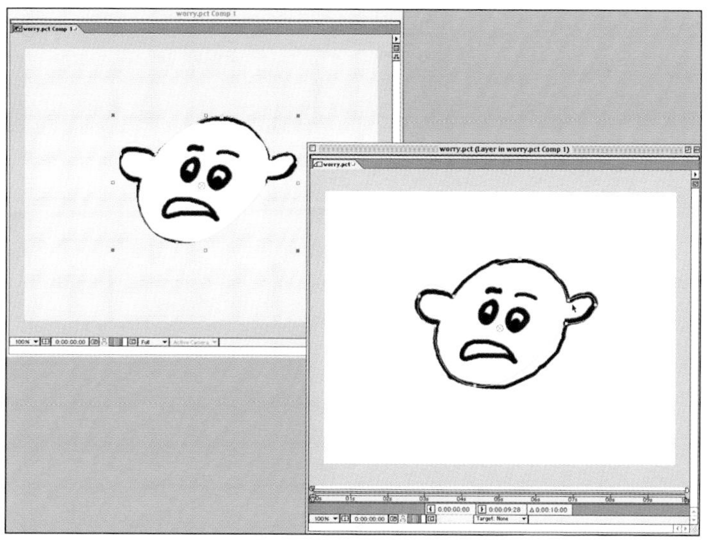

Changes made in the Layer window will update in the Composition window.

10 Highlight worry.pct in the Timeline window and click on the triangle to the left of the layer's name to show the layer's attributes.

You will see the Mask track appear. You can also press the M key to reveal only the Mask track.

11 Click on the triangle to the left of Masks.

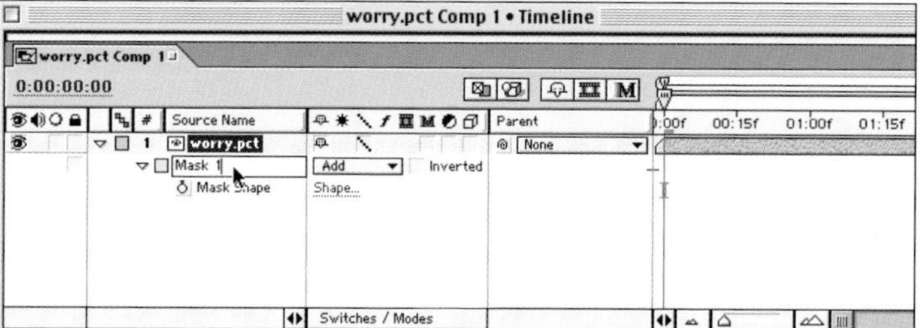

Click M to make the Mask track visible.

12 Highlight Mask 1 and press Enter on your keyboard. Now name the mask **HeadLine**. Press Enter again to accept the new name.

13 Repeat steps 9 and 11 on the mouth, eye, and pupils.

Don't close the paths for the eyebrows. After you've made the path, simply switch to the Move tool [the V key] or Cmd/Ctrl + click anywhere in the Layer window. Leave them as curved lines. Unclosed paths are good for small details.

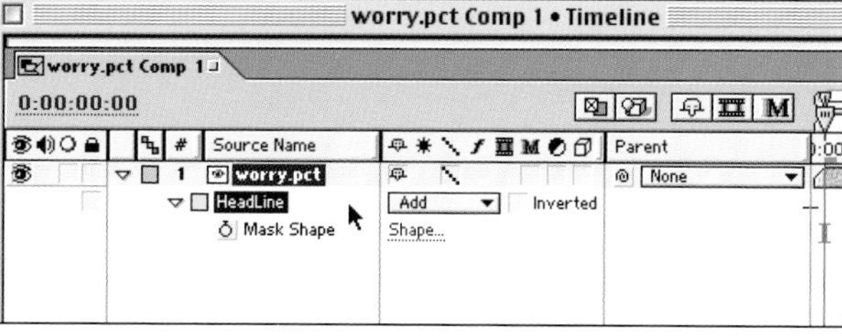

Change the name of Mask 1 to HeadLine.

14 Change the colors of the paths by clicking on the square to the left of each path's name in the Timeline window.

Using different colored paths makes it easier to see what you are doing.

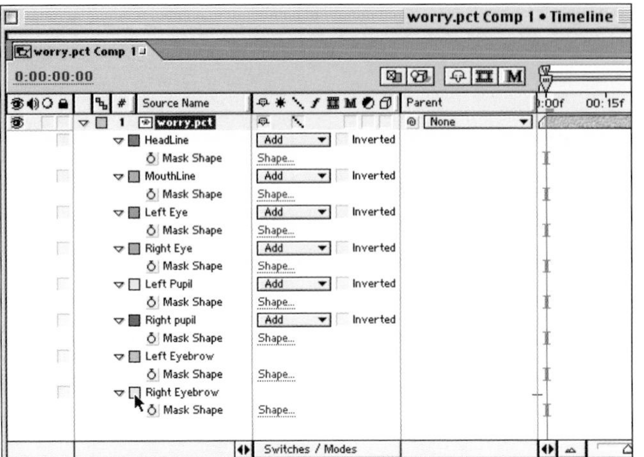

Organize your paths with custom colors and names.

Stroking the Paths

Now that the paths are made, you will replace the worry.pct with a simple color and stroke the lines for that cartoon feeling.

1 Import **PinkPaper.pct** from the accompanying CD-ROM.

2 Highlight worry.pct in the Timeline window.

3 While holding the Option key, drag PinkPaper.pct anywhere into the Composition window. Let go of the drag before you release the Option key.

Note: The Option-drag method is the only way to replace footage in the Timeline.

4 Press the letter M on the keyboard to show the paths.

5 Change the mask colors again if you need to see them better against the new color. I changed the mouth to a darker green and made the pupils darker.

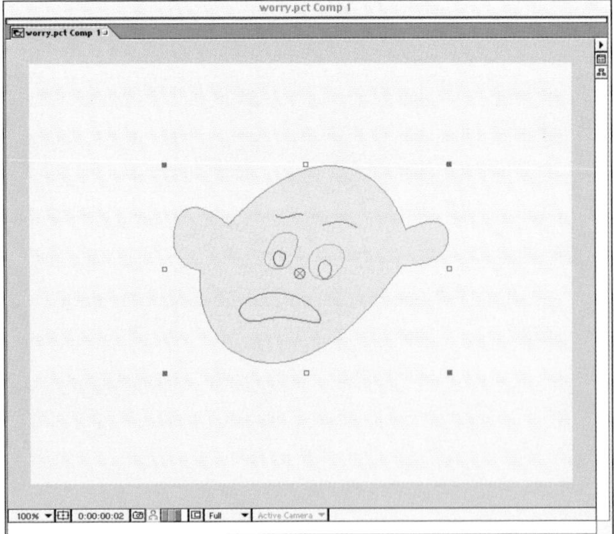

Replace worry.pct with PinkPaper.pct.

6 Choose Effect > Render > Stroke. You can also drag this effect from the Effects palette onto the selected layer in the Composition or Timeline window.

The Effect Controls window will appear. Notice the white line only around the head. The default setting is for a white stroke, but you will change that to black.

Note: Either the F3 key or Cmd+Shift/Ctrl+Shift + T will open the Effect Controls window for the currently selected layer.

7 In the Effect Controls window, check the ALL MASKS check box, change the color to black, and change the brush size to 4.

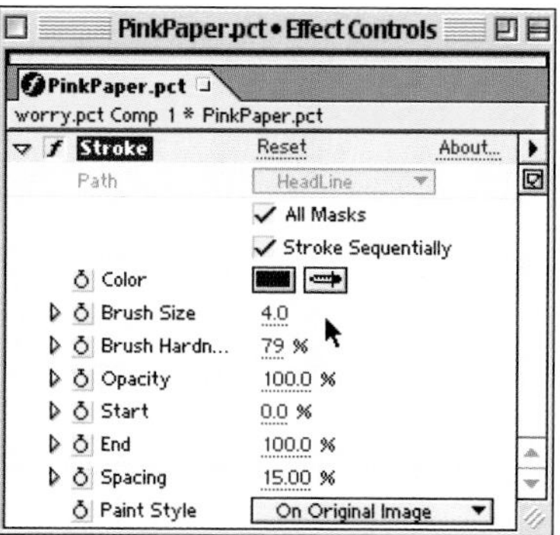

Adjust settings for the Effect Controls window.

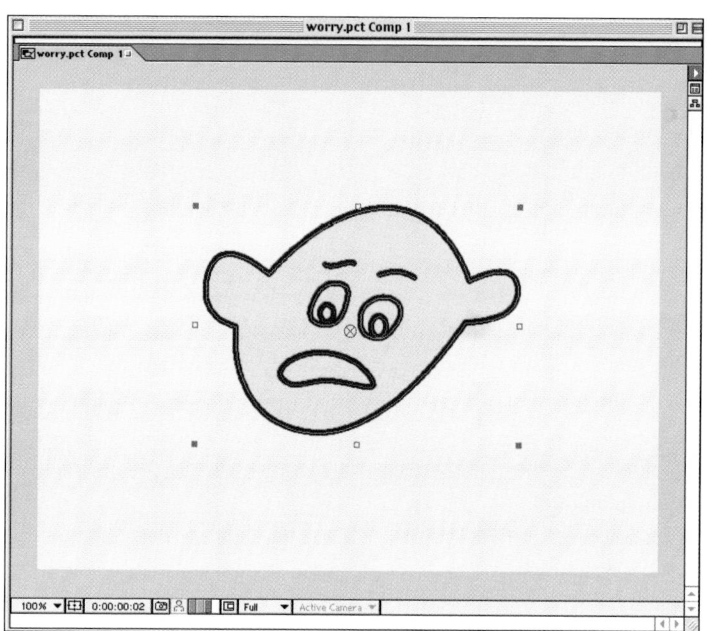

Stroke the paths with the color black.

Manipulating the Lines

You can see that the sketch almost looks like a real cartoon. Now you will make it move.

1. In the Timeline window, double-click PinkPaper.pct to bring up the Footage window.

   You will adjust the lines in this window.

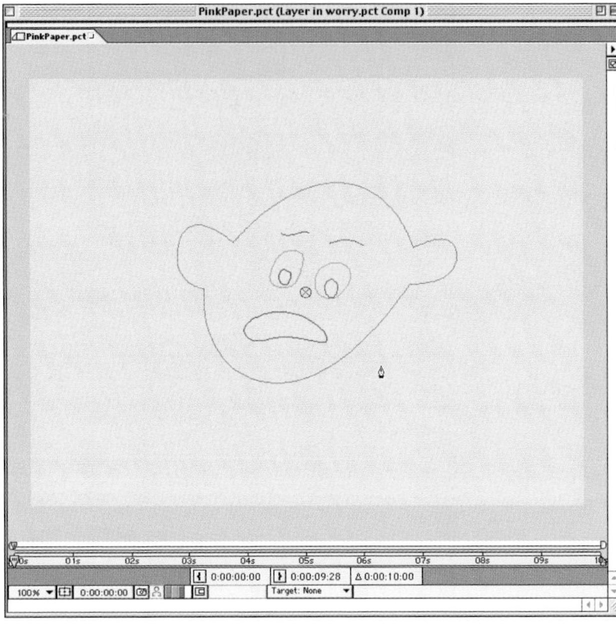

Apply the PinkPaper.pct Layer window to the masks.

2. In the Timeline window, click the stopwatch next to each Mask Shape track.

   This will set an initial keyframe for each line.

3. With the Arrow tool, click directly on a path to move a section of the path or draw a marquee around a point (or set of points) to manipulate only the points you need.

4. With the Arrow tool, double-click on a path or group of points to reveal Transform controls. You can scale or rotate the points. Press Enter on the keyboard to accept.

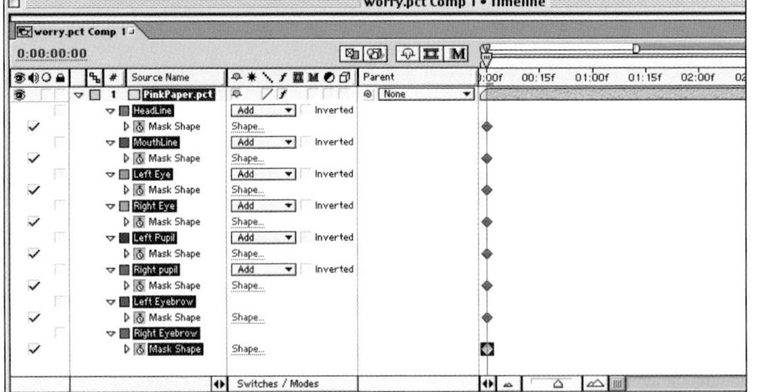

Set keyframe markers in the Mask Shape tracks.

Note: Hold the Cmd key and click on a point with the Arrow tool to extend or retract the handles for that point. If you want to only have one handle move at a time, use the Ctrl key.

5 Make any adjustments to the paths to bring the face into a "neutral" facial expression.

You will return to this expression later.

6 Advance the Time Marker in the Timeline window to frame 06:00.

This takes you forward in time so that you can make a new facial expression. After Effects will interpolate the position of the masks in the in-between frames.

Adjust the handles on a point.

7 Click on the Mouth path and adjust the handles.

A few twists can turn that frown around. Feel free to experiment at this point to create any expression you like by adjusting each path. I moved the eyebrows and eyes as well.

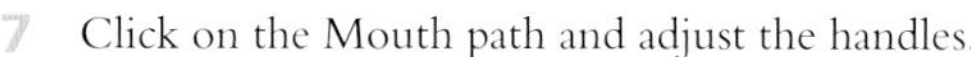

Note: Even if you do not change a path (like HeadLine) on frame 06:00, put a keyframe there anyway. This will help with interpolation later on.

Adjust the paths to create a new facial expression.

8 Advance the Time Marker in the Timeline window to frame 00:10.

Select the points that make up the left ear, double-click them (or press Cmd/Ctrl + T), and rotate them a bit. After you've rotated your points, double-click or press Cmd/Ctrl + T to finalize your changes.

9 Repeat step 8 on the right ear.

Note: You might need to adjust the Composition window's zoom level to make subtle adjustments.

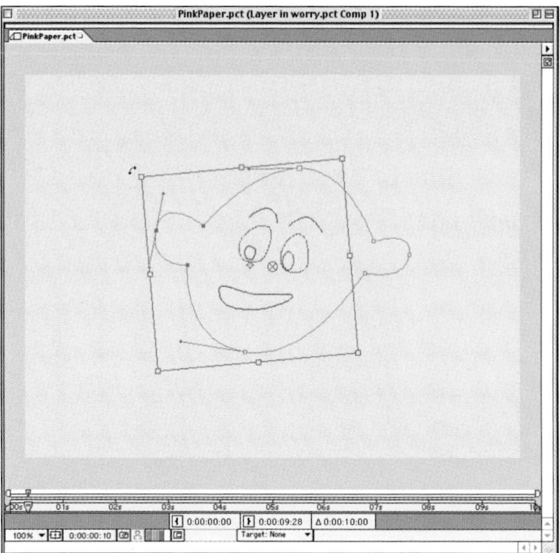

Rotate a group of points.

10 Now skip ahead in time to 02:18. On this frame, use the techniques described in steps 7 through 9 to create a *very* different facial expression from the one on frame 06:00.

This is where your own personal style should come in. In the finished project on the CD-ROM (worryface.aep), frame 06:00 is fairly jolly, whereas frame 02:18 is downright diabolical.

If you want, you can go back and introduce intermediate keyframes as desired to add more personality. For example, I changed the mouthline often but did not move any other paths until frame 02:18. You'll also notice that I added another intermediate facial expression at frame 02:24.

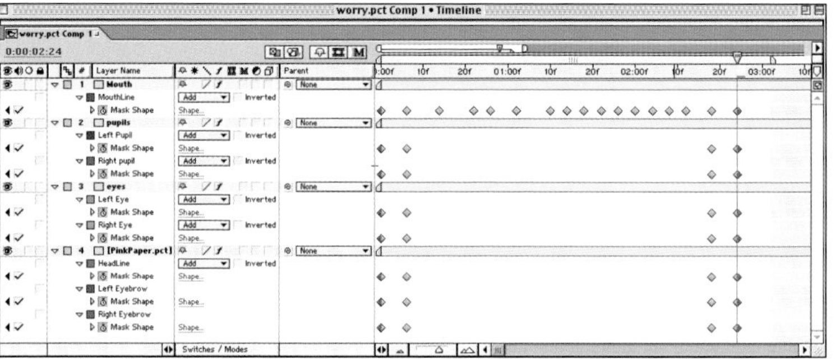

The mouth is moving a lot, but significant facial expression changes only occur at the very beginning and very end of the animation.

11 Let's end the animation with the same facial expression it began with. Return to frame 00:00 and drag a selection marquee around all of the mask keyframes on that frame. Copy these keyframes, move the Timeline marker to 03:00 seconds, and paste them down.

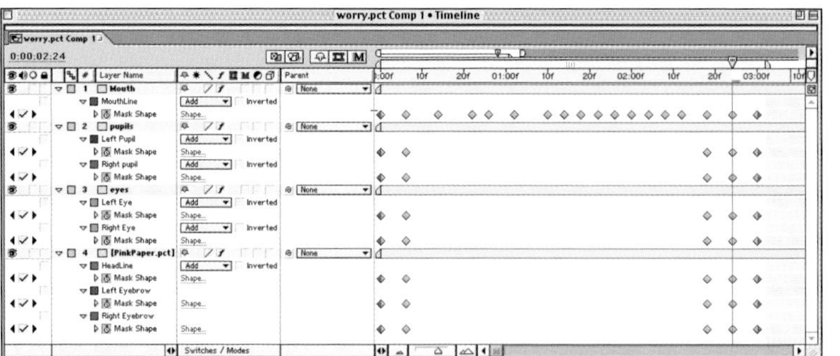

Paste the keyframes from frame 00:00 to frame 03:00.

12 To check out your animation, click on the RAM preview button in the Time Controls palette by choosing Composition > Preview > RAM Preview or by pressing 0 on the numeric keypad.

13 Select all keyframes and apply the Easy Ease Animation Assistant (Animation Menu > Keyframe Assistant > Easy Ease). This softens the motion a bit to make it more organic.

14 After applying Easy Ease, create another RAM Preview to see the difference.

Although After Effects' standard mask interpolation methods are decent, there's a little bit of jumpiness to the mask movement between 06:00 and 02:18. This jumpiness could be minor or major, depending on how you built your own animation. Add keyframes as needed to smooth out your animation.

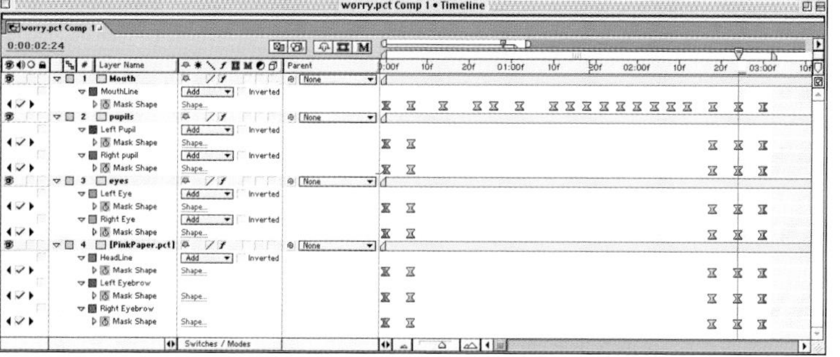

Apply Easy Ease to the keyframes.

Coloring

To make the head features different colors, you must duplicate each layer and delete the masks you don't need from the new layer.

1 Duplicate the Pink Paper.pct layer in the Timeline [Cmd/Ctrl + D].

2 Rename the top layer **Mouth**.

3 Press the letter M on the keyboard to reveal the paths.

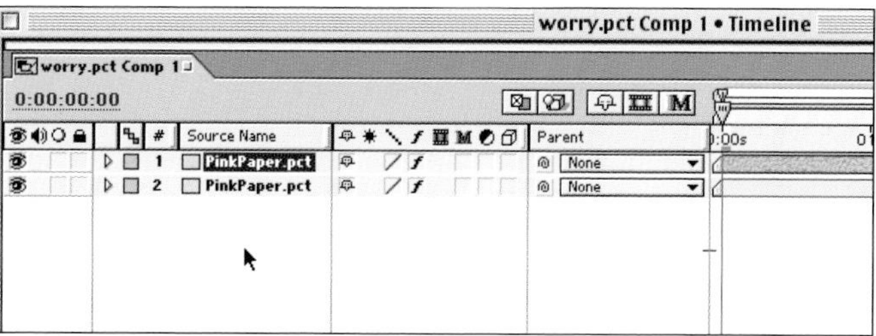

Duplicate the layers in the Timeline window.

4 Select all of the paths on this layer—*except* the Mouth mask—in the Timeline window. Select Clear from the Edit menu.

Now you should have a Mouth layer with a single MouthLine path. It is separated so that you can make it a different color.

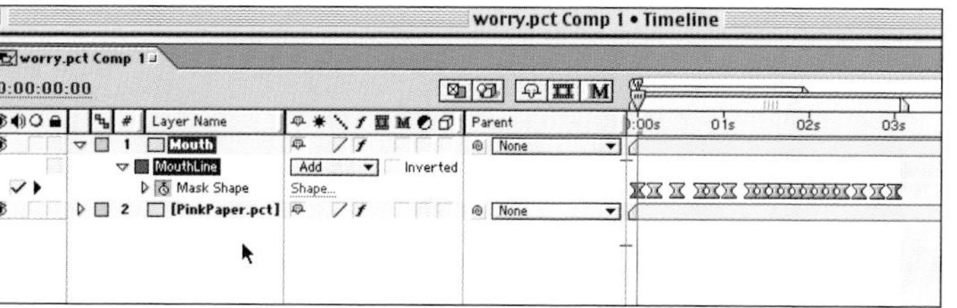

The Mouth layer with its only path.

5 Clear the Mouthline path from layer 2.

Now the Mouthline is only on layer 1.

6 Select the Mouth layer and choose Tint from the Effect menu (Effect > Image Control > Tint).

This changes the color of the layer.

7 Open the Effect Controls window and select the Tint filter. Drag it to the top of the stack, above Stroke. This applies the Tint before the Stroke.

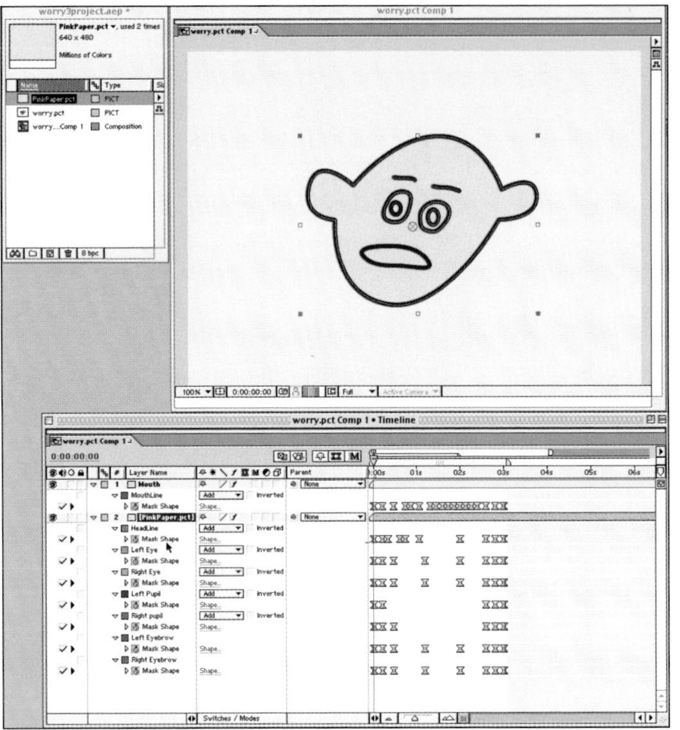

Create a separate layer for each different-colored shape.

8 Click on the Map White To color box and change the color to red. Set the Amount to 84%.

9 Repeat step 4 for each part that needs a new color.

You might want to color the eyes and pupils separately.

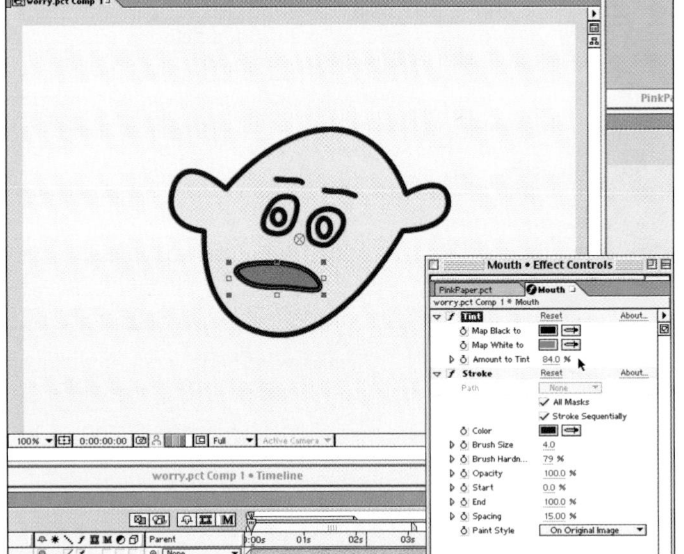

Change the color box to red and then reduce the intensity.

Production Bundle Users: Smart Mask Interpolation

If you use the Production Bundle version of After Effects 5.5, you can employ a different way of animating mask shapes: Smart Mask Interpolation. Smart Mask Interpolation is a keyframe assistant that creates new keyframes as it animates for you. It offers a number of controls that affect how mask vertices are interpolated, often resulting in smoother animations.

Note: Smart Mask Interpolation is only available in After Effects 5.5. If you are using an earlier version, you will have to create additional keyframes manually to smooth out your mask shapes.

1. Open the Smart Mask Interpolation palette by choosing Animation > Keyframe Assistant > Smart Mask Interpolation.
2. Set the Keyframe Rate to 4 so that four new keyframes are created per second. Disable Keyframe Fields (you're only dealing with full frames here) and Use Linear Vertex Paths (you want your mask vertices to curve around as needed). Bending resistance should be set to zero percent because you want your animated masks to bend as much as possible rather than stretch. Quality should almost always be set to 100%. Don't add any mask vertices—this will speed rendering and keep the shapes intact—and set the Matching Method to Curve because none of the masks are very straight. Enabling the last two options—Use 1:1 Vertex Matches and First Vertices Match—will ensure that After Effects accurately matches the vertices on the starting and ending mask shapes.

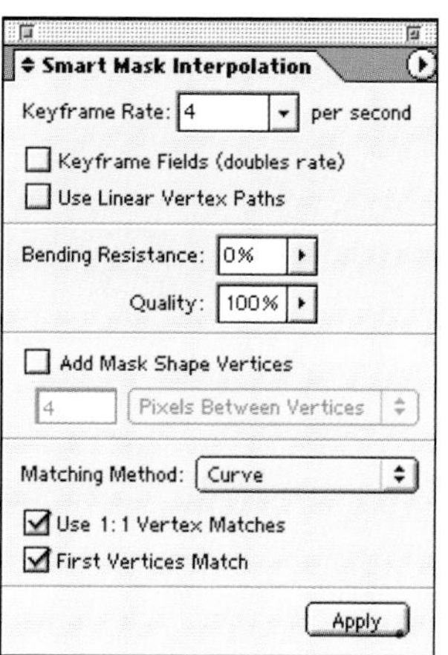

Use these settings in the Smart Mask Interpolation palette.

3. Select all layers except layer 1, which already has enough mouth shape keyframes, and press the M key to reveal all Mask Shape keyframes.
4. Drag a selection marquee around the keyframes at 06:00 and 02:18.

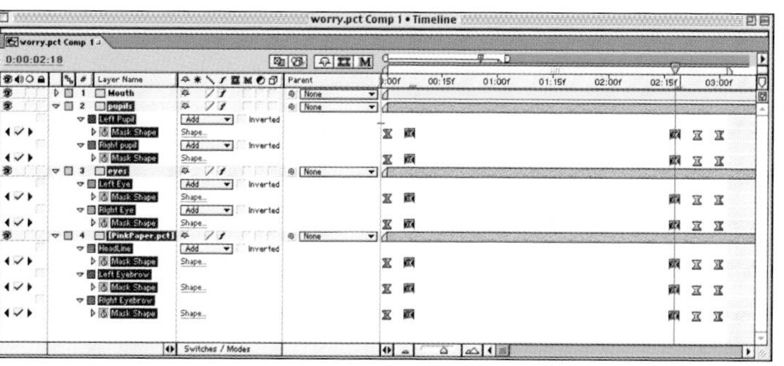

Select the keyframes that will be interpolated.

5 Click the Apply button in the Smart Mask Interpolation palette.

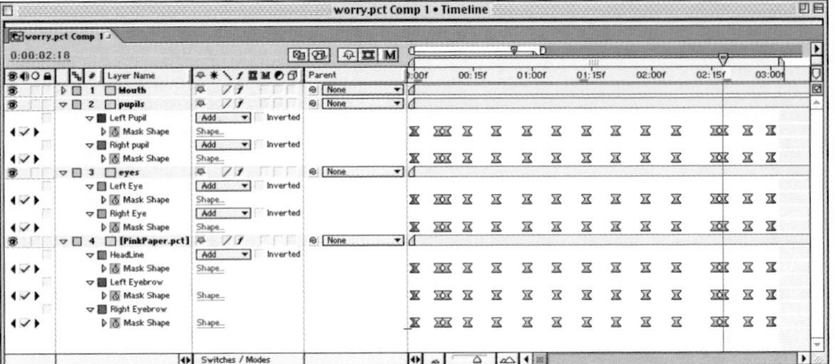

Smart Mask Interpolation generates the intervening keyframes.

6 Create a RAM Preview to see the results.

This new animation not only should look smoother and more organic, but there are now plenty of intermediate keyframes for further tweaking and editing.

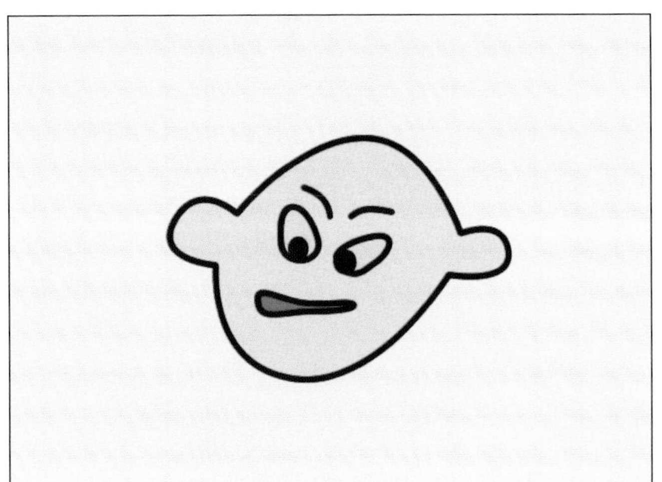

Adjust the colors for a finished angry face.

Modifications

It must be noted that all of the "Coloring" section can be eliminated if you use the Fill plug-in (Effect > Render > Fill). With it, you can do all of the coloring on one layer without the need to duplicate layers. The Bevel Alpha effect with a little Fast Blur effect can shade your lines nicely. On the accompanying CD-ROM is the **cel_modify_project.aep** file. It has a few new composites that show different methods and styles.

A different figure with just Stroke.

A shaded face with Fast Blur and Bevel Alpha.

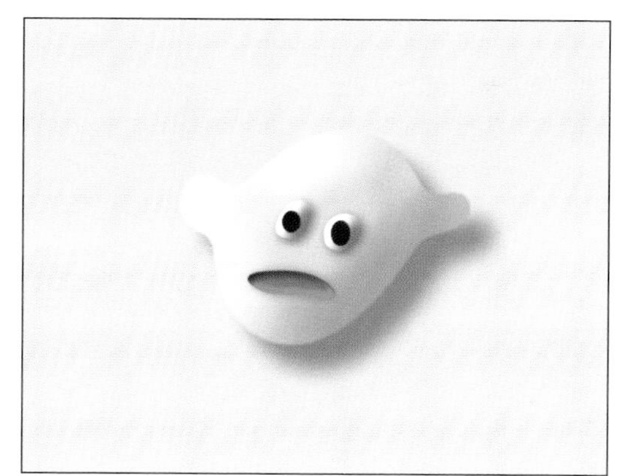

A version of the face with no Stroke.

ALGORITHMIC VIDEO DISTORTION

"Check your camera. There seems to be a malfunction."

—PRIVATE GORMAN, *ALIENS*

Using Static, Noise, and Expressions to Create Video Distortions

Although most video professionals take great pains to acquire the cleanest source footage possible, every once in a while a project will demand some grunge. Due to storyline or style, an effects artist is sometimes called on to "dirty up" clean video footage. Examples of this look include the video cameras worn by the marines in the film *Aliens* and the more artistic video distortion effects used by music video director Chris Cunningham (for such electronic music acts as Autechre and Aphex Twin).

Project 2

Algorithmic Video Distortion

by Nathan Moody

The original dark and stormy hillside panorama.

The same panorama shown through the lens of a panning video camera...with some serious malfunctions.

How It Works

Although there are third-party plug-ins that can accomplish the "dirty" video footage effect, all you need to accomplish these effects automatically is some audio static, some visual noise, and a few expressions. This project will start with animating a single still image in a realistic way and then will focus on using both keyframes and expressions to drive parameters of various effects. This technique virtually eliminates keyframing by hand. This tutorial can be used as a model for driving nearly any other kind of 2D visual effect. Throughout this project, alternatives will be offered for those readers who own the Production Bundle edition of After Effects. This project should be completed on a computer system with headphones or speakers.

Getting Started

The footage to which video distortion will be applied is a simple camera pan of a hillside on an overcast day. The clouds are moving slightly, casting subtle shadows on the ground, and the footage is super clean. However, this footage will be created by animating a still Photoshop file rather than using actual video.

The primary source footage is a single Photoshop file, **Hillside.psd**, located on the accompanying CD-ROM. This source image is a panoramic composite of three separate images shot with a digital camera. After some initial retouching and removal of lens distortion, these shots were stitched together into a single wide image (1,346 pixels wide by 486 pixels tall). The sky was then masked out, and a new cloudy sky was added. This new composite will serve as your primary background.

1. Copy this project's folder from the CD-ROM onto your hard drive and launch After Effects.

2. Create a new project (File > New > New Project) [Cmd+Option/Ctrl+Alt + N] and name it **distressedVideo_new.aep**. Save it to your hard drive, preferably in the folder that was just copied to your hard drive.

3. Choose File > Import [Cmd/Ctrl + I] and navigate to this project's folder on your hard drive. In the source_footage subfolder, you will find the file **Hillside.psd**. From the Import As pop-up menu in the Import dialog box, choose the Composition option.

   This will retain all of the Photoshop files' layer states rather than importing each layer separately or flattening the file.

4. Press Return, Enter, or click the Import button (or Open button in Windows). In the Project window, you will see a new composition called Hillside.psd and a folder with the same name, which holds the file's individual Photoshop layers.

5. In the Project window, select the Hillside.psd composition and press the Return key; its label will highlight, allowing you to rename it. Rename the composition **1_Hillside.psd**.

   This will help you follow which compositions are nested later on in this exercise.

6. Double-click on the 1_Hillside.psd composition in the Project window to open its Composition and Timeline windows.

The original Photoshop footage file, imported as a composition.

7 Open the Composition window wide enough to see the whole image. For speed's sake, set the Resolution of the Composition window to Half, either from the pop-up menu at the bottom of the window or by selecting View > Resolution > Half [Cmd+Shift/Ctrl+Shift + J].

Note: You might need to reduce the magnification of the Composition window to 50% or 25% (by using the Zoom pop-up menu on the lower-left corner of the Composition window).

8 Open the Composition Settings dialog box (Composition > Composition Settings) [Cmd/Ctrl + K] and set the Duration of the 1_Hillside.psd composition to 0:00:08:00 (8 seconds).

This should also be the new length of any composition you create during this exercise.

9 Click OK to close the Composition Settings dialog box. If the layers of your composition are now longer or shorter than the composition itself, go to the Timeline window and select all the layers (Edit > Select All) [Cmd/Ctrl + A], press the End key to go to the last frame of the composition, and then press Option +] (close bracket) on the Mac or Alt +] in Windows.

Note: If you maximize your Composition window and view the 1_Hillside.psd composition at 50% magnification or less, you'll notice that the bounding box of the clouds layer is wider than the composition itself. This is because Photoshop has a feature called Big Data that allows pixel information *beyond* the canvas area to be retained when layers are pasted or moved from one image to another. Because the clouds will be panned subtly from left to right, the clouds layer needs to be wider than the composition itself. Now the clouds need to be animated so that they will move from left to right.

This snaps all the layers' out points to the current frame.

10 Select the clouds layer in the Timeline and make sure the time indicator is at 0:00:00:00 (or frame 1) by pressing the Home key.

11 Open the Position property for the clouds layer.

This can be done by clicking on the triangle next to the layer name to expose its parameter groups and then clicking on the triangle next to the Transform group. This can also be accomplished by selecting the clouds layer and simply pressing the P key.

12 Create an initial keyframe at 0:00:00:00 by clicking once on the Position property stopwatch icon, choosing Animation > Add Keyframe, or pressing Opt+P (Mac) or Alt+Shift+P (Windows).

13 Set the X value of the clouds layer to 658 by clicking on the first value in the Position track and entering the new value.

14 Go to the last frame in the Timeline (0:00:07:29) by pressing the End key. Create a new keyframe at 0:00:07:29 by setting the X Position of the clouds layer to 740.

This will move the clouds 81 pixels over 8 seconds.

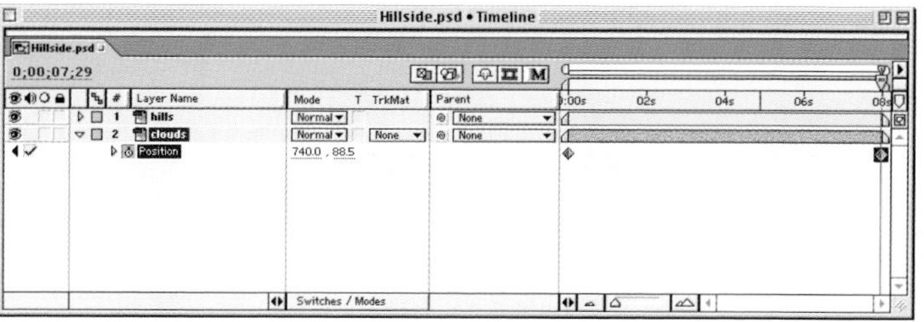

These Position keyframes determine the cloud's slow pan across the scene.

15 Click the RAM preview button in the Time Controls palette by choosing Composition > Preview > RAM Preview or by pressing 0 on the numeric keypad.

This will show you the slow, subtle move of the clouds crossing the sky.

Note: Reset the Composition window's magnification setting to 50% and the resolution to Half to see the preview easily. You can reduce the resolution of the Composition window further if you don't have enough RAM to render the entire movie.

Introducing Camera Movement

With a fairly realistic background finished, it's time to simulate a realistic right-to-left camera pan in a new composition that is a bit more output-friendly than 1,300 pixels wide.

The goal is to simulate a camera, in a fixed position, being panned from right to left. Although you could simply move the scene right to left using Position keyframes, this would give the effect of a camera simply dollying right to left, not panning. The most obvious place to start with this sort of effect is to create a *virtual* camera and take advantage of After Effects' new 3D filters.

The reason that 1_Hillside.psd isn't just panned left to right is to impart a very subtle change in perspective as the camera pans, especially at the far left and right edges of the shot. In this example, this effect is not easy to see, but it is an important distinction when simulating a real camera lens distortion in After Effects.

1 Create a new composition and name it **2_hillsFakePan**.

Again, numbering compositions helps keep track of nesting at a glance. Like the first composition, it should be 8 seconds long, but it should be properly sized for square pixels at the default NTSC D1 resolution: 720×486. According to the NTSC format, make sure the frame rate is 29.97 frames per second.

Note: This composition is much smaller than 1_Hillside.psd, so you might want to increase the Composition window's size, resolution, and magnification settings at this time.

2 Drag the 1_Hillside.psd composition from the Project window into the Timeline of the 2_hillsFakePan composition.

This ensures that the nested composition is exactly centered in the new composition.

3 Enable the 3D option for the 1_Hillside.psd layer by clicking the 3D Layer switch in the rightmost column in the Switches area in the Timeline.

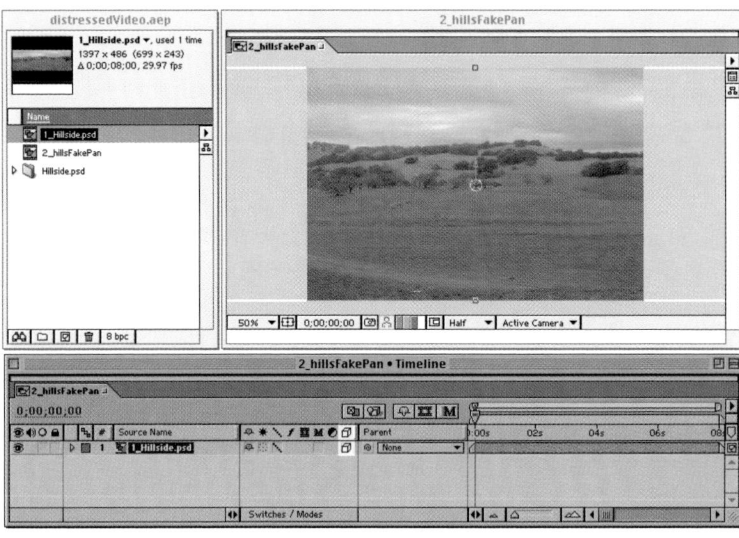

The new composition with the original panorama composition nested within it. Note the enabled 3D Layer switch in the Timeline.

4 Choose Layer > New > Camera [Cmd+Option+Shift/ Ctrl+Alt+Shift + C]. This will create a virtual camera called Camera 1, which you will use for the pan. Choose 35mm from the preset menu (to simulate a 35mm film size). Leave all other settings at their defaults and click OK. Make sure Active Camera view is selected in the View menu at the bottom of the Composition window.

5 Go to time 0:00:00:00 [Home key], select the Camera 1 layer, and inspect its Position and Orientation and Rotation properties by pressing the P and R keys, respectively, while holding down the Shift key. Create a keyframe for only its Y Rotation.

6 Set the Camera 1 layer's Z position to 580 and its Y rotation to 8.5 degrees.

These camera settings should yield a slightly rotated view of the 1_Hillside.psd layer's right half while making sure there are no gaps around this layer that reveal the background color.

7 Go to time 0:00:07:29 [End key], create a keyframe for Camera 1's Y Rotation, and set its value to –7 degrees.

This will pan Camera 1 across the background Composition layer. There is one slight problem, however; a camera's lens is curved and introduces a subtle curved distortion to whatever it is capturing. Without this curvature to the image, the camera pan doesn't look *quite* realistic enough (although it will stretch very slightly in perspective). Luckily, After Effects now comes with a filter built to do just that: Optics Compensation.

8 Set the current time marker to 0:00 and create a new adjustment layer (Layer > New > Adjustment Layer; no keyboard shortcut). Name this layer **Lens Curvature**. Make sure it is the topmost layer.

After Effects' adjustment layers, unlike Photoshop's, can hold *any* effect and apply it to all layers beneath it.

9 With the Lens Curvature layer selected, apply the Optics Compensation effect (Effect > Distort > Optics Compensation). You can also drag this effect from the Effects Palette onto the selected layer in the Composition or Timeline windows. Choose 50 for the Field of View and check the Reverse Lens Distortion option. Leave all other controls at their default values.

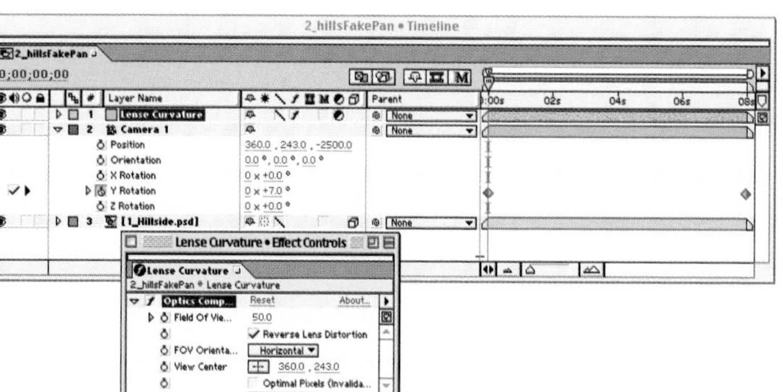

The Timeline and Effects windows show the combined camera effect: some slight panning and a subtle lens distortion for added realism.

This will *introduce* optical distortion rather than remove it. This emulates a 50mm lens, with which the hillside stills were originally shot (independent from the original 35mm film size). You can see the difference easily by simply toggling the visibly of the Lens Curvature layer on and off in the Timeline.

10 Create a RAM Preview.

You'll see that the difference is subtle, but the center of the frame is "pushed back" slightly in a bulge, lending some additional physical realism to the effect.

Note: You might want to temporarily set the Composition window to Full resolution and zoom up to 100% magnification to see this effect more clearly.

In the next section, we'll manipulate multiple copies of the 2_hillsFakePan composition. This could be pretty taxing on your computer, at least slowing down previews quite a bit. To speed up workflow, it might be time to pre-render this composition.

11 Select the 2_hillsFakePan composition in the Project window, and choose Composition > Pre-Render. This will automatically open the Render Queue window.

12 Make sure that the Render Settings module is set to Lossless and that the Output Module is using best-quality Animation compression without audio.

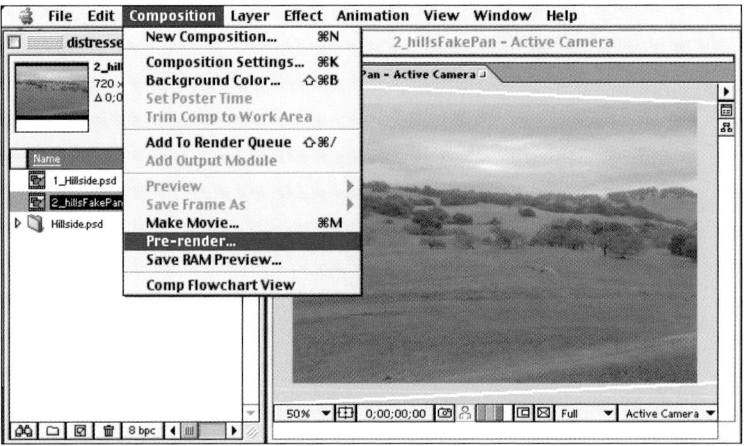

Pre-rendering this composition will speed up both previewing and final rendering.

13 Click on the arrow to the left of the Output Module to inspect its settings. You will notice that the Post-Render Action popup menu is already set to Import & Replace Usage. This could also be set to just Import, because we have not yet nested this composition in another. For now, leave this setting as it is.

14 Click the Render button.

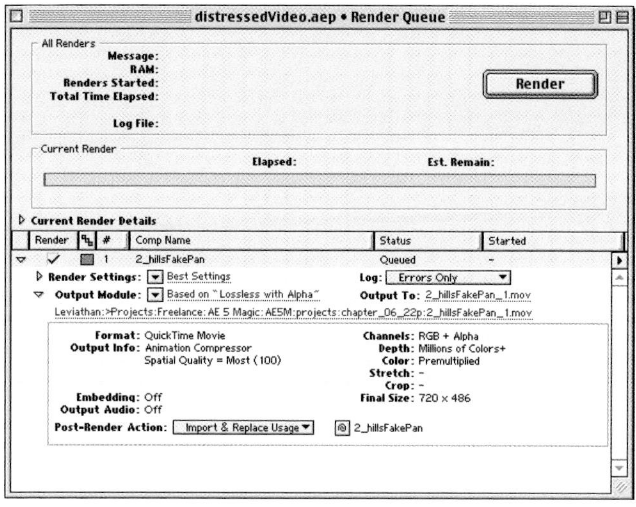

The Post-Render Action parameter in a render's Output Module automatically imports pre-rendered movies or image sequences.

15 After the render is complete, you'll notice that a new file— 2_hillsFakePan_1.mov—has now been imported into the Project.

Note: The Post-Render Action feature is specific to After Effects 5.5. In After Effects 5.0, simply add the 2_hillsFakePan composition to the Render Queue, render it, and then import it back in.

Adding Sound

Now that the source is clean and somewhat convincing, it's time to royally mess things up. Using the concept that this camera might have been outside a while and is on the fritz, the next phase involves setting up an audio source that will drive the video distortion effects.

It is interesting to note that, from this point, all animation will be accomplished without any keyframes, relying instead on expressions.

1 Choose File > Import [Cmd/Ctrl + I] and open the source_footage folder in this project's folder. Select **staticConstant.wav** and press the Import (Mac) or Open (Windows) button.

2 Play the audio file by double-clicking on it in the Project window and pressing the Playback button in the resulting QuickTime window.

It contains nothing but 8 seconds of pure white noise at a constant volume. Not very interesting…yet.

3 Create a new composition and name it **3_videoNoise**. Like the previous composition, make it 8 seconds long, 720×486 pixels in size, and with a frame rate of 29.97. Into its Timeline, drag the 2_hillsFakePan_1.mov footage item from the previous exercise and the staticConstant.wav audio file. Make sure the Background color [Cmd+Shift/Ctrl+Shift + B] of this composition is white; this will be important in the next exercise.

For audio to drive a visual effect, there needs to be some variation in its audio level. Although the Production Bundle's excellent Motion Math can create keyframes based on audio amplitude, the Standard version of After Effects is only sensitive to changes in audio level (that is, the volume control of an audio layer). Because both aural and visual noise is chaotic, expressions will allow you to *automatically* introduce random variations into the static soundtrack's volume.

4 Select the staticConstant.wav audio and inspect its Levels track by pressing the L key. Click once on the Levels property to select it and apply an expression to this track (Animation > Add Expression) [Option+Shift/Alt+Shift + =].

5 In the resulting Expression field, type the following:

gauss_random([-48,-48],[-12,-12])

This creates Gaussian-distributed random values (placed along a bell curve of probability) for the left and right channels of this layer (the original clip is in stereo) in decibels.

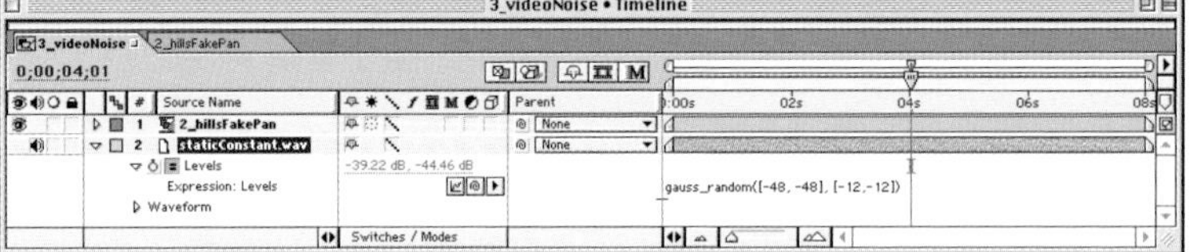

This single line of expressions code will animate the volume of the audio clip automatically.

It's important to note that this function has two sets of numbers. The first bracketed pair of numbers represents the minimum volume for the left and right channels, respectively. The second bracketed pair of numbers is the maximum allowed volume. The central comma separates these "min" and "max" values, and the parentheses enclose the values.

> **Note:** It is imperative to understand that the maximum allowable volume for 16-bit digital audio is 0dB (zero decibels) and that the minimum volume is generally assumed to be –96 decibels. The reasons for this are relatively unimportant, but it figures heavily into how the expressions are written. For example, digital audio volume is *always* expressed in negative numbers, a critical fact when writing expressions involving audio. Also, dividing anything by a layer's audio level at maximum volume (0dB) will cause After Effects to disable the script because it's trying to divide by zero.

6 Create a RAM preview to listen to the results.

The audio will dip and jump in volume as if someone is playing with the volume knob of an off-station radio tuner.

> **Note:** The default audio preview duration is 4 seconds. You can change this to 8 seconds (so that you can preview the whole clip) by selecting Edit > Preferences > Previews and changing the Audio Preview Duration to 00:00:08:00. If you don't have a lot of RAM, set your Audio Preview settings to 22.05kHz, 8-bit, and Mono.

Introducing Noise

The next step is to drive a visual effect—video noise—with these randomly altered audio levels.

1 With the current time set at 0:00, in the 3_videoNoise composition, create a new Solid (Layer > New > Solid) [Cmd/Ctrl + Y] that is half the full size of the composition. It is critical to make sure its color is exactly 50% gray. Call it **noiseLayer**.

2 Make sure this layer is the topmost layer in the Timeline and set its Scale property to 200%, keeping the proportions locked.

By scaling up the smaller file, the noise effect you are about to apply will be stretched and therefore easier to see.

3 Apply the Noise Effect to this layer (Effect > Stylize > Noise, or drag-and-drop from the Effects Palette). Bring the Noise amount up to 100% and leave the default checkboxes as they are.

4 In the Timeline, press the Switches/Mode toggle near the bottom of the window to reveal the layers' transfer modes. Change the mode of noiseLayer to Soft Light.

This will result in an overlay-like result, in which the solid's gray background will never appear (even though it is currently overwhelmed by noise).

5 Inspect the Opacity property of noiseLayer by selecting the layer and pressing the T key. Click on the Opacity property in the Timeline window and add an expression to the Opacity property of noiseLayer. Type in this:

```
div(-700, this_comp.layer("staticConstant.wav").audio_levels[0])
```

This expression is dividing the number –700 by the staticConstant.wav layer's left channel volume and is applying it to the Opacity track of noiseLayer. This division is necessary to translate a –96dB to 0dB scale of audio levels to a 0% to 100%. Because Opacity only has one parameter—a single percentage—either the left (**audio_levels[0]**) or right channel (**audio_levels[1]**) can be used to determine transparency but not both.

The value of –700 was chosen to make the noise obvious but without obliterating all the detail behind it. Because the audio level of staticConstant.wav is scripted to be between –48 and –12, the Opacity of noiseLayer would range from 14% (–700 divided by –48) to 58% (–700 divided by –12).

Note: In After Effects 5.5, the keyboard shortcut for cycling down through the transfer modes, from Normal down toward Luminescent Premul, is Shift+ Plus/Equals (+ and =). Cycling in the reverse order can be done by pressing Shift-Minus/Underscore (- and _).

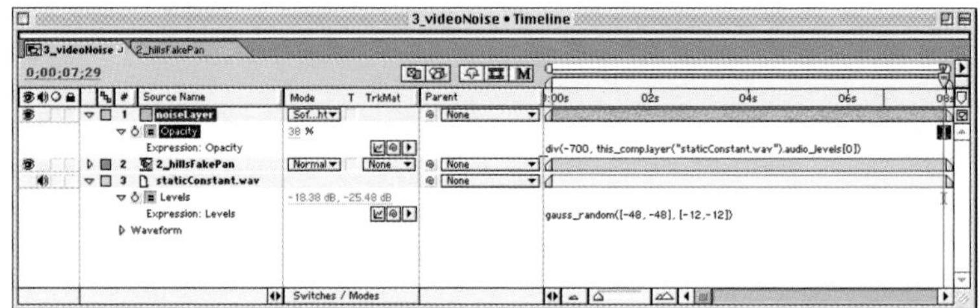

The Opacity track is using expressions to base its values on *another* Expression in the composition.

Note: If you can't read the expression clearly, temporarily move your current time marker out of the way (to the end of the Timeline window, for example). Because you're not dealing with keyframes when writing expressions, moving the time marker won't matter.

6 Create a RAM preview.

The noise is pretty heavy, but that is primarily for demonstration purposes. Feel free to cut back on the noise if you want by lowering the numeric constant of –700 in the noiseLayer.

A final layer in this composition will make the source footage appear to be even more low resolution: introducing fake interlacing.

7 Import the file **RasterLines.psd** from the source_footage folder. (File > Import or Cmd/Ctrl + I).

This file is nothing but a 720×486 image with alternating black-and-white lines, each 2 pixels high.

8 Set the current time marker at 0:00 and drag RasterLines.psd from the Project window into the Timeline, making sure it will be the topmost image (Layer 1 in the layer stack).

9 Set this layer's transfer mode to Overlay and reduce its Opacity to 25%.

The noiseLayer's Opacity is now tied directly to the volume of the audio.

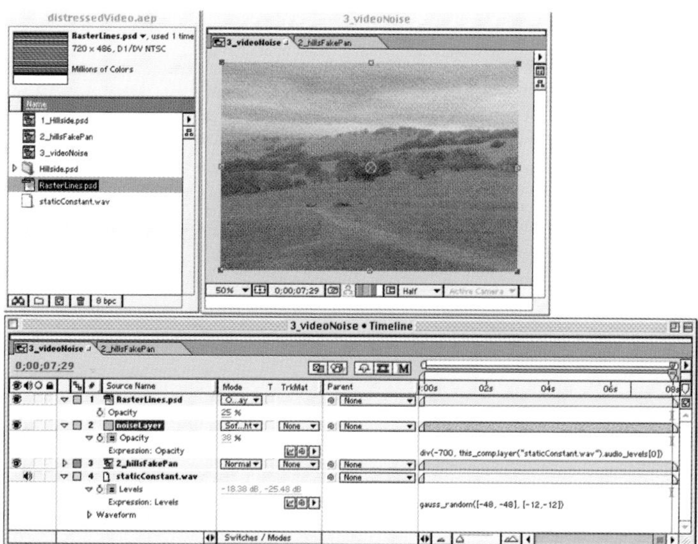

Introducing fake interlacing makes the footage appear even more low resolution.

Introducing Color Offset

The Shift Channels effect and expressions can be combined for an even more convincing video distortion technique. I first saw this general technique used by Eric Henry in his excellent *Wood Technology…* short film a couple years ago, as a transition effect. Then, having observed how color channels sometimes diverge in poor video signals, the application of this technique to video distortion became clear.

Because After Effects works in an additive RGB colorspace, screening layers together against white can create quite interesting visual effects. What's more, separating the red, green, and blue channels of an image and placing them together in Screen mode will reconstruct a color-accurate RGB image. This exercise uses this technique to introduce offsets into only a single color channel at a time, and it is the reason why the background for all the compositions in this project should have white backgrounds.

This is also the reason why using an adjustment layer is beneficial: The Noise effect doesn't have to be applied to each layer individually. Effects applied to adjustment layers affect all of the layers beneath the adjustment layer in the layer stack.

1. In the 3_videoNoise composition, select the 2_hillsFakePan_1.mov layer.
2. Apply the Shift Channels effect (Effect > Channel > Shift Channels, or drag-and-drop from the Effects Palette) to the 2_hillsFakePan_1.mov layer. Leave the Alpha and Red channels alone, but set the Take Green From and Take Blue From options to Full Off.
3. Set the blending mode of the 2_hillsFakePan_1.mov layer to Screen (there will be no immediate change in the Composition window). Rename this layer **hills_R** by selecting the layer in the Timeline and pressing the Return key.
4. Duplicate this layer and name the duplicate **hills_G**.

The Shift Channels effect enables you to composite red, green, and blue layers together to make a complete RGB image.

5 Open its Effect Controls window (Effect > Effect Controls) [Cmd+Shift/Ctrl+Shift + T], set Take Red From to Full Off, and change the Take Green From option to Green.

In the Composition window, the image will appear to be tinted yellow: the additive result of screening red on green.

6 Back in the Timeline window, duplicate this layer, name the duplicate **hills_B**, and open its Effect Controls window. Set Take Green From to Full Off and change the Take Blue From option to Blue.

This results in a return to a full-color (albeit distressed) image.

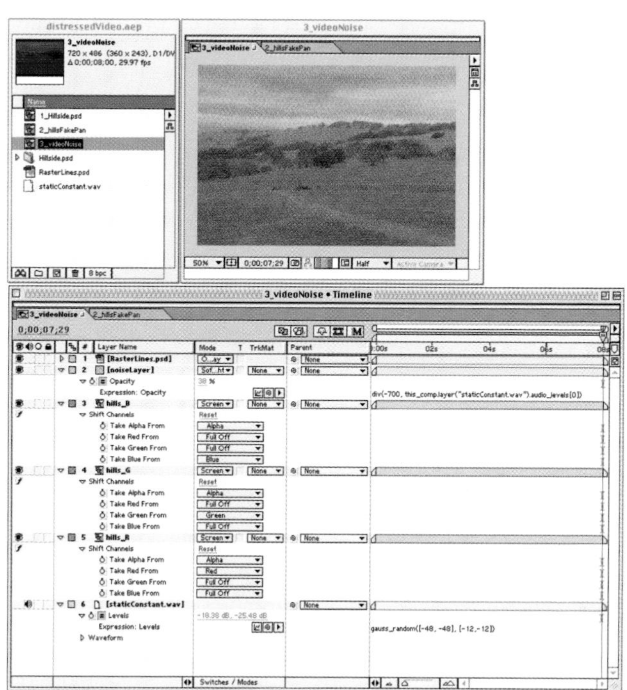

The image appears as a full-color image once again... still covered in grimy noise and interlaced lines, of course.

7 Open the Position property for the hills_R layer (P key), click the Position property to select it, and add an expression (Animation > Add Expression) [Option+Shift/Alt+Shift + =]. Type in the following expression for the hills_R layer's Position track:

```
[position[0], sub (position[1], (div(-300,
➥this_comp.layer("staticConstant.wav").audio_levels[1]))]
```

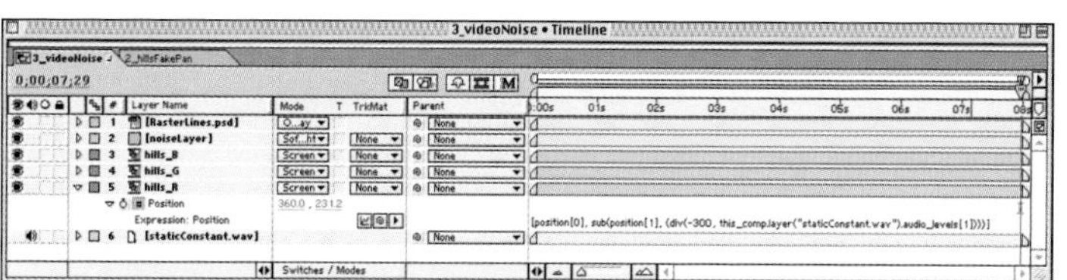

Having separated the original image into three R, G, and B layers, expressions will offset the red color channel based on the volume of the audio clip's right channel.

This expression is doing conceptually the same thing as the last expression you wrote: modulating a layer parameter based on audio level. Unlike Opacity, however, Position has *two* values: X (**position[0]**) and Y (**position[1]**). This expression states that the first value, X, isn't modified at all, so its value will be left unchanged.

```
[position[0], sub (position[1], (div(-300,
➥this_comp.layer("staticConstant.wav").audio_levels[1]))))]
```

The second value, Y, will be modified by subtracting the current value dividing a numerical constant (the number –300) by the right channel of the staticConstant.wav layer.

You might see some color shifting in the composition; there might be an upward yellow ghosting effect. This gives the impression of the hillside image's red channel being offset due to interference. This occurs because you've allowed the audio's right-channel volume to affect the red channel's Y position. The louder the right audio channel's volume, the farther the hills_R layer will be shifted upward. For example, if the right audio channel's level is –20, the resulting new Y position would be as follows:

(current Y position: 240) minus
(–300 divided by –20 = 15), or 225.

The numerical constant of –300 is negative because the audio clip's volume is measured in negative decibels, so dividing two negative numbers returns a positive result. If the staticConstant.wav layer's audio level were to be divided by a positive number (like 300), it would shift the hills_R layer *downward* because the result would be negative.

8 Select the hills_B layer, click on its Position property, and type in the following expression:

```
[sub (position[0], (div(300, this_comp.layer
➥("staticConstant.wav").audio_levels[0]))), position[1]]
```

This expression is similar to the first one except the X value is being modified by the *left* audio level of the staticConstant.wav layer. The Y position is not affected at all:

Now there might be a right-hand shift of blue values in the Composition window. The louder the left audio channel's volume, the farther the blue channel (the hills_B layer) will be shifted toward the right. If the staticConstant.wav layer's audio level were to be divided by a negative number (like –300), it would shift the hills_B layer toward the left.

9 Save your project and then create a RAM preview.

That nice, clean camera pan you started with now suffers from all sorts of problems. Every special effect added to the clean footage has been created without making a single keyframe, but expressions still afford the capability to enter numeric values to alter the subtlety or severity of these effects.

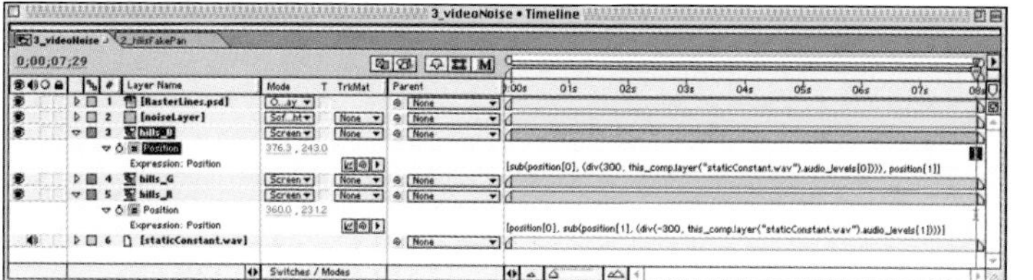

While the green color layer stays put, the red and blue color layers will be offset in different directions by the volume of the left and right audio channels, respectively.

Note: To see similar effects at work, see Aphex Twin's "Come to Daddy" and Autechre's "Second Bad Vilbel." These music videos were both directed by Chris Cunningham... although some of his work is clearly based on simply editing together video clips of poor quality!

Better Glitches Through Displacement: Production Bundle Users Only

Anyone who's seen poor video reception knows that images often jump, scroll, and do other visual acrobatics. This can easily be achieved by using the Production Bundle's Displacement Map effect, the secret weapon of professional effects artists.

Displacement mapping offsets or moves pixels in one image based on the brightness values in another image. The *target* is the image to be manipulated with the effect, and the *displacement map* is the image whose brightness determines the amount of offset. Black pixels in the displacement map move pixels in the direction indicated in the Effect Controls, while white pixels in the displacement map move pixels in the target in the opposite direction. This effect slopes off in severity where the displacement image is 50% gray, which imposes no offset in the target at all.

In Photoshop, the Displace filter does this to individual images. In After Effects, things get scary when entire animation sequences or video footage can be manipulated using the Displacement Map effect.

The caveat to this exercise, however, is that it is important to have a good animated displacement map to work with. This project comes with a sample sequence of images made just for this purpose. In general, for this kind of effect, the displacement map should be mostly 50% gray with some extremely high contrast areas of pure blacks and whites.

1 Open the Import dialog box (File > Import > File) [Cmd/Ctrl + I]; in the source_footage folder there is a subfolder named displaceSequence. Open this folder and, leaving the menu set to Footage, select the first file in the series **disp01.psd**.

   This is the first in a sequence of Photoshop files.

These are some of the images in the displacement map sequence: mostly gray for little overall effect but with a few very dark and very light highlights for significant pixel offset.

2 Under the Import As option, activate the Photoshop Sequence check box and click the Import (Mac) or Open (Windows) button. A sequence named disp[1-10].psd appears in the Project window.

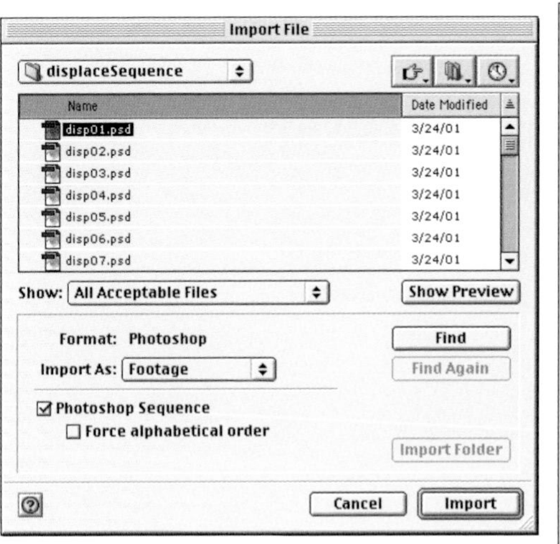

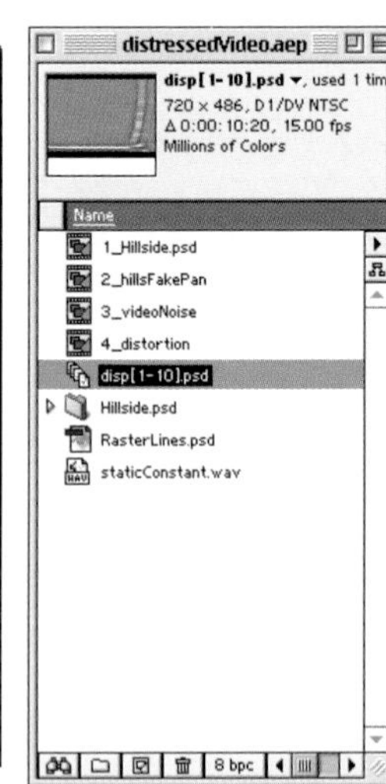

Importing the displacement map images as a sequence enables them to be manipulated like any other type of motion footage.

3 Select the disp[1-10].psd sequence in the project window and open the Interpret Footage dialog box (File > Interpret Footage > Main) [Cmd/Ctrl + F].

This command enables deep control over the playback and appearance of footage in the composition.

4 Set the clip's frame rate to 15 frames per second and have it loop 12 times. Click OK.

This will slow down the sequence enough to prevent it from becoming too jarring and will also make it exactly 8 seconds long.

5 Create a new composition (Composition > New Composition) [Cmd/Ctrl + N] of the same size as the previous one: 720×468, 8 seconds long. Name the composition **4_distortion**.

6 Drag the 3_videoNoise composition and the disp[1-10].psd sequence into this new composition's Timeline; the order of the layers is unimportant.

7 Disable the visibility of the disp[1-10].psd layer by turning off the eye icon in the Timeline's Video switch.

It only needs to be present in the composition for the displacement effect and will not be rendered in the final output.

8 Select the 3_videoNoise layer and apply the Displacement Map effect (Effect > Distort > Displacement Map, or drag-and-drop from the Effects Palette).

9 Inspect the effect's parameters in the Timeline [E key]. Add an expression (Animation > Add Expression) [Option+Shift/Alt+Shift + =] to the Max Horizontal Displacement property.

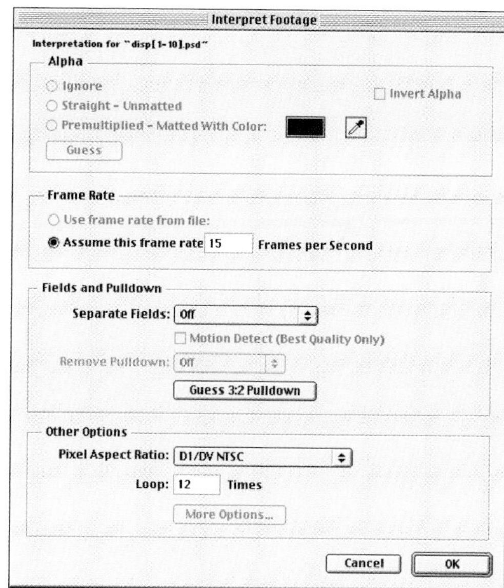

Using the Interpret Footage command, a brief piece of footage can be looped to extend for the length of any composition.

10 Type the following expression into the Max Horizontal Displacement property:

```
div(-100, (comp("3_videoNoise").layer
➥("staticConstant.wav").audio_levels[0])
```

This simple expression divides the audio level of the staticConstant.wav layer's left channel by –100 and makes this value the greatest possible horizontal offset that the displacement map will create. Note that the path name has to include the composition in which the staticConstant.wav layer resides because it is not in this composition (using **comp("3_videoNoise")** instead of **this_comp**). The louder the audio, the greater the displacement effect. Because the expression for the staticConstant.wav layer is designed to not exceed –12dB, this effect will not exceed 8.33 pixels of offset.

11 Add an expression (Animation > Add Expression) [Option+Shift/Alt+Shift + =] to the Max Vertical Displacement track and type in the following expression:

```
div(100, (comp("3_videoNoise").layer
➥("staticConstant.wav").audio_levels[1])
```

This expression will vertically offset pixels based on the audio level of the staticConstant.wav layer's right channel.

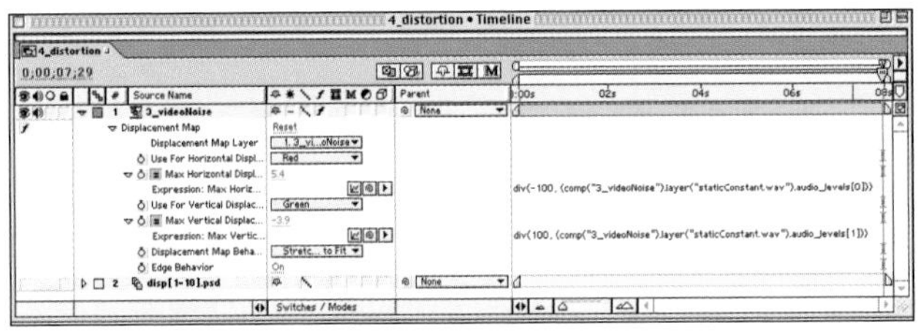

These expressions will displace the pixels in the target layer, but the amount of the effect is driven by the audio clip's left and right channel levels.

12 Save the project and then create a RAM preview to see the full effect.

The cumulative effects of the video distortion include noise, interlacing, color channel offsets, and even some overall image distortion.

LOOKING AT THE PROJECT'S STRUCTURE

Before rendering out the project to a QuickTime movie, open the Flowchart view by selecting Window > Project Flowchart View (there is also a toggle button on the right side of the Composition window). The Flowchart view gives a direct view of the actual structure of the project. The pop-up menu on the right-hand side of this window lets the user customize the view to make it easier to read.

To expand the contents of the Flowchart view, click on the plus (+) symbol on each composition (represented as dark gray). The more you expand compositions nested within one another, you'll eventually see every single composition, layer, solid, and scene object in your project and how they relate to one another.

Looking at the project, you can see that there are four main compositions, four pieces of footage (the two Photoshop layers, the raster line image, and the audio track), one solid (for the visual noise), one adjustment layer, and one camera. Not only that, you can see each effect applied to each component of the project. For complex projects, this can often be a helpful visualization tool, and it is critical when such projects are traded between artists.

hills/Hillside.psd
clouds/Hillside.psd
1: hills
2: clouds
1_Hillside.psd
1: Lense Curvature
Optics Compensation
2: Camera 1
3: 1_Hillside.psd
RasterLines.psd
2_hillsFakePan
staticConstant.wav
1: RasterLines.psd
2: noiseLayer
Noise
3: hills_B
Shift Channels
4: hills_G
Shift Channels
5: hills_R
Shift Channels
6: staticConstant.wav
3_videoNoise
disp[1-10].psd
1: 3_videoNoise
Displacement Map
2: disp[1-10].psd
4_distortion

The Flowchart view is a great way to visually correlate how nested compositions and their layers interact with, and relate to, one another.

MODIFICATIONS

A suggested modification to the Production Bundle version of this project is to go back to the 3_videoNoise composition, turn off the noiseLayer completely, and then create a preview of the 4_distortion composition. The effect is a bit different: It's easier to see the background plate, but it's glitchy enough to still indicate that there are some transmission problems.

Removing a layer of noise clarifies the footage but still allows the glitches to show through.

Swap the hillside footage out with footage of a talking head for a low-resolution videophone effect. For this modification, also make sure to remove the Optics Compensation adjustment layer and the camera.

This project's techniques are great for simulating low-grade video conferencing systems because the human face is easily recognizable even when distorted.

Displacement mapping is an amazing technique with millions of uses. How it works is fairly straightforward, but it's hard to completely understand without seeing the displacement map and its resulting effect. On the accompanying CD_ROM, this project includes a folder called modified_examples, and in it you will find two QuickTime files that show a simple displacement effect. The **grid_displace.mov** movie is extremely simple: two opposing Venetian blind wipes, alternately revealing white and black backgrounds. The **hotel_displaced.mov** movie shows this grid displacing a piece of video footage (the Venetian Hotel, appropriately enough). Although the final effect is pretty complex looking, correlating what's going on in the final movie and its displacement map makes it much easier to understand how the effect works.

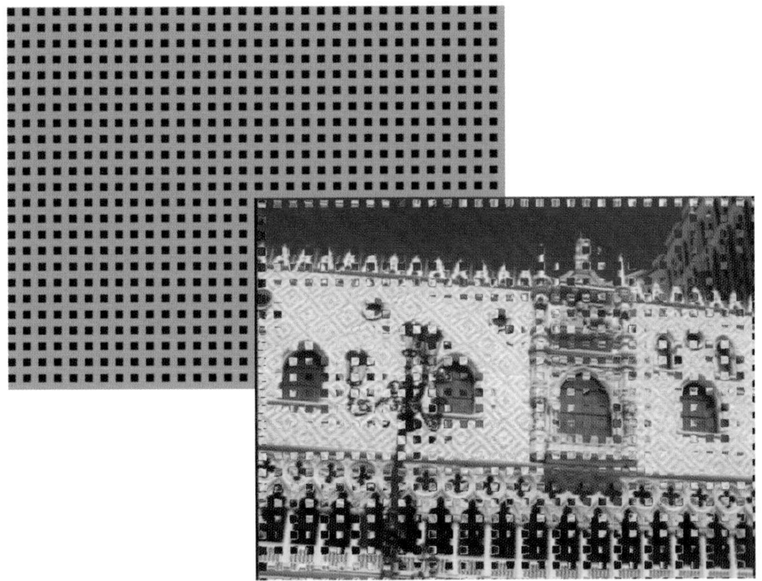

These movies show the direct correlation between gray, black, and white values in a displacement map and the resulting effect applied to real footage.

This project has also made extensive use of expressions to drive audio levels, effects (like displacement mapping), and object transformations (such as Opacity and Position). In this project's modified_examples folder on the accompanying CD-ROM, there is a further audio-related expressions project called **audio_ducking.aep**. *Audio ducking* is a recording technique in which one audio source is made quieter during the peaks of another audio source; the term comes from when an audio engineer would manually "duck" a fader by hand. Using expressions, a randomly modulated track of white noise (the same one from this tutorial) is used to inversely affect a piece of music. A high-pass audio filter is used to make the music sound more "brittle," filtering out its lower frequencies to give the impression of poor radio reception.

As with the earlier examples, this expression is complicated by 0dB being maximum volume and –96dB being the minimum volume. Take a look and figure out the flow of logic in the code.

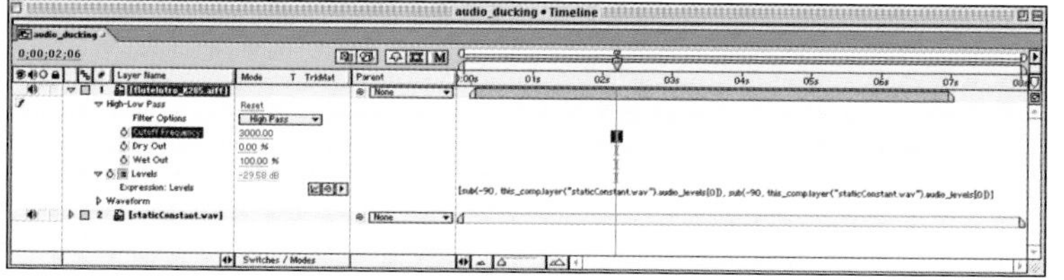

This expression creates an inverse relationship between the static track and the flute sound.

SWF EXPORT FROM AFTER EFFECTS

"I'm not bad. I'm just drawn that way."

—JESSICA RABBIT,
WHO FRAMED ROGER RABBIT

Repurposing After Effects Files for Use in Flash

One of the primary advantages of any digital medium is the potential to repurpose imagery or content from one means of delivery to another. In the world of design, this potentially means that a single visual language (logos, type treatments, print ads, and so on) can be developed once and then simply applied to a specific delivery method (printing, video, online, and so on). After Effects now has the capability to export SWF (Shockwave Flash, usually pronounced *swiff*) files, allowing motion-graphic artists to take their video or desktop multimedia work onto the World Wide Web.

This lesson will show how a short interstitial (used as a short introduction between episodes or commercial breaks) is translated from its original After Effects form into an optimized SWF and how this project can be optimized for web playback.

Project 3

SWF Export from After Effects

by Nathan Moody

How It Works

The reality of translating After Effects work to SWF files is never as quite as simple or as elegant as this "single-sourcing" theory sounds. For example, many broadcast designers create their work by starting with vector artwork, usually EPS files created from Illustrator or Freehand. This is also true of most Flash artists and animators as well. This at least provides original art assets that can be used for video, multimedia, and SWF media.

There are vast differences, however, between how QuickTime (or similar systems such as Windows Media Player) and Flash render their content. These differences can be summarized as follows: QuickTime and AVI movies have their pixels rendered before playback, whereas SWF files have their pixels rendered during playback.

After Effects normally renders its output as an absolute number of pixels: 720×486, 640×480, and so on. Each pixel is calculated in After Effects and rendered into a file, where each pixel is saved as part of a frame. QuickTime and AVI movies have fixed resolutions, requiring a single viewing size that is optimal. The advantage of prerendered pixels is that complex effects, such as blurs, glows, and complex compositing, can be shown without taxing the computer's processor because it has all been precalculated. As long as the device can keep up with the movie's data rate (*x* number of pixels blasted to the screen *y* times per second), everything should play smoothly.

On the other hand, SWF movies represent shapes and forms as *vectors*, mathematically described angles and curves with certain color characteristics. SWF movies are rendered on the fly, during playback, by a SWF Player (Flash Player, QuickTime Player, and so on), or by a browser's Flash plug-in on the viewer's computer. Flash movies are resolution independent and can be dynamically scaled to accommodate any size of playback window. The advantage of SWF movies is that the files are miniscule compared to QuickTime or AVI files of comparable length, but SWF playback relies on the client/playback device's computing power to render its vector shapes. (RAM helps, but processor power is a much bigger factor in playback speed.) This is why SWF files remain one of the best ways to deliver rich content over low-bandwidth Internet connections.

Note: Mac OS users will find that SWF playback, in many cases, is quite slower than for their comrades on Windows machines. This is because the Flash plug-in for browsers and the Flash Player standalone application are not fully optimized for Mac OS playback. You'll see a significant increase in playback speed watching SWFs on the Windows platform. This is a critical tip in preparing media for the web: If your movie plays back really well on your Macintosh, it will *scream* when running in Windows.

Getting Started

Before starting into the tutorial portion of this lesson, it is useful to take a look at After Effects' new SWF Export feature and discuss when and where this feature is best used.

After Effects' sophisticated numerical controls make it an excellent tool for creating complex, linear (noninteractive) SWF movies. Its capability to encode URLs into frames allows for simple, linear hyperlinking that will take the user to a different location after the movie is done playing. The main danger here is that many users are quickly tiring of the ubiquitous splash-page movies found on many SWF-enhanced web sites. Be sure what you create is short enough, small enough, and compelling enough to prevent your viewer from instinctively clicking that Skip Intro button.

Given that After Effects cannot embed hyperlinks in objects (although it can trigger URL redirects on certain frames, as you'll see later) or support interactive scripting, do not expect it to be able to export a functional animated interface. The main exception to this limitation is when small, intricate After Effects files are exported as SWFs and then imported back into Flash or LiveMotion as movie clips. This approach will let the artist build animations in After Effects' environment and do sophisticated scripting in a better tool: the best of both worlds.

When planning your After Effects project, consider whether it will need to be deployed online and build it appropriately. The SWF Export command is *not* well suited for putting your whole demo reel online. It *is* suited for evolving an ongoing campaign or corporate identity from print or video to the web.

Introducing *The Gambler*

The Gambler is an online animated series that profiles a randy "lover, not a fighter" antihero in 1970's Las Vegas. The producer of the show is unsure whether the series' niche and audience will be primarily online or on video, and he wants to hedge his bets by producing media that can be viewed both ways. Coupled with the lead animator's comfort level with After Effects as an animation tool, the show is made to be delivered both online and on video.

To this end, all the production design has been done in Illustrator: character design, backgrounds, everything. These assets are made in Illustrator and are rendered out to full-resolution DV QuickTime movies. However, they are also exported as SWF files for the show's web site.

Note: SWF files can be further edited and manipulated in either Adobe LiveMotion or Macromedia Flash. In fact, you'll be dipping into Flash later in this project to check your output results. If you don't have either program, it won't affect the outcome of this tutorial. However, if you do have either of these applications, I'd recommend running it alongside After Effects for this lesson.

Looking at the Project: The Good, the Bad...

Given that this animation is inherently simple by design, you're not going to spend much time figuring out the specifics of how its was animated. You'll focus instead on how this composition is structured, and you'll analyze how well (or how poorly) it will translate into the SWF format.

Again, this piece was created specifically to be exported as both a DV-compressed QuickTime movie and as a SWF (complete with audio). To accommodate for Flash output, only two types of layers are being used: imported Adobe Illustrator artwork and After Effects solids. That's it—no pixels to be found.

Note: Take note of how the mandalaCW and mandalaCCW layers spin in opposite directions through the use of a simple expression. The pickwhip was used to link the two layers' rotation values together, and then the expression was multiplied by –1 to impart rotation in the opposite direction. This is another example of how animating with basic expressions can be *faster* than setting keyframes by hand.

1. Open the **theGambler_final.aep** project file from this chapter's folder on the accompanying CD-ROM.

2. In the Project window, double-click on the composition called Gambler_martini; you'll see a finished animation ready for output.

   The animation has a few layers moving around, and near the end of the piece, the gambler lifts his orange martini (hey, it's only a cartoon) as his logo comes into view.

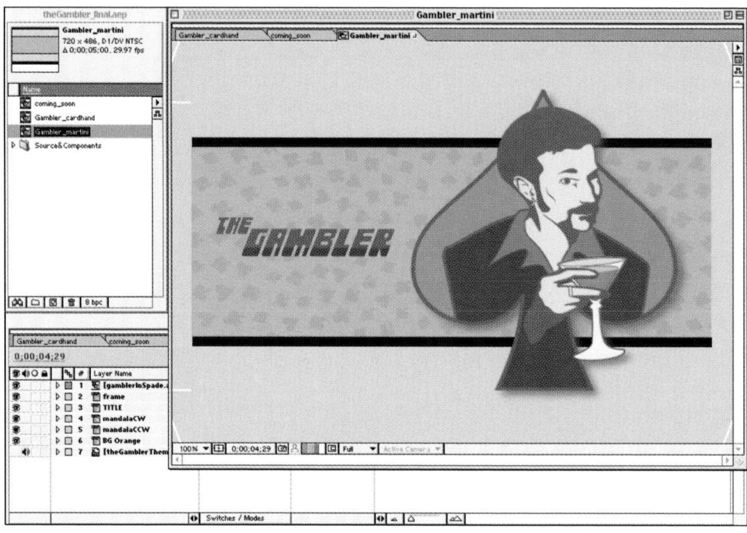

This relatively simple, animated interstitial has been built completely with Illustrator shapes to facilitate SWF Export.

3. In the Timeline window, move your time indicator all the way to the last frame of the animation [End key]. Now, zoom in the Timeline's view as much as possible (by using the Zoom slider or by moving the left edge of the Time View bracket).

   You'll see that there is a layer-time marker on Layer 3 (Gambler_Title.ai) at time 0:00:04:29, marked "URL."

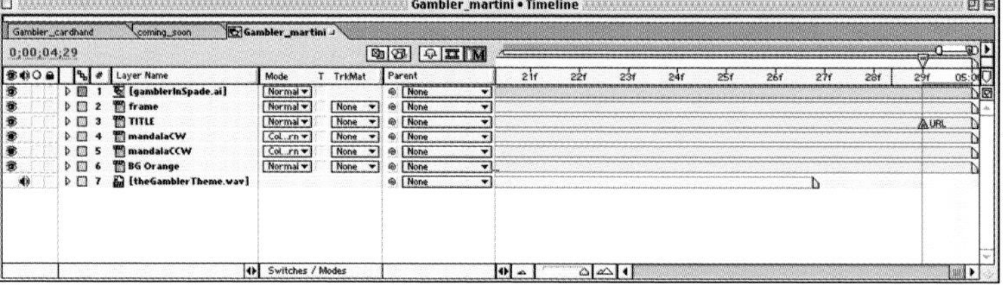

Layer-time markers can be used to produce simple URL links in exported SWF files.

4 Double-click on this layer-time marker to open its dialog box.

You'll see that it has a URL embedded in it; the last section of this lesson discusses its particulars.

Note: Chapter links, which can also be embedded in layer-time markers, can be used with QuickTime; they are most often used as a control for CD-ROMs and DVDs. They have no impact on SWF Export or viewing the movie in a browser. It's worth mentioning that composition-time markers have no linking functionality whatsoever; they are organization tools only.

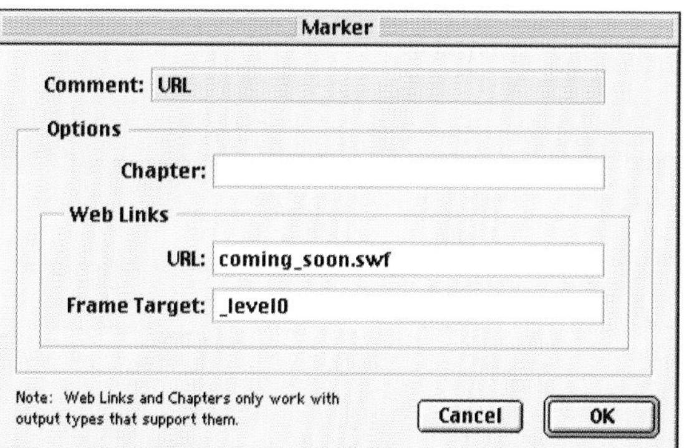

Time-layer markers support relative and absolute links as well as the capability to determine in which window or frame the link will be resolved.

5 Zoom the Timeline all the way back out to the full length of the composition and select Layer 1 (gamblerInSpade.ai). Press the E key to inspect its effects.

This layer has a Drop Shadow effect applied to it. This is, in fact, the only effect applied in the whole composition. But let's take a moment to discuss why this minor effect is a potential problem.

SWF files easily accept vector or EPS artwork, but pixels are another story. This simple drop shadow not only generates pixels on its own, but these pixels are semi-opaque and are composited on a background with multiple solids. The SWF format is going to have a difficult time dealing with this because its format cannot assign transparency to individual pixels (although it can for vector shapes). Bitmapped graphics themselves can have an overall transparency or opacity value, but there is no accommodation for image-based masking or alpha channels in which color and brightness are figured on a per-pixel basis.

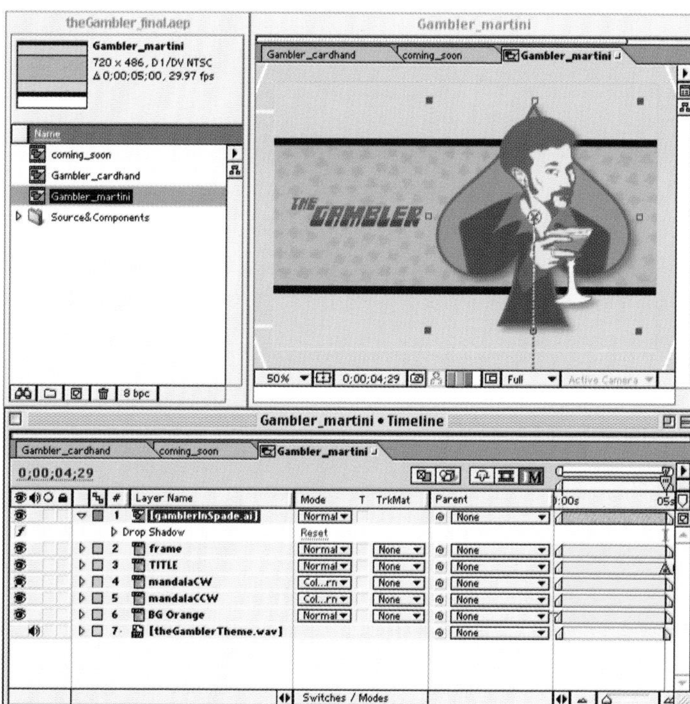

The Drop Shadow effect is pixel based and can create problems when exporting vector-based SWFs.

So, you will probably want to lose the Drop Shadow effect for efficiency's sake, but yet another potential problem raises its ugly head: Motion Blur is also activated for the Gambler_Main composition. That is also a pixel-based effect. It might be time to examine some global ways of dealing with all these raster-heavy effects.

After Effects offers two solutions to these kinds of problems. One alternative is to simply ignore any setting or effect that will generate pixels, which is the route you'll take here (it will save on render time, anyway). Another solution is to rasterize all unsupported features as pixel-based imagery.

6 Select the SWF Export command (File > Export > Macromedia Flash [SWF]), name the file **gambler_martini_IGNORE.swf**, and save the file to somewhere on your hard drive.

7 Inspect the next dialog: SWF Settings.

You'll see that the second option down is the Unsupported Features preference, which can be set to either ignore or rasterize effects and features that generate pixels.

Don't close or resolve the dialog box yet.

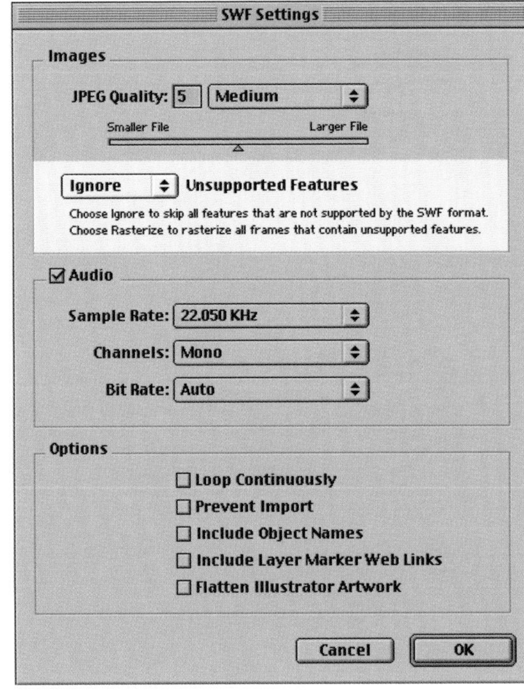

The option to ignore or rasterize unsupported features is a major factor in determining how the SWF file will look... and how big it will be.

Looking at the Project: ...And the Ugly

After Effects has an interesting habit that will make some animations very difficult to export: It always renders nested compositions as pixels. If you have any precomped layers or nested compositions in the composition you're trying to export, even if they are composed completely of vector or EPS shapes, you'll essentially have a large raster image in each frame.

Let's take a shot at exporting this composition as it stands.

1 In the SWF Settings dialog box (which is hopefully still open from the last section), set the JPEG quality to 5 and ignore all unsupported features. Select 22.050 KHz audio and mono, with Bit Rate set to Auto, for the soundtrack. Leave all the other Options unchecked.

   You'll notice that, although it might take a little while, this kind of rendering is much faster than actually rendering QuickTime movies. This is because After Effects is simply referring to the original Illustrator vector shapes and is reproducing those colors, points, and curves in the SWF format.

   You'll also notice that two separate files have been created. Gambler_martini.swf is the actual SWF movie file, and Gambler_martiniR.html is an HTML document that enables you to view the SWF movie in a web page.

2 Double-click on the Gambler_martiniR.html file; it should open in a browser. (Drop-launch the file onto your preferred browser if this does not work.)

Note: MacOS users will find that the HTML files created by After Effects will be associated with the default browser specified in the Internet Control Panel. To alter this setting, go to the Apple menu and choose Control Panels > Internet. Click on the Web tab, and you will see the Default Browser pop-up menu at the bottom of the dialog box.

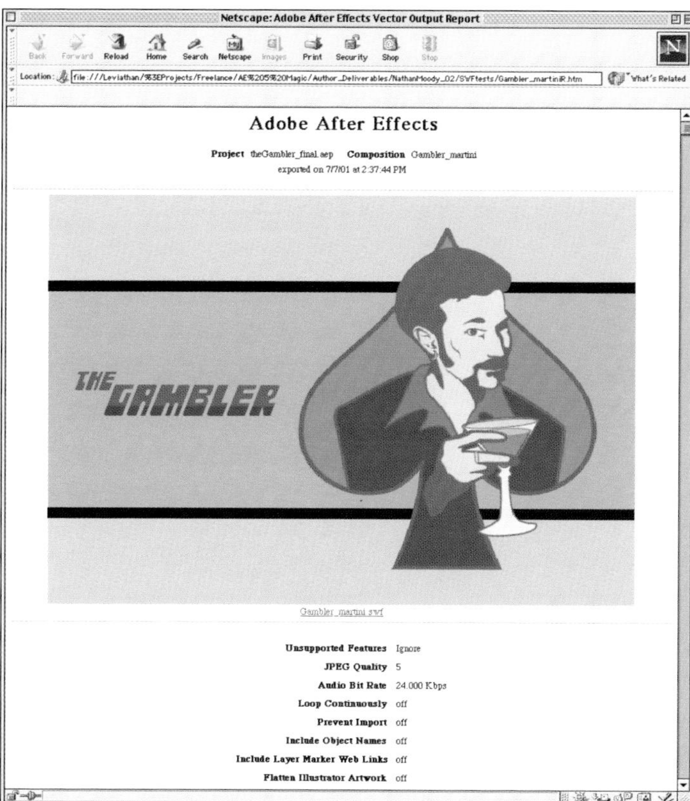

After Effects conveniently exports an HTML document showing the SWF and all of your export settings.

You'll see the animation play in a web page, but more interesting is all of the great information After Effects exports with each SWF render: all of your preference and file settings, render completion time, and even the name of the project and composition. Clicking on the hyperlink below the SWF will open it in its own browser window, if desired. This is very useful, especially for showing intermediate work to supervisors or sharing your work with other artists.

The best part about this web page, however, is its list of the unsupported features that the plug-in encountered, on a per-frame basis.

3 Scroll down the page, and you'll see a very long table with all sorts of error messages.

This is extremely helpful for troubleshooting After Effects projects and seeing how certain effects are (or aren't) handled.

Now for the bad news.

Note: If you want to see the animation play again—it currently is not set to loop continuously—press your browser's Reload button.

Time	Name - Unsupported Feature
0;00;00;00	1: gamblerInSpade.ai - multiple or unsupported effects 2: frame - motion blur 3: TITLE - motion blur 4: card_suits.ai - unsupported layer mode 5: card_suits.ai - unsupported layer mode 6: BG Orange - motion blur
0;00;00;01	1: gamblerInSpade.ai - multiple or unsupported effects 2: frame - motion blur 3: TITLE - motion blur 4: card_suits.ai - unsupported layer mode 5: card_suits.ai - unsupported layer mode 6: BG Orange - motion blur
0;00;00;02	1: gamblerInSpade.ai - multiple or unsupported effects 2: frame - motion blur 3: TITLE - motion blur 4: card_suits.ai - unsupported layer mode 5: card_suits.ai - unsupported layer mode 6: BG Orange - motion blur
0;00;00;03	1: gamblerInSpade.ai - multiple or unsupported effects 2: frame - motion blur 3: TITLE - motion blur 4: card_suits.ai - unsupported layer mode 5: card_suits.ai - unsupported layer mode 6: BG Orange - motion blur
0;00;00;04	1: gamblerInSpade.ai - multiple or unsupported effects 2: frame - motion blur 3: TITLE - motion blur 4: card_suits.ai - unsupported layer mode 5: card_suits.ai - unsupported layer mode 6: BG Orange - motion blur
0;00;00;05	1: gamblerInSpade.ai - multiple or unsupported effects 2: frame - motion blur 3: TITLE - motion blur 4: card_suits.ai - unsupported layer mode 5: card_suits.ai - unsupported layer mode 6: BG Orange - motion blur
0;00;00;06	1: gamblerInSpade.ai - multiple or unsupported effects 2: frame - motion blur 3: TITLE - motion blur 4: card_suits.ai - unsupported layer mode 5: card_suits.ai - unsupported layer mode 6: BG Orange - motion blur
0;00;00;07	1: gamblerInSpade.ai - multiple or unsupported effects 2: frame - motion blur 3: TITLE - motion blur 4: card_suits.ai - unsupported layer mode 5: card_suits.ai - unsupported layer mode 6: BG Orange - motion blur
0;00;00;08	1: gamblerInSpade.ai - multiple or unsupported effects 2: frame - motion blur 3: TITLE - motion blur 4: card_suits.ai - unsupported layer mode 5: card_suits.ai - unsupported layer mode 6: BG Orange - motion blur
0;00;00;09	1: gamblerInSpade.ai - multiple or unsupported effects 2: frame - motion blur 3: TITLE - motion blur 4: card_suits.ai - unsupported layer mode 5: card_suits.ai - unsupported layer mode 6: BG Orange - motion blur
	1: gamblerInSpade.ai - multiple or unsupported effects

After Effects goes to great lengths to detail exactly which unsupported features were encountered during export.

4 Look at the file size of your SWF: over 900KB, almost 1MB! Second, take a very close look at the SWF's upper-right corner and take account of what's happened.

In After Effects, the spiraling mandala of card suits in the background is a reddish-orange color, thanks to the Color Burn mode. Flash and the SWF format have no idea what blending modes are, so it has completely ignored these layers (as per our instructions).

There are some blocky artifacts around edge regions of the gambler himself but nowhere else. These are JPEG compression artifacts, evidence of the aforementioned tendency to rasterize nested compositions. The emblem with the character in it had to be precomped to allow for a drop shadow on the entire image.

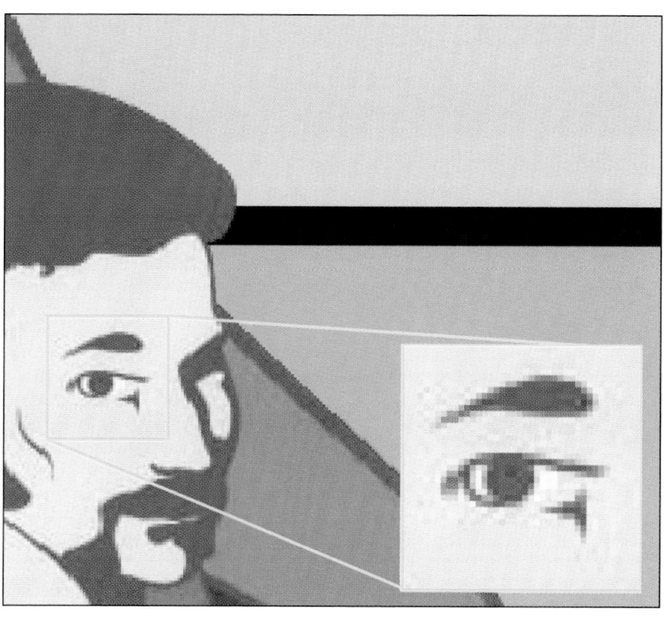

Even though all elements were created in Illustrator, some shapes become rasterized—and compressed as JPEGs.

There is another quite subtle issue with this SWF file: its pixel aspect ratio. Because it was created with DV in mind, its pixel aspect ratio is not square, making it look wider than it should on a computer monitor. Take a look at the following figure to compare how NTSC and DV pixel aspects differ.

A subtle but noticeable difference can be seen between square pixels for standard NTSC video and nonsquare pixels in digital D1 and DV footage. SWF Export does not correct for rectangular pixel aspect ratios.

If you needed to re-render a QuickTime movie for a different pixel aspect ratio, that's nothing a little precompositing can't cure. However, as you've already learned, precomps become rasterized, so that's not a viable alternative. Each frame would be a different JPEG, at which point it's better delivered as a QuickTime or AVI movie.

The two quickest workarounds for this problem lie outside of After Effects. One solution is to scale the SWF in the browser by simply entering new width parameters in a web page's OBJECT or EMBED tags. Alternatively, in Flash, all its frames can be imported (or cut and pasted) into a movie clip, and then its instance can be scaled after it is placed in a Scene. Because SWFs are vector-based, they hold up very well to resizing like this, although text-heavy SWFs might become hard to read.

A final workflow suggestion is to create such clips with square aspect ratios from the start and then precomp them into a new composition with a DV-aspect pixel ratio for high-resolution output. This enables your SWF files to come out better, but it's not of much use for altering preexisting After Effects projects and compositions.

5 Back in After Effects, re-export the Gambler_martini composition and name the SWF **Gambler_martini_raster**. When the SWF Settings dialog box appears, choose Rasterize for the Unsupported Features option.

6 Open the resulting HTML file in a browser.

Now you have your drop shadow and your mandala back. However, look at the file size: over 3.5MB! What happened? Between your precomp, the mandala layers' unsupported color mode, and the drop shadow, every single frame has been saved as a JPEG. Not exactly what the SWF file format was meant to deliver over the web, is it?

All in all, this composition (and its resulting SWF) is quite a mess. Now, you haven't optimized any of After Effects' output settings, which could help a bit, but even the 900KB+ original file size is not good for a 5-second online clip. It might be time to move on to greener pastures.

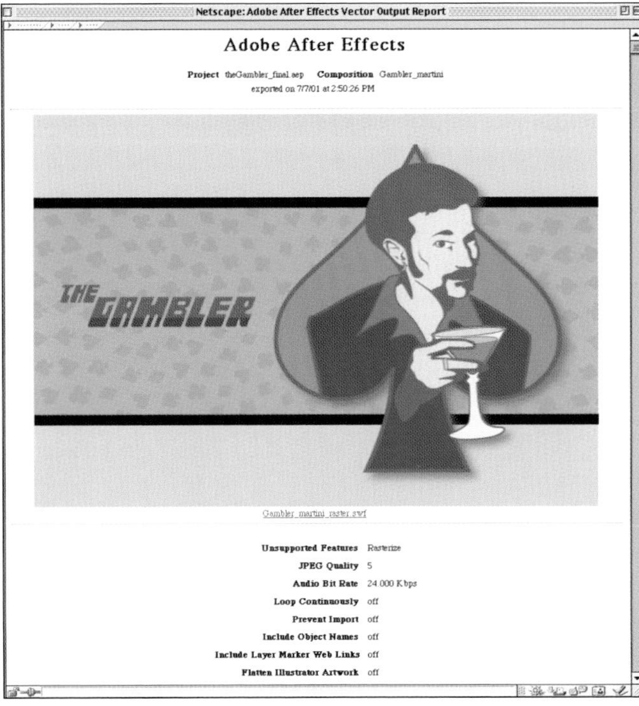

Rasterizing the unsupported features brings back every detail from the original After Effects file.

REINTRODUCING *THE GAMBLER*

The preceding example showed some of the pitfalls that artists and animators will encounter with the SWF Export feature in After Effects. Retrofitting compositions made for other media (specifically DV) can have some serious limitations.

Luckily, there is an alternate composition in this project with which you will have much better luck: Gambler_cardhand. Luckily, it was also built as a short interstitial, and it will fit the same role for the show as the previous composition.

1. Set the Composition window's resolution to Half and view it at 50%. Then create a RAM preview [0 on the numeric keypad].

   This animation is a simple move of the gambler's profile from left to right, with an occasional blink and a hand of cards moving over his lower face.

   There is not a drop shadow in sight, no motion blur to be found, and no troublesome precomps. Even all of the blending modes have been set to Normal, and the pixel aspect ratio of this composition is square. This clip is a good example of a composition that has been built for SWF export first and DV output second. Altering the composition to a nonsquare pixel ratio can be accomplished by nesting it in a DV-aspect composition (and scaling the precomp accordingly).

2. Select File > Export > Macromedia Flash (SWF) and save the resulting SWF to your hard drive.

3. In the SWF Settings dialog box, reset the Unsupported Features option back to Ignore. There should be no surprises at output time.

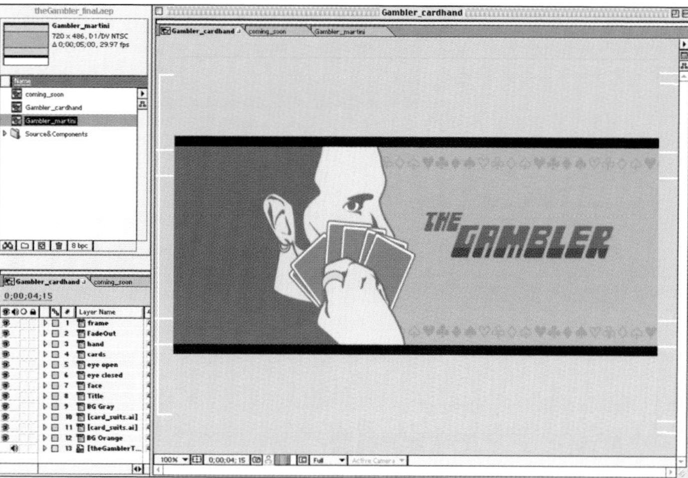

This second composition is cleaner, simpler, and lacks any pixel-based effects and nested compositions.

4. Open the HTML file that After Effects has produced in a browser.

   The first thing you'll notice is that the SWF looks exactly like the original and plays back at a decent speed. If you scroll to the bottom the HTML file, the table of unsupported features is missing: Everything you've done in the After Effects project has been translated perfectly into the SWF format. Most importantly, the file size of this animation is less than 60KB, a dramatic improvement over your last attempt with the previous composition.

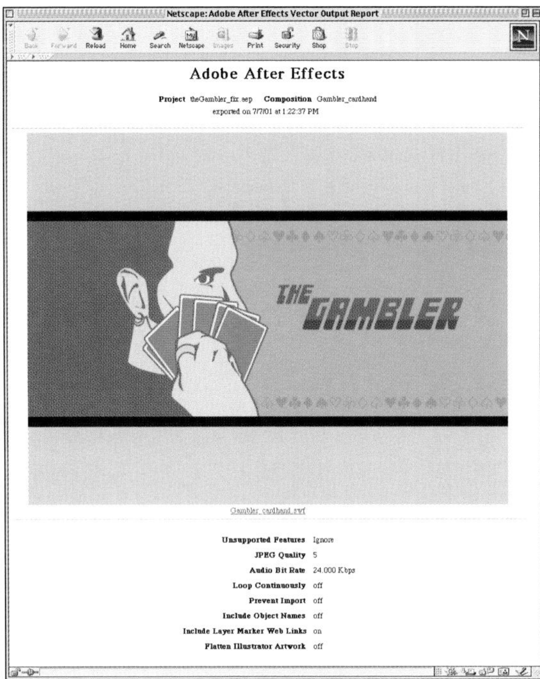

This SWF is completely vector based. There are no horizontal scroll bars in this browser window, which means there are no unsupported features to report.

Up Close and Personal: Examining SWF Output in Flash

The SWF file you just created is ready to go on a web site. You can even copy and paste the EMBED and OBJECT tags right out of the Gambler_cardhandR.htm file into a new HTML page. However, many animators will want to import this SWF into Flash or LiveMotion to be used in a larger interactive piece. Let's examine how After Effects' SWF output imports into these applications, and let's see what you can learn about optimizing your SWF movies.

If you have Flash or LiveMotion, this is a good time to launch the application and follow along, but these steps will be "shorthanded" for those who do not have access to one of these tools. This lesson will use Flash.

First, the Movie Properties of a Flash movie must be set to whatever the After Effects project dictates.

1 Before importing the SWF, your Flash movie should be set to 30 frames per second, and its dimensions should be 720 pixels wide by 540 pixels tall.

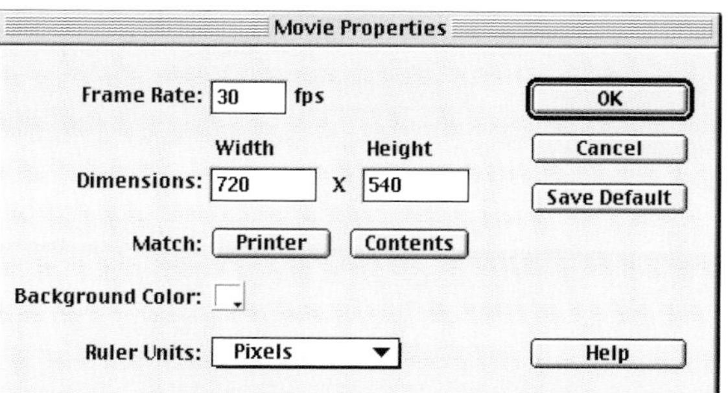

In Flash, these settings will accommodate your exported SWF for further study and editing.

2 Import the SWF into Flash.

At first glance, there are no big surprises. The clip is indeed 150 frames long. (Remember that Flash starts frame numbering at 1, not zero.) There are some shapes beyond the stage area, but that's to be expected because you're moving around some objects that are bigger than the active stage.

Your exported SWF, in Flash, shows the full extent of all shapes on the stage.

One thing that will immediately be a concern to some Flash artists is that all the components of the animation are imported on a single layer, and *every* frame is a keyframe. This means that customization or refinement of motion or movement must be done in After Effects because the imported SWF contains only frame and image information, not tweening.

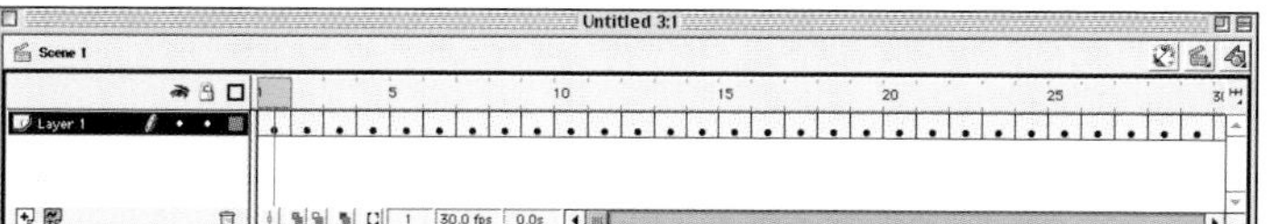

Notice that every frame contains a keyframe, and all the frames are in a single layer.

3 Open the Library to see the components that this SWF brought with it. The Library contains 1,777 symbols!

What's even more interesting is that not every symbol is different. The first 130 to 140 symbols are unique: they comprise every line, arc, stroke, and fill contained in the imported artwork. You'll also find a few large red boxes in the Library; they were not imported into your original After Effects project, but the SWF uses them as masks to accomplish certain shape compositing tasks. At a certain point (after Symbol 140 or so), however, every 22nd symbol seems to be the same: For example, Symbol 1733, Symbol 1755, and Symbol 1777 are all the beige "letterboxing" bars on the top and bottom of our animation. If you save this Flash project, you'll see that all of this winds up yielding a FLA file well over 3MB in size.

Note: The most unfortunate result of importing this SWF into Flash is that its audio does not get imported into Flash. If you are building a larger Flash movie and want to present this SWF with audio, the best way to accomplish this is by using the Load Movie ActionScript command, which will load and play external SWFs into another SWF at runtime.

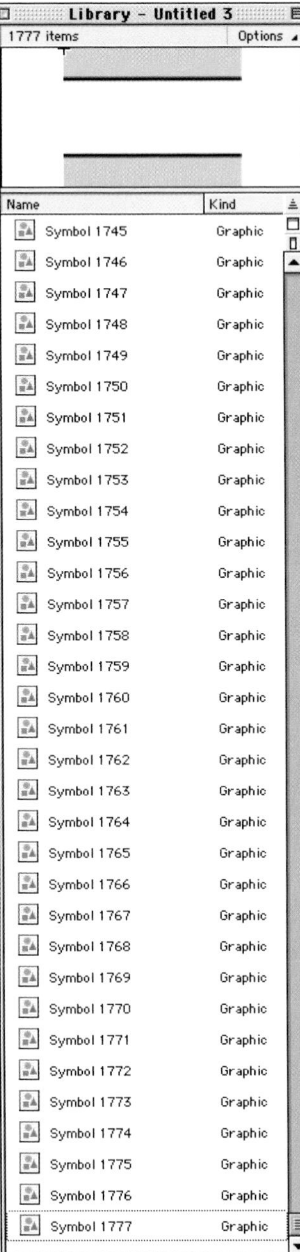

Every object on every frame gets its own symbol. This exported SWF, brought into Flash, has more than 1,700 symbols.

Finishing the SWF Animation

So, having looked in-depth at your gambler SWF in Flash, it's time to get back into After Effects and complete your animation. You'll take the interactivity that After Effects offers you and link a separate SWF into your main Gambler_cardhand composition.

Note: Loading external SWF files into other SWFs using the GetMovie ActionScript feature is an effective way to create modular content, which can be edited separately and modified according to project and client needs.

1 In After Effects, open the Gambler_cardhand composition and double-click on the layer-time marker at frame 0:00:04:29 in the Title layer.

This URL is a relative link to another SWF file in the same directory. The Frame Target, _level0, refers to the SWF's main Timeline. When this animation reaches this frame, this marker will trigger an ActionScript command to automatically load a separate SWF into this movie.

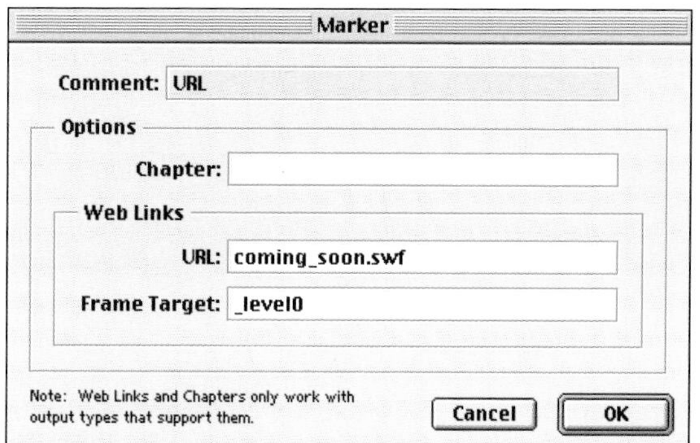

This layer-time marker's Web Links settings will translate into an ActionScript command that will load a new SWF right into the current one.

2 Click OK to close this dialog box.

3 In the Project window, double-click on the coming_soon composition.

This composition is an extremely simple title card that states the release date of the full animated series.

As you can guess from this composition's name, this is the SWF that will get loaded into the Gambler_cardhand SWF. For this trick to work, you'll have to export each of them separately and put them both into the same directory.

Note: For those After Effects artists who are unfamiliar with Flash (or who are intimidated by its scripting capabilities), there is good news. Both After Effects' Expressions and Flash's ActionScripting language are built on JavaScript-style syntax. With some minor adjustments for each application, an artist or programmer only needs to learn one type of syntax to be able to program effectively in JavaScript, ActionScript, and Expressions. Purchasing a single book on basic JavaScript is a great investment for any artist working in dynamic digital media.

4 In the Timeline window for the coming_soon composition, there is a layer-time marker at time 0:00:02:29 in the coming_soon.ai layer. Double-click on this marker to open its dialog box.

This marker is a little different than the previous one: It is loading a true URL for a web page, not a SWF file. Its Frame Target is set to _blank, which will open a new browser window with the listed URL.

Note: Sometimes a layer-time marker's GetMovie action gets triggered before the image content of the frame loads. To prevent a single-frame "ghosted" text (the last frame of the Opacity tween before the coming_soon.ai layer becomes transparent), make sure all keyframes are set one frame before the layer-time marker.

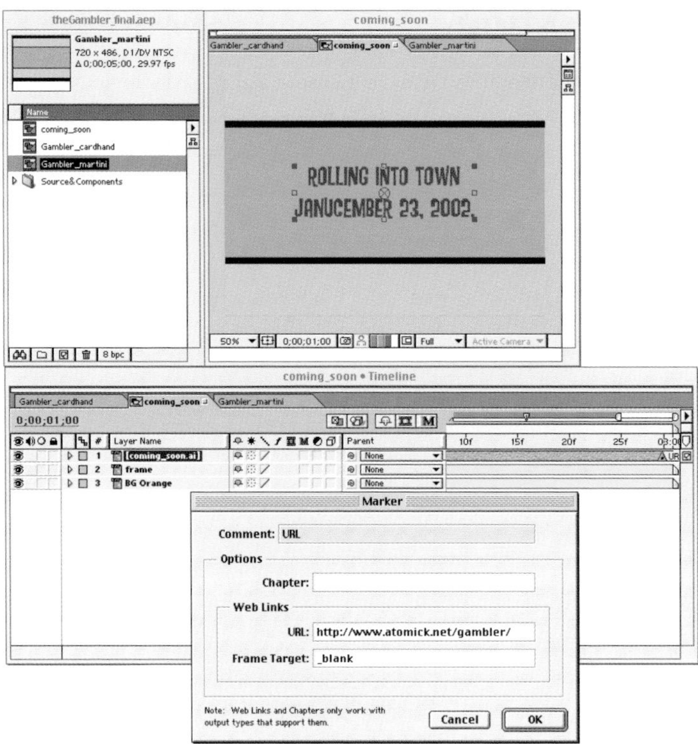

This type of web link will resolve as a standard URL.

5 Export the Gambler_cardhand composition and make sure to check the Include Layer Marker Web Links option.

6 Do the same to the coming_soon composition. Because the coming_soon.swf file points at a real URL, enable an Internet connection.

7 Open the Gambler_cardhandR.htm file in a browser. If you have Flash, simply double-clicking the Gambler_cardhand.swf file will open it in Flash Player, which will still respect URL hyperlinks.

You'll see the gambler animation play first, then the "coming soon" animation will load in its place, and finally a live web page will be loaded from over the Internet.

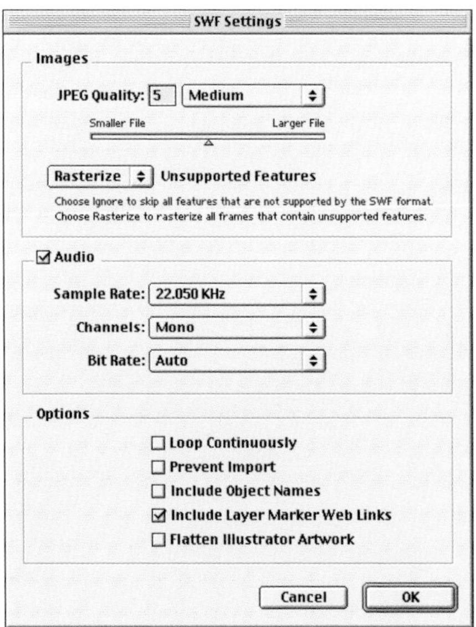

Include Layer Marker Web Links must be checked to enable hyperlinking and ActionScript commands.

Final Analysis: Workflow for SWF Export

- It is almost always better to build After Effects compositions *specifically* for SWF deployment. It is easier to manipulate such compositions to conform to video specifications than the other way around (although it can be done).
- In building projects that will be brought into Flash or LiveMotion, it's most helpful to still consider After Effects a specialized animation tool and Flash or LiveMotion an integration and editing environment. It is most efficient to only animate what is actually moving in After Effects and then mix those components with static elements imported or copied directly from Adobe Illustrator or Macromedia Freehand. Likewise, final audio tracks need to be imported into Flash, although working with them in After Effects will help achieve synch.
- If you want to play an After Effects–exported SWF within a larger Flash movie, it makes more sense to do so using the Load Movie or GetMovie ActionScript commands. This will avoid the loss of audio that will occur when a SWF file is imported into Flash. You can even link several individual SWF files together in After Effects itself through the use of layer-time markers.
- Leaving the Include Object Names and Flatten Illustrator Artwork options unchecked in the SWF Settings dialog will usually yield smaller files.
- Creating complex motion is what After Effects is all about, so use it for what it is good for. Simple animations might be better done entirely within Flash or LiveMotion if those packages are available. This mainly pertains to file size; SWFs exported from After Effects are not completely optimized for file size.

Modifications

You should continue to experiment with this project and get a handle on the SWF Export feature's strengths and weaknesses. The gambler's lovely purple 1966 GTO is also included in the After Effects project (in the project's Footage folder) for your further animation edification, as are all of the original Illustrator files.

The gambler's regal wheels are included for further animation edification.

GREEN-SCREEN COMPOSITING AND OTHER KEYING TECHNIQUES

"It's not easy being green."

—KERMIT THE FROG

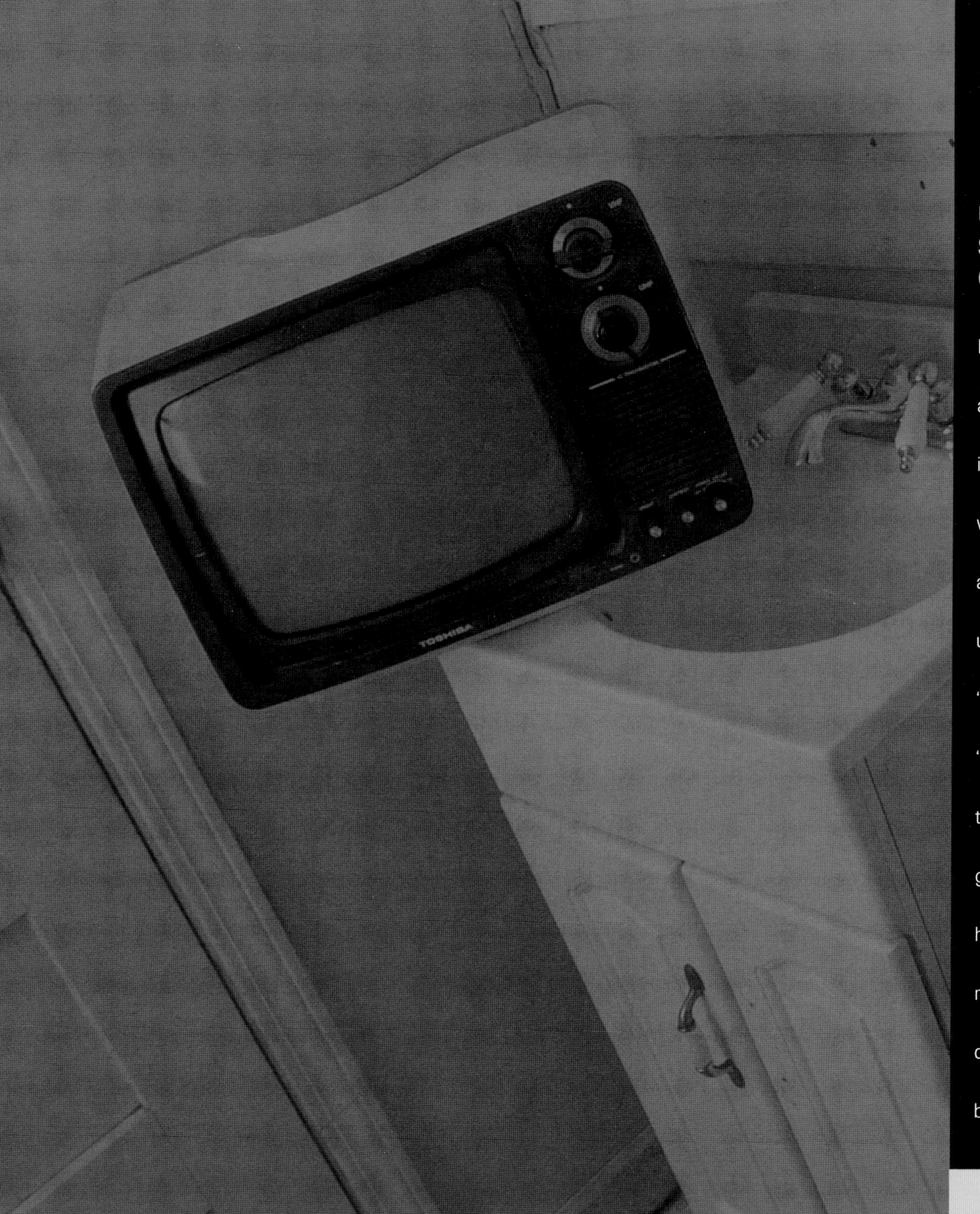

Using Keying Techniques to Simplify Pulling a Matte from a Green/Blue Screen

Every piece of footage is different and presents a different challenge to the After Effects artist in pulling a matte (or mask). The use of the word "mask" here is incorrect when talking about keying in visual effects. I stand by the use of the word "matte" *only* here. You cannot "pull a mask" in After Effects; you can only "pull a matte." This project will show you how to pull a matte from a green screen and will give you some other options that you might not have already thought of for pulling a decent matte for your composite. Keep in mind that all of the techniques used can also be applied to blue screens.

Project 4

Green-Screen Compositing and Other Keying Techniques

by Sherry Hitch

How It Works

This lesson is divided into three parts: showing how to pull a green-screen matte using the tools available in the After Effects Standard version, showing a similar task using the Production Bundle's Keying Pack effects, and showing a final look at using Color Range to pull a matte. Just remember one thing when putting together any composite in After Effects: Try to keep it simple! If you can do that, your compositions will result in faster render times, and when you have to go back and open up the same project a month down the road, it won't take an eternity to figure out what you were doing.

Getting Started

The first few steps will help you determine which route will be the best approach to pulling a matte. Before starting, be sure you know on what format your footage was shot or filmed. Was it filmed on 35mm film? Digital video? Beta SP? This is important to know because it will determine how you want to set up your composition in terms of a frame rate and how After Effects will interpret your footage. In addition to the Project Settings window, the Interpret Footage dialog box (File > Interpret Footage) [Cmd/Ctrl + F] can help you determine what kind of footage you are dealing with, including the footage's frame rate, field dominance, and more. If you accidentally have an incorrect frame rate or wrong field dominance, this can impact how the sequence will play back once rendered out. If you set up any keyframes, it can also impact your timing by throwing off all of your keyframes. This footage was shot on 35 mm and then transferred to Digi-beta, thus giving us footage at 24 frames per second.

1 Open After Effects and import (File > Import) [Cmd/Ctrl + I] both footage sequences from Lesson_1 on the accompanying CD-ROM: **lesson1_foreground.mov** and **lesson1_background.mov**.

2 From the Project window, create a new composition (Composition > New Composition) [Cmd/Ctrl + I].

Remember to put the layers you want in the distance on the bottom and the layers you want in the foreground on top of the Timeline window.

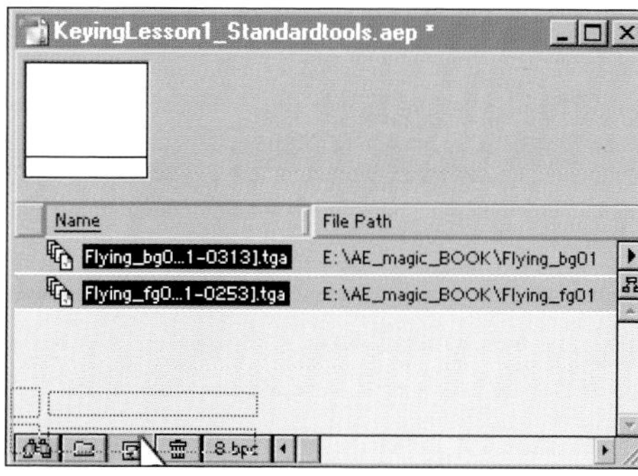

Drag the footage over the New Composition icon to create a new composition.

Note: You can drag both footages over the New Composition icon at the bottom of the Project window to create a new composition that automatically corresponds to the footage's size (D1) and frame rate (24fps). Make sure that these line up to the way you first brought your footage into the project. You can also rename the composition at this stage, because your composition will automatically be renamed to match the first frame of your sequence.

3 Create a RAM preview to examine the footage and to see what problems you might encounter with your footage. You might see something that "whizzes" past camera, or that the shot pans up and you see outside the actual green screen. Save your project as **GSLesson1**.

Note: The keyboard command for RAM preview is the 0 (zero) key on the numeric keypad.

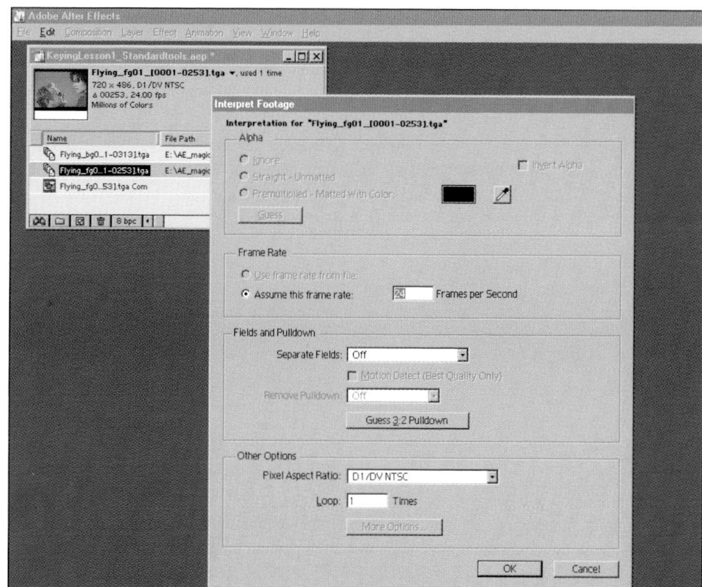

Use the Interpret Footage dialog box to determine the frame rate of your footage, 24 frames per second.

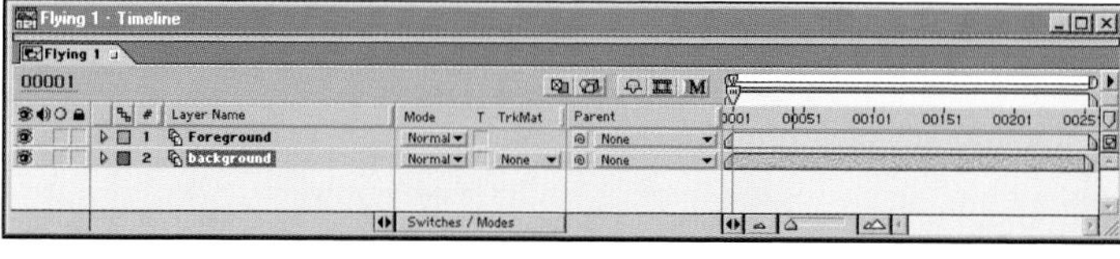

Put all the layers for the foreground on top of the Timeline window; put the layers for the distance on the bottom.

Lesson 1: Pulling a Green-Screen Matte with the Standard Version Keying Tools

Now you need to experiment with the various keying tools in After Effects to determine which tool is the best for pulling a matte. Because this is a book that tries to teach techniques without the addition of third-party plug-ins, I would like to show you how you can pull a matte effectively without having to rely on buying expensive plug-ins, starting with only the Standard version of After Effects.

For this lesson, continue using the Lesson 1 footage you just imported.

"Velocity Rules", 2001
The American Film Institute, Rocks & Rules Productions
Director Patty Jenkins, Cinematographer Guy Livneh

Use the Standard version of After Effects to create this final composite.

1. In the Timeline window, select your Green Screen layer, lesson1_foreground.mov, so that it is highlighted. Select the Color Key effect (Effect > Keying > Color Key or drag-and-drop from the Effects Palette onto the selected layer in the Composition or Timeline windows.*)*.

   This filter will be able to "key out," or remove, any color you want.

2. Click on the Eyedropper tool in the Color Key Effect Controls window and drag it over the green screen.

   Before you press the mouse to select the color, take a look at the Info palette to note the different values of green as you drag the Eyedropper tool around on the green screen. Try choosing a value with the largest green value and then go ahead and select the color. At first, there won't be much that is keyed out (where the black dots begin to appear). You will have to go in and raise the tolerance level in the Effect Controls window.

3. Select a Color Tolerance value around 76.

   This increases the areas of green to be included with this particular shade of green.

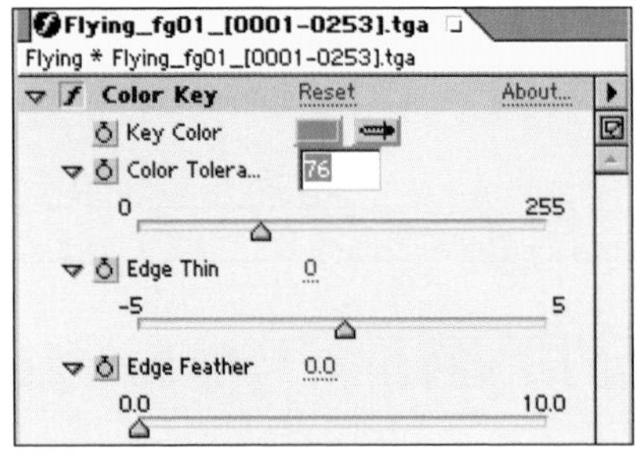

Select a green from the Color Key Effect Controls.

4 Increase the Edge Feather to 1.5.

This will soften the edge of the matte and remove those sharp edges. You now need to get rid of the green hue around the subjects, which you can no doubt see most vividly in their hair. You need a filter that has the capability to select the green color and modify that particular color.

For this next step, you will want to adjust the Hue to try and take out as much of the leftover green spill as possible.

5 Open Change Color (Effect > Image Control > Change Color or drag-and-drop from the Effects Palette). Using the Color Picker, choose a color on the edge, such as around the hair. I entered the following (the numbers on the left are HLS, the ones on the right are RGB):

Hue: **64**	Red: **117 (49%)**
Saturation: **90**	Green: **174 (68%)**
Luminance: **119 (47%)**	Blue: **79 (31%)**

The same goes for the rest of the values applied within this filter. Try altering the Matching Tolerance and Matching Softness settings and then take a peek at the view of the Color Correction Mask on the pull-down menu within the filter. Notice that the edge that marks the presence of green is all white. The goal is to make sure you have a solid black and white image to show you the alpha channel. The white area represents the area of the composition that you want to keep in the shot; the black area represents the area of the original green screen footage that you want to get rid of.

Note: Notice that you aren't bothering with the Edge Thin parameter. This is primarily because it takes off a bit too much around the edges sometimes, and you can lose important detail. Edge detail is the primary factor in determining whether or not your composite is successful. You can generally get better control by just adjusting the Tolerance and Feather options. You don't want to bite off too much from the edges of the hair—you want to keep its wispiness.

6 Set these values if you need further assistance:

Matching Tolerance: **10.1%**

Matching Softness: **1.6%**

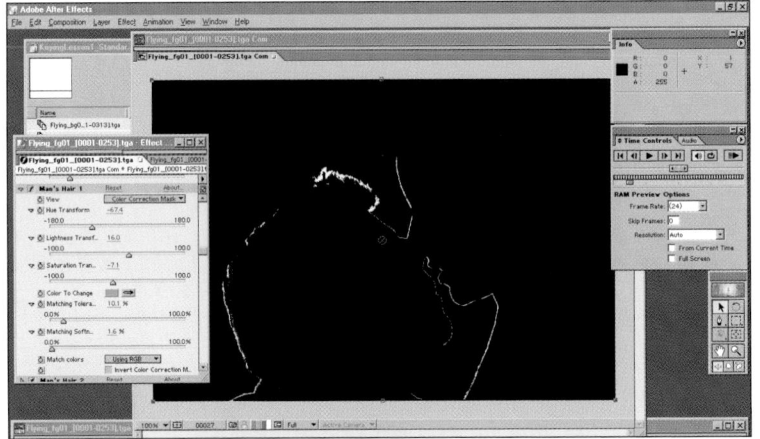

View the matte of the Change Color filter.

7 Set the following transforms:

Hue: **–67.4**

Lightness: **16.0**

Saturation: **–7.1**

Reducing the Hue value will change the green to another color, increasing the Lightness will bump the brightness of the edge up a bit, and decreasing the saturation will take down the bright tones.

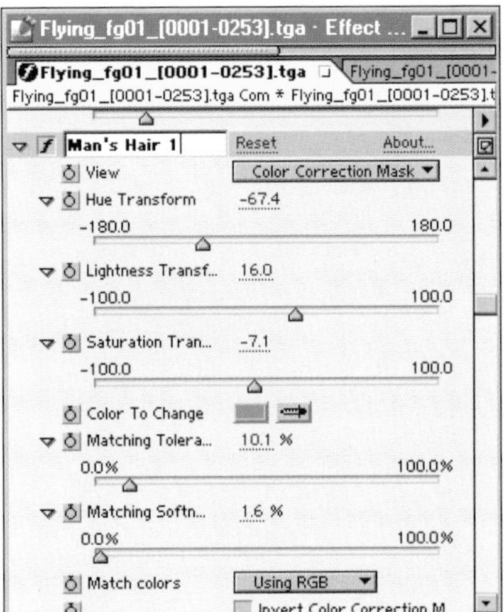

Change the Transform settings in the Effect Controls window.

Note: You can keep duplicating the Change Color filter in the same Effects window (by selecting the filter and then Ctrl+D) to further tweak the green values to get rid of the spill even more.

Once you are happy with the amount of green you have taken away, you need to do a trick to shrink the matte, eliminating most of the foreground edge artifacts without using a Production Bundle plug-in such as the Matte Choker.

Tip: You can rename your effects within the Effect Controls window. Select the filter name in the Effect Controls window and then press Return to change the name, just as you would change the name of a layer in the Timeline window. This is helpful for describing the uses of multiple effects on a single layer.

8 Duplicate the Green Screen layer that you have just keyed by selecting the layer in the Timeline and then pressing Ctrl+D.

Now Layers 1 and 2 are the same. Next you are going to select the bottom layer of the two (Layer 2) and use a track matte.

9 Be sure that you are viewing the Modes panel by clicking on the Switches/Modes toggle at the bottom of the Switches panel in the Timeline window, or by choosing Panels > Modes from the Timeline window menu. Use the track matte called Alpha Matte.

You will notice that the overall image shrinks by a few pixels, and the eyeball on the first layer disappears, making Layer 1 invisible in the composition but working in conjunction with Layer 2. You can even take a snapshot and do a before and after comparison of applying the track matte to see by how much the matte really has shrunk.

Note: Using Alpha matte is just a little trick used to shrink a matte without using any special filters. You can even subtly shrink the matte by reducing the scale of Layer 1 back ever so slightly, like .5 percent.

10 Delete all the Change Color effects.

You really do not need all the Change Color filters that are on Layer 1 because that layer is only being used for its Alpha channel. In other words, you will not see the actual color video of this layer. Anything to do with color correction here is pointless because you are only using its alpha channel to further tweak your true layer.

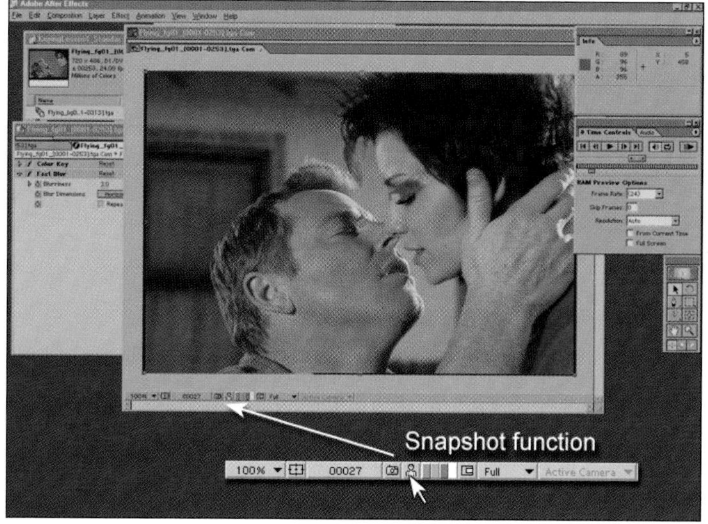

Use the Snapshot function to toggle between two different frames.

Note: You can also use a color correction filter, such as Levels or Curves, (both are under Effect > Adjust) to tweak the overall color of Layer 2 and further get rid of the green if need be.

Now that you have figured out how to choke a matte without a matte choker tool, you can apply a few properties and filters to Layer 1 to further tweak the edge of your matte. You can do the following:

- Scale, which will shrink the matte even more, as previously mentioned.
- Nudge Layer 1's position by a fraction of a pixel. This is useful if there is a heavy matte line on one side versus the other side of the matte.
- Apply the Fast Blur filter, which will soften the edges of the matte.

Lesson 2: Pulling a Green-Screen Matte with the Production Bundle Keying Tools

The Production Bundle comes with more tools to have even more control over pulling mattes. Once again, without the expensive third-party plug-ins, I would like to show you a few different techniques using the Production Bundle effects. Some of the methodology will be applied in much the same way as pulling a key with the Standard version. I will give you two different methods using two different keyers.

You want to import the same material as in the previous section.

1. Open After Effects and import both footage sequences from Lesson_2 on the accompanying CD-ROM: **lesson2_background.mov** and **lesson2_foreground.mov**.
2. From the Project window, create a new composition.
3. Put the layer you want to pull a matte from on top of the background layer in the layer stack of the Timeline window.

"Velocity Rules", 2001
The American Film Institute, Rocks & Rules Productions
Director Patty Jenkins, Cinematographer Guy Livneh

Use the color difference keyer in the Production Bundle version of After Effects for this final composite.

Pulling a Matte Using the Color Difference Matte

I quite like the Color Difference Matte plug-in within the Production Bundle, due to the various options it presents for the artist to view (background, foreground, matte, and final composite). For this example, view the Lesson 2 footage.

1. In the Timeline, select your Green Screen layer so that it is highlighted. With the foreground element selected, apply the Color Difference Key effect (Effect > Keying > Color Difference Key or drag-and-drop from the Effects Palette).

Tip: In Windows, you can highlight the layer in the Timeline and then right-click to bring up multiple menus, including the Effect menu. This can also be done in the Mac OS by Ctrl+clicking on a selected layer.

2. Starting in the Color Difference Matte with Source View selected, select the Eyedropper tool and move it over the Composition window to select where the green is most saturated.

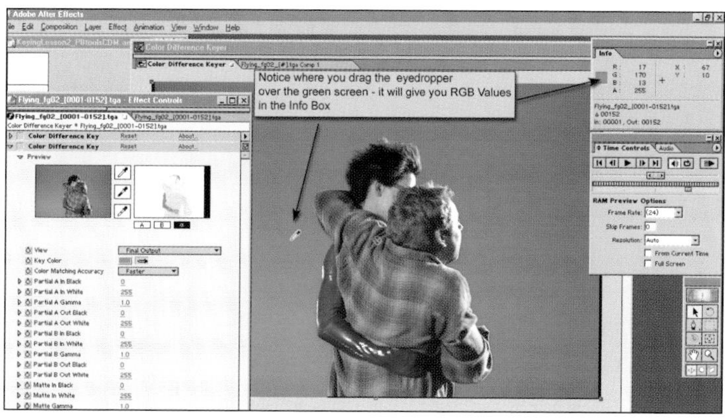

Select the green color in the Composition window.

Tip: Use the Info palette to view the RGB values to pick where the green has the highest value.

3. Under Color Matching Accuracy, choose More Accurate.

   Notice the two windows containing your green-screen element within the filter. Below the window on the right are the different matte views:

   - A = Shows the areas of transparency that don't contain a second different color.
   - B = Shows the areas based on the key color (that is, green).
   - X = This is the combined matte of A and B, and it shows the final matte.

4. Click X to view the final matte.

5. Pick the second Eyedropper tool and click in the small black and white window on where the background would be.

Note: There are three different Eyedropper tools between the two windows within the filter. On top there is a clear Eyedropper tool. This is the selected color to key; you already did this in step 3. Second, there is an Eyedropper tool filled with black, which is the backdrop color. Third, there is an Eyedropper tool filled with white, which is the foreground holdout matte.

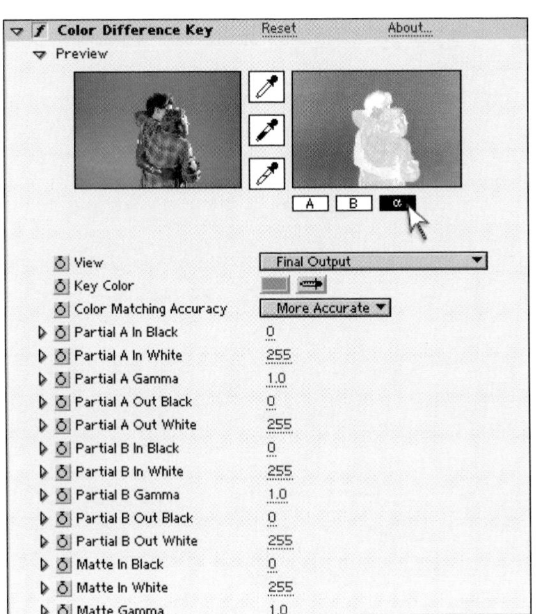

Select the final view X window.

6. Select the third Eyedropper tool and select the foreground subject. Repeat this step to get rid of all the gray areas on the subject.

   The gray areas on the subject are the areas that will become transparent, revealing the background layer. You want your entire foreground matte to be white.

7. Click on View in the View pop-up menu and show Matte Corrected to see what you've just accomplished. You can also select the Final Output view to show your key.

   You might notice some spill around the edges and some leftover green "garbage" in the corners. You will eliminate that garbage in the next part of this lesson.

Note: You might notice that the background brightens up some more, so you might need to go back with the black Eyedropper tool to bring the background back down to all black. Even if you don't get the entire background completely black, remember that there are other methods and tools that you will use in the next few steps to choke the matte. It's a lot more difficult to add information back into your foreground matte.

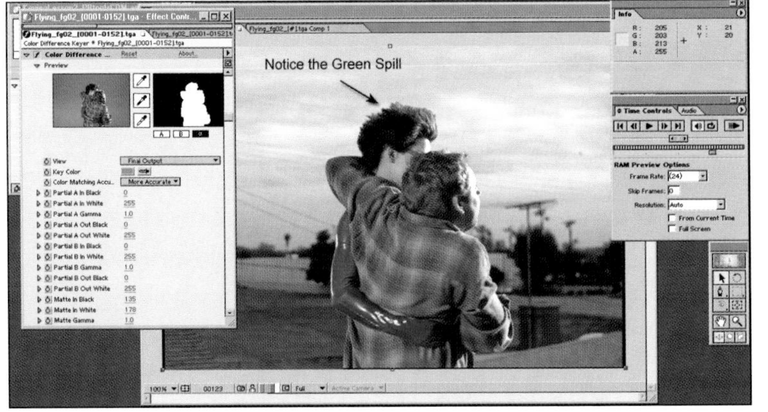

Green spill left over from keying.

Spill Suppression and the Other "Garbage" Left Behind

For every green screen or blue screen shot, there is bound to be "spill" on your subject. Color spill results in light being reflected off the green screen (or whatever color screen you are using) and projected onto the foreground subjects. Spill is a natural by-product of color-screening methods, and luckily After Effects' Keying Pack has an effect written specifically to deal with this inevitable problem.

1. Select the Foreground layer and apply the Spill Suppressor effect (Effect > Keying > Spill Suppressor or drag-and-drop from the Effects Palette.).

   The filter will default to blue, but make sure you select the green you previously keyed with the Eyedropper tool once the filter has been selected.

Zoom in to pick the green for the Spill Suppressor.

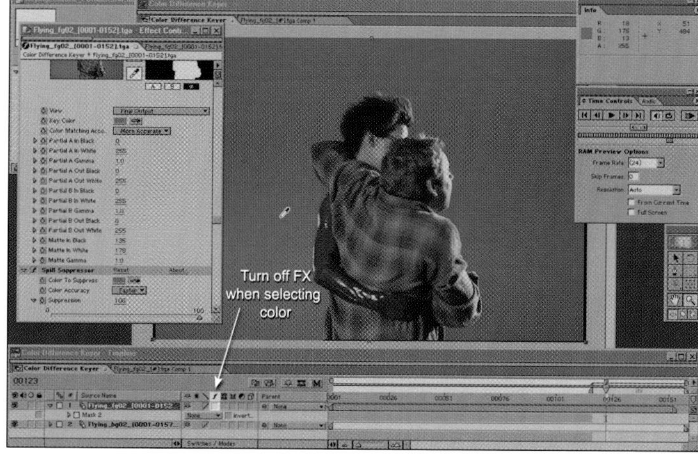

Turn off FX when selecting color for Spill Suppressor.

Tip: It's a good idea to disable the Spill Suppressor filter within the Effect Controls window when choosing a color to suppress in the main menu before selecting the tone of green you want to get rid of around the edges. This is because it defaults to blue and will throw off the color accuracy when choosing a color in the main Composition window. You can sample the green shown in the Key Color swatch in the Color Difference Key's effect controls.

It's also a good idea to zoom in to maybe 400% to pick the perfect pixel if you are selecting a color from the Composition window.

Note: As an alternate method, you can turn off the effects of your layer to get back to your original plate with the green screen and then use the Eyedropper tool to select the green color that needs to be removed around the edges.

2 Make sure the effect's Suppression is set to 100 for maximum results.

Now you will notice some gray around the edges and possibly in the corners where the green spill was knocked down but was still showing up in the background. You obviously want this to go away.

3 Select the Simple Choker effect (Effect > Matte Tools > Simple Choker or drag-and-drop from the Effects Palette).

Positive numbers in the Choke Matte parameter decrease the edge of your matte line; negative numbers increase the matte line. You definitely want a value on the positive side for this example in order to decrease the amount of noise around the foreground subjects.

Remove the gray around the edges.

4 Use a simple Choke Matte value of .45.

You don't want to lose too much detail in the hair. Notice that you will still have some garbage over to the right side of the frame, where the lighting on the green screen becomes uneven. This can easily be removed by creating a mask.

5 Double-click on Layer 1 to bring up the Layer window.

Tip: It's a good idea to occasionally check the view of the Simple Choker to view the matte, so you can see if you're right on track and not getting any holes.

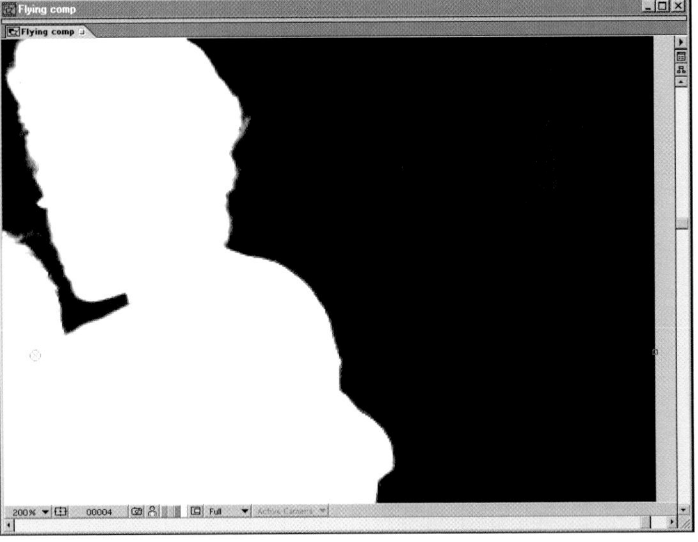

Mask out the "garbage" on the right side of the frame.

6 Using the toolbox, select the Rectangle tool Mask and create a box over on the right-hand side.

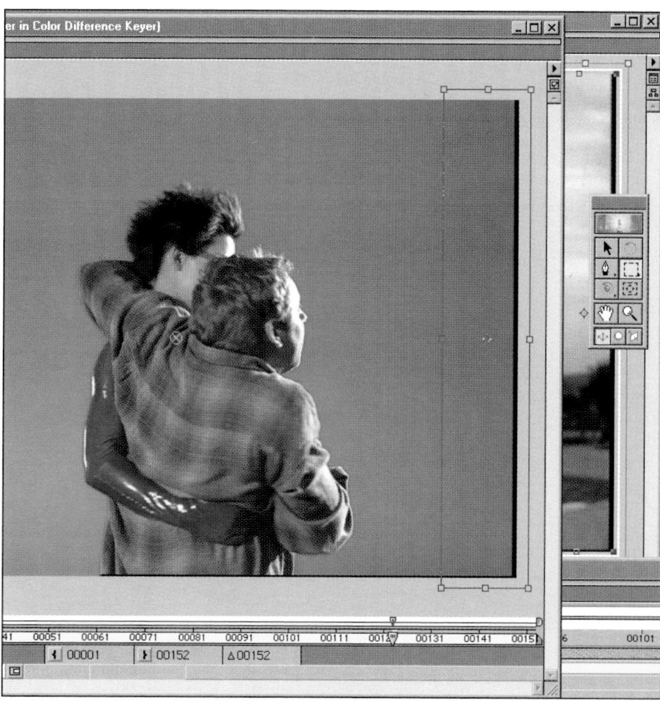

Create a Mask Shape to mask out the dark area.

7 In the Timeline window, twirl the arrow of your layer down to reveal the Mask Shape. Select Subtract from the Mask Modes pop-up menu because this is the area you do not want to be shown.

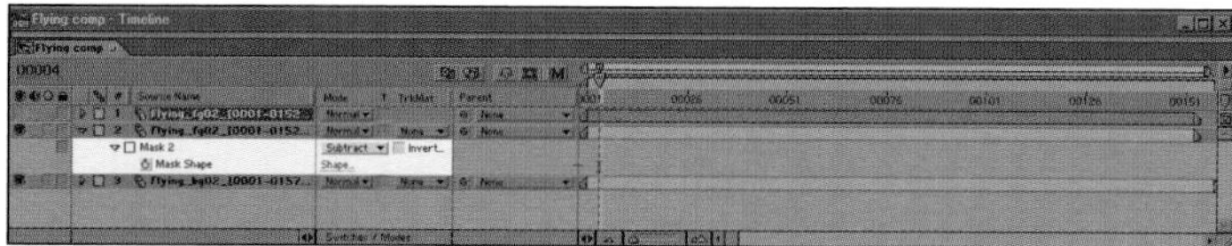

Press the M key to inspect your mask values in the Timeline.

Note: You might also want to scrub through the footage to make sure your subject doesn't cross over into the masked area; otherwise, you will need to set keyframes to allow your foreground subject to pass through (by clicking on the stopwatch next to the words "Mask Shape").

Correcting Color

Apart from pulling a decent green-screen matte, correcting for matte-induced color shifting is always the second hardest step in getting your compositions to look acceptable to the eye. I will go into further detail about all sorts of ways to color correct and blend your elements together for one nice composition in Project 5, "Adding a Realistic Touch to a Composite." For this particular example, I will just show you the basics of how to bring your composition into the final stretch.

You will go ahead and continue using Lesson 2 for this lesson.

1. Turn off the effects on the Green Screen layer by deselecting the effects switch in the Switches panel for that layer, take a snapshot, and then click the Effects filters back on again. Toggle between the two and notice the difference in the overall blue tones.

   This occurred after you applied the Spill Suppression tool; the overall blue levels became much more saturated and deeper in color value.

   Toggle between the sample using Spill Suppressor and the sample not using it.

See the difference in tones.

2. Knock back the Spill Suppression effect's Suppression value ever so slightly from 100 to 85.

   This will kick back a lot of the overall green that was lost by bumping it all the way to 100.

3. To knock back the deep blue color that is coming out, go to Effect > Adjust > Hue/Saturation and enter the following values:

   Master hue: **–12**
   Master Saturation: **–18**

4 Go to Effect > Adjust > Curves and, based on your own estimate, try adjusting the color to match the original blue value.

For further help, you can load a Photoshop Curves file named **ColorDiffKeyCurves.ACV** that I saved in the Lesson_2 folder on the accompanying CD-ROM.

You can continue further on the composition by adding your own specialties to make it look how you want. For example, I added a Sun Flare in the upper-right corner on the background plate to match the hard lighting on the subjects and to give it a warm overall feeling.

Load the saved Curves file.

Lesson 3: Pulling a Matte Using the Color Range

I often use this approach for doing quick-and-dirty keys on things that aren't all that detail oriented because you can pull a quick key just by selecting any color you want to key. (For this example, use the Lesson_3 footage on the accompanying CD-ROM.)

1 Import both footage sequences from the Lesson_3 folder on the accompanying CD-ROM: **lesson3_foreground.mov** and **lesson3_background.tga**. Again, create a new composition (Composition > New Composition) [Cmd/Ctrl + I] and drag the footage into the Timeline window. Make sure the background is on the bottom and the Green Screen layer is on the top.

Unlike the previous lessons, this section uses a still background element.

2 In the Timeline, select your Green Screen layer so that it is highlighted.

Use the Color Range Keyer in the Production Bundle version of After Effects for this final render.

3 Apply the Color Range effect (Effect > Keying > Color Range or drag-and-drop from the Effects Palette.).

Notice a thumbnail window with three Eyedropper tools beside it.

4 Click on the top Eyedropper tool. Now click in the thumbnail window approximately where the green-screen area is.

This is the tool you use to select whatever color to key. You can see where there are still bits of light gray and white where the background should be completely black. The next Eyedropper tool down has a plus (+) sign beside it; this is an Additive Eyedropper used to select additional amounts of green to remove.

You can experiment with all three different Color Space methods to see which one will best suit the footage you are working with. I used the LAB method for this project.

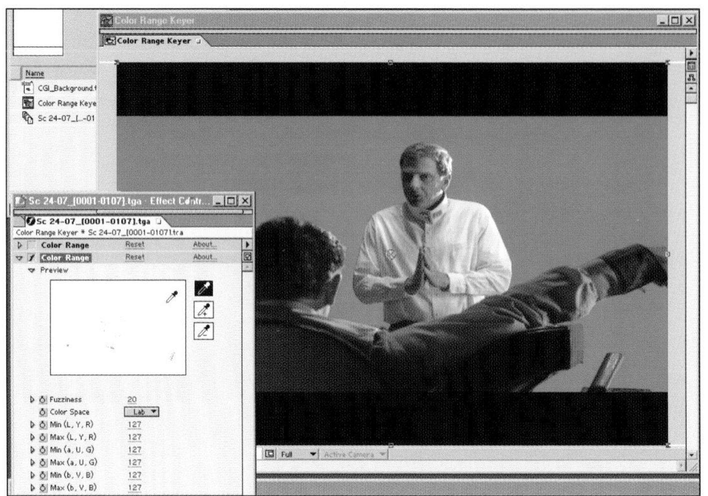

Choose a Color Range approximation on the green screen.

Note: The slider tool for Effect Controls can go much beyond the values originally clicked on. The higher you go with the value, the more the edges and green will go away. Just remember to be careful not to go to a value that's too high; otherwise, you might end up with holes in your matte or lose too much detail along the edges.

Note: In case you need it (if you accidentally drag the Additive Eyedropper tool over to where your foreground subject is or you start to see holes in your matte), you can use the third Eyedropper tool (a subtractive tool, marked with a minus [-] sign) to bring your foreground back.

5 Use the Solo button in the timeline and the Show Alpha Channel button in the Composition window to get an accurate account of how well your matte is shaping up. First, select the Solo button to view this layer only, then select the View Alpha Channel button. When you're done, deselect the Solo and Alpha buttons before moving on to the next step.

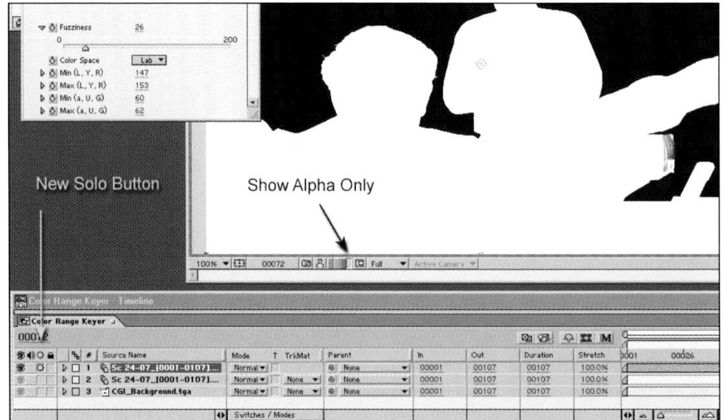

Use both the Solo and Show Alpha Channel buttons to quickly view the Alpha channel.

6 Duplicate your Green Screen layer by selecting the layer and pressing Ctrl/Cmd+D.

Now you have Layers 1 and 2, which are your Green Screen layers. These will rectify the significant spill on the shininess of the arm of the chair it is keying out as well as the background. You will need to create a second layer of the footage and add a holdout matte for the arm of the chair.

7 Double-click on Layer 2 to bring up the Layer window so you can begin to mask out the arm of the chair. Once you are happy with the mask outline of the arm of the chair, close your layer window.

8 Remove the Color Range filter on Layer 2.

Because Layer 2 is underneath Layer 1 and is your holdout matte, you will want to remove the Color Range filter on this particular layer so that nothing is keyed out and shows through to the background. You can switch the video on and off on each Foreground layer to view what it contains.

9 Go back to the Spill Suppression section and apply the concepts covered there with what you have just accomplished using the Color Range filter. Be sure to apply the spill suppression to both foreground layers, so that they remain the same in color values to one another.

You wouldn't want all of that spill to show through!

10 Don't forget to save your project.

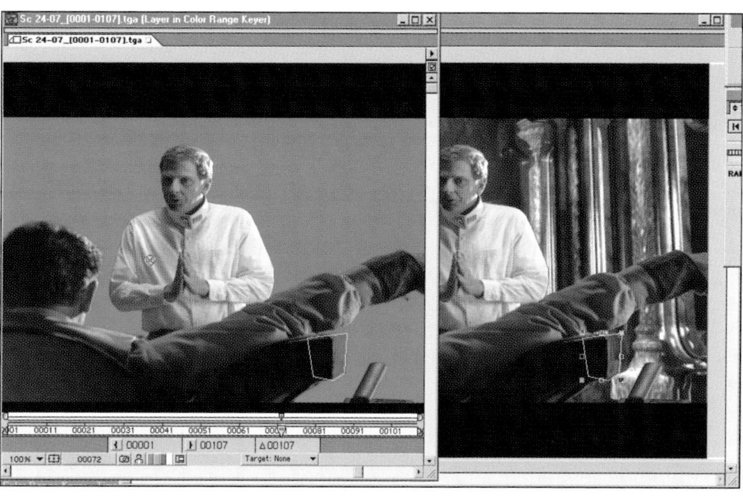

Use the Masking tool to create a holdout matte (or garbage matte).

Note: Remember to use the Mask Feather option for a soft edge. A value of 1 is usually sufficient for something of this nature. Also remember to check along the sequence for any camera movement because you might need to keyframe your mask (by clicking on the stopwatch next to the words "Mask Shape").

Note: You might want to add a touch of the matte choker here to the non-masked foreground layer because it borders the green screen and it might give you some trouble along the edges.

Modifications

What I have shown you are some examples of how to pull a key of a green screen using both the Standard version and the Production Bundle version of After Effects. Keep in mind that there are always several ways to go about pulling a matte, beginning with how well your subject was actually shot against a green or blue screen.

As important as how your green screen or blue screen was shot is the format you decide to use. Digital video is becoming increasingly popular and is much cheaper than shooting on film. Just remember that with most digital video cameras, you will have interlacing fields to contend with, which might cause some problems on the edge of the subject you are shooting against the green screen. Just try to remember the tips previously discussed to help you out so you can deal with it when the time comes.

I'm sure you will find your own techniques the more you try different combinations of plug-ins and the more experience you gain; just remember to try to keep it simple. The more layers and filters you apply to your composition, the slower it will be to move around your composition and to render. Try starting out with the basics to get the best results you can and then work your way to improvements from there.

Remember that nothing is ever shot exactly the same way (a light might change, the camera or even its lens might change, or an actor might stand on a different marker than before). Therefore, the values and techniques to pulling a matte will always differ from shot to shot. You can combine any of the techniques discussed in this project to come up with a valid solution for any shot. Some mattes might be very easy to pull, while others might take a heck of a lot more time to get a decent result, but that's the nature of the beast known as compositing…it takes a lot of patience!

Other Tools That Will Help Your Blue or Green Screen

I have been fortunate over the years to have a chance to try some different third-party filters that take keying to the next level within After Effects. If you find yourself doing a lot of blue-screen or green-screen compositing, I would suggest saving enough money to get some of these filters. They can make keying a little bit easier and quicker on some of those tougher shots in the long run.

Here are some of my favorites:

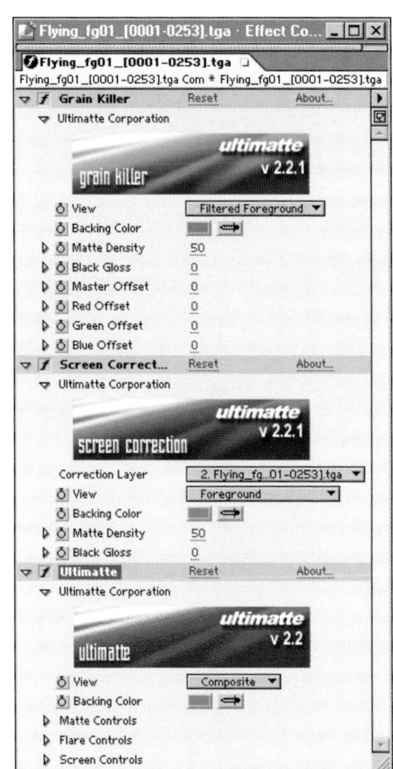

Ultimatte's Keyer package (**www.ultimatte.com**).

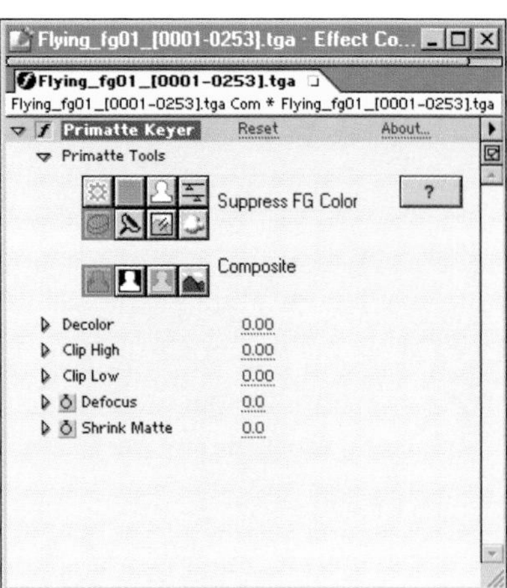

Pinnacle System's Primatte Keyer (**www.commotionpro.com**).

Digital Film Tools Composite Suite (**www.digitalfilmtools.com**).

Boris After Effects Effects from Artel Software (**www.borisfx.com**).

Here are some others that also are available:

- ADI's X-Matte (Mac only)
- Zbig
- Kaleidafex Matte Pack (Mac only)

Note: Check out the accompanying CD-ROM for appendixes on Difference mattes and instructions for building your own green screen.

ADDING A REALISTIC TOUCH TO A COMPOSITE

"Is it live or is it Memorex?"

—MEMOREX AD

Combining CGI and Live Action

The combination of CGI and live action seems to be more and more commonplace in everything from corporate videos to television, not to mention its more obvious use in films. More and more composites are showing up in films these days and for reasons other than a sci-fi type of shot in which someone needs to be beamed aboard a spaceship. You are seeing more and more of the "invisible" type of effects in which the effects aren't that obvious. These are the effects that actually help a filmmaker tell a story without having to spend oodles of money to travel all over the world to shoot a film. I like to refer to these types of effects as *Forest Gump* effects. Remember Tom Hanks meeting former presidents and becoming involved in many events from the 1960s? Or how about Gary Sinese playing a disabled vet without any legs? Both are examples of composites that tend to lead people to believe that what they are seeing on screen is actually real, and these effects are the ones that help tell a story.

Project 5

Adding a Realistic Touch to a Composite

by Sherry Hitch

How It Works

This project will deal with various elements in compositing, using tips and tricks needed to add realism to a shot. From CGI 3D-generated elements to plate elements that were shot separately, this project goes over the things you need to know about blending them all together to create a realistic composite.

Getting Started

With every shot comes the challenge of how best to approach putting the layers together in After Effects to produce a realistic composite. This project covers a few of the basics that are essential to pulling off a believable composite. Using a Green Screen layer, a CGI layer, and an element shot on film, you will combine all three layers to produce a realistic final composite.

Once again, as I mentioned in Project 4, "Green-Screen Compositing and Other Keying Techniques," remember to keep it simple. If you do so, it will give way to faster render times and less convoluted composites, and when you open the project up a month later, you'll still be able to understand what you were doing and pick up from where you left off with no problems.

Note: If you are unclear about the best approach to pulling a key with After Effect's Keying Pack effects, refer to Project 4 for more information on how to pull a green-screen matte. Depending on which version of After Effects you have, that project explains how to pull a matte with both the Standard and Production Bundle versions.

Starting Footage

Let's begin by bringing in all the elements needed to create the shot.

Before getting started, be sure you know on what format your footage was taped or filmed. Was it filmed on 35mm? Shot on digital video? Is it PAL Video (European format)? NTSC? High definition? 3:2 pull-down footage (film that is either transferred one-to-one per frame to video or that is interpreted to video and has fields within the frames to make up the difference between a frame rate of 24 and a frame rate of 30 for television)? All of this is important to know because it will determine how you interpret your footage and frame rate for each composite. Knowing these answers before you start the composition will definitely help prevent problems down the line. As a start, however, clicking on a piece of footage in the Project window will give you some basic information, such as frame rate, resolution, pixel aspect ratio, and duration.

1 Open After Effects and import (File > Import) [Cmd/Ctrl + I] the three items needed for this lesson from the accompanying CD-ROM.

- Background footage (**cgi_bg.tga**)
- Foreground green screen (**greenscreen.mov**)
- Smoke FX (**smoke.mov**)

Note: To bring in multiple sequences, you can use Ctrl+Alt+I on Windows (or Cmd+Option+I on the Mac) as a shortcut.

Tip: Another cool way to import your footage is to open up Explorer for Windows (or Finder for Mac) and literally drag the folder with the sequence into the Project window.

You want to change the current 24fps frame rate of the footage to a more video friendly 29.97fps.

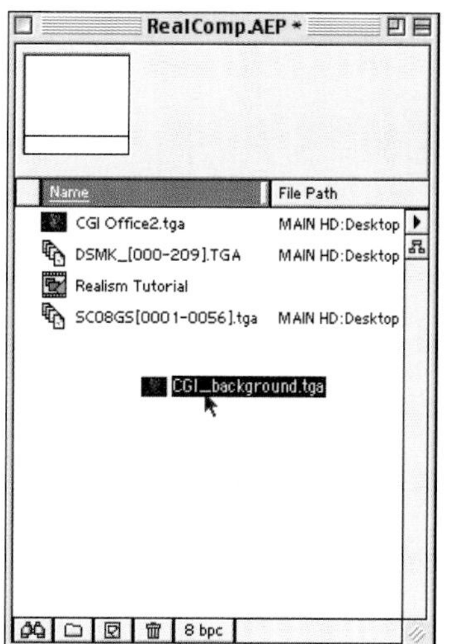

Dragging footage from open folders into the After Effects Project window.

2 Open the Interpret Footage dialog box (File > Interpret Footage > Main) [Cmd/Ctrl + F]. For this exercise, you will set the following information for each piece of footage:

greenscreen.mov: **29.97fps**
cgi_bg.tga: **No frame rate because it is a still image**
smoke.mov: **29.97fps**

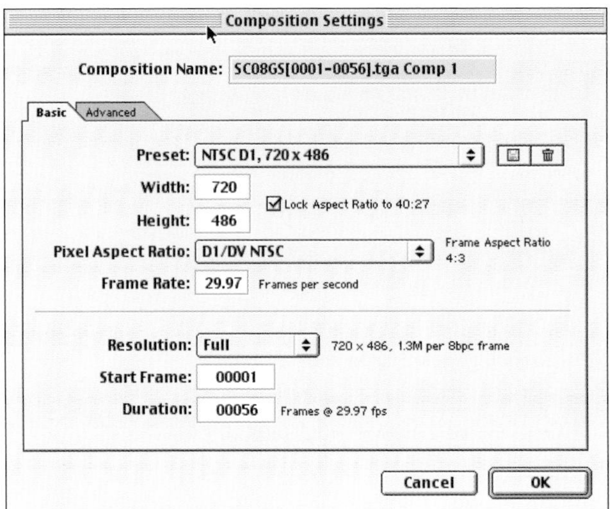

Composition settings.

Note: Your composition settings will default to whatever you used last unless you have interpreted your footage to 29.97 first and then dragged your sequence on top of the Project window's Create a New Composition icon.

3 Open the Project window and create a new composition by dragging both pieces of footage over the Create a New Composition icon at the bottom of the Project window.

Looking into the Timeline window, remember to put the layers you want in the distance on the bottom and the layers that you want in the foreground on top. Now let's see what you've got to work with.

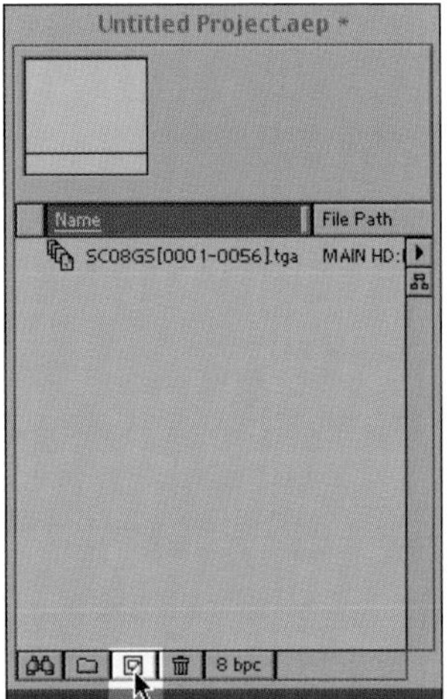

The Create a New Composition icon below the Project window.

Note: You can also rename your Composition window at this point to a more suitable name to help you organize your composite. To do so, select Ctrl+K in Windows or Cmd+K on the Mac.

4 Create a RAM preview. This will help you identify any problems you might encounter with your footage.

Note: The hotkey for this is the 0 (zero) key on the numeric keypad.

Don't forget to save your project after this first bit of setup. Now let's get started!

Setting Up the Composition

You want to figure out the best approach in setting up the composite, and you must try to remember to keep it simple.

Having viewed your footage by building a RAM preview, you have figured out what problems you might encounter before you begin your full composite. Now let's break down each piece of footage and decide on the best approach.

Here's what you have to work with:

- **greenscreen.mov.** Your foreground green-screen footage
- **smoke.mov.** A smoke element to be seen rather subtly
- **cgi_bg.tga.** CG background to be used for the virtual environment

The Green Screen Layer

Naturally, this foreground element will be your layer closest to the camera and thus the topmost layer in the Timeline window, so let's go ahead and pull the green-screen matte first. Again, refer to Project 4 if you need help.

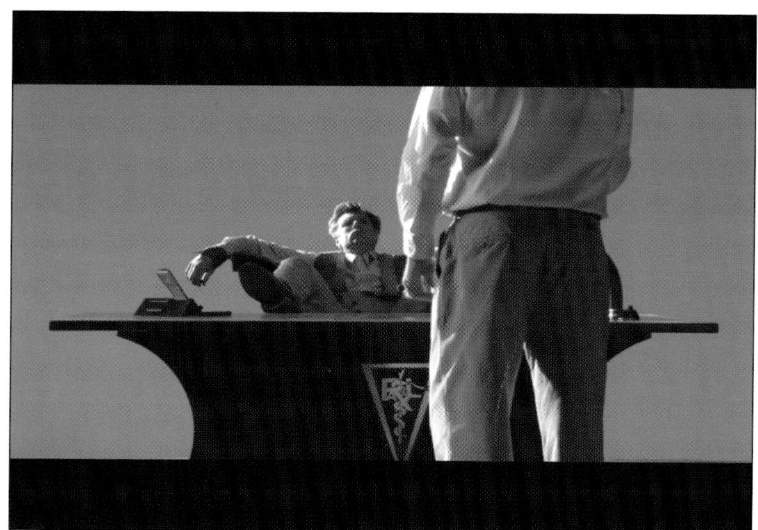

The Green Screen layer.

1 After you have the green actually keyed out, click on the Solo button in the Time Layout window and the Alpha button in the Composition window.

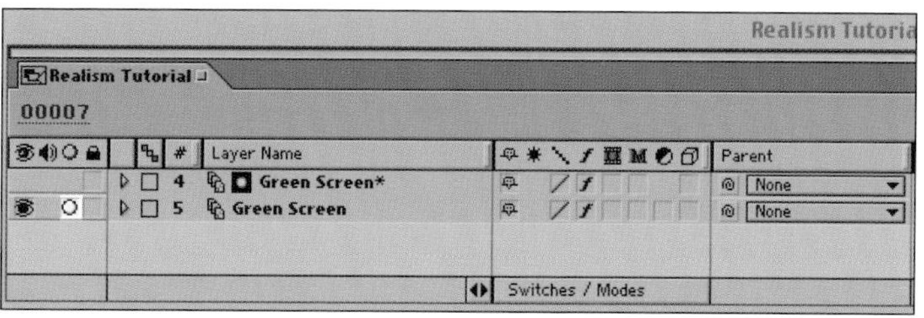

Use the Solo button to view the layer by itself.

Take a look at the matte to see how you're coming along. You should not see any "matte holes" in the live action; you should have a solid white matte that represents the live action, with the black representing the areas you want to see in the background and the rest of the environment.

If you see any areas of the foreground element that show through to the background (this is represented as dark or black areas that are supposed to be solid white), you might need to cut back on the matte choker. It is also possible to duplicate the Green Screen layer, removing any green-screen keying filters and only apply the spill suppressor, then apply a custom mask shape to fix the holes in your matte. This masking will prevent the holes from showing through to the background layer. As mentioned in Project 4, this is called a holdout matte.

The white Alpha Channel button used to view the matte.

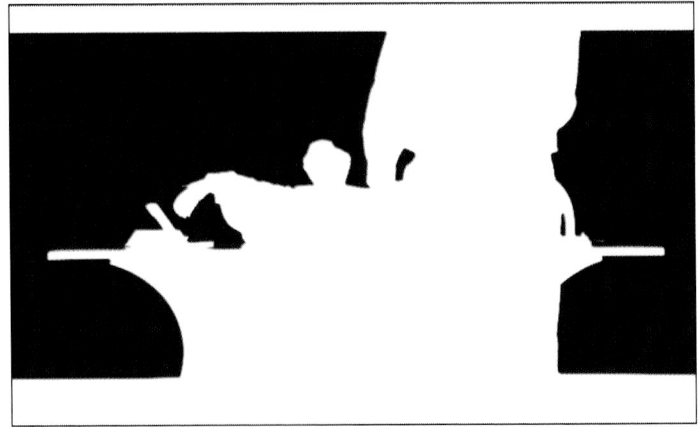

What the matte of the Green Screen layer looks like after the key is pulled.

Note: When you create a holdout matte, it's a good idea to know whether the shot is a locked-off shot or a moving shot when setting up the mask. If it is a moving shot, you might need to set keyframes for your mask as you advance over frames throughout the composition. In this case, of course, the shot is locked off and stationary, so there's no need to keyframe the mask.

Tip: Because a lot of layers could be involved in any composite, you might want to rename your layers in the composition to be more suited to what you are doing with them. This helps ensure that when you open up the composition a few weeks down the road, you can remember what you were doing. To do this, simply select the layer and hit the Return key.

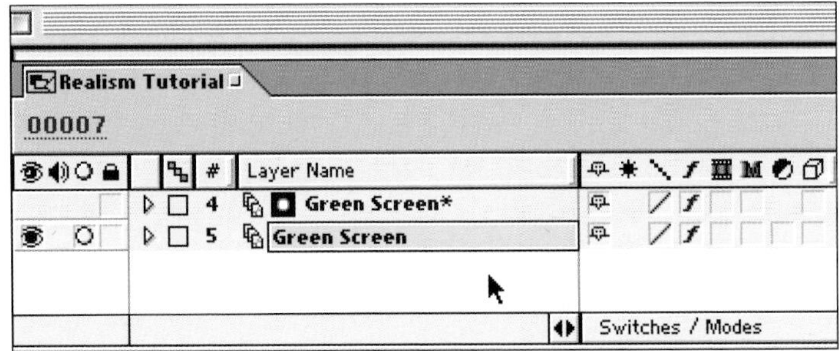

Renaming a layer to help you get organized.

Now look at the holdout matte to see the color on the table. Due to the Spill Suppression tool, it might look to be a little too deep blue because it was trying to get rid of the green spill. Now some color correction might be needed because you want the table top to blend in and look a little more real.

2 Open Levels (Effect > Adjust > Levels) and adjust the color to be slightly less deep blue.

Try inputting the following values to start with. You can adjust from there for further tweaking.

RGB > Output Black: **4.0**
Blue > Blue Output White: **230**

Tip: Another good alternative is using the Hue/Saturation effect (Effect > Adjust > Hue & Saturation), which only affects the green tones you want to remove.

Now take a good look at the matte, the pulled key, and everything associated with pulling the key. You want to get in the practice of double-checking layers that you might have split in the process of getting a key to work to make sure they match.

Note: Because you are slightly changing the values on the holdout matte, you might need to do the same to the regular Green Screen layer as well.

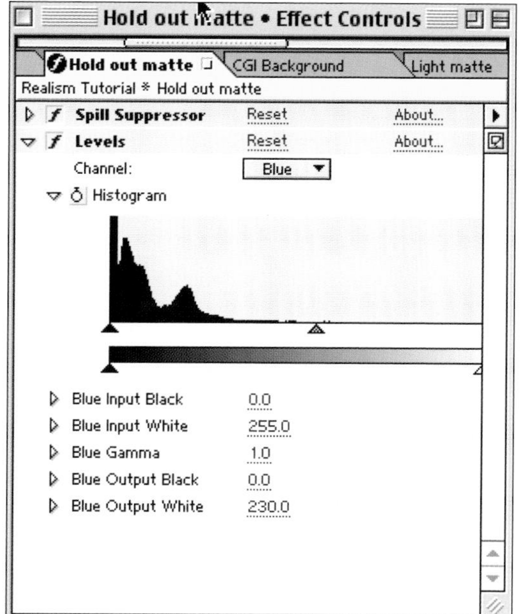

Tweaking the layer's levels.

The Background Layer

Now that you have your foreground, you'll want to adjust your background layer in the composition. For this exercise, you want to use the CGI still called **cgi_bg.tga**.

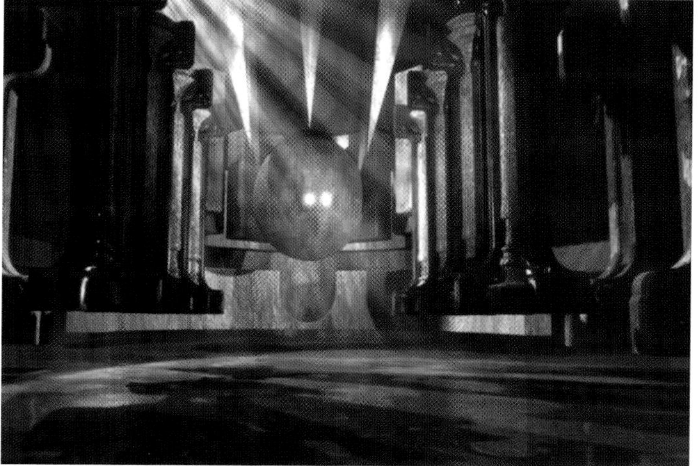

The CGI-rendered background.

1 From the Project window, drag the cgi_bg.tga layer into the Timeline window. With After Effects, you can drag it right to the bottom layer. (You'll see a dark bar showing where the new layer will be placed.)

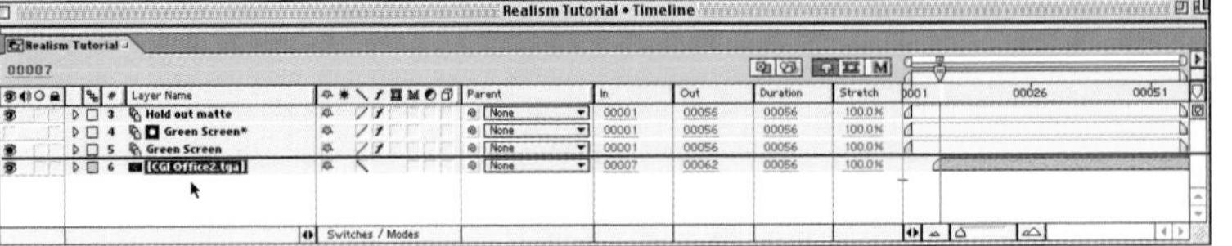

Dragging the background layer to the bottom of the composition.

You want this to be the bottom layer because it is the layer furthest from the camera.

You should be able to see your background as it is, past the Green Screen layer, straight through to the back of the composition.

Tip: As a safety precaution, it's wise to lock the other layers you have in place already for the time being while you tweak the background layer. This will prevent you from accidentally moving or applying unnecessary features to the other layers you already have set up. This can be done while you tweak one layer and then you can unlock them later for further blending.

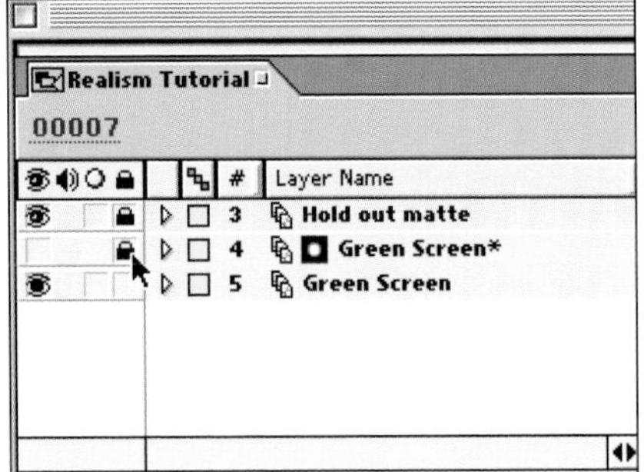

Using the Lock feature.

Now, just by looking at your background in general (and at any composite you might do hereafter), chances are you might need to adjust properties, such as Scale and Position, as well as the levels, color, saturation, blur amount, and so on. To start with in this exercise, you want to make some adjustments to the background layer.

2 Set the Layer Position to X = 322, Y = 256.

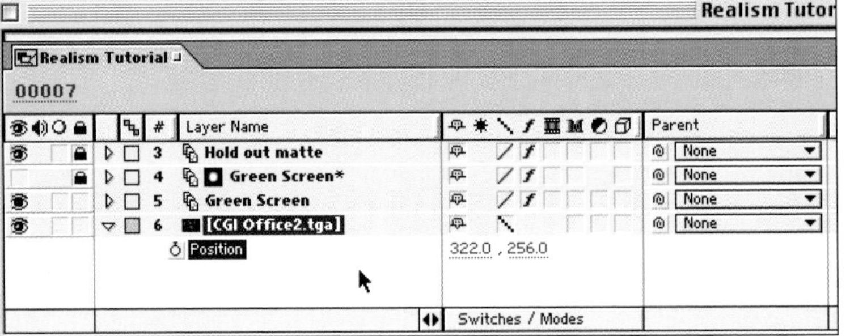

Setting the Layer Position.

Position is moved sometimes because you want to line up the background with your foreground that was shot more accurately to represent what you would actually see through the camera lens. In this instance, you have a background that was rendered oversized from CGI to give the compositor more free reign in lining up the two layers more accurately. This is also helpful when doing a camera move within a composite.

3 Set the Layer Scale to 80%, keeping the layer's proportions locked.

Because this layer was rendered oversized to give you full control, you can size it to a percentage that feels and looks natural. Feel free to adjust it to different sizes to get a look and feel that you want in particular.

4 Open Levels (Effect > Adjust > Levels) and set Input Black 6.7.

Any type of color-correction filter can be used here to adjust the color to blend more with your foreground elements. You can also use other filters to accomplish this task, such as Curves or Color Balance.

5 Open Blur (Effect > Blur & Sharpen > Gaussian Blur) and set Blurriness to 0.3.

A blur is applied to give the composite more of a sense of depth of field. When looking through a camera lens, depending on which lens is used and how far away your subject is from the camera, you will have a different Field of View on how blurry your background is. Sometimes, if camera data is given on set, this effect can be applied in camera within a 3D package for a more accurate representation of the blur. Most other times, the compositor must compensate for this and visually correct the background.

Tip: When applying a blur, be careful not to overcompensate and blur a background too much; otherwise, your foreground element might look pasted into the shot or too fake.

Tip: On the Mac OS, use the Ctrl key and click on the word Position and then Edit Value to adjust X and Y values independently of each other in the same dialog box. On Windows, you can right-click on the word Position.

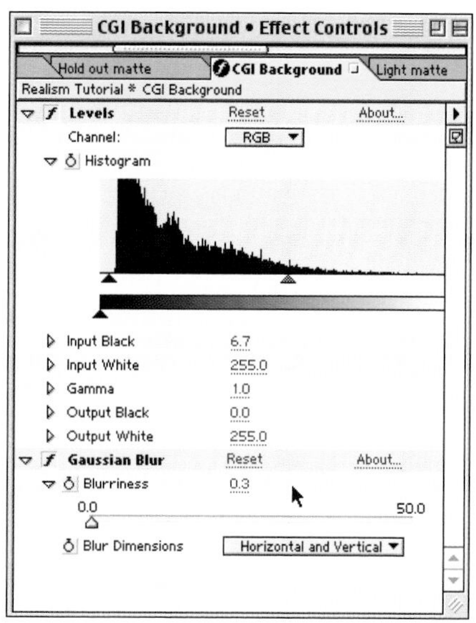

Adjusting the effect's values.

Note: Other filters can be used here as well, depending on the composition and the elements involved. I often find that I need to use a bit of desaturation on a lot of elements rendered from 3D. 3D elements are often rendered out as very sharp (that is, in focus) and very colorful, which makes them look nicer on their own but less realistic when composited with live footage. Desaturating rendered 3D elements can help them more closely match live-action footage. Blurring is also a common trick, as is adding small amounts of noise. You'll get to that trick in a moment.

THE STOCK ELEMENT

Truly realistic composites usually require additional elements besides the composited foreground and background elements. Sometimes these elements can also come from a stock library that you might accumulate (from years of producing such footage for other projects) or that you might purchase from stock-footage suppliers. Firms such as VCE and ArtBeats have such stock elements that you can purchase online.

The background element has light rays streaming down from the ceiling, made visible by airborne particles in the room. Unfortunately, as a still image, there is no movement of these particles as you would see in real life. The footage element called **smoke.mov** will be used to simulate moving atmospheric particles seen through the bright light source in the background.

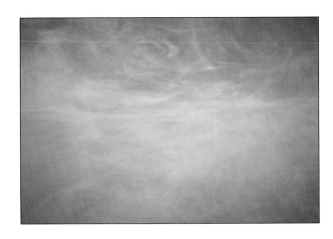

The filmed stock smoke element.

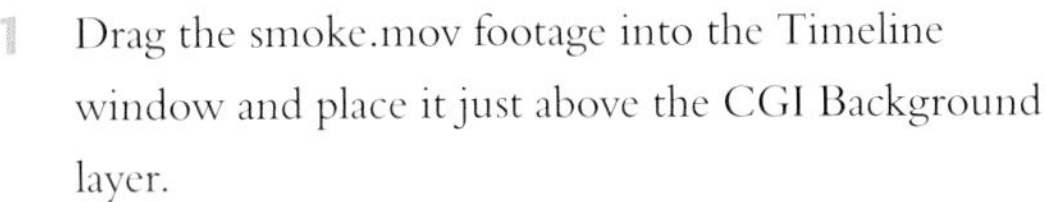

1 Drag the smoke.mov footage into the Timeline window and place it just above the CGI Background layer.

Because the purpose of this layer is to show the smoke through the light, you want to use the CGI Background also as a track matte.

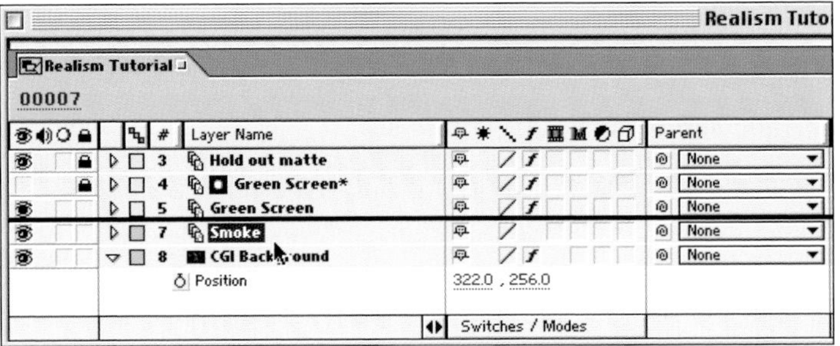

Placing the Smoke element into the composition.

2 Duplicate the CGI Background layer (Edit > Duplicate) [Cmd/Ctrl + D] and change its name to **Light Matte**.

3 Change the position of this duplicated CGI Background layer and move it to above the smoke layer.

You will notice that your smoke layer has disappeared because it is beneath the second CGI layer.

You now need to adjust the Contrast of this new Light Matte layer, so that only the strong rays of light are showing. (This is because you want to use only the strong rays of light for the smoke to be seen through.)

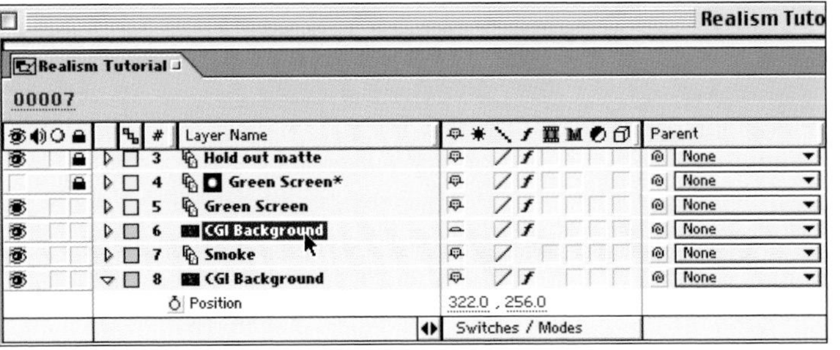

Moving the duplicated background layer to above the smoke layer.

4 Apply the Brightness & Contrast effect to this layer (Effect > Adjust > Brightness & Contrast or drag and drop from the Effects palette). Adjust the Contrast lever to 35.

Notice how the dark areas seem to drop out. This can be adjusted to your liking.

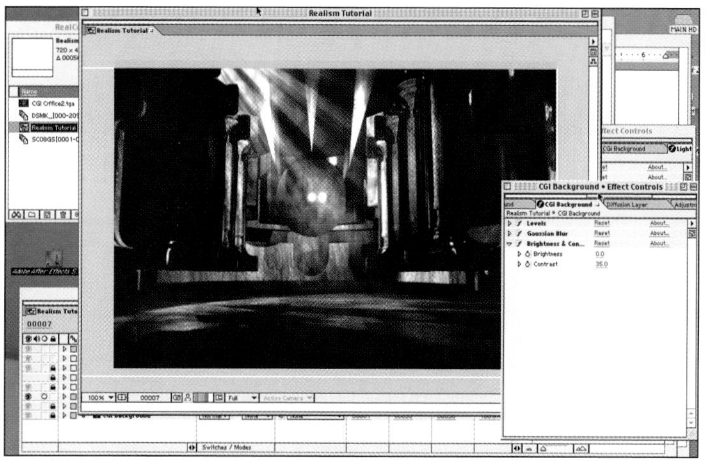

Adjusting the Brightness & Contrast of the duplicated layer.

Tip: If you are working on a slow machine, you can keep this effect while speeding up rendering by removing the previous Levels and Gaussian Blur effects and setting the Contrast slider to a higher value.

5 Go back to your Smoke layer and, in the Timeline under Switches and Modes, go to Track Matte and select Luma Matte.

Now you have the smoke only showing up in the areas that are bright.

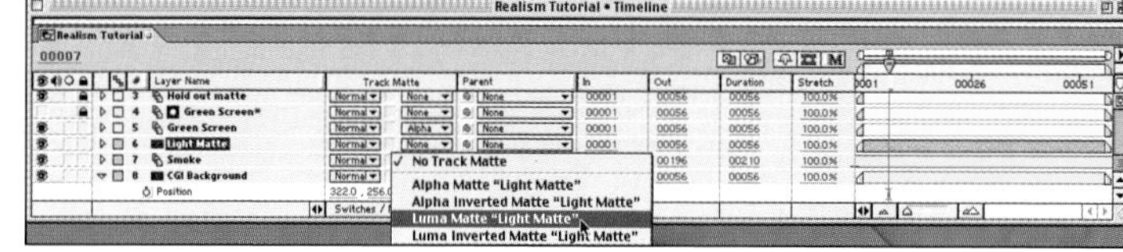

Setting the Track Matte to Luma Matte.

6 Apply a transfer mode to further blend the smoke layer. For this particular exercise, I used Screen mode.

7 Lock the layers used in this process until you want to do some further tweaking.

Note: You can further adjust the smoke layer on its own by reducing its Opacity down a bit if it feels too strong. You can use the Snapshot function in the Composition window to do comparisons to get the right look and feel.

Tip: You can also render out other types of floating particles for this shot from other software packages to further enhance the look in the light. If you want the effect to be less subtle, also try increasing the contrast of the smoke.mov footage using the Levels effect.

Better Matching the Live Action

Now that you have everything set up, you can go in many other directions. Some folks might consider this composite finished, but not me. Let's take it a step further for a better blend. Now you want to add a touch that will mimic a diffusion filter on a camera lens. You want to "bloom out" the highlights on your live action.

1. Go back to the Green Screen layer and unlock the actual Green Screen layer. After this layer is selected, duplicate it, change the name of the duplicated layer to Diffusion Layer, and move this layer to the top of the composition. Be sure the track matte is set to None.

   You do this because this will be the frontmost layer visible to the camera.

2. In the Timeline window, use the Solo button (between the Audio and Lock toggles) on this layer, so that you can now work with just this layer.

3. Open up the Effects window for this layer. Now you want to use the Luma Key effect found in the Production Bundle (Effect > Keying > Luma Key or drag and drop from the Effects palette).

   You want to key out all the dark areas to leave only the bright white-hot areas.

4. Under Key Type, use Key Out Darker. Adjust the Threshold to 80 and the Edge Feather to 6.0.

   You want to blur this layer to achieve a "blooming out" of your light areas to help create the diffusion filter effect.

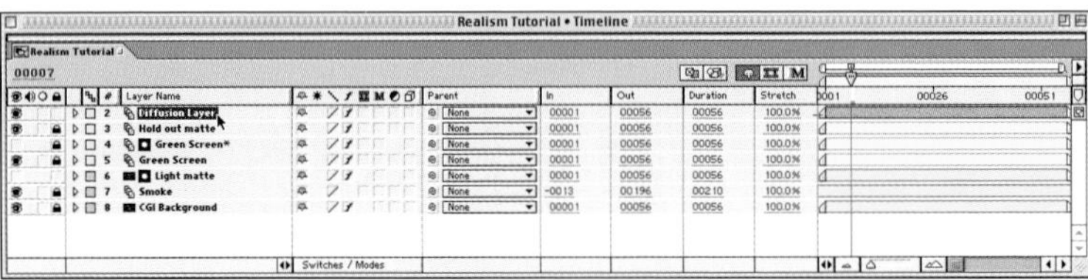

Creating the Diffusion layer by duplicating the keyed Green Screen layer.

Tip: Using the new Solo button feature in After Effects can come in very handy when you start getting multiple layers in a composition together. It prevents you from accidentally leaving off a layer or turning on a layer that is unnecessary. This is a great improvement from the old way of doing this sort of thing using the eye.

5 Select Effect > Blur & Sharpen > Gaussian Blur and enter a value of 7 for Blurriness.

6 Turn off the Solo button to take a look at what you have done.

You're nearly there, but you aren't quite finished with this look yet...

7 Go to the transfer modes and use Screen. (You could also use Add if you want, but it might be a little too strong.) In addition to this step, you can make this effect more subtle by turning down the Diffusion layer's Opacity to 60%.

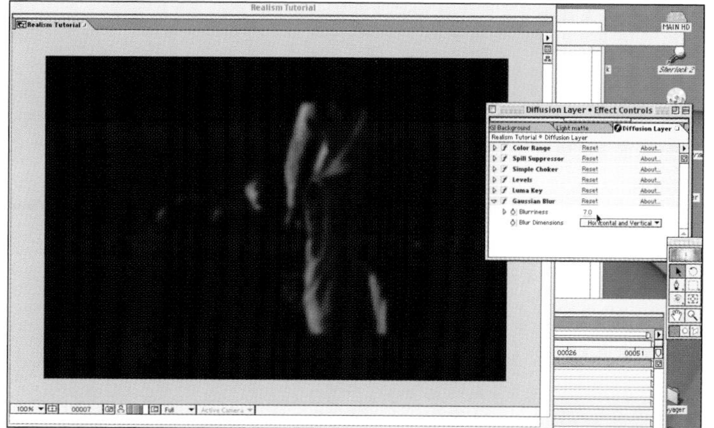

The end result of the Diffusion layer on its own.

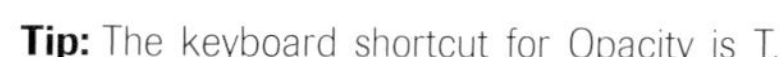

Tip: The keyboard shortcut for Opacity is T.

A Final Touch

Once again, some folks might consider this composite finished, but there is one more final step to blend the live action and the CGI element together: some subtle film grain. Even if something is shot with a perfectly still camera, there is always some moving noise in the image, whether it's video noise from a camera's light sensors or actual film grain. Because CGI is purely digital, it can easily be noticed as fake if it does not have that same graininess.

1 Because you want the noise to be applied to all layers, you'll make an Adjustment layer (Layer > New > Adjustment Layer). Place it on top of all other layers in the Timeline window.

Note: Depending on where you are in the composition when you add this layer, a new layer or solid will start at that particular frame you are on in the Timeline. Be sure to have the Adjustment layer starting on frame 1 (time 0:00:00:00) for the filter to take effect over the entire composition.

This exercise is built around having only the basic tools within After Effects, so you are going to use noise to simulate film grain. Remember to keep it subtle!

2 Go to Effect > Stylize > Noise and set the following parameters:

Color Noise: **Off**
Noise Amount: **3.0%**

This final choice is definitely an option but not necessary. You can add one more tiny bit of blur on top of the noise to slightly blur the noise that has been added, but remember that this will also blur your entire image. Keep it simple, keep it subtle, and it will be alright!

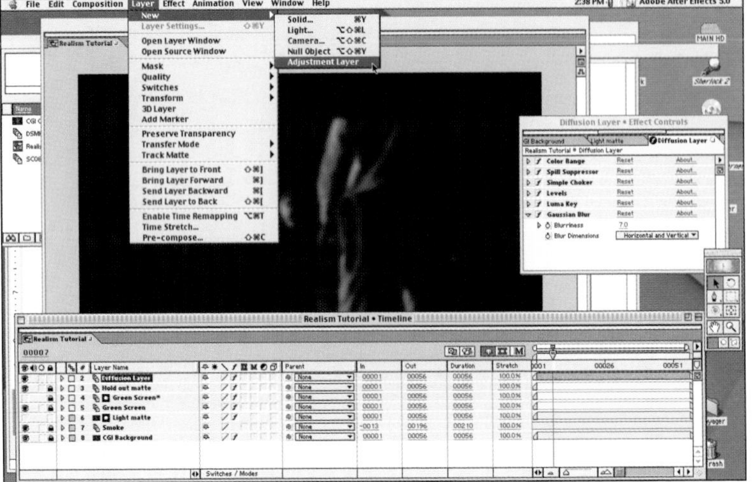

Creating an Adjustment layer.

Modifications

What I have shown you is a start to blending together a few layers of a composite to make it look more real, utilizing the plug-ins that come with After Effects. I truly believe that most composites can actually be done by using just these basic tools within After Effects, as long as you keep it simple and apply as many tricks within this book as you can.

Of course, there are many, many third-party plug-ins that are great to have for achieving a particular look. By all means, use them! They might save you a few steps or might simply be cool to play around with. Some of my favorite compositing enhancement plug-ins are as follows:

- Puffin Composite Wizard (**www.commotionpro.com**)
- Puffin Image Lounge (**www.commotionpro.com**)
- Final Effects (**www.media100.com**)
- DigiEffects Cinelook (**www.digieffects.com**)
- Digital Film Tools Composite Suite (**www.digitalfilmtools.com**)
- The Foundry's Tinderbox 1.0 (**www.thefoundry.co.uk**)

Each of these packages has a unique set of plug-ins that can get the job done, depending on what you or your client is looking for. You can add film grain, a true camera blur, a rack focus, and a long list of various atmospheric particles and effects.

For all the shots I've done for television and film, I've always felt that I could keep tweaking a shot until the end of time. Unfortunately, there comes a time when the client likes it just the way it is or when the deadline approaches a little sooner than expected. When doing a realistic composition, it's also a good idea to get a second opinion; just having a second set of eyes can sometimes catch something you might not have noticed before. You can spend hours looking at the same shot, trying to go over every detail, when maybe you forgot to blur the slightest element or had something else in the frame that was not meant to be there. Staying objective about your shot is critical.

ANIMATING LAYERS FROM PHOTOSHOP AND ILLUSTRATOR

"I see plans within plans."

—FRANK HERBERT, *DUNE*

Multilayered Data Screen

Many projects call for a complex, highly textured background against which other elements can be placed. One common example of this type of background is a field of complex data calculations, often used for simulated computer interfaces or for conveying the abstract impression of digital technology. This project will illustrate the construction of a multi-layered data field that communicates a sense of depth and mystery, as well as imparting the impression of random motion that would occur with actual calculations.

Project 6

Animating Layers From Photoshop and Illustrator

by Nori-zso Tolson and Terry Green,
twenty2product

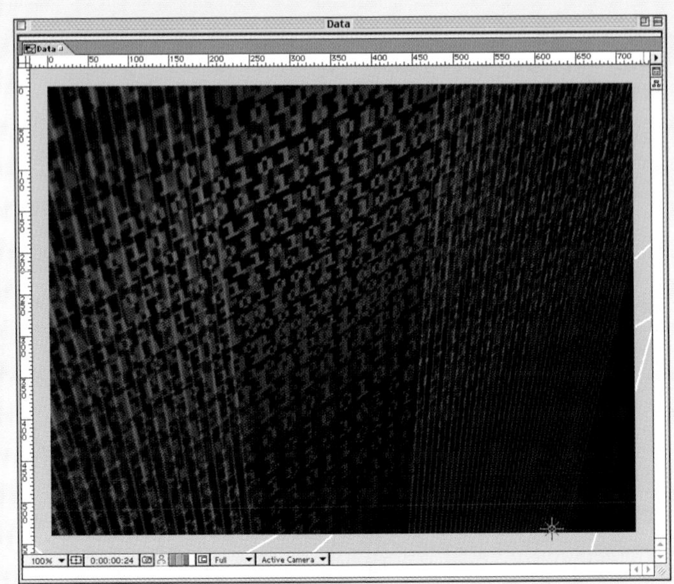

How It Works

You will be animating lines of randomly sequenced 1s and 0s traveling at different rates across the screen. Another layer will move in the foreground to create a sense of depth. Lighting will be added to support the feeling of vast space and infinity. There's an example of the finished movie that you can refer to after you copy it onto your hard drive from the accompanying CD-ROM.

The primary footage source is a layered file that was made in Adobe Illustrator. The file consists of three layers of randomly sequenced 1s and 0s. Because Illustrator files are described by vectors instead of pixels, this file can be rasterized at any size within After Effects without sacrificing image quality, so you can use it for both the small distant type and the large close-up type.

Getting Started

How you import your layered files is the most important part of this project, and yet it is the simplest thing to do. After Effects lets you import your layered Photoshop and Illustrator files as compositions; this is how a single Illustrator file containing layers will serve as the basis for the entire animation.

Note: If you would prefer to use randomly sequenced letters, feel free to create your own layered files in Illustrator or Photoshop or to make low-resolution proxy files. Just be sure that all three layers of characters line up with one another. Take a look at the **datalayers.ai** file as a reference for setting up your own layered Illustrator or Photoshop file.

Importing Layered Files

First, locate this project's folder on the accompanying CD-ROM. Within it, you'll find a file named **datalayers.ai**. The file you'll be using contains three layers of 1s and 0s that are lined up with each other. There is also a project named **VLines.aep** that you will be importing into the project you are working on. Within the same folder is the finished After Effects project named **dataproject.aep** and a small QuickTime movie, called **Data.mov**, of the finished project. You should copy all of the source files for this project from the accompanying CD-ROM onto your local drive for speed and ease of use.

1. Launch AE or, if you already have, close any other open projects. Change your import preferences (Edit > Preferences > Import). In the Still Footage section of the resulting dialog box, click on the second button (next to the text field with timecode numbers) and change it to 0:00:00:05 by typing **5** into the text entry box.

   The full timecode will appear to the right of the text entry box. This will set all imported still footage (- NT) to be the same length: 5 frames. By changing the import settings in the preferences, you save yourself the trouble of changing every layer in a composition separately to the needed length. This is especially useful in projects that have many layers of short edits.

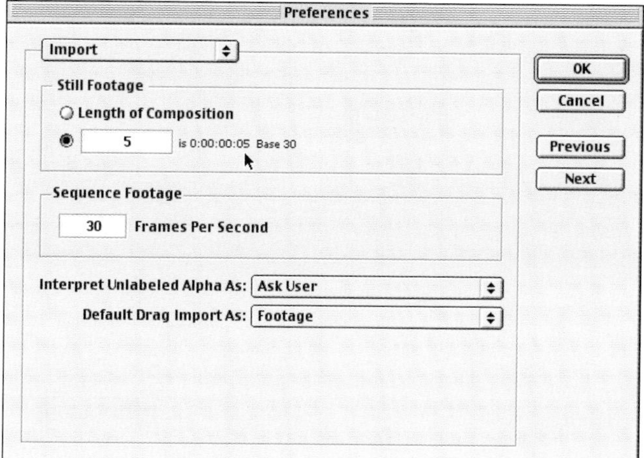

Change the default duration length of the imported layers.

2. Create a new project in After Effects (File > New > New Project) [Cmd+Option/Ctrl+Alt + N].

3 Click Import (Mac) or Open (Windows) to import the layered Illustrator file named datalayers.ai in the project's folder (File > Import > File). In the lower half of the Import dialog box, change the Import As option from Footage to Composition. A folder and a composition will appear in the Project window. The folder contains each of the separate layers that were within the file you imported. The composition has each of those layers on a separate track with the original positions and settings assigned to them.

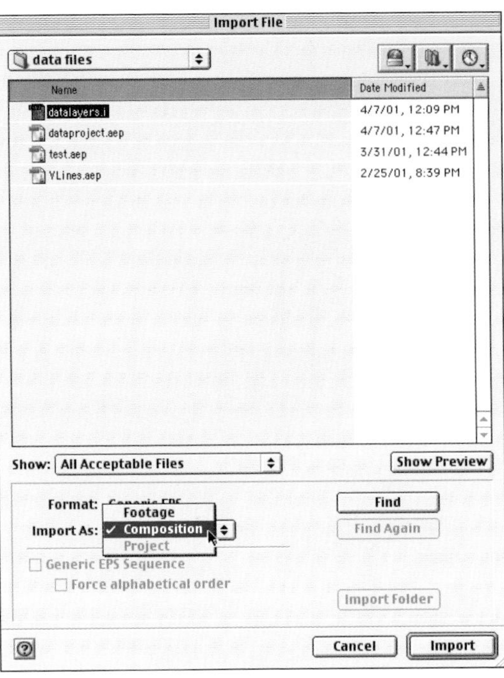

Import a layered file as a composition.

Note: A layered footage item must be selected for this option to be enabled.

4 Select the datalayers.ai composition and change the Composition settings (Composition > Composition Settings) [Cmd/Ctrl + K]. Change the size of the composition to 1,440 pixels wide by 1,080 pixels high. You'll need to deselect the Lock Aspect Ratio check box to type this custom resolution. Then set the duration to 5 seconds (0:00:05:00). If the Time is currently displayed in Frames, you'll need to close Composition Settings, go to File > Project Settings, select Timecode Base: 30fps, and click OK. Then return to the composition settings and change the duration of the composition to 5:00. It will be helpful to change the resolution pop-up to Half or Third to make viewing speedier because the composition is so large.

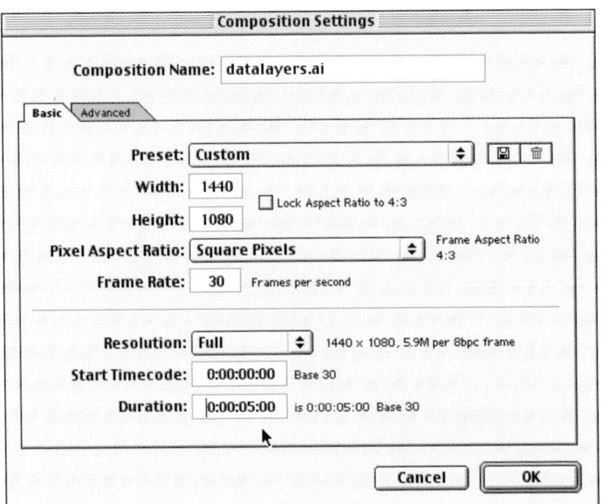

Change the Composition settings.

Note: Generally, the frame rate is determined by the animation's usage. Unless you have a professional video card to play movies at full size and at real time, you might have to make a movie that is half-sized and rendered at 15 frames per second to see it play at full speed.

You're going to be scaling up the size of the data here and using it as a nested composition in another composition.

5 Save the project and name it **Data Project.aep**.

> **Note:** When you import a layered file as a composition, After Effects creates your layers in the exact order and position that you set in Illustrator or Photoshop. The folder that appears with the individual layers is rearranged alphabetically, and each layer is centered to itself rather than its relationship to the finished layout.

> **Note:** After Effects 5.5 now has an Options button for its 3D rendering plug-ins on the Advanced tab of the Composition Settings dialog. Clicking on it will offer two options: Faster and More Accurate anti-aliasing. More Accurate is the preferred setting, and it will better render layers at extreme angles to the camera.
>
> For this example, the Standard 3D rendering plug-in will suffice... there aren't enough significant layer transformations to require the more time-intensive Advanced 3D plug-in.

Building the First Composition, datalayers.ai

You'll be setting up three individual compositions before you actually set up the final project. Because these files can be very slow to display, you can turn off the Visibility of some or all of the layers while you're changing settings and moving them around. Just click on the Video Switch to the left of each file to toggle a layer's Visibility on and off.

1 Because these compositions are so large, set the magnification to 25% or 50% at the bottom of the Composition window. You can also change the resolution from Full to Half or Quarter in that window so that it will display more quickly.

The first composition will use the datalayers.ai composition. Each of the layers should be 5 frames long.

2 Double-click on the datalayers.ai composition in the Project window to open the Composition and Timeline windows. Remove the mask layer by selecting it in the Timeline and pressing the Delete key.

You'll need the mask layer later, but for now it is in the way.

3 Select all of the layers in the Timeline window [Cmd/Ctrl + A] and press the S key to reveal their Scale tracks.

4 Clicking on any layer's numerical Scale value, change the layers' Scale from 100% to 200%, keeping the layer's proportions locked. Press S again to hide Scale.

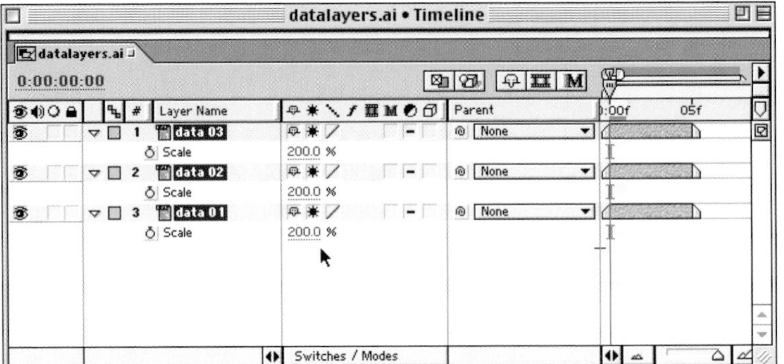

Change the Scale of all three layers to 200%.

Note: The layers now fill the composition frame and look very "jaggie" as a result of the Scale change.

5 While all of the layers are still selected, click on the Continuous Rasterization switch for any layer.

The Continuous Rasterization switch is the second from the left, marked by a starburst icon, in the Switches panel in the Timeline window. With this switch turned on, an Illustrator file can be scaled to any size and will be antialiased without losing any resolution.

6 Drag data 02 and data 03 (by their layer duration bars) down the Timeline so that they follow each other sequentially.

They need to follow one another in time. Which one comes first is not important, but they can't stay above one another. They must be moved forward in time so that data 01 starts at 0, data 02 starts at frame 5, and data 03 starts at frame 10. You can open the In/Out panel to view the in and out points of each layer as you do this, or you can watch the in and out times in the Info palette while dragging the layers.

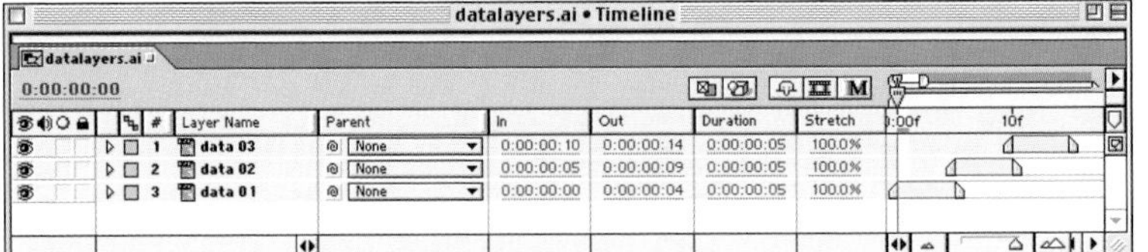

Open the In/Out panel and move the layers down the Timeline.

Tip: Use the following keyboard shortcuts:

i = Go to the in point of the selected layer

o = Go to the out point of the selected layer

Press Shift as you drag a layer to snap it to the current time marker.

7 Duplicate each layer in the Timeline window [Cmd/Ctrl + D] and then drag these duplicates further along the Timeline so that one layer will start where the previous one ends. The layers shouldn't overlap. One begins at the previous one's out point. Vary the order of the three layers so that the repeating patterns will be less obvious.

Repeat step 6 as many times as needed to fill the Timeline with these layers. This process will take a bit of time; with 5-frame layers, you'll need at least 30 layers total to fill up the Timeline. Close the In/Out panel when you're finished arranging the layers. This is a good time to save your project.

8 Turn on the Video switch of all layers before you close the composition (if you've turned them off for a speedier display). You can preview the composition at this point to see what's been built so far.

At this point, you have a full screen of changing data. As an option, you could make a new composition that's the screen size you need and drag the datalayers.ai composition into your new composition and scale it down in size. This would give you a static screen of 1s and 0s flashing back and forth. It could be used in an area of a pseudo computer interface to make it look as though some sort of calculation is going on. But you're going to make another composition to be used as a source layer in the final composition. It will separate the flashing numbers into moving lines of data that travel in opposite directions and will create a more complex and interesting data animation.

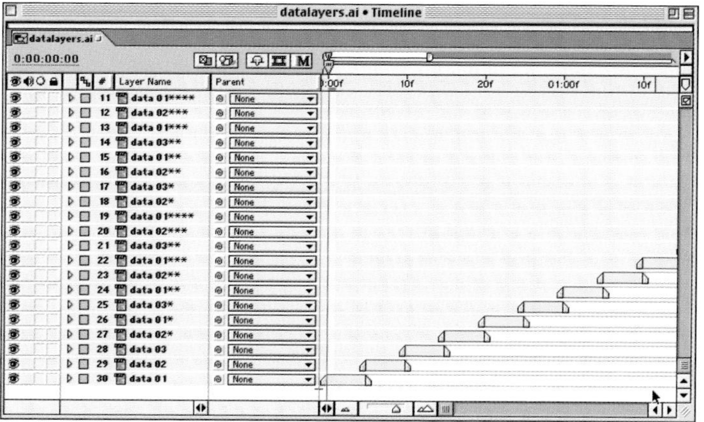

Duplicate the data layers in random order.

Note: To speed up the layer duplicating, you can select any number of layers by Shift-selecting and duplicating them at once. Drag the whole group down the Timeline to more quickly fill the 5 seconds. By duplicating the layers in the Timeline window rather than dragging new layers over from the folder, the layers will already be arranged correctly along the timeline.

Building the Second Composition, H lines

In this second composition, you will use the datalayers.ai composition as a base and then use masks to isolate every other line.

1 Make a new composition [Cmd/Ctrl + N]. It should be the same as the last composition: 1,440 pixels wide by 1,080 pixels high and 5 seconds in duration. Name it **H lines**, referring to the horizontal animation you'll be setting up. Set the frame rate to 29.97 or to whatever frame rate you've decided is best for your purposes. Just be sure to keep them all consistent.

2 Drag and drop the datalayers.ai composition into the H lines Timeline window to ensure proper centering.

Making the Mask

In this section, you will isolate every other line of the datalayers.ai composition. You will then be able to show every second line moving from left to right, and the remaining lines will move from right to left.

1 In the Project window, drag the mask/datalayers.ai layer from the datalayers.ai folder into the H lines composition; it should be above the datalayers.ai layer. Rename this layer **mask**.

2 Select the mask layer and press the S key to reveal its Scale property; change its scale from 100% to 200%, keeping proportions preserved. Then enable Continuous Rasterization for this layer so that you can see how it will look.

3 Select the datalayers.ai layer and press the Switches/Modes toggle in the Timeline to view the Track Matte pop-up menu. Set the Track Matte for the datalayers.ai layer to Alpha Matte mask/datalayers.ai. Be sure to extend the duration of the mask layer so that its out point is at 4:29.

Using the mask layer as a track matte makes every other line visible.

This will use the shapes in the mask layer to determine what areas of the datalayers.ai layer are visible. Because this is being used as an Alpha matte, the layer's alpha information is being used to determine the matte shape. Take a look at the mask layer by itself and view its alpha channel to see what shape is creating the matte. The video switch of the matte layer gets turned off when a track matte is set, and an icon is added next to the layer name.

Note: The layer assigned as a track matte must always stay directly above the layer using it in the layer stack to maintain the relationship.

Duplicating Layers to Animate

In this section, you will begin by animating the datalayers.ai layer so that it travels across the screen from left to right.

When you animate the datalayers.ai layer to have it move from left to right, you must have a copy of that same layer following it so that the far right edge isn't just revealing the empty screen as it moves. The alternative would be to make files that are twice as wide as the screen, but by now you know how slow to display that would be. By using the Parent feature, you can attach a duplicate layer to the first, and it will automatically move at the same speed.

1. Select the datalayers.ai layer, press P to reveal Position, and change the coordinate values (X = 0 and Y = 540) so that the data layer is halfway across the window. Click in the stopwatch at frame 0 on the Timeline to set a keyframe.
2. Press End to go to 0:00:04:29 on the Timeline and change the Position coordinates to X = 720, Y = 540. This will cause datalayers.ai to fill the whole window. When you change the Position coordinates, a new keyframe will be automatically set, so there's no need to click the stopwatch at that point.
3. Duplicate both the mask and datalayers.ai layers (Edit > Duplicate) [Cmd/Ctrl + D] and press Home to go to 0:00:00:00 on the Timeline.

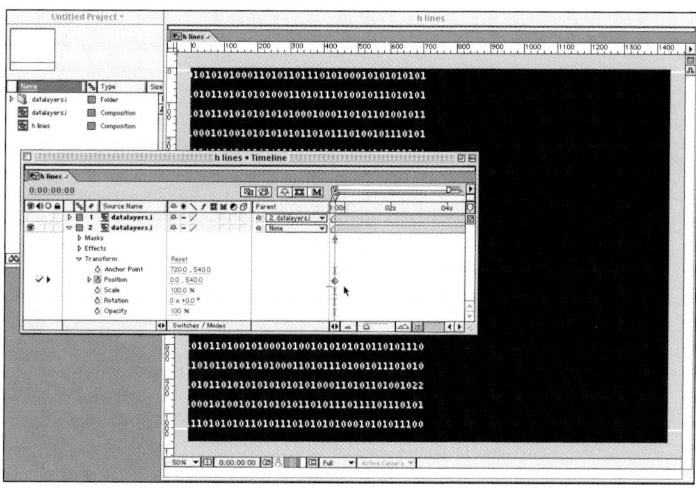

Set keyframes for the first datalayer.

4 Bring both layers to the top by first selecting both layers and then choosing Layer > Bring Layer to Front [Cmd+Shift/Ctrl+Shift + [ ]. It's very important that the position of these layers relative to one another in the layer stack is maintained to preserve the Track Matte relationships set up between them.

5 Click on datalayers.ai (Layer 4), press the Return key on the keyboard, and type in the new name. Rename datalayers.ai (Layer 4) **Data R1** and datalayers.ai (Layer 2) **Data R2**. Renaming the mask layers is unnecessary.

The source name is the original file name as listed in the Project window. If you select the source name and hit Return or Enter, you can type in a new name. This new name becomes the layer name.

It's important to give your layers names that help identify them. Some projects might have 50 or more layers, and using descriptive layer names really helps to find your way around the project.

Note: You can toggle back and forth between the source name and the new layer name by clicking either one at the top of the column of layer names in the Timeline window.

6 Select the Data R2 layer and press P to reveal position. Click off the stopwatch to remove the keyframes.

7 Select the Data R2 layer. Set its Position to X = 2144, Y = 540 so that it fills the right half of the window; do not create any keyframes for this layer. If the Parent panel is not displayed, go to the Timeline window menu and select Panels > Parent.

8 In the Timeline, click on the Data R2 layer's Parent pop-up menu (to the right of the Swtiches/Modes panel). Select Data R1 as the Data R2 layer's parent.

When a parent layer is animated to move from one position to another, it will drag the child layer along at the same rate and for the same distance. Data R2 has been offset so that its beginning position is different from that of Data R1, so it will follow the animation set for Data R2, but will begin the motion from its original position. This is why it's not necessary to set any keyframes for the child layers.

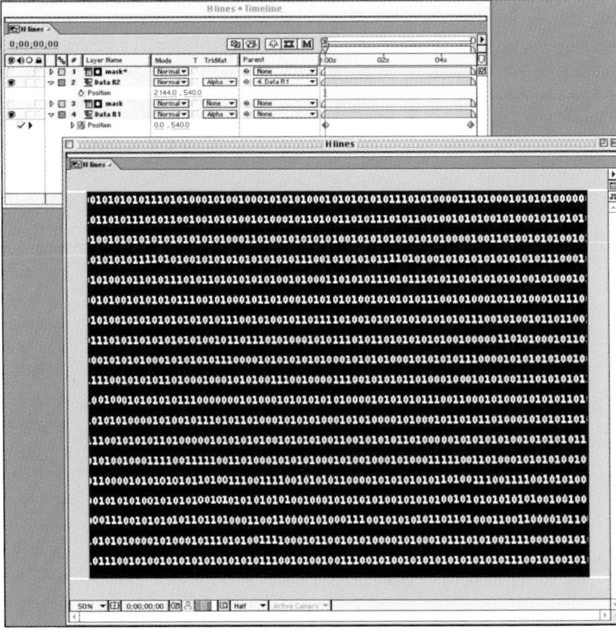

Position Data R2 to line up with the edge of Data R1, filling the empty half of the screen.

Duplicating the Second Set of Layers

You'll duplicate the first layer again to make another Parent layer that will move in the opposite direction at a slower speed. You'll also change the Mask settings so that the alternate lines of data will be revealed.

1. Collapse the layer outlines to clean up the Timeline window.

2. Duplicate all the layers in the Timeline by first selecting Edit > Select A [Cmd/Ctrl + A] and then Edit > Duplicate [Cmd/Ctrl + D].

3. Change the name of the duplicated layer Data R1 to **Data L1** and change the name of the duplicated layer Data R2 to **Data L2**.

   By renaming the layers, you can keep track of which ones are moving left and which are moving right, and you can be certain that you have the correct layers selected to be the parent of the trailing layer.

4. Change the Track Mattes for Data L1 and Data L2 to Alpha Inverted Matte. The Track Matte menu option will read: Alpha Inverted Matte mask/datalayers.ai.

   Changing the TrkMat setting causes the alternate lines of type to be revealed in the duplicated layers because the matte is now based on the inverse of the alpha channel in the mask layer. Be sure that each Data layer has a mask layer above it. The order of the layers is very important.

5. Select layer Data L1 and press the P key to inspect its Position property. Leave the first keyframe as it is but go to its keyframe at 0:00:04:29 on the Timeline and change its value to X = –320, Y = 540 so that it moves in the opposite direction. Because layer Data L2 has already had its Parent layer changed to Data L1, it will follow this new change in movement. Save the project and preview the animation. You'll see the screen filled with data, every other one traveling in opposite directions.

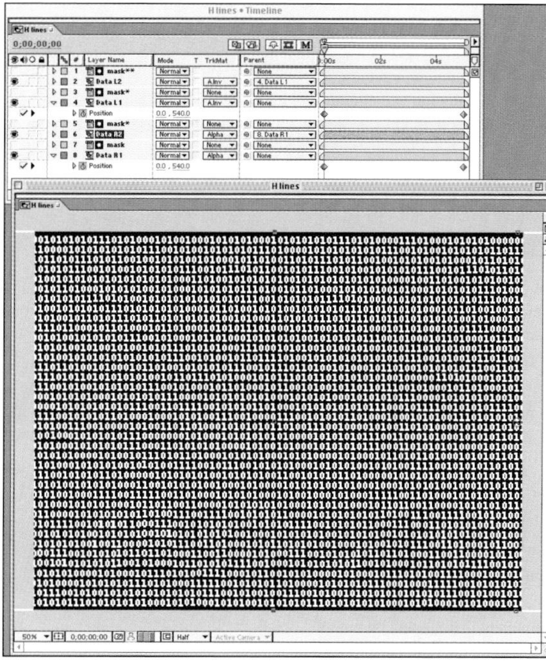

Duplicate the layers, change the Track Mattes, and then set new layers for the parents.

Tip: It might be helpful to turn off the video switches for R1 and R2 to view L1 and L2 to better see what's happening here.

6 Change the Parent layer of Data L2 to Data L1. This will cause it to follow Data L1 in the opposite direction of Data R1 and Data R2 now that the position keyframes have been changed.

Setting Up the Composition

Using your first two compositions, you'll be able to set up your animating data within a smaller composition in extreme perspectives that will fill the screen.

1 Make a new composition [Cmd/Ctrl + N]. It should be the same 5 seconds in duration, but change the size to 720 pixels wide by 540 pixels high. Name it **Data**. Set the frame rate to be the same as your other compositions and click OK when finished to close the Composition Settings dialog box.

   You're going to rotate and tilt the animating data field, so you needed to make it larger than the final composition size it will be used in. Otherwise, it would not fill the entire screen, and you would see all its edges when it's in perspective. When it's twice as big, the range in size from the closest to farthest can be much more dramatic.

Note: You will have to determine the final size of your movie based on your hardware and the project requirements. If desired, you can continue with this project at this size and then put a scaled version of the final composition into a differently sized composition to render the movie at a smaller size.

2 Drag the H lines composition to the Data composition's Timeline window.

3 In the Timeline window, click on the H lines layer's 3DLayer switch icon to turn it into a 3D layer.

   This will give you additional Z-axis settings under the layer's Transform properties.

4 In the Timeline window, select the H lines layer and press P to set its Position to X = 640, Y = 170, Z = 0. Then press R to set its X rotation to 60 degrees and the Y rotation to –30 degrees.

You won't animate the position or rotation of this layer in this project, but feel free to experiment with different angles and try adding some keyframes to change this layer's angle over time.

5 If you preview the animation at this point, you will see the 1s and 0s changing back and forth as each line of data moves in the opposite direction of the line above and below it as before but in dramatic perspective.

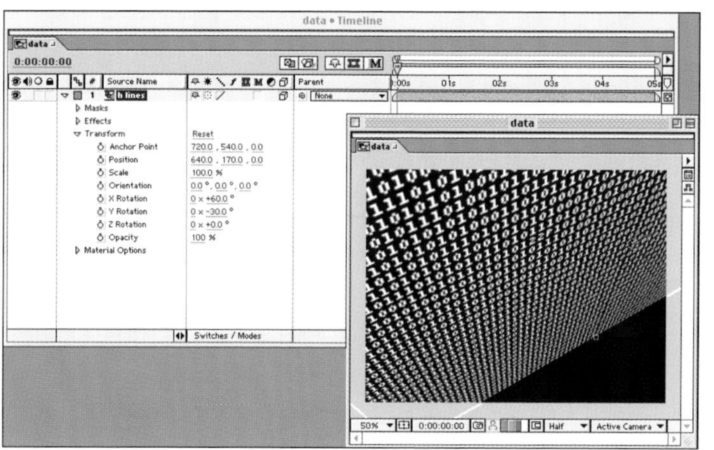

Add 3D settings to the composition.

Note: As an experiment, you could set the X rotation at 30 degrees at frame 0, changing to 60 degrees at 4:29. This would cause the numbers to start at less of a tilt forward and lean more dramatically forward throughout the animation. By changing the Y rotation to 0 and centering the H lines composition, you would have a screen of numbers that went straight across the screen, filled the frame, and tilted forward at the top. By experimenting with different settings, you can compare the effect of a bird's-eye view versus a low-angle point of view.

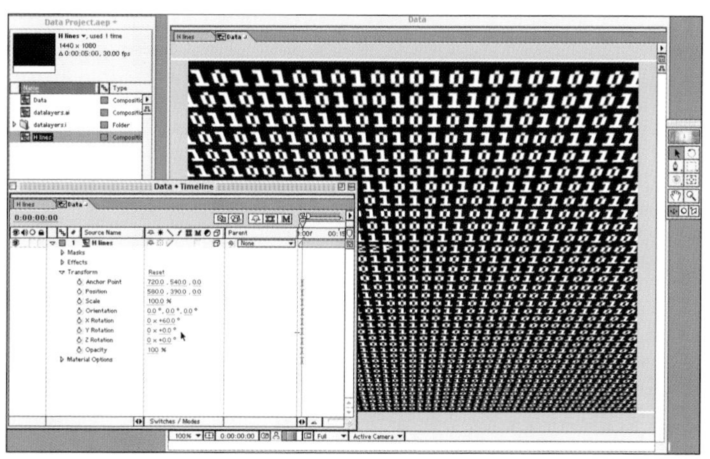

An alternate experiment in which the Y rotation and the position of the H lines in the composition have been changed.

6 Press Home to go to 0:00 and add a light (Layer > New > Light) [Cmd+Option+Shift/Ctrl+Alt+Shift+L]. Change the Light Type to Spot and the color to green (such as R 76, G 128, B 0). Set the Cone angle to 100. Name it **greenlight**. The other light settings can be left at their default settings. Click OK to close the dialog box.

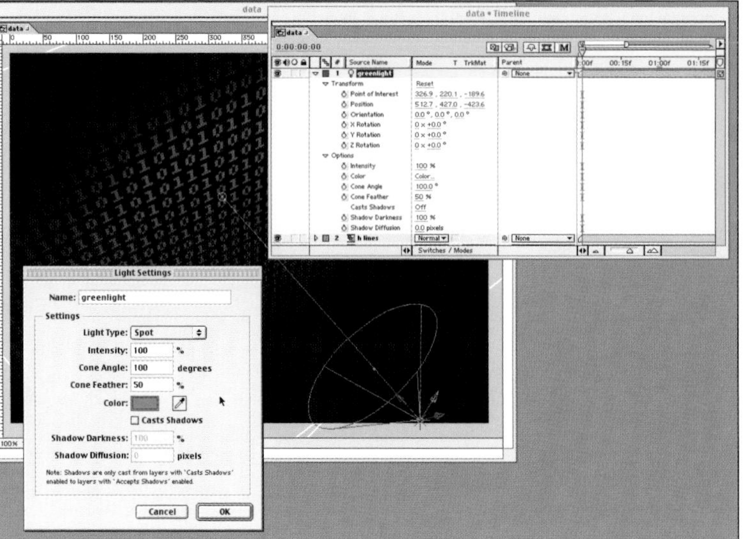

Add a green light to the composition.

Note: The light gives the animation a more dramatic or mysterious appearance. The light's position and color could be animated for more interest.

7 In the greenlight layer, under Transform, set the Point of Interest to X = –210, Y = –253, Z = –190 and its Position to X = 512, Y = 427, Z = –423. Then collapse all layer outlines.

Note: You can animate the light's position and color over time for different effects; feel free to experiment. If you want to experiment with different approaches, you can make a data field with an entirely different look and feel by making your type blue by adding a new solid (Layer > New > Solid), changing its color to blue, and using H lines as a track matte. A yellow spotlight was added and two additional light blue solid layers. The bottom layer acts as a surface for the spotlight to act on by clicking on its 3D Layer, and the layer above it has its mode set to ADD to brighten up the background.

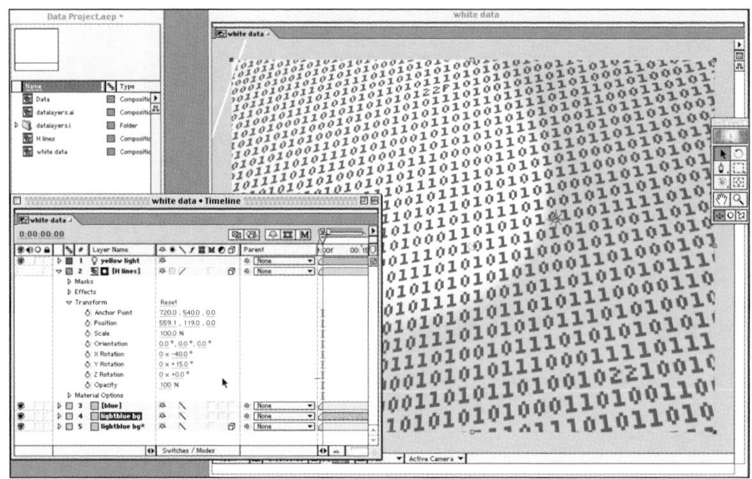

An example of a variation with blue type, altered 3D, and a light background.

Adding the Top Layers

The next two layers will give an additional sense of depth to the animation. The datalayers.ai composition will be used in the foreground, scaled up in size and made more transparent, and animating vertical lines will be placed on top of that using a project called VLines.aep.

Note: Remember that you can turn off the Visibility for all the layers while you change settings so that you don't have to wait for everything to redraw.

1. Press Home to go to 0:00 and drag the datalayers.ai composition onto the Data composition's Timeline window.

   This will add another, closer layer of data for greater depth.

2. Add a new Mask (Layer > Mask > New Mask) [Cmd+Shift/Ctrl+Shift + N] or just press M in the Timeline window.

   This mask will have soft edges to give the impression of the numbers fading away into the distance.

3. Select the datalayers.ai layer and press M to reveal the Mask Shape in the Time Layout window. Click on datalayers.ai to open the Layer window. Using the Rectangular Selection tool, draw a mask that includes the top two thirds of the layer. It will be easier if you are viewing the layer at 25%.

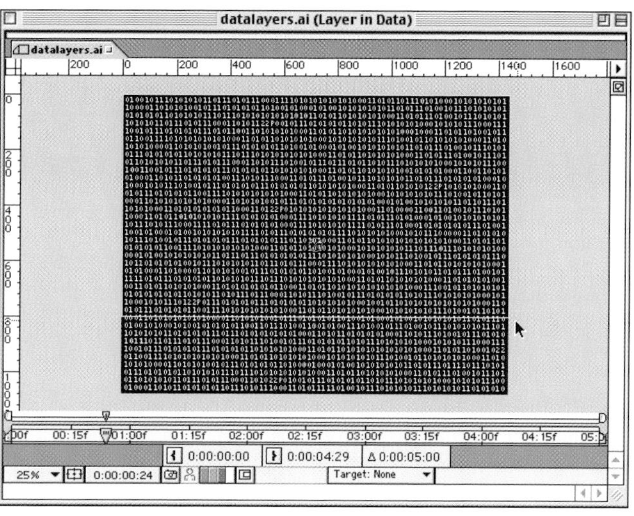

Add a mask to the datalayers.ai layer.

4. Open the Mask Feather dialog box (Layer > Mask > Mask Feather) [Cmd+Shift/Ctrl+Shift + F] while the mask is selected. Uncheck the Lock option, set just the Vertical feather to 200, and click OK.

5. Click on the datalayers.ai 3D switch icon to turn it on.

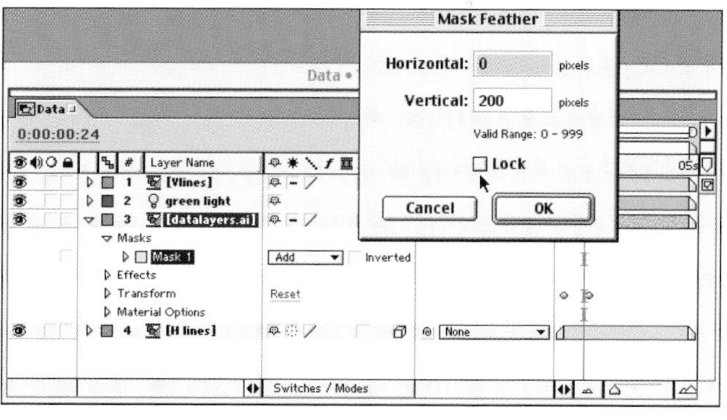

Uncheck the Lock option and set just the Vertical feather to 200.

6 Open Transform and set a keyframe for this layer's Position at 0:00:00:00 on the Timeline to X = 290, Y = 471, Z = 0. In this layer's Scale track, click on the chain-link icon to disable its proportion constraints; set the values to Width 200, Height 200, Depth 100, and its Opacity to 20%. Set the X Rotation to +45 and the Y Rotation to –45. You can do this by using keyboard shortcuts to access the individual values [S = scale, O = opacity, R = rotation].

Note: You can also set the scale by choosing Layer > Transform > Scale, or Control-clicking/right-clicking on the Scale values and choosing Edit Values. The Preserve pop-up menu should be set to "None" in the dialog box before entering the new values. If you are using After Effects 5.0, this is the only way to unconstrain the layer's proportions.

7 In the Timeline window, click on the arrow to the left of the datalayers.ai layer to display Masks, Effects Transform, and Material Options. Open Material Options and turn off Accepts Lights. (Just click where it says On and it will change to Off.)

This is a very faint transparent layer. Not making it green from the light will help distinguish it from the layer of green type behind it.

8 At 0:00:01:00 on the Timeline, change Position to X = 290, Y = 278, Z = 0 and collapse the layer outline.

Note: This is another good place to experiment with motion. For example, this layer could slowly scroll upward throughout the animation or suddenly jerk into position as you've set it up.

This will cause the layer to slide into place. It could have continued moving throughout the 5 seconds, but I thought it would be more interesting to break up the pace. It would be a good idea to save and preview your work at this point.

Composition 3

This composition will be used as the top layer in the final movie. It's a large screen of thin vertical lines that will make the final composition more interesting. It was made by adding new solids (Layer > New > Solid) to a composition that were 1 pixel wide by 2,000 pixels tall (the height of the composition), but you could also just make a series of perpendicular lines in Illustrator or Photoshop.

1. Import the Project named **VLines.aep** (File > Import) [Cmd/Ctrl + I] from this project's folder on your hard drive.
2. Open the folder in the Project window and drag the VLines.aep composition onto the Data composition's Timeline window at 0:00 to the top of the layer stack.
3. Add a new Mask, as in the previous layer. Repeat steps 2, 3, and 4 from the previous section.
4. Click on the 3D Layer switch for this layer and repeat step 7 from the previous section to turn off Accepts Lights.
5. Inspect this layer's Transform properties. At 0:00:00:00 on the Timeline, set the Position to X = 360, Y = 580, Z = 0. Set its Opacity to 40%. Set keyframes for the X Rotation to 45 degrees and the Y Rotation to –45 degrees.

Note: You've been setting the angle of rotation the same for each layer, but you could try different angles and change them over time. Changing the X rotation to –60 causes the lines to lean back and go through the layers of data.

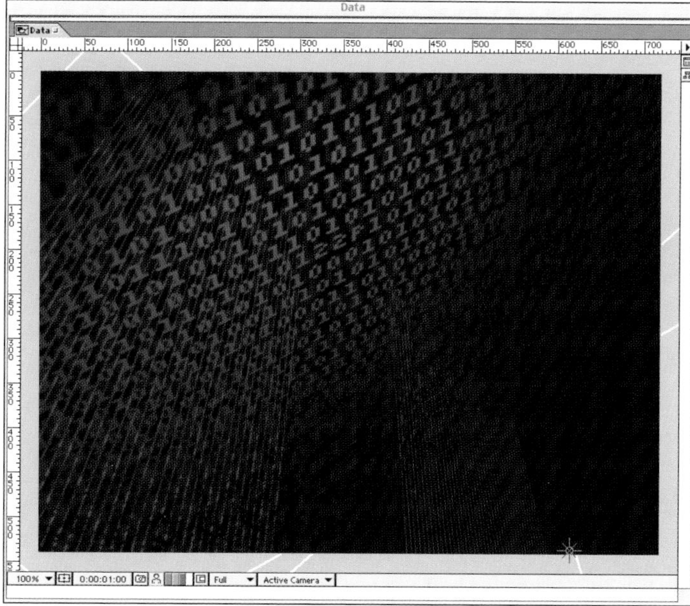

An example of a variation in which the angle of the lines looks like they are piercing the wall of data.

6. At 0:00:004:29 on the Timeline, change its X Rotation to 0 degrees and its Y Rotation to 0 degrees. This will automatically add a second keyframe.

   This animates the lines square to the screen and separates them from the planes of data in the background.

7. To render the movie, go to the Composition menu and select Make Movie [Cmd/Ctrl + M]. Then click OK to close dialog box.

8. The Render Queue window will open. Click on Render Settings, where you can choose the quality of the render and whether to render on fields or frames. How you choose the settings depends on what you'll be doing with the movie, but you should be sure that the frame rate is consistent with your composition's setting.

9. Next, in the Render Queue window, click on Output Module. This is where you choose the compressor for your movie. Unless you have a video card with its own CODEC, just choose animation compression. Then click the Render button to begin rendering the movie.

   You can take a look at a small version of the final movie by opening **Data.mov**.

Note: Changing the angles and duration of these animations can be motivated by editing to musical cues to achieve different moods. You could use masks to reveal one line at a time to a percussive beat for impact. A slow vertical-wipe on one of the lines to a thoughtful piano piece could give the feeling of rain.

Note: If you want to render a small version of this movie, you can make a new medium-size composition (320×240) and drag the final composition into it, scale it down to size, and render it.

Modifications

This technique could be used with a screen of text as well as data. In this example, a layout was done in Photoshop with names of many different countries arranged to line up so that they could dissolve or cut from one to another, just as the 1s and 0s did. The lines of text were isolated with masks as in the H lines composition. Wide bands of color were added in addition to fine lines.

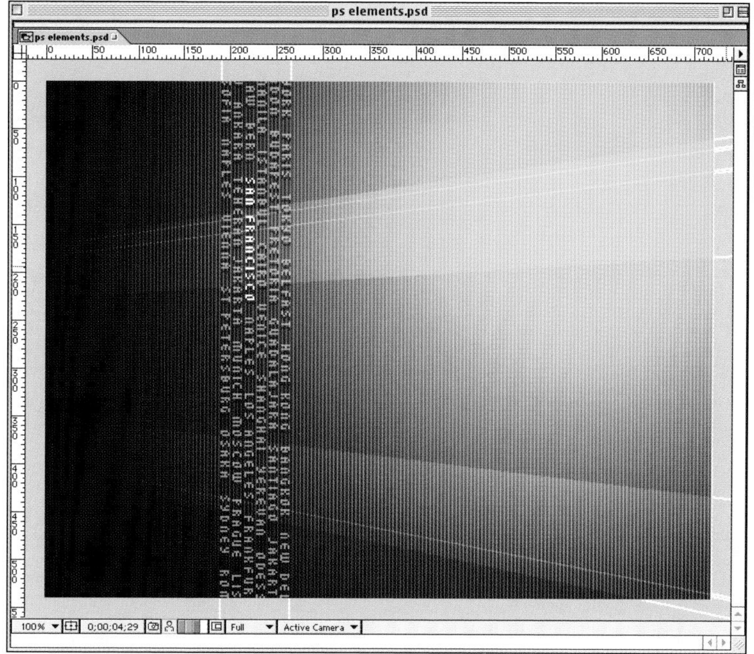

Use this project to create a text animation.

LOGO ANIMATION WITH 3D

"We can't all be heroes because somebody has to sit on the curb and clap as they go by."

—WILL ROGERS

Melwood Pictures 2K Film Logo

Have you ever designed a logo ID at film resolution for a big-time studio? In this project, you will learn how to use the new 3D features in After Effects to create a film company's logo animation using dazzling light and shadow effects, Hollywood style.

Project 7

Logo Animation with 3D

by Kory Jones, Reality Check Studios

How It Works

This project illustrates a full-resolution film project. There are some steps you can take to optimize your workflow and After Effects' performance. To work efficiently on a film-resolution file, view it at 25% in the Composition window and change the resolution to a custom setting, showing every 12 pixels horizontally and every 8 pixels vertically. When you work on the position of layers in 3D, you can speed up redraw by using the Draft 3D feature. Unfortunately, when animating lights or working with shadows, you must stay in the fully rendered mode.

Getting Started

Copy this project's folder to your hard drive from the accompanying CD-ROM. This folder contains the source files you'll need to work the project as well as the After Effects files and the completed animation for reference.

Note: This project suggests some alternatives that use the Knoll Light Factory (**www.commotionpro.com**) and Final Effects (**www.media100.com**) plug-ins. They provide some cool effects that After Effects can't quite reproduce. These plug-ins are not necessary to complete the project, but they do provide some interesting "extras."

The Shadow Layer

The first layer you'll create is the Shadow layer. This layer is the base on which you'll construct the rest of the logo.

1 Launch After Effects and create a new project. Import (File > Import) [Cmd/Ctrl + I] the file **MelwoodLogoBlack.ai** from this project's folder on your hard drive.

The logo was created in Adobe Illustrator with crop marks around it at 2048×1107 points.

Note: If you choose points as your units of measure in Illustrator, they will relate directly to the number of pixels in the After Effects composition. The crop marks enable you to scale the logo to the correct size relative to the canvas it will use in After Effects. If you do this, you won't have to precompose your layers to use blurs or other effects that need a big canvas area.

2 Drag the Illustrator logo to the New Composition button at the bottom of the Project window to create a new composition.

This will automatically set your composition to the correct size of 2048×1107. This is a full-resolution film frame at a 1.85 aspect ratio.

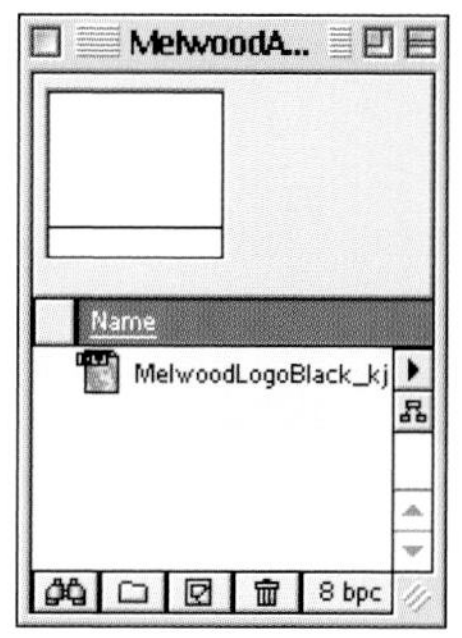

The Illustrator file added and ready to roll.

3 Use Cmd/Ctrl + K to bring up the Composition Settings dialog box and double-check that your Frame Rate is 24 for film. Change the Duration of your composition to 10 seconds. Make sure you are working in Timecode Base 24 so that you get an accurate representation of the number of frames per second for film. You can set this parameter in the Project Settings under the File menu [Cmd+Option+Shift+K or Ctrl+Alt+Shift+K]. Name the composition **00_ShadowBackground Comp** and click OK.

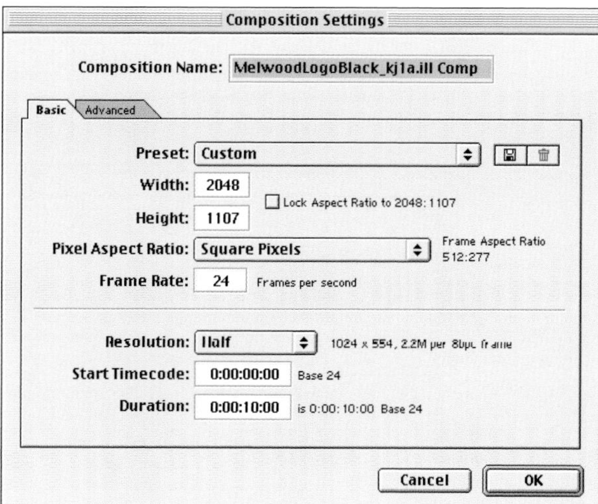

The composition is set and ready to be renamed.

The black Illustrator logo is the layer you will use to cast a shadow. Now you need to create a background on which to cast the shadow.

Note: Keeping your compositions, folders, and files named and organized will be crucial as you do more complex projects. I use the numbers at the beginning of my composition names to organize my subcompositions in the order they get stacked from back to front. Notice that the names of my files consistently use my initials and then a version number, followed by the three-letter extension for the type of file. If every file you create is named this way and there is a consistent method for organizing the folders that hold these files, you will be able to quickly make revisions or find a file in a project that is years old.

4 Create a New Solid (Layer > New > Solid) [Cmd/Ctrl + Y] and set its Width to 3000 pixels, its Height to 1500 pixels, and the Color to white.

The solid needs to be bigger than the size of the composition because it will be moved back in 3D space and tilted back at the top. If you were to move a solid exactly the same size as the Composition window back in space, it would appear smaller, and the edges would be visible.

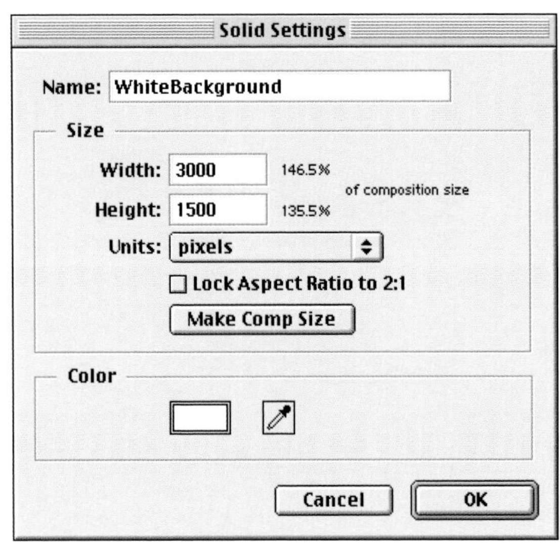

That's a good-size solid.

5 In the Timeline window, toggle on the 3D Layer buttons for both layers. This gives the layers additional controls for manipulating them in 3D space, including Z position and X and Y rotation.

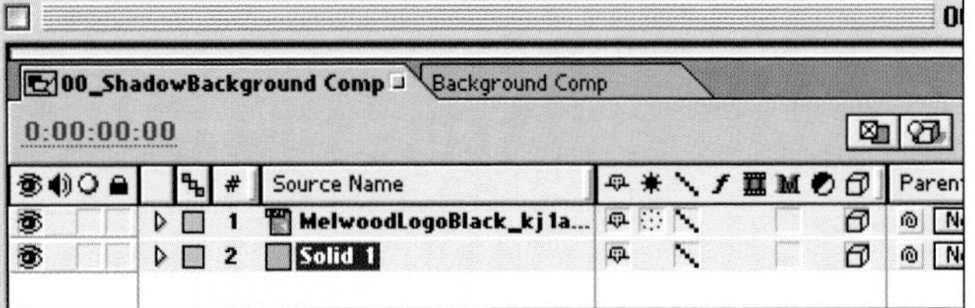

The little 3D box icon shows you that both layers have 3D activated.

6 Change the 3D View pop-up to the Right view.

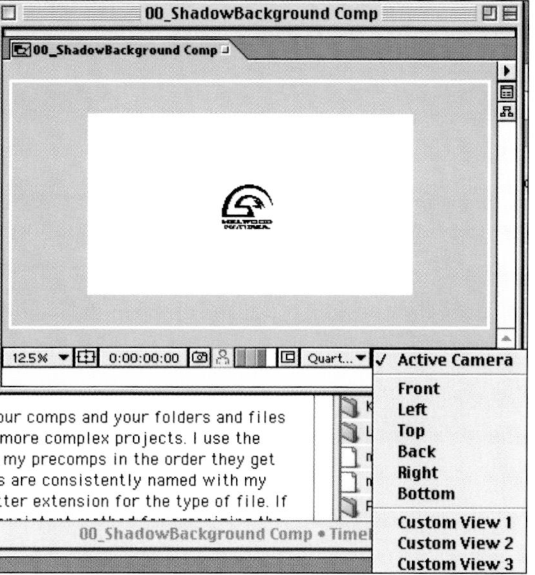

Use the pull-down menu at the lower right of the Composition window to control the view.

Note: Versions of After Effects prior to 5.0 had a simple approach toward compositing. The closer a layer was to the bottom of the Layer window, the closer it was to be back of the composition. The addition of 3D world space to the compositing environment added another level of complexity. It is now possible for the lowest layer in your composition window to be in front of the layers above it if the 3D feature is enabled on all the layers. This gives you much more control, but you need to view the compositing world space from different sides to see how the layers are situated in space.

7 Inspect the background layer's Position track in the Timeline window [P key]. Reposition the background layer to X = 1024, Y = 442, and Z = 192.

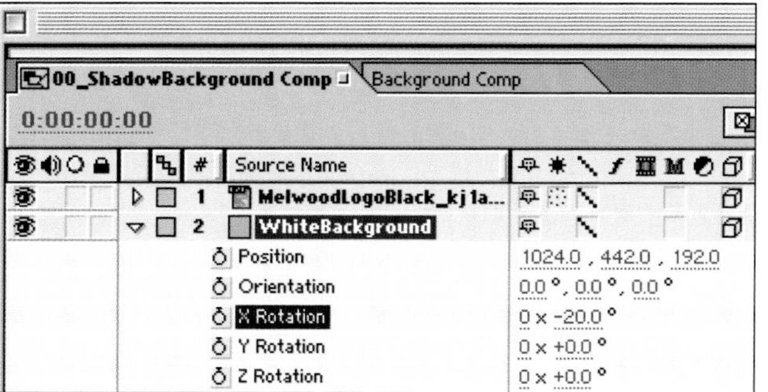

All of the layer's transform properties are revealed, including your new Position values.

Because you are now viewing your composition from the right side, you can see that the background layer is behind the logo layer.

8 In the Composition window, change the 3D View pop-up to Custom View 1 to see the 3D world from a 3/4 side view.

If you are new to 3D, you should go through each of the views. It will give you a better sense of the 3D world. You can also try multiple views under Workspace in the Windows menu. When you are done, go back to Custom View 1.

9 Select the MelwoodLogoBlack layer.

Note that in addition to the selection indicators visible on 2D layers, there are red, green, and blue arrows coming out of the anchor point of the layer.

In the 3D worldspace, you have the X- and Y-axes, just as in 2D. In addition, 3D has the Z-axis, which controls front-to-back motion. The red arrow corresponds to the X-axis, the green to the Y, and the blue to the Z. If you move your selection tool over the blue arrow, you'll see the letter Z appended to your cursor to let you know which axis you will move the layer in.

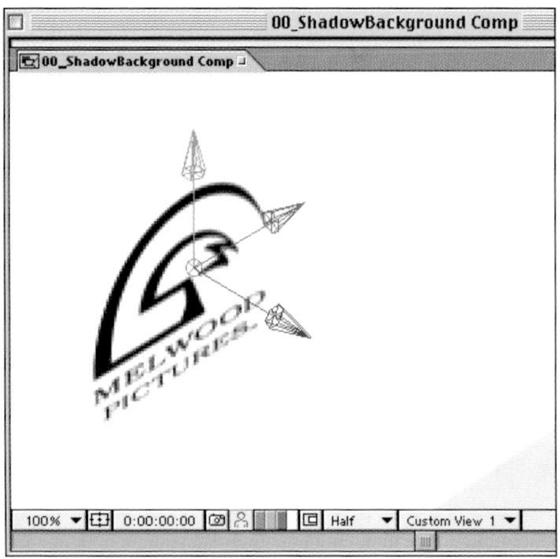

At its most basic, this is what the world of 3D looks like in After Effects.

10 Click and drag the blue arrow toward the upper left.

You'll see the layer move toward the background and eventually disappear behind it.

11 Select the Logo layer in the Timeline window and press the P key to display the position data for the layer. The parameters represent X, Y, and Z positions, left to right. Reset the last number, the layer's Z position, to 0.

Rotations in 3D work the same as translations. The arrows enable you to rotate the layer on a single axis. If you use the tool on the layer without selecting a specific axis, you will rotate the object on all three axes at once.

12 Select the Rotation tool in the Tool palette [W key] and use it to change the orientation of the Logo layer.

Note: The standard engine that handles 3D in After Effects does not resolve the intersection of layers in space. When the anchor point of the logo layer passes behind the background layer's anchor point, the logo is considered to be behind the background and disappears. For After Effects to resolve intersections, users of 5.5 now have the option of switching to the Advanced 3D rendering plug-in. Go into your Composition Settings [Cmd/Ctrl + K], click on the Advanced tab, and switch the pull-down menu selection under 3D Rendering Plug-in to Advanced 3D. Not only does this plug-in calculate intersections, it can also calculate shadow maps, which enable the user to define the softness of shadows cast by a layer.

This project does not require intersections or shadow maps, so the standard 3D renderer will suffice here.

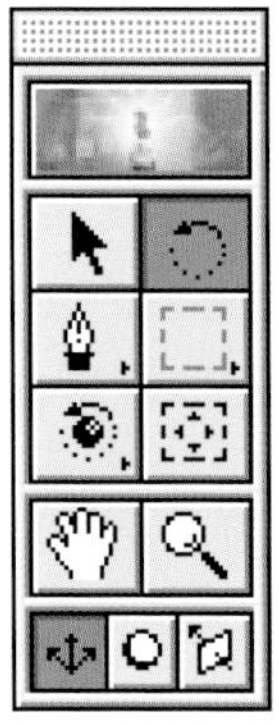

The shortcut for this tool is W, which Adobe documents as standing for "Wotate." Those waskily wabbits.

13 Use the R key to show the layer's Orientation and Rotation values and then reset them to 0.

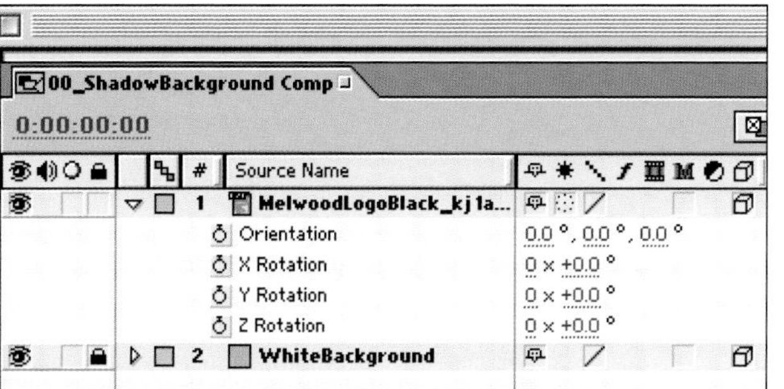

For a 3D layer, the R key reveals both Orientation and Rotation (on three axes).

14 In the Timeline window, lock both this layer and the background (so that you don't accidentally move them) and return to the Active Camera view in the 3D View pop-up.

15 Add a new light to the project by going to the Layer menu and selecting New > Light [Cmd+Option+Shift+L or Ctrl+Alt+Shift+L]. In the Light Settings dialog box, change the light's name to **Light Warm** and change the color to a warm orange.

16 Set the light's Cone Angle to 65° and its Cone Feather to 76%, enable Cast Shadows, and set its Shadow Darkness to 8%. Click OK.

Note that the default light type is a spotlight. There are two parameters that control what a spotlight is illuminating, the Position and the Point of Interest. The Position is the point the light comes from and the Point of Interest controls the direction the light is aiming.

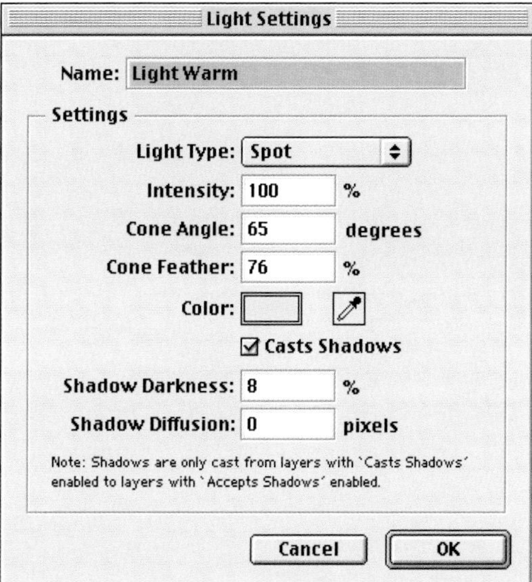

I'm in the habit of naming things object first, modifier second, so that I can see all of the same objects together in an alphabetical list.

17 Select Light Warm in the Timeline window and inspect the Transform parameters. Use the following settings:

Point of Interest: **X = 1066.2, Y = 604.9, Z = 38.7**

Position: **X = 646.5, Y = 579.9, Z = –397.6**

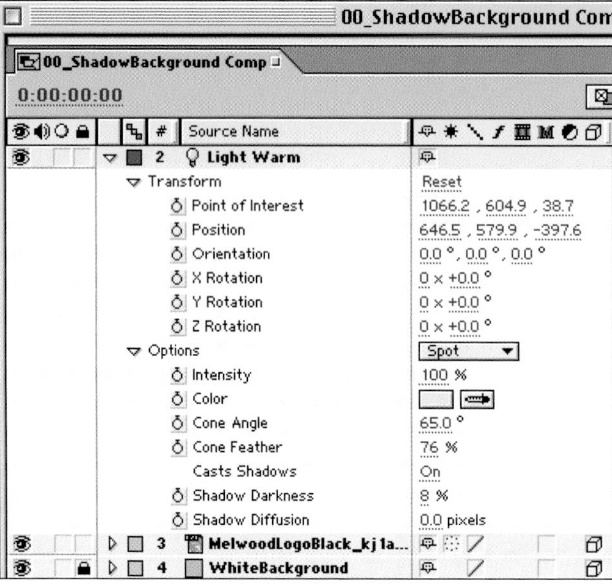

You can drag the light Position and Point of Interest in the Composition window, but setting numerical values is more accurate when you already know the settings.

18 Repeat the process (steps 15 through 18) to create Light Cool with a blue color. Change the parameters as shown in the accompanying image.

Next, the Logo layer needs to have the Cast Shadows feature enabled under the Material Options toggle. For the Casts Shadows parameter, set the toggle to On.

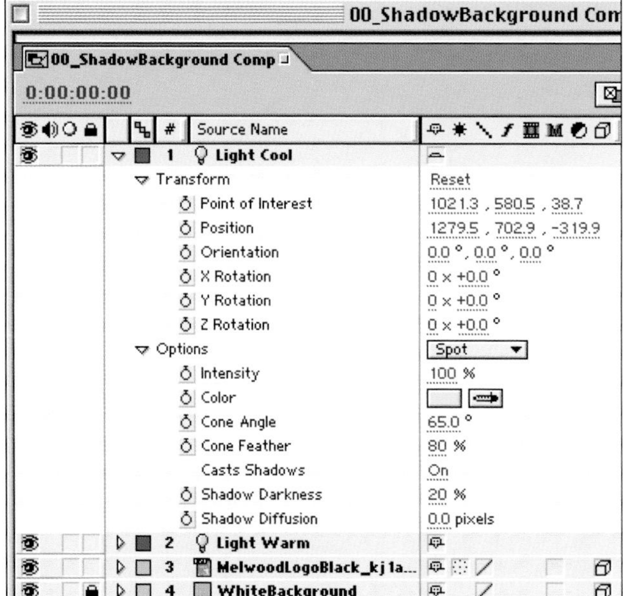

Enter the correct settings for your cool light.

19. In the Timeline, set the logo layer's Transfer mode to Screen.

    This will create a layer that doesn't have any effect on the composition except to cast a shadow on the background.

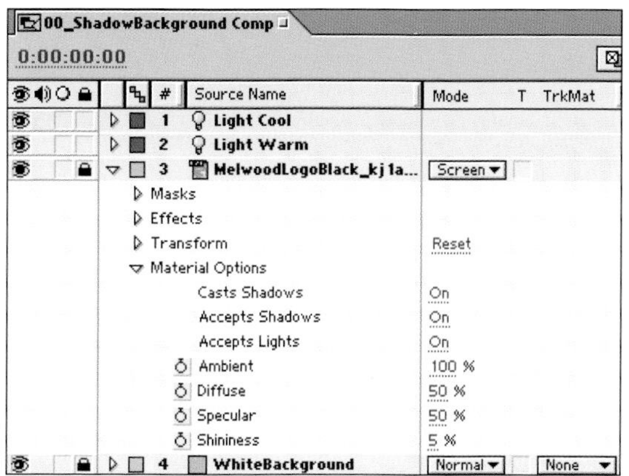

Note that, under Mode, the pull-down has been set to Screen.

Prerendering the Background

Because the animation calls for the logo to be built out of light, having a black logo over the background would not work. Isolating the background and rendering it separately from the logo has a couple of advantages. You are able to prerender the background at a low resolution and use a movie instead of a precomposition; this saves time as you build the rest of the animation. It also provides an opportunity to adjust the levels or to make other tweaks without having to affect the foreground.

1. Move the time marker to 2 seconds (0:00:02:00 or frame 48) and then toggle down the Transform and Options parameters for both lights. Set keyframes for Point of Interest, Position, Intensity, and Cone Angle for both lights.

At this point, your background should look like this (at a low-resolution view).

2. Select both lights and use the U key.

   This will hide all the parameters of the lights except the ones with animation channels and will keep your Timeline window more manageable.

3. Move the time marker to the beginning of the animation and set the keyframes for both lights as shown in the accompanying figure.

1 Light Warm	
Point of Interest	980.5 , 588.6 , 38.7
Position	1179.4 , 588.1 , -243.6
Intensity	0 %
Cone Angle	90.0 °
2 Light Cool	
Point of Interest	923.4 , 588.6 , 38.7
Position	814.2 , 388.0 , -215.8
Intensity	0 %
Cone Angle	90.0 °

Use these settings with keyframes at the beginning of your animation.

4 Move the time marker to the end of the animation and set the Position keyframes for both lights as shown in the accompanying figure.

1 Light Warm	
Position	745.3, 671.7, -497.4
2 Light Cool	
Position	1378.2, 794.8, -419.7

Use these settings with keyframes at the end of your animation.

There are now four animated channels for each light. The Point of Interest animates to aim the lights at the logo. The animated Position of the lights relative to the tilted background creates the moving spotlight effect. As is typical with most film logos, the animation starts in black, so you animate the Intensity to turn the lights on. The Cone Angle animates from wide to narrow to focus the light on the area the logo will build.

5 Build a RAM Preview by pressing the RAM Preview button in the Time Controls palette or by pressing the 0 key on the numeric keypad.

Note: 3D takes longer to render than normal compositing techniques. If you are on a slower machine, you might want to change the resolution to a custom setting (as discussed in the "How It Works" section at the beginning of this project) or press Shift + 0 to build a RAM Preview at a lower frame.

Now it's time to refine the motion path for the light's position and the velocity for all the keyframes. You probably noticed there was a visible pop in the animated preview at 2 seconds when the Point of Interest, Intensity, and Cone stop animating. You'll fix this problem by setting these keyframes to ease in.

6 Select both lights and use the U key to show the animated channels. Select the keyframes for Point of Interest, Intensity, and Cone at the 2-second mark for both lights. If you have the Production Bundle version of After Effects, Ctrl+click (right-click in Windows) and hold to see a pop-up menu for options to affect the selected keyframes. Choose the Easy Ease In option under Keyframe Assistant. If you are using the Standard version of After Effects and don't see this option, select Keyframe Interpolation instead and then, under the Temporal Interpolation pull-down menu, choose Continuous Bezier. If you want more ease, you can add it by twirling down the arrow next to each parameter and pulling the handle on the curve under this keyframe further to the left.

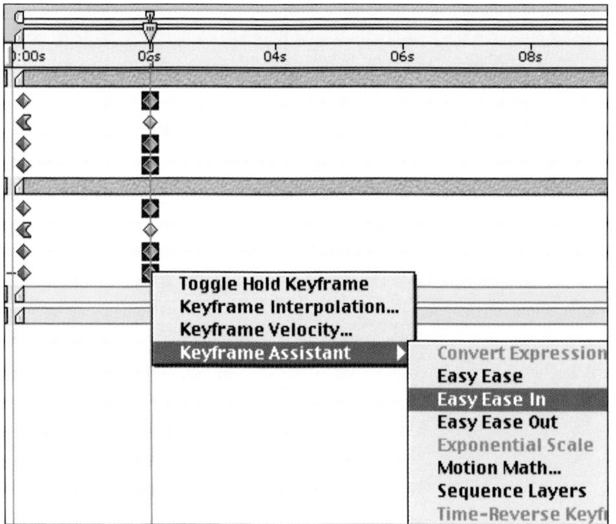

Context menus are the speediest way to choose keyframe options such as Easy Ease In.

The Bezier handles work just as they do in the 2D world, except they now enable you to tweak a path in all three dimensions.

7 Turn off this Visibility of all the objects in the composition *except* Light Warm (by clicking on their Visibility icons in the Timeline window) and then select the Light Warm layer.

8 Change the view to Custom 1 and press the spacebar. You will see the light animate along its path. Continue switching between the Front, Right, and Top views to smooth the Bezier handles for the motion path until it is smooth.

Note: Bezier handles take a bit of practice for the uninitiated. Go slowly if you're new to editing them so as not to lose your selection; if you do lose it, highlight the corresponding keyframe on the Timeline and it should reappear. If you're still having a problem at that point, open View Options with the wing menu at the upper right of the Composition window (the little black triangle) and make sure that all six check boxes at the top are checked.

9 Repeat the process with Light Cool.

Note: Select both lights and look at their motion paths from the Right, Front, Top, and Custom 1 views by changing the 3D View pop-up. If you don't see motion paths, click the black arrow at the upper right of the Composition window and make sure they are activated.

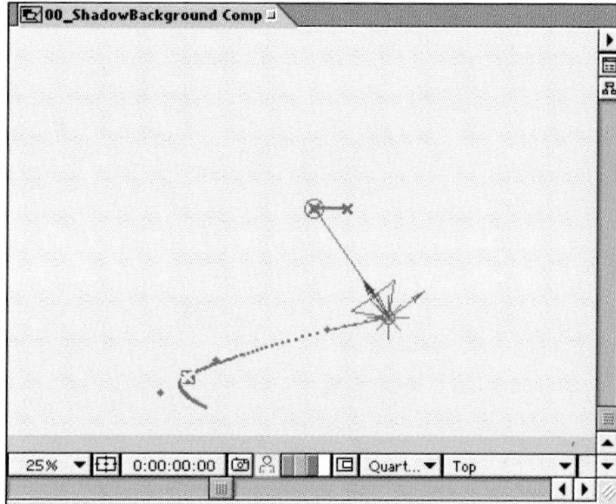

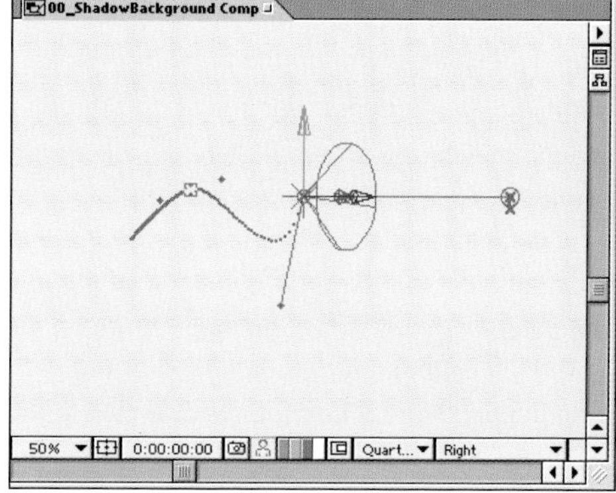

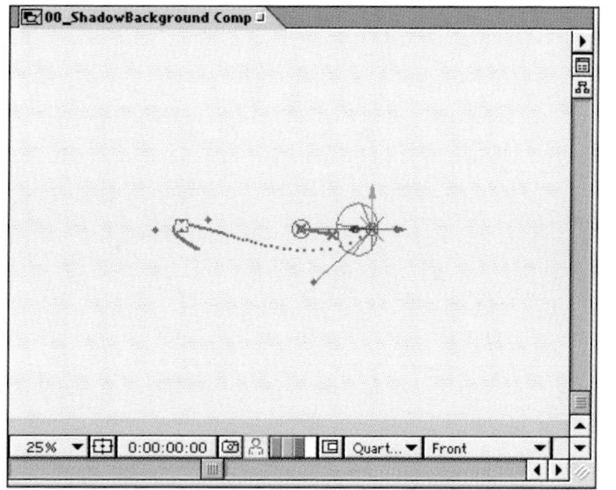

Shown are the Top, Front, and Right views, respectively.

10 Inspect the velocity curves for the Position of both lights. Adjust the curves to match those illustrated in the accompanying image.

The high velocity at the beginning of the animation brings the lights on moving very quickly. Higher speed creates a more dynamic move.

11 Render this composition out by pressing Cmd/Ctrl + M and choosing a name. Set the Render Settings pull-down menu (in the Render Queue window) to Best Settings and then click on this to bring up the Render Settings dialog box. Change the Resolution pull-down to Quarter. Click OK.

12 Set the Output Module to Lossless and click the white twirly arrow next to Output Module. At the Post-Render Actions pull-down at the bottom, choose Import. Now click the Render button at the top to render and import this movie.

13 Create a new composition by dragging the 00_ShadowLayer Composition to the New Composition button at the bottom of the Project window. Rename the new composition **01_LogoReveal Comp**.

This will force the new composition to have the same frame rate, size, and length as the source composition.

14 Drag the 1/4 rez background movie to the new composition and then select it and use Cmd/Ctrl + Option + F to fit the movie to the window. Turn off the Visibility of 00_Shadow.

Now you have a background to work on top of that renders very quickly. Later, when you render the final, you can turn off the small movie and turn on the original composition, and you will get the benefit of the higher-resolution composition.

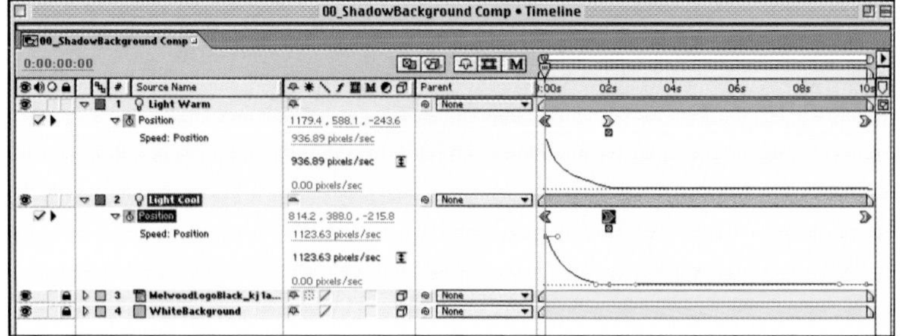

The lights start quickly and then ease into position.

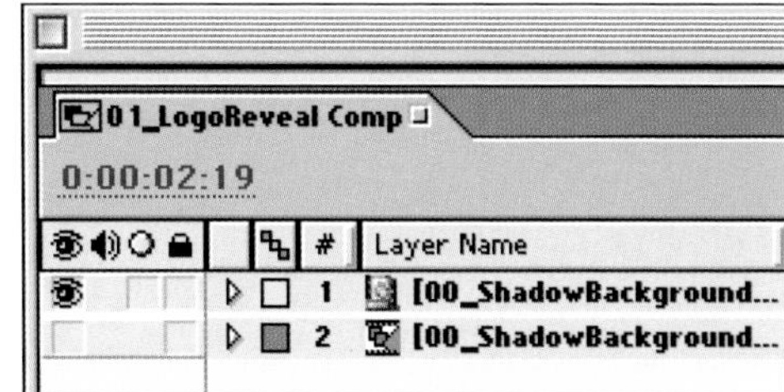

Our lower-resolution layer is on top and active; the high-resolution version waits below until you have completed your edits.

Animating the Logo

The design calls for the logo to build out of light. The first step in this process is to break down the individual pieces of the logo in the order they will appear. I broke down the logo into five layers in Illustrator—the text, ground, trunk, leaves, and sky—and saved the file as MelwoodLogo.ai.

Note: An important thing to realize about the final rendered movie, as it appears on the accompanying CD-ROM, is that a number of third-party filters were used in its creation, most notably the Knoll Lens Flare Pro and Final Effects Light Burst effects. The rest of this project will deviate from the look of the rendered movie in order to use filters available to all After Effects artists.

1 Import **MelwoodLogo.ai** into After Effects as a composition.

This will force all the layers to import at the same time and be neatly organized in a folder.

2 Throw away the composition created by the import; you need only the individual layers. Rename the folder **Melwood Logo Layers**.

3 Create a new folder in the Project window called **Source**. Put everything except your compositions in this folder so that you can toggle it shut when you are not using the imported items.

Your Project window should now look like the accompanying figure.

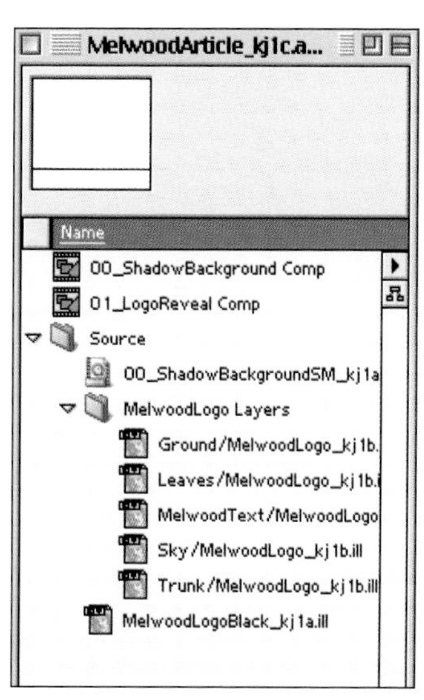

All five Illustrator layers now appear in a single folder together.

4 Open the Logo Layers folder and select all the Illustrator layers. Move the time marker to 0:00:00:00 and drag all the layers to the Timeline window. Arrange them from bottom to top as shown in the figure.

All of the effects for building the logo will happen with these graphic elements. Notice that the text simply fades up from 0% Opacity at time 0:00:00:00 to 100% Opacity at time 0:00:02:19 (frame 67). This should be a gradual transition.

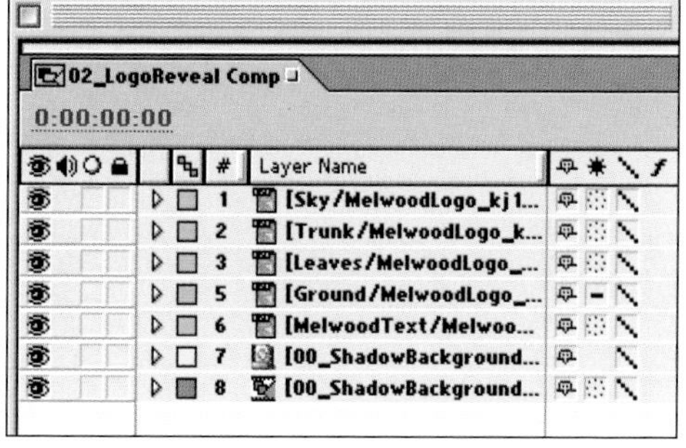

The project now contains two compositions, a QuickTime movie and five Illustrator layers grouped together (along with the original stand-alone Illustrator logo file).

5 Set the keyframes for this animation and then set them to ease in and out as you did earlier with your light positions so that there will be no pops—hard, sudden stops in the animation.

6 Use the Q key with the Ground layer selected to choose the Rectangular Mask tool from the Tool palette. Turn off the Visibility for all the layers except the ground.

7 Draw a rectangular mask just bigger than the yellow line of the ground.

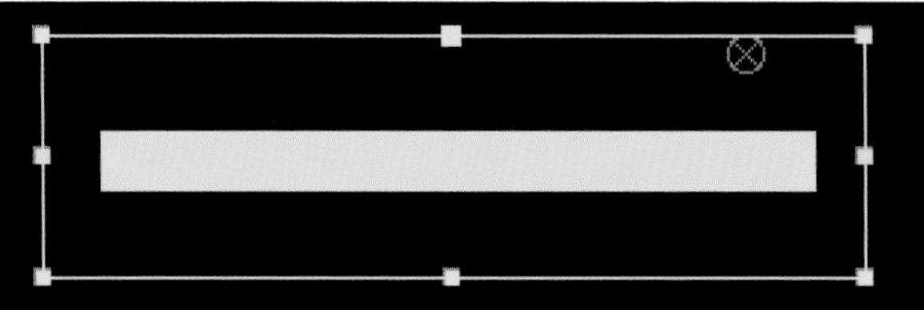

The yellow mask is bigger than the yellow line.

8 Select the Ground layer in the Timeline window and use the M key to toggle down the Mask Shape animation channel. Change the Transfer mode from Add to None.

This will enable you to see the ground as you animate the revealing of the ground.

9 In the Composition window, move the mask just to the right of the ground, create an initial keyframe for the Mask Shape track at time 0:00:00:00 (frame 1), and then move the time thumb to 0:00:01:19 (frame 43). Click and drag on the mask until it is back over the ground; this will automatically create a new keyframe.

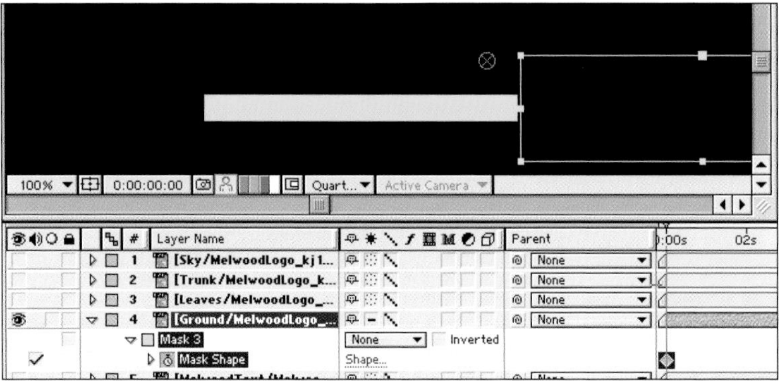

In the first frame, the mask is been offset to the right of the yellow stripe.

10 Set the Transfer mode of the mask back to Add and then build a RAM Preview of the animation.

You will see that the ground is now revealed from right to left.

11 Add a new solid to the composition, making it the same size as the composition itself, and name it **Ground Hilite**. Move the layer to right above the Ground layer in the Timeline window.

Note: I used a lens flare from Knoll Light Factory to hide the leading edge of the reveal in a bright light. Go to **www.commotionpro.com** if you'd like to learn more about it. For this lesson, however, you'll use the PS+ Lens Flare effect that ships with After Effects.

12 Apply the PS+ Lens Flare effect (Effect > Render > PS+ Lens Flare or choose PS+ Lens Flare from the Effects palette) to the Ground Hilite layer. Set its Lens Type to 35mm prime and its Brightness to 50%. Click OK.

Note: If you'd like to follow along using the Light Factory demo, select Options at the top of the Effect window (which opens automatically when you apply the filter). Press the Load button in the effect's dialog box. Navigate to the After Effects plug-ins folder and find the folder called Knoll Custom Light Effects. Pick one of the many interesting presets that ship with this effect.

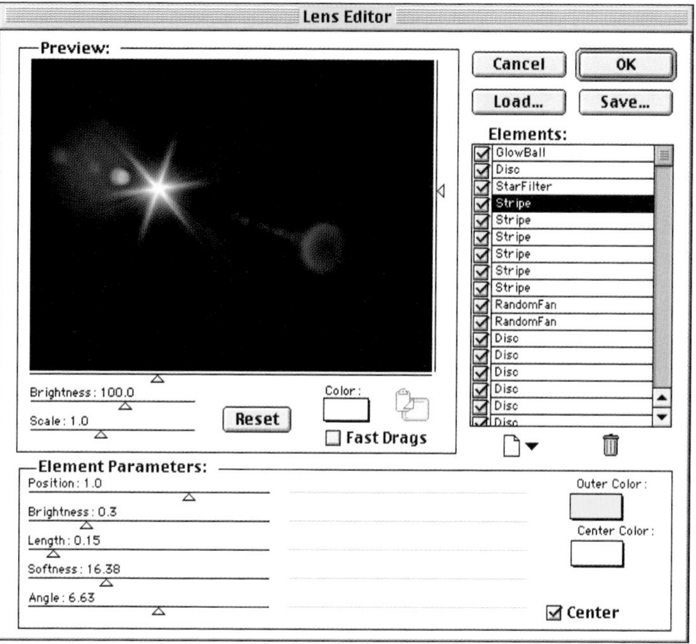

Knoll Light Factory has a complete user interface of its own, accessed via the Options link at the top of the effect setting.

13 Inspect the effect's parameters in the Timeline window [E key]. Return to time 0:00:00:00 (frame 1) and create an initial keyframe in the Flare Center and Flare Brightness tracks.

You want the lens flare to follow the left-hand side of the Ground layer's mask and highlight its leading edge as it draws on from right to left. The most accurate way to do this is to use the information that already exists in the Ground layer's mask track.

14 Select the Ground layer and press the M key to inspect its Mask Shape track. Your time indicator should still be on time 0:00:00:00. Press the Shape link next to the Mask Shape track and view the Left value of the bounding box.

In my final composition, it's 1050. Also, look at the Top and Bottom values and average them: The average of mine comes out to 590. Close this dialog box.

15 Double-click on the first Flare Center keyframe. Enter the mask's Left edge parameter into the X value (in my case, 1050) and enter in the average of the Top and Bottom mask values into the Y value (I'll use 590). Click OK.

You'll find that your lens flare now perfectly conforms to the left edge of the mask and is also vertically centered on the mask.

16 Go to time 0:00:01:19 and view the Ground layer's final Left edge in the Mask Shape dialog box, just as you did in step 14.

17 In the Ground Hilite layer, enter this value into the Flare Center's X value at time 0:00:01:19 (in my composition, it's 800).

The PS+ Lens Flare effect cannot have a Flare Brightness value of less than 10. For this reason, the in point of the Ground Hilite layer needs to be time 0:00:00:01 so that the first frame can be truly black. This will also make the flare's appearance coincide with that of the ground itself.

18 Simply select the Ground Hilite layer, move the time indicator to 0:00:00:01 (you can do this by pressing the Home key followed by the Page Down key), and press Option/Alt + [(open bracket).

19 Create a keyframe for the Flare Brightness track at this frame and enter a value of 10 (the minimum). Move three frames ahead (the Page Down key will move ahead one frame at a time) and set the Brightness to 50. Set an identical keyframe at 0:00:01:19 and then move to 0:00:01:22 and set the Flare Brightness back down to 10.

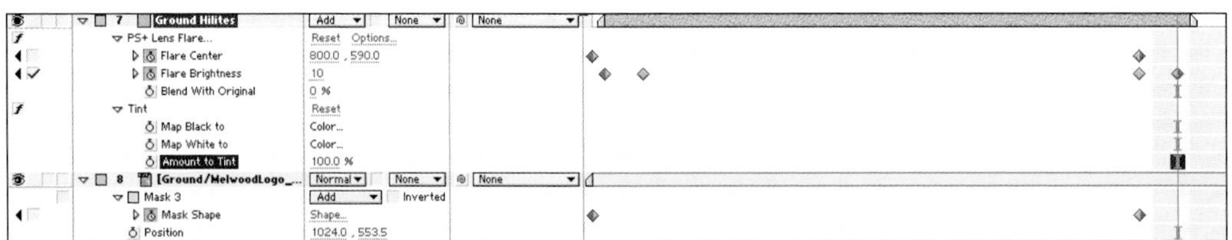

The Ground Hilite layer ends right at its final keyframe.

20 To make the Flare completely disappear, set the layer's out point to that frame by pressing Option/ Alt +] (close bracket).

The principles used to "paint on" the sky and trunk are similar to those used for the ground. I'm going to leave the implementation up to you, but there are a few guidelines to follow.

21 Check the rendered final movie (**MelwoodLogo_ Final.mov** on the accompanying CD-ROM) to get rough timings and then animate the masks and flares for these two layers.

In the final composition, they are called Sky Hilites and Trunk Hilites, respectively.

22 Tint the lens flares with the color of the actual elements to more closely match the final render.

The motion path for the sky is a bit trickier than a straight path; it needs to paint on in an arc that matches that of the final sky shape.

23 Add a small, temporary solid to the composition and then animate its position to follow the curve of the sky. (In the finished project, this layer is called Sky Tracker.)

Once you have the position and velocity of the solid correct, you can copy and paste the position keyframes to the Flare Center. You can also use the solid as a visual reference to animate the mask. As long as the leading edge of the mask is under the solid, it will be covered by the flare.

The leaves are a little trickier, however.

Note: To more closely follow the look of the final rendered movie, you can apply the Tint effect (Effect > Image Control > Tint) and map white to the yellow of the Ground layer at 60%.

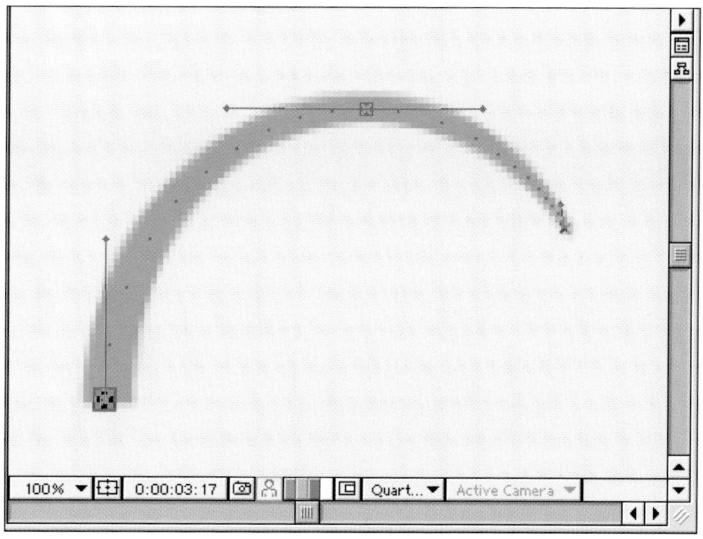

Three keys are created here at the beginning, middle, and end. Use Bezier handles to adjust the slope of the path to fit the sky element.

24 Draw a circle mask on the Leaves layer with the center at the center of the leaves. Tweak the curve so that it matches the outer curve of the leaves.

You'll work a little bit backward here so that your perfectly fitting mask will be kept accurate.

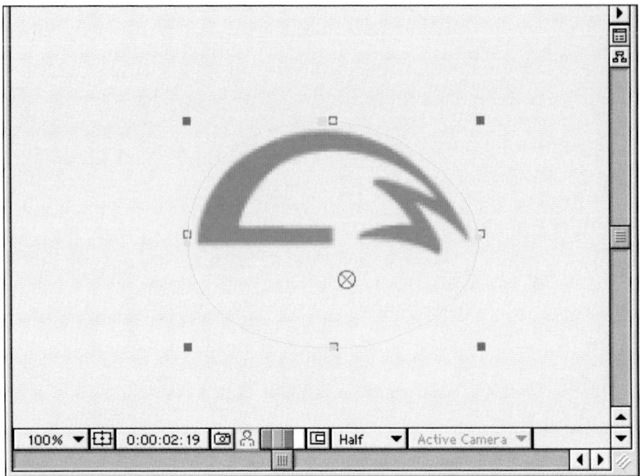

A circle mask encompasses the Leaves layer.

Note: You might notice some banding in the background spotlights for the final project, even rendered at a small size. This problem is compounded in a film frame. To fix this, I set my project to render at 16-bit by Option-clicking on the 8bpc button at the bottom of the Project window. Your render times will increase, and you will have to double-check that all of your plug-ins are 16-bit compatible, but if you do, you will be working with trillions of colors so that the banding caused by a limited color range will be avoided. To take advantage of this expanded color space, you need to use a file format such as Cineon or Digital Voodoo that can store the additional information.

25 Create a keyframe at 0:00:02:19 and then move back in time to 0:00:01:17 and shrink the elliptical mask down enough so that it is *inside* the leaves, obscuring the whole shape. Cmd/Ctrl + T will directly transform the mask shape in the Composition window.

As far as a light effect for the leaves, you're going to leave them as-is for this lesson. After experimenting with different motions for the flare, I decided that it just wasn't working with the design. I duplicated the layer and then precomped it. If you have Final Effects Light Burst, put a black solid behind the leaves in the precomp and then use the Final Effects Light Burst filter to create a light effect. In the main composition, change the layers Transfer mode of the precomp to Add. Because the mask is the same for both layers, the effect is that the light is coming from the leading edge of the mask. You had to precomp the layer over black because the filter's light rays would not have gone outside the mask area.

You can find this precomp in the final project on the accompanying CD-ROM. See what effects *you* can invent!

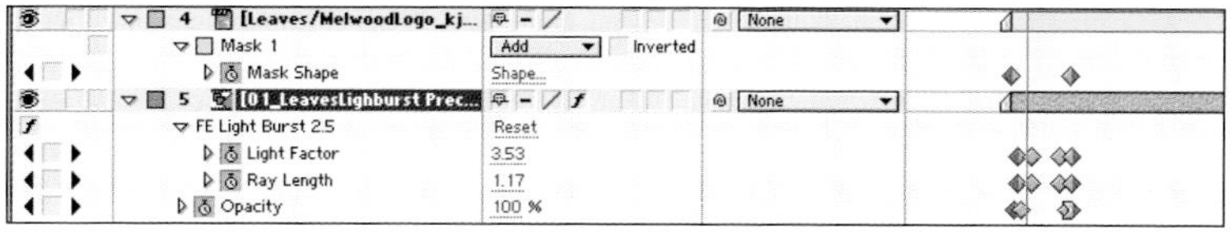

Keyframes are set for Light Factor and Ray Length of Final Effects Light Burst, as well as layer Opacity.

MODIFICATIONS

Alternative 1. The principles you used to animate the lights in this scene and to navigate the 3D world space can be used to animate solids, stills, movies, or even the camera. Try adding a camera to the Shadow Background animation and then moving into the final position over the first 15 frames. Be sure to check the velocity so that the camera eases to a stop and there is no pop in the animation.

Alternative 2. Check out the 3D Invigorator Demo plug-in from Zaxwerks (**www.zaxwerks.com**). It will enable you to extrude and bevel illustrator files in true 3D space. Experiment with a subtle beveled edge on the logo layers. You can use the exact same layers provided in the Melwood Logo Illustrator file. By applying a reflection map in the filter and animating its position, you can get a subtle highlight on the bevels that adds life to the logo. Render a 10-second movie with animated reflections and lights for each of the layers and then replace the stills in your final project with the movies. Your new animated logo will truly look 3D.

3D IMAGES AND 3D LAYERS

"Man's mind stretched to a new idea never goes back to its original dimensions."

—OLIVER WENDELL HOLMES, JR. (1841–1935)

Controlling Animation 3D Layers

After Effects has been a great compositing tool for many years, with animators often relying on its toolset for final composites. As an animator and artist, however, creating a combination of 3D-rendered imagery and real video is an art all its own. By using various 3D-rendered formats, such as SoftImage PIC, RLA, and Electric Image EI, you can retain the red, green, blue, and alpha (RGBA) channels as well as Z-depth, object IDs, texture coordinates, and more in your renders.

Note: The Standard Version of After Effects reads and displays the RGBA information. The Production Bundle allows users to access and manipulate additional channel information combined in certain imported file types by using 3D channel plug-ins. Both versions allow for the creation of 3D layers.

Project 8

3D Images and 3D Layers

by Dan Ablan

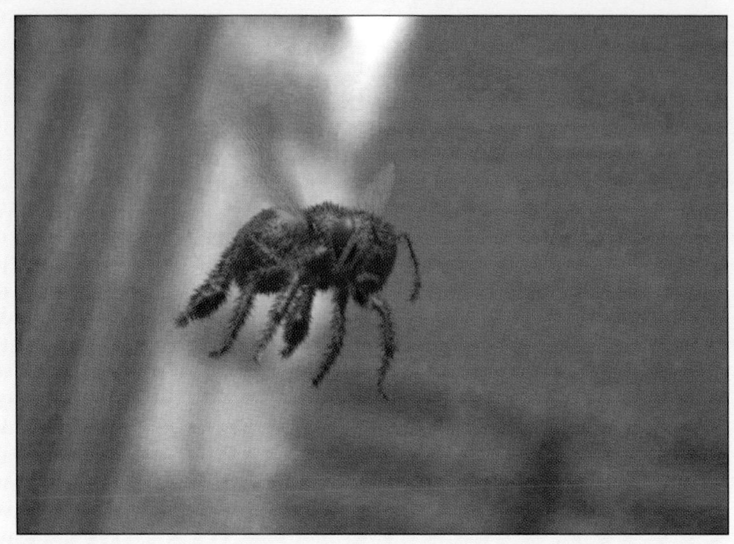

How It Works

In this project, using a clip of video and a prerendered 3D animation, you will learn to light an animation to match its background composite. The additional Z-depth information saved with the animation file will enable you to add specific controls for specularity and blurs.

Note: You might be asking yourself why you don't just light and render the 3D over the video in your favorite 3D application. Simply put—control. Rendering the 3D as an RLA sequence and later compositing it in After Effects gives you control without the need to rerender. You can change lighting, shadows, glows, blurs, create masks, and more.

Getting Started

In this section, you'll set up the animation. Most 3D applications allow you to use a video clip behind an animation. This project will concentrate on the postprocess in After Effects, but it's important to know how to get the proper 3D file. Check to see if your 3D application has an RLA saver option. If so, use this type of file. Don't worry about lighting or shadows, the RLA file type will store information that enables you to light the render later in After Effects. For this project, you'll be using the **Bee.rla** and **ChiTown.jpg** image sequences found on the accompanying CD-ROM.

Setting Up the Composition

When you begin any project in After Effects, you need to start with a composition. This project will be using a resolution for video and will match the prerendered 3D animation sequence.

You'll begin by selecting New from the File menu to create a new composition.

1 In After Effects, create a new composition called **BeeComp** at 720×486. Make the composition 10 seconds long.

2 Select File > Import and then File. Load the **ChiTown.jpg** sequence. Be sure to select the JPG Sequence option at the bottom left of the Import File dialog box. When the Interpret Alpha dialog box appears, leave it set at the default. Repeat for the **Bee.rla** sequence.

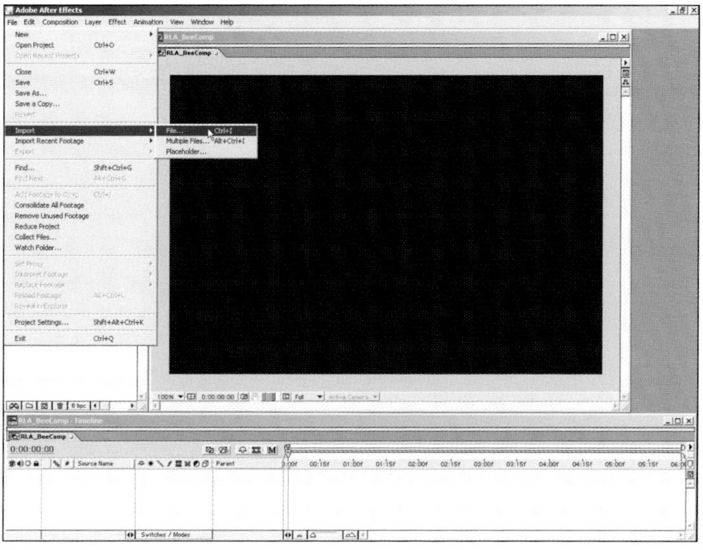

Import the ChiTown.jpg and Bee.rla image sequences.

3 Drag the ChiTown.jpg sequence onto the composition. It should be centered in the composition frame.

Set up the shot first by putting the ChiTown.jpg sequence into the composition.

4 Add the Bee.rla sequence to the composition at frame 0 and advance ahead to frame 250. Also, because this composition is using frames rather than timecode, change the project settings to follow along with this project.

At this point, press the spacebar to make a quick RAM preview to see how the composition is coming along.

Advancing forward in the composition shows the bee over the moving background sequence.

Working with 3D Layers

At this point, your project is set up and ready to be enhanced. In After Effects 5.0 and 5.5, layers can be 3D, meaning they can take on properties of other items such as Z-axis movement and lights.

1 Right-click or Ctrl+click directly on the Bee.rla layer in the composition window to select the 3D Layer. You can also use the 3D Layer switch in the Switches panel to select the layer.

Note: You can also right-click on the file listing in the Timeline to make a layer a 3D layer.

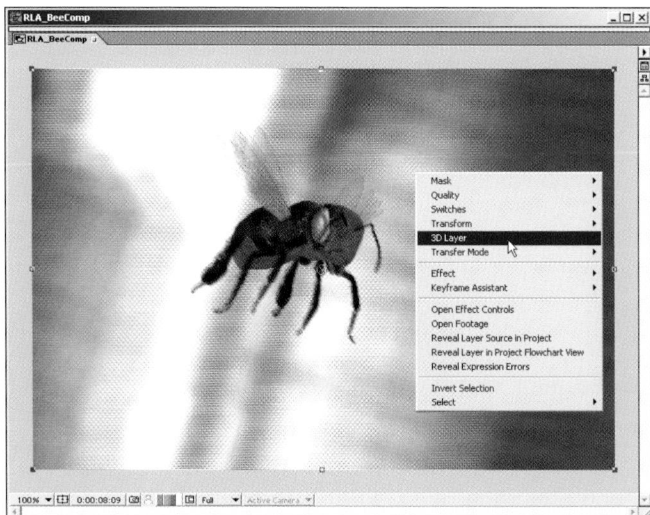

Make the Bee.rla sequence a 3D layer.

2 Go to the Timeline at frame 0 (current time marker) and expand the Bee.rla layer. Making this layer a 3D layer added a Material Options list. Right-click anywhere in the Timeline and select New > Light to add a light to the composition.

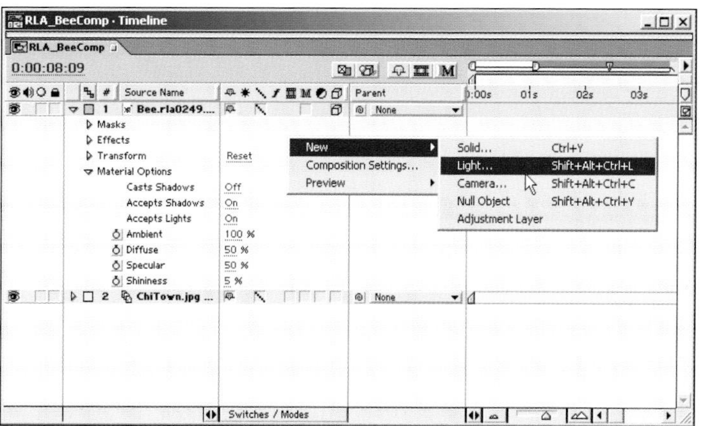

A light is added to the composition. This light will now affect the 3D layer.

Note: If you're working on a Macintosh with a one-button mouse, hold the Ctrl key while clicking the mouse to simulate right-button mouse commands.

Note: While the Bee.rla layer is expanded, notice the available options now that a light has been added, options such as Ambient, Diffuse, Specular, and Shininess. These are referred to in the user interface as Material Options. The options will not appear until the Light Settings panel has been closed. Then you'll need to expand the arrowhead next to Material Options for the properties.

3 The default name for the light is Light1, which is fine. Set the Light Properties as follows:

Light Type: **Spot**
Intensity: **160**
Cone Angle: **85**
Cone Feather: **85**
Color: **White**
Cast Shadows: **On**
Shadow Darkness: **100**
Shadow Diffusion: **20**

4 Click OK to close the panel.

No light outside is ever really pure white. After Effects' lights let you change your colors, and one great way to do it is to use the Eyedropper.

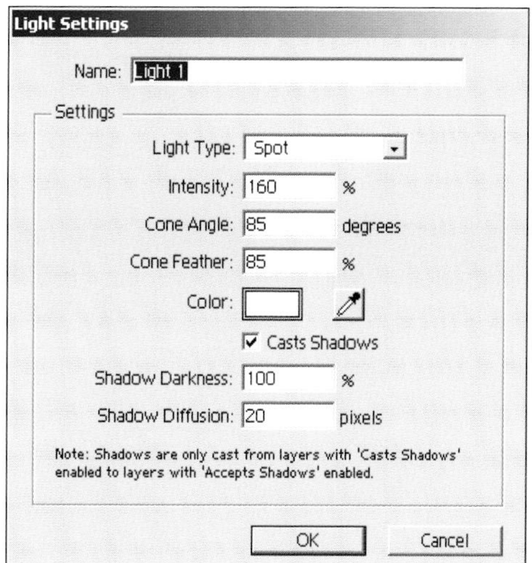

Set the basic Light Properties to light the Bee.rla layer.

5 Double-click the Light layer to call up its settings and select the Eyedropper tool. The current time can be brought to about frame 200 or so for easy bee visibility. Click on an area of the sky or a building highlight in the Composition window. This will sample the color data and change the light color to match.

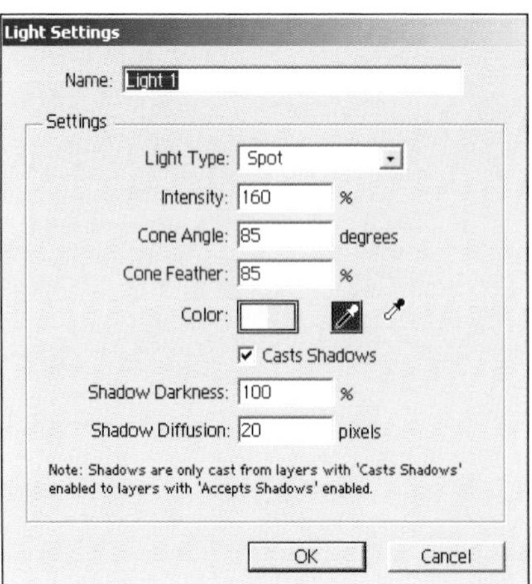

A great way to set the light color for a Layer light is to sample the color from the background video using the Eyedropper.

6 In the Timeline, expand the light's Transform properties and move the light to the following:

Position: **X = 163, Y = 105, Z = –221**
Orientation: **X = 330, Y = 2.0, Z = 0**

7 Move the Point of Interest to the body of the bee. This will help brighten the 3D layer.

With this light now in place, you can adjust and tweak its settings to your eye. Increase and decrease the Intensity, Color, and Shadows. Then go a step further and play with the 3D layer's Material Properties such as Specularity, Diffuse, and Shininess. You can experiment with these settings to see how they affect your composition.

8 Remember to collapse the Light1 and Bee.rla layer properties when you're finished making adjustments. Then press the spacebar to make a quick RAM preview.

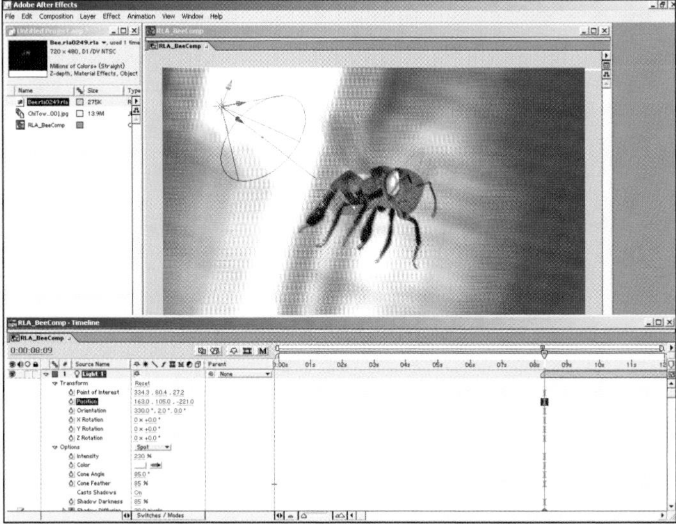

Move the light up and to the left of the bee to simulate the natural light in the video clip behind it.

Creating the Fill Light

Although the added light created a main key light to help the bee blend into the background video clip, an additional light should be added to simulate bounced light or radiosity effects.

1. Right-click anywhere in the Timeline window and, with the current time set at frame 0, add another light named **Light2**.

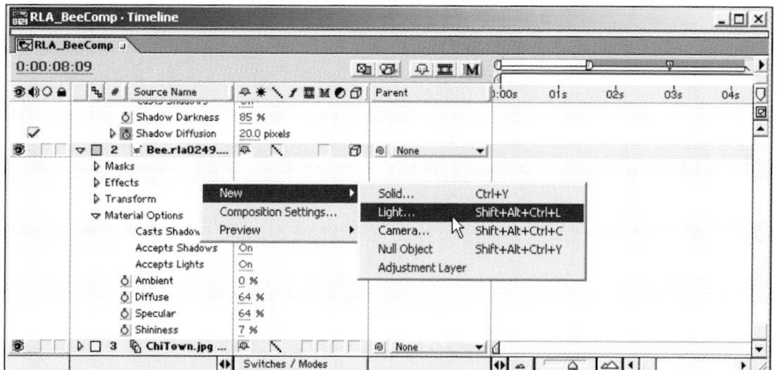

A second light is added to create a bounced fill light on the other side of the bee.

2. Set the following for Light2:

   Light Type: **Spot**
   Intensity: **250**
   Cone Angle: **90**
   Cone Feather: **50**
   Color: **R132, G158, B198**
   Cast Shadows: **On**
   Shadow Darkness: **100**
   Shadow Diffusion: **0**

3. Click OK to close the dialog box.

4. In the Timeline, expand the second light's Transform commands and set the light to the following:

   Point of Interest: **X = 460.3, Y = 190, Z = 137.8**
   Position: **X = 590, Y = 130, Z = –95**
   Orientation: **X = 0, Y = 0, Z = 0**

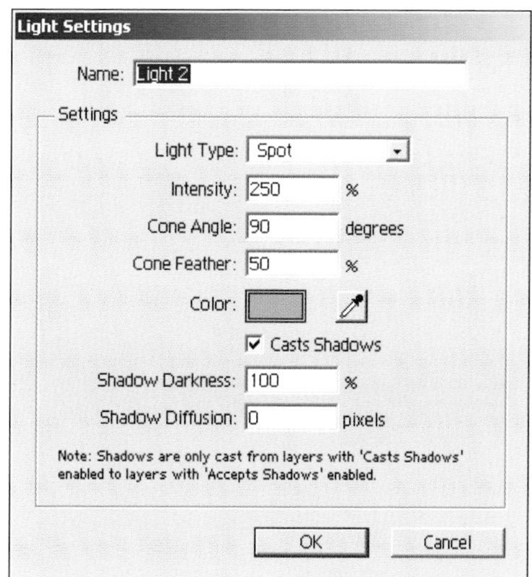

The second light has a color to match the blue tint of the background video clip.

5 Close the Light2 properties and save the project.

At any point, you can change a light's values, position, and rotation. Now that you have two lights in place—one key light and one fill light—the bee looks a bit overlit. This is where you can take advantage of a "dark" light.

Using the Point of Interest control on the second light, you can target the light to the tip of the bee's head.

Dark or Negative Lights

The lighting of the bee is about what you need for the moment, but it's losing some of the depth of the 3D image because of too much light. The bottom of the bee should not be lit as much as the top and side. Therefore, you can add a negative light to take away or darken the Bee.rla layer.

1 Add another light to the composition and name it **DarkLight**. Add this at frame 0 for the entire composition.

2 Set the following for DarkLight:

Light Type: **Spot**
Intensity: **–360**
Cone Angle: **90**
Cone Feather: **50**
Color: **R169, G162, B169**
Cast Shadows: **On**
Shadow Darkness: **100**
Shadow Diffusion: **30**

3 Click OK to close the dialog box.

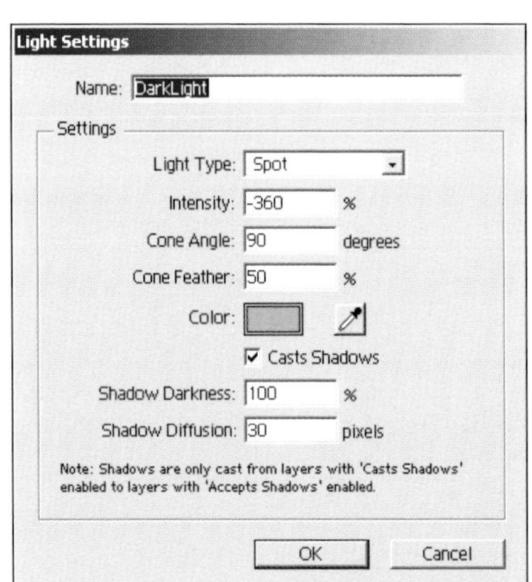

A negative light can be added to take away lighting effects.

4 Set the light's position to the following:

Point of Interest: **X= 365, Y = 387, Z = –19**
Position: **X= 390, Y = 365, Z = –250**
Orientation: **X= 0, Y = 0, Z = 0**

Now the lower belly of the bee is shaded and less lit, giving it more depth.

5 Save the project and then press the spacebar to make a quick RAM preview.

This project showed you how to take a 3D-rendered object and use a special file type (RLA) that holds buffer information. This information is read by After Effects and enables you to adjust lighting on the pre-rendered model. The result of this is a composite that matches the background composite sequence, which in this case is video of city buildings.

6 Once you have the composition and sequence lighting to your liking, render it out from the Make Movie selection. An AVI or QuickTime will provide a nice-quality preview. From there, render out in full resolution to match your final output device.

RLA images are extremely useful when working with 3D animations and After Effects. This project showed you that even just lighting alone can be faster and easier after you render. But using a 3D animation in After Effects can go much further than lighting RLA images.

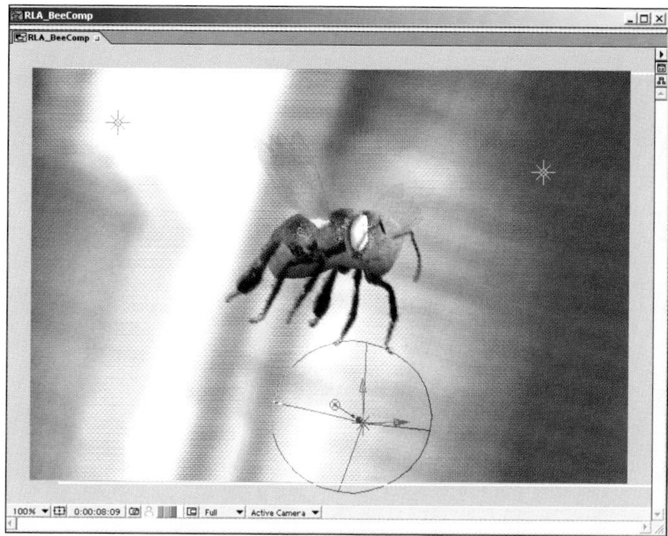

The added negative light helps give depth to the bee. Remember that the bee is a 3D render, and too much light on it will flatten the look.

Modifications

You can use the stored information from the RLA to extract a 3D channel such as Texture UV, Z-Depth, Surface Normals, and more. These channels can then be used for additional enhancements such as glows, blurs, shadows, and even filters.

The next time you have a chance to render a 3D animation, render it as a SoftImage PIC, RLA, or Electric Image (EI) file and take it to the next level in After Effects. You can use this technique for compositing 3D people into real environments, 3D cars onto roadways, and more. It's also a very useful technique for architectural visualization. Perhaps your client needs to see what a new proposed building would look like next to existing buildings? A rendered RLA sequence composited over real video or film is an excellent way to deliver your message.

"I go from the extreme to the extremities!"

—LARRY THE WINE HEAD, 1988

BUILDING VIRTUAL SETS

Constructing a Three-Dimensional Environment

After Effects is not a full 3D program, but it can be used to do some powerful things in a 3D environment using 2D pictures. This project will show you how to construct a simple "3D set" that won't require the usual pain and anguish of modeling, texture mapping, and lengthy rendering. In doing this, you will learn how to manipulate After Effects' new camera, lights, and 3D layer functions.

Project 9

Building Virtual Sets

by Ben Stokes

How It Works

In this tutorial, a three-dimensional environment will be constructed completely within After Effects. This virtual set will be built using only still photographs. Then you will light the scene and animate a camera move through the scene.

Note: There are significant limits to what can be achieved using only two-dimensional pictures to create a three-dimensional space. For example, After Effects has no way to deal intelligently with intersecting layers; layers that cross and overlap simply become "sliced off" at the intersection. This lesson includes some workarounds for that particular problem, but it is important for you to be aware of it.

Getting Started

Make a fresh pot of coffee. Get comfortable. There are two projects on the CD: One is a partially constructed set, and the other is the finished project. You will use the partially constructed set for this lesson.

The files for this lesson are on the CD in the this project's folder. There are two AE project files, **Final.aep** and **startbuilding.aep**, and a folder entitled "elements." There is also a movie called **Final_Comp.mov**. Copy this project's entire folder to your hard drive.

Construction of a Room

1 Open the project **startbuilding.aep**. Open the composition Final Comp.

Take a moment to look at what is in the project. There are five layers, which make up the walls and floor of a room. Notice that all of the layers have their 3D buttons turned on.

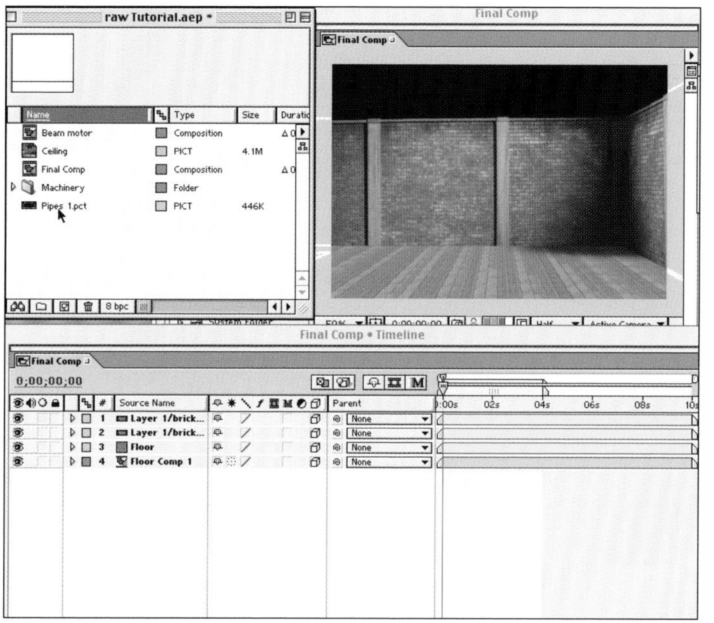

Open Final Comp.

2 Drag the clip Ceiling over to the Final Comp Composition window. Place it in the center (you will notice it snap to the center of the composition automatically) and make sure it is the bottommost layer. Reveal the Transform channels for that layer in the Timeline window. Check the 3D button for the Ceiling layer.

Notice that the options under Transform change.

3 Move the cursor over the center of the layer Ceiling in the Composition window. As you move the cursor over the axes of this layer (at its center), you will see the letters X, Y, and Z appear next to your cursor. When your cursor displays the letter Z, click and drag on the Ceiling layer.

You will see the layer get smaller as you drag down and to the left.

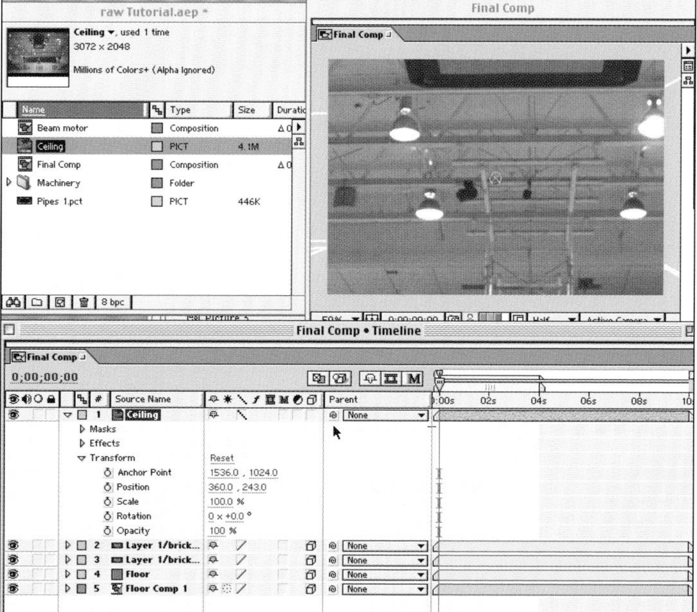

Drag the picture Ceiling to the stage.

4 Move the layer backward on the Z-axis and watch the layer's Position values change in both the Timeline window and the Info palette.

5 Drag the Ceiling layer back until Z is set to 3000 or simply click on the third Position value in the Timeline and enter this value manually.

Tip: The Shift key will enable you to move it faster.

6 Select the Y-axis and move the layer up to –400.

Position the cursor to highlight the Z-axis.

7 Rotate the layer on the X-axis until the orientation reads 50.0°. Scale the Ceiling layer up to 125%, keeping the layer's proportions locked.

Now let's take a look at the positions of these layers from above.

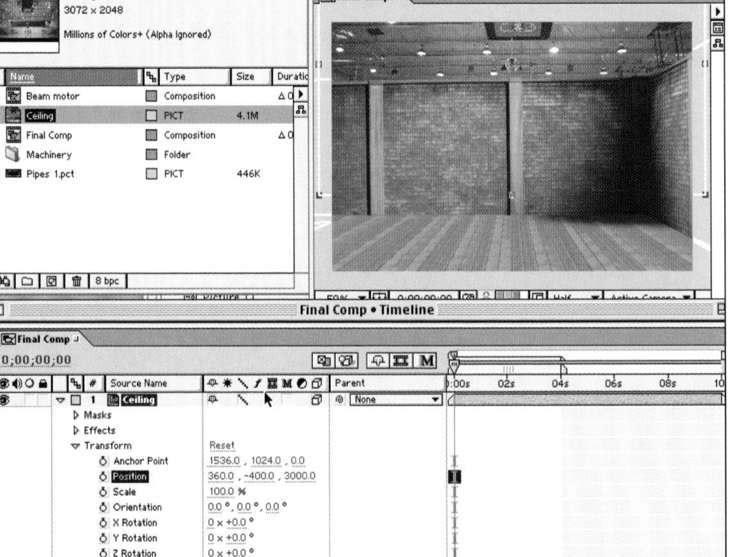

Move the Ceiling layer back on the Z and up on the Y.

8 Go to the 3D View pop-up menu at the lower-left corner of the Composition window (it currently reads "Active Camera") and click and hold down your mouse button. Select Top.

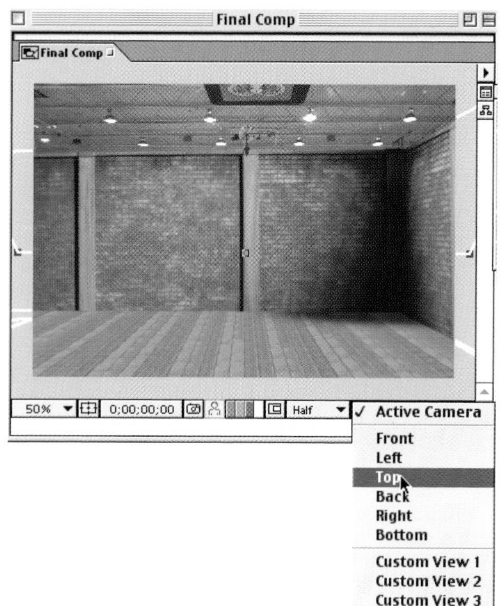

Choose Top from the 3D View menu.

You will see a wireframe representation of all the layers. This is because they are outside of the visible area of the composition.

Note: If you do not see anything at first, zoom out to reveal more of the Composition window. Then you can see all the layers as they are laid out from overhead.

9 Go back to the Active Camera view in the 3D View pop-up.

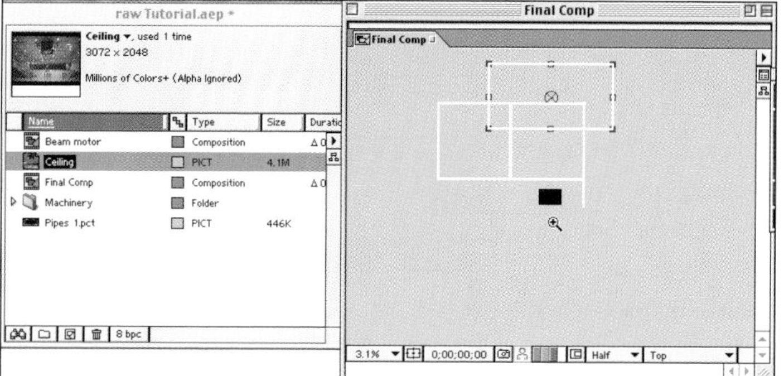

Zoom out to see everything.

Adding the Foreground Objects

With the virtual set's backdrops, floors, and walls in place, it is time to add some foreground props.

1 From the Project window, drag the composition Beam motor to the stage.

Drag Beam motor to the stage.

2 Check the Beam motor layer's 3D box, reveal its Transform channels, and open the layer's Position dialog box. (Right-click on the Position values on a PC; use Ctrl+click on a Mac.) Set its Position to X = 80.0, Y = 0.0, Z = 2500.0 and scale it up to 170%.

Alter the Beam motor composition's settings.

3 From the Project window, drag Pipes 1.pct over, center it, and check its 3D box, open Transform. Set its Position to X = 56.0, Y = 150.9, Z = 1305.5.

4 Duplicate the Pipes 1.pct layer (Edit > Duplicate) [Cmd/Ctrl + D]. This duplicate is automatically selected in the Timeline. Inspect its Position layer [the P key] and change this duplicate's Z position to 1859.3.

5 Duplicate this second duplicate layer and change only its X position to 536.0.

6 Duplicate this third duplicate layer. Set its Position to X = 601.2, Y = 307.9, Z = –181.5, and scale it down to 80.5%.

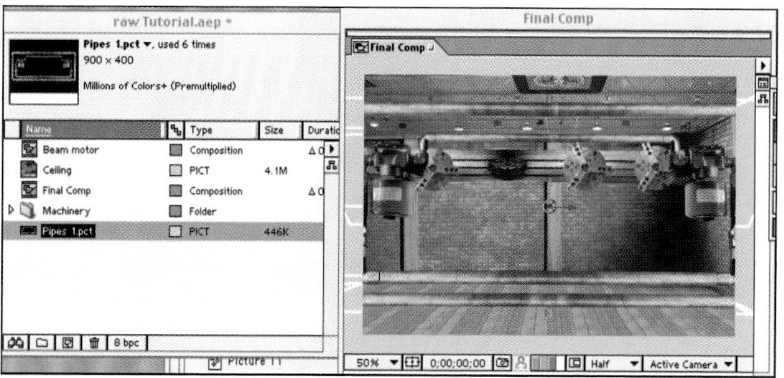

Drag Pipes 1.pct over to the stage.

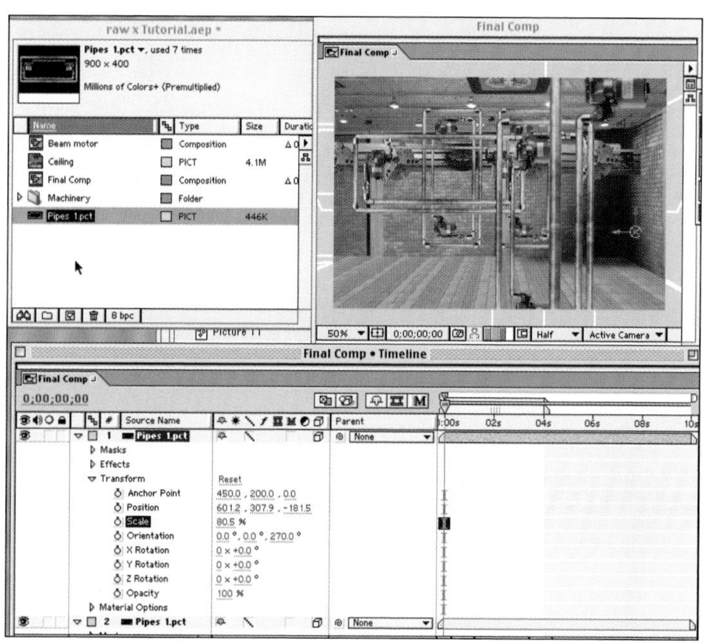

Duplicate and move Pipes 1.pct to create several layers.

7 From the Project window, open the composition called Other parts. This will show you another way to bring set elements in.

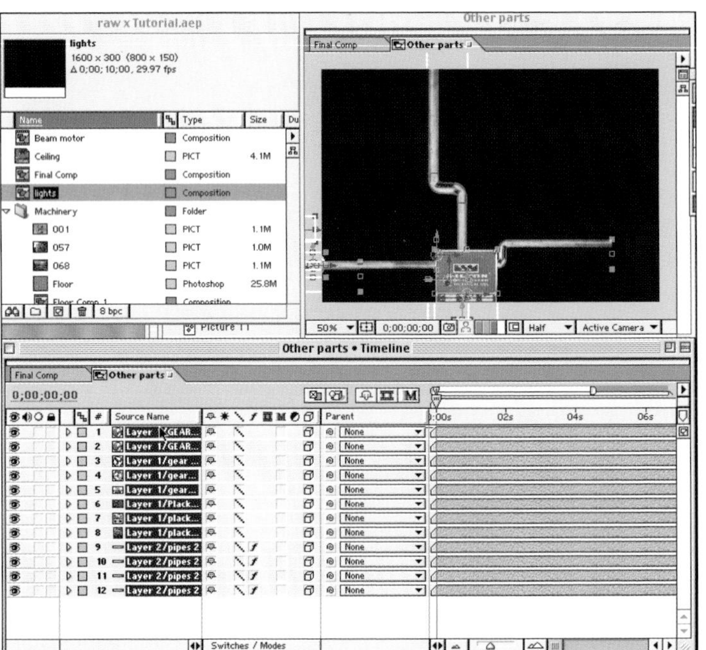

Select all the layers in the Other Parts composition.

8 Select all layers in the Other Parts composition. Copy and go back to Final Comp. Paste the layers into Final Comp.

Copying and pasting 3D layers keeps them in the same position and relation to each other, even if they come from different compositions.

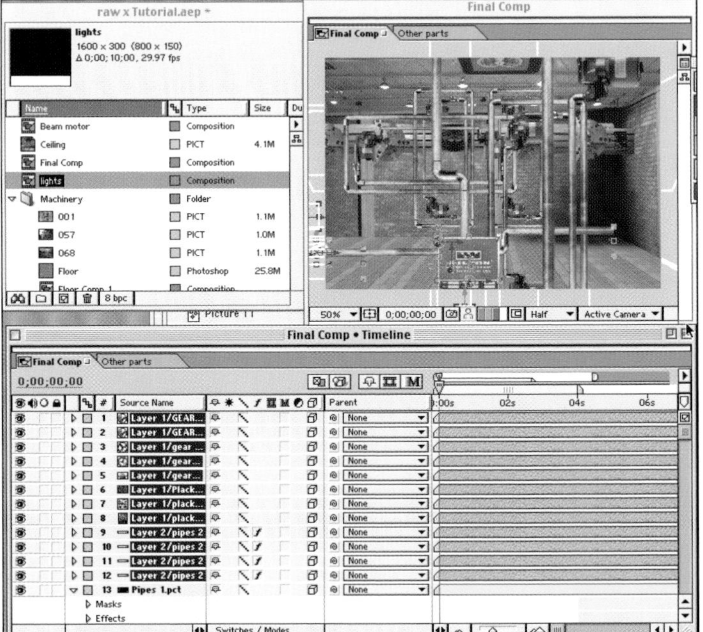

Paste the layers into the composition Final Comp.

Adding and Animating the Camera

To enable you to change your perspective, you will need a camera. You are already working in a three-dimensional environment, but you only see from the default front view until you add a camera.

1. Add a camera to the Final Comp (Layer > New > Camera) [Option+Shift+Cmd/Alt+Shift+Ctrl + C].

   You will get a Camera Settings dialog box.

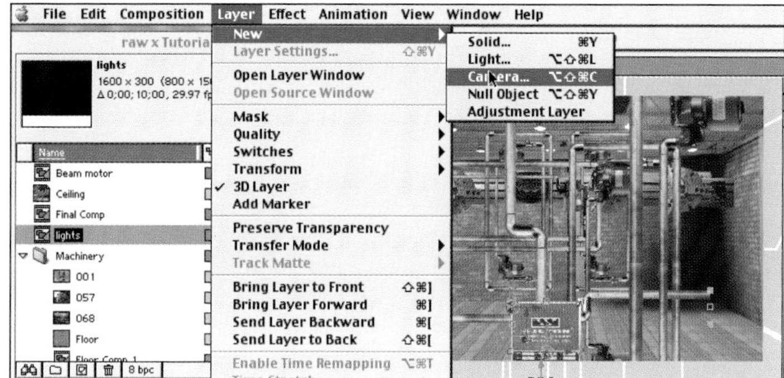

Adding a camera.

2. Set your camera to the 50mm preset and click OK.

   Notice that the camera is now the topmost layer.

3. Make sure that Active Camera is selected in the Composition window's 3D View pop-up.

4. Reveal the camera's Transform channels and set its Point of Interest to X = 230.2, Y = 418.2, and Z = 217.3. Set its Position to X = 238.9, Y = 453.1, and Z = –782.0.

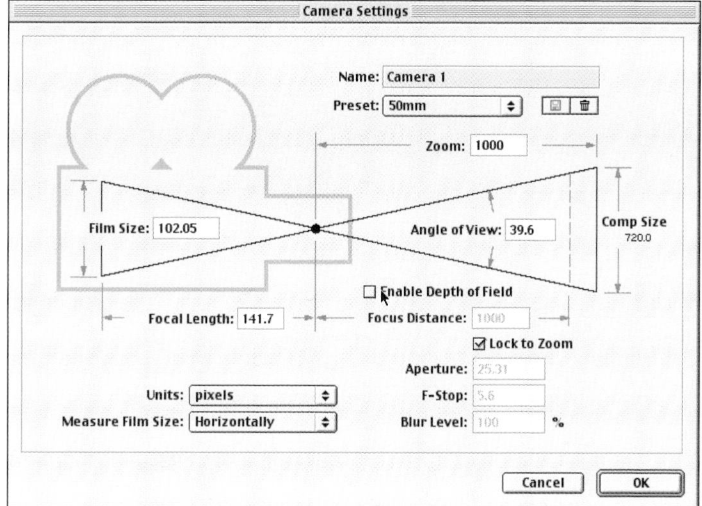

The settings in the Camera Settings dialog box.

5 Create initial keyframes at 0:00:00:00 for the camera's Point of Interest and its Position channels by clicking on the stopwatch for Point of Interest and Position. (Make sure the time marker is at frame 00.00.00.)

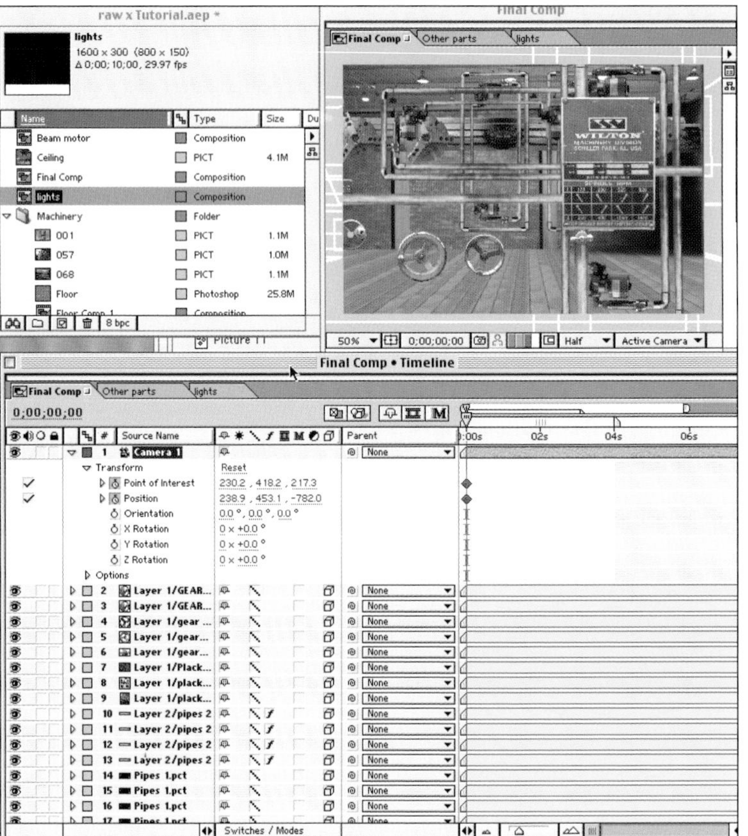

Click the stopwatch for the Point of Interest and Position channels to create initial keyframes at 0:00:00:00.

Creating Keyframes for the Camera

Before assigning the final camera animation to this project, let's take a moment to experiment with a few methods of camera movement.

1 Move the time marker to 2 seconds in the Timeline. Click on the Orbit Camera tool in the Tools palette.

By holding the mouse button down over the tool's icon, you get three camera movement tools in a pop-up menu.

2 Using the Track XY Camera mode (the second option in the Orbit tool's pop-up), click and drag anywhere in the Composition window.

This will pan the camera and thus our point of view. Notice that keyframes appear in both the camera's Point of Interest and its Position.

3 Go back to the Orbit Camera tool's icon and switch to the Track Z Camera tool from its pop-up menu. Zoom in a bit. Now click on the Orbit tool.

You might have gone off the edge of our little set by now. Undo this move (or simply delete the keyframes you just made) and the camera will go back to its starting position.

In the final project, the camera has an animated zoom-through of the space. This was achieved using the Orbit, Zoom, and Pan tools as shown here. You are encouraged to create your own keyframes for the camera and to create your own camera move through this virtual space.

Alternatively, you can copy and paste the camera from the composition entitled Lights, Camera in this project.

If you paste this camera into the composition, it will be the current camera if it is the topmost layer.

Rotating the camera with the Orbit tool.

Note: Whenever there are multiple cameras in a single composition, After Effects treats the topmost camera as the Active Camera.

Adding Lights

Now it's time for my favorite part of the process—lighting. This set can take on a totally different look, depending on the lighting. You will darken it and make it more mysterious and moody with colored lights.

1 Create a new light (Layer > New > Light) [Option+Shift+Cmd/Alt+Shift+Ctrl + L].

The options can be left as they are, or you can set your own color preference. The lights have X, Y, and Z axes, and just like the camera, they have points of interest and orientation settings.

You can move the light and its Point of Interest, but be careful… you might have to move it out of view to get the effect you want. This can make it hard to find again. You can always set its Position and Point of Interest to X = 0.0, Y = 0.0, Z = 0.0 in the Transform options to get the Point of Interest back.

If you want the lights to be exactly like the final project, you can copy the four lights from the Lights, Camera composition. However, I recommend that you try lighting the scene yourself first. You can animate the lights with keys, just like anything in After Effects.

If you use the lights and camera from the Lights, Camera composition (transferred via copy-and-paste from the composition Lights, Camera), your composition should look like the final QuickTime movie (Final_Comp.mov) on the CD.

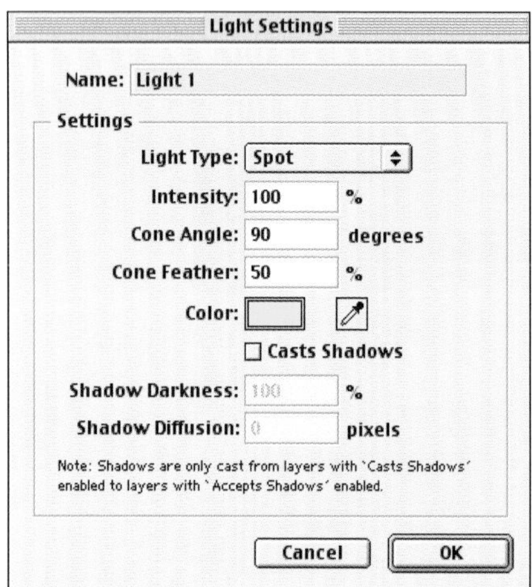

Setting the light options.

The lit scene!

Modifications

Try moving different foreground elements around. Arrange the layers in your own way. Try moving the camera to explore this set thoroughly. Experiment with lighting; multiple lights of different colors will create additive color effects.

Using red and yellow lights gives the scene a much more warm and friendly environment. Setting the camera to a wider lens setting makes the space feel much more open. This will give you fewer places to position the camera without going off the edge of the set. You can duplicate the walls and floor to extend the set. Going more telephoto with the camera has the opposite effect, making all of the layers seem to pile up on each other.

Related to lighting, you should play with the materials option settings of the 3D elements. Experiment with the Ambient, Diffuse, Specular, Shininess, and Metal parameters. Attempt to make the pipes look more metallic and make less-reflective objects, like the walls and flat plaques, reflect more of the lights' inherent colors.

One thing to keep in mind is that by using flat 2D pictures to build a set in 3D, you are "cheating," and if you go too far around a layer, it will be obvious that it is paper thin. This may or may not be a bad thing in some cases, but this set is built on creating the illusion of depth, so a complete, 360-degree orbit around the set won't work.

The modified scene.

"Every motion must only be considered as a relative motion."

—ALBERT EINSTEIN (1879–1955), FROM THE GENERAL THEORY OF RELATIVITY (1920)

MOTION GRAPHICS—THE NEXT LEVEL

Taking Graphics from 2D to 3D in After Effects

This tutorial showcases a number of features that were new in After Effects 5 for tasks that were very difficult—or impossible—to accomplish in previous versions of the program. Starting with a composition of simple geometric shapes from Adobe Illustrator, you'll go from the world of 2D to the world of 3D. Along the way, you'll use parental hierarchy, a camera, and an expression or two as you create a dynamic 3D animation in After Effects.

Project 10

Motion Graphics—The Next Level

by Fred Lewis

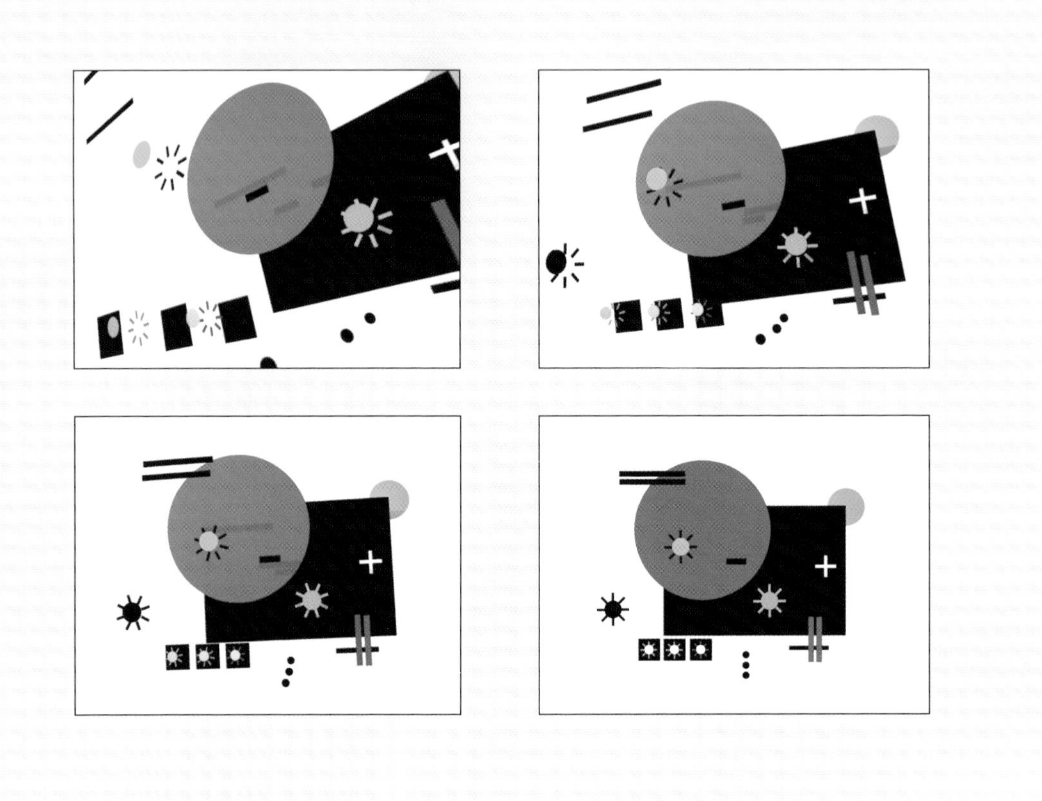

How It Works

Even in a 3D animation, the final rendered frame is still essentially a flat 2D image. The 2D composition of that image is important. Here, you'll take a composition that was originally designed in 2D (in Adobe Illustrator) and translate it into 3D without losing the 2D composition of the image. To be able to do that, you must first do some initial setup work.

Getting Started

The single source file you'll be using is an Adobe Illustrator file called SourceShapes.ai, which is on the accompanying CD-ROM.

1 Copy **SourceShapes.ai** from the accompanying CD-ROM to a local hard disk on your machine.

2 Open After Effects. Choose File > Save As. In the Save Project As dialog box, save the project (as any name you choose) to the same place on your hard disk where you copied the SourceShapes.ai file.

3 Import the SourceShapes.ai Illustrator file as a composition. (In the Import dialog box, set the Import As pop-up menu to Composition.)

This creates a new composition in After Effects that contains the shape layers from the Illustrator file, arranged as they were in Illustrator. In the Project window, you can see this new composition, SourceShapes.ai, as well as a new folder containing all of the imported source shapes from the Illustrator file, which are now being used by the composition. Double-click the icon for the SourceShapes.ai composition to open its Composition and Timeline windows.

4 Set the background color to white because the composition was meant to have a white background (Composition > Background Color) [Cmd/Ctrl + Shift + B].

The bottom layer in the Timeline window, "comp size," is an empty layer. In Illustrator, this layer contained crop marks, which defined the outer boundary of the animation. Now that the file has been imported, this layer no longer is needed.

5 Select and delete the comp size layer.

6 Set the composition's display resolution to Half (in the Resolution pop-up, at the bottom of the Composition window, or by entering Cmd/Ctrl + Shift + J). Then zoom to 50% either using the Magnification pop-up in the lower-left corner of the Composition window or by pressing the comma key [,] to zoom out.

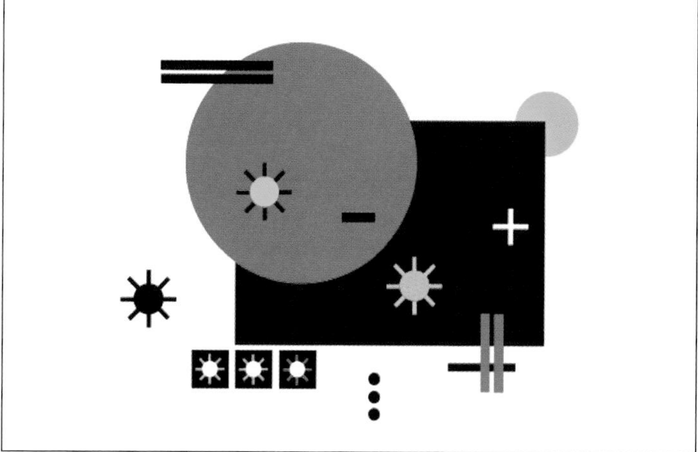

Import SourceShapes.ai.

Note: The Composition option in the Import dialog box pop-up menu is only available when importing multilayered files. Because SourceShapes.ai is a file that has multiple layers, this option is available.

Viewing the composition at half resolution while you work on it will speed up redraw to approximately four times as fast as normal, but this is for preview purposes only; it will not alter the quality of the final output.

7 Press Cmd/Ctrl + K to open the composition settings to alter the duration of the composition to 6:00 (or choose Composition > Composition Settings from the menu bar). Then make sure all layers are visible for the entire length of the composition. If they're not, move the current-time marker to the end of the composition at 5:29, which can be reached by pressing your End key, selecting all [Cmd/Ctrl + A], and pressing Option/Alt +] (right bracket).

Note: To see the full length of the Timeline at this point, you might need to zoom out in the Timeline window.

8 Turn on the 3D switch for all of the shape layers. Select All [Cmd/Ctrl + A] and click on a 3D switch (looks like a cube) for any shape layer in the Timeline.

Because the shape layers are all selected, all 3D switches are now turned on. You also want to enable Continuous Rasterization for the shape layers. This will make the shape layers resolution independent so that you can zoom in on them as much as you want, without worrying about aliasing. Why? Because Continuous Rasterization looks at the previous nested composition and the source files before rasterizing; if they contain a higher resolution source, that resolution is preserved. In this case, your source is shapes created as Illustrator vectors, which means they are resolution independent and can be scaled up infinitely without losing their smooth, antialiased characteristics.

9 Click on a Collapse Transformations switch for any shape layer in the Timeline.

All shape layers' Collapse switches are now turned on.

10 Deselect all layers [Cmd/Ctrl + Shift + A].

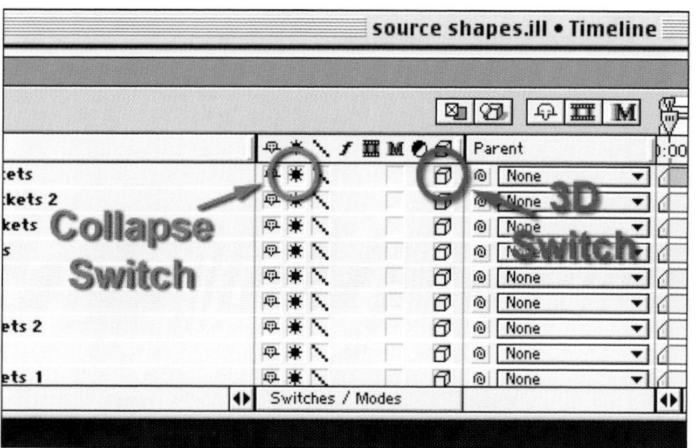

Turn on the 3D switches and Collapse switches for all layers.

Setting Up a New Camera

You'll be using a 3D camera to animate your point of view of the shapes. Later, when you move the camera, the view will change accordingly.

1 Press Home to move the current-time marker to frame 0 in the Timeline window. Choose Layer > New > Camera.

The Camera Settings dialog box opens.

2 In the Camera Settings dialog box, set Units to millimeters, set Film Size to 35, and set Focal Length to 30. The Angle of View should now be 60.51.

Be sure not to directly manipulate the Zoom value.

This will give you the digital equivalent of a 30mm lens on a standard 35mm-film camera—a medium wide-angle view. (On a 35mm-film camera, a 50mm lens is considered a "normal" lens. Shorter lens lengths are more "wide angle," and longer lens lengths are more "telephoto.")

3 Click OK to close the Camera Settings dialog box.

Note that a Camera 1 layer has been added to your Timeline window.

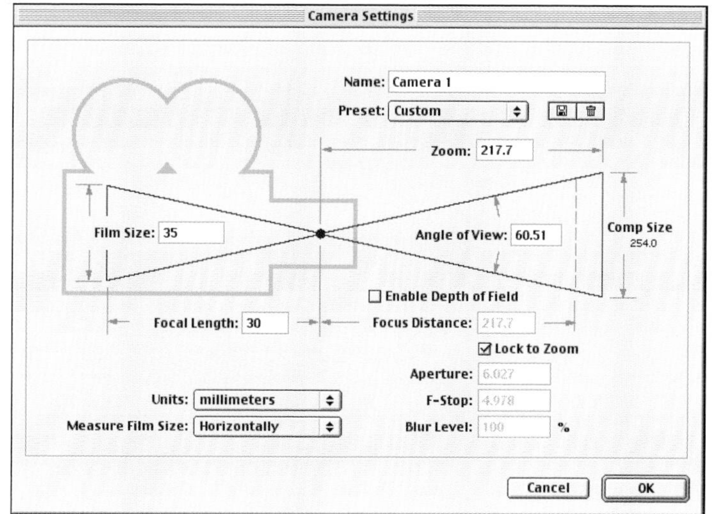

Make adjustments in the Camera Settings dialog box.

Applying an Expression

Each animation property in After Effects can now be controlled either by keyframes or by a formula, called an expression. Expressions can reference other channels, allowing the action of one channel to dictate the behavior of another. Simple expressions can be created easily via a method similar to drag-and-drop, using a tool called the pickwhip. More complex expressions can be created either completely from scratch or by pasting and editing provided examples. Expressions save you a lot of time, enabling you to create animations without keyframes.

Now that a camera exists, you will apply an expression to the Scale channels of all the shape layers; this will cause them to scale as they are moved toward or away from the camera. This will cause the apparent size and position of each shape to stay the same within the camera view. (The reason for doing this will be apparent soon.) The expression you need to apply has already been written and has been included on the accompanying CD-ROM in a text file called **scale_expression.txt**.

1. Label the camera **Camera 1** in the Timeline window (if this isn't already entered as its default name). Note that your camera should start from frame 0 and be the length of the composition; otherwise, it will be effectively turned off for the frames on which it doesn't appear. If this isn't the case, just press Opt/Alt + Home to set the camera's start frame at 0:00.

2. Lock the camera (so that it cannot be selected), select all [Cmd/Ctrl + A], and type **S**. Then deselect all [Cmd/Ctrl + Shift + A].

   This will expose the Scale channels of all of the shape layers in the Timeline.

3. Open the text file **scale_expression.txt** in any text editor, such as SimpleText on the Mac or Notepad in Windows.

4. Select all text in this file and copy it into the Clipboard [Cmd/Ctrl + C].

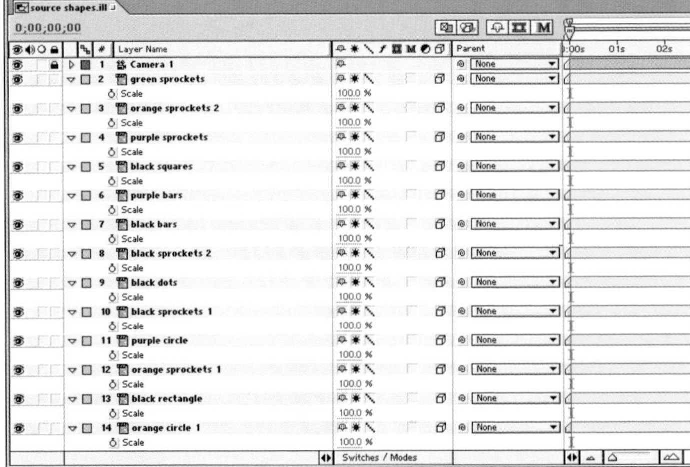

Lock the camera and expose the Scale channels in the Timeline.

5. Back in After Effects, Option/Alt + click the Stopwatch icon for the Scale channel of the shape layer called purple circle (layer 11 in the Timeline).

   This creates a new expression for the Scale channel.

6. Paste [Cmd/Ctrl + V]. This pastes the expression you copied from the text file. Press the Enter key to officially enter the newly pasted expression. (Be sure to press the Enter key in this case, not the Return key.)

   The text you have pasted is now controlling the Scale channel of the layer. The next section explains how.

Paste the purple circle layer with the expression into its Scale channel.

Note to 5.0 Users: Inside the _AEv5_Projects folder for this chapter is scale_expression_5.txt—this uses the more complex Vector Math operators that After Effects 5.5 doesn't require.

Understanding What the Expression Does

Before you apply this expression to the rest of the shape layers, let's take a look at what this expression is really doing in the Composition window. You can see that the arrangement of shapes is still exactly as it was when you first imported it. You are now viewing the scene through the new camera you created previously. But when that camera was created, it automatically positioned itself so that the composition would still look the same.

1. With purple circle (layer 11) still selected in the Timeline, press the P key to reveal its position channel.

Note: Since this is a 3D layer, it has three values for position (X, Y, and Z). The Z value is currently zero, which is the default.

2. Change the Z value to –400.

   This brings the layer closer to the camera, but the purple circle does not appear to change size. This is because the expression you have pasted is automatically scaling the layer to make it appear to stay the same within the camera view. The purple circle does get in front of other layers that used to be on top of it, but that is the only change you can see.

Set the purple circle layer's Z position value to –400.

3. Set the Z value back to zero [Cmd/Ctrl + Z].

   Let's look at the scene from a different point of view.

4 From the Window menu, choose Workspace > Two Comp Views. Now in addition to the Camera view, on the left, you will see Custom View 1 on the right. Select Custom View 3 in the Right Composition window. If you haven't tried out the custom views and Workspaces yet, now is a good time; they are presets designed to give you a helpful perspective on the 3D contents of your scene. All the other presets are orthogonal views at right axes to the layer; these three views are at more natural diagonal positions.

You are now seeing the same scene from an alternate viewpoint, from above and at an angle. Here you can see the camera (a gray box in the lower-left corner of the view) and the arrangement of shapes in 3D perspective. The currently selected layer is highlighted (meaning its X, Y, and Z axes are visible).

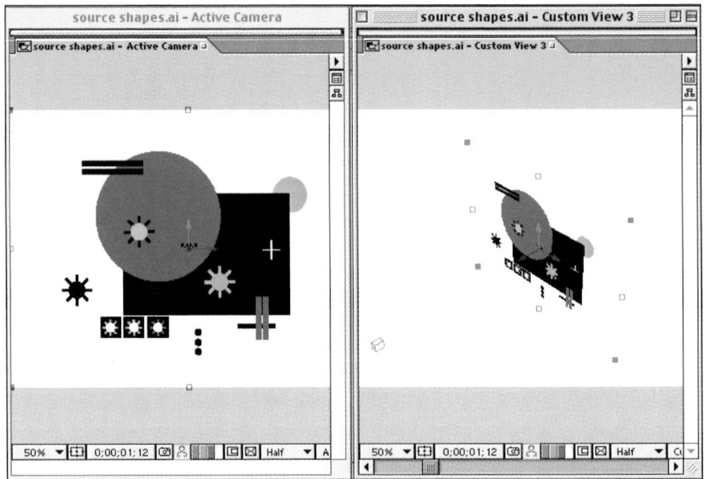

Select Custom View 3 from the View pop-up on the right. By default, the windows are a little on the narrow side; you can define your own custom workspaces if you have a more generous size monitor.

5 Set the Z value to –400 again [Cmd/Ctrl + Shift + Z].

You can now see that the layer (and its purple circle) have indeed moved closer to the camera, but the circle has shrunk to compensate for the change in perspective. This is what the expression is doing, and it is why you didn't see the circle change size in the camera view.

6 Drag the Z-axis handle (the blue arrow) of the selected layer, moving it toward or away from the camera.

You can see the purple circle change size as you do this.

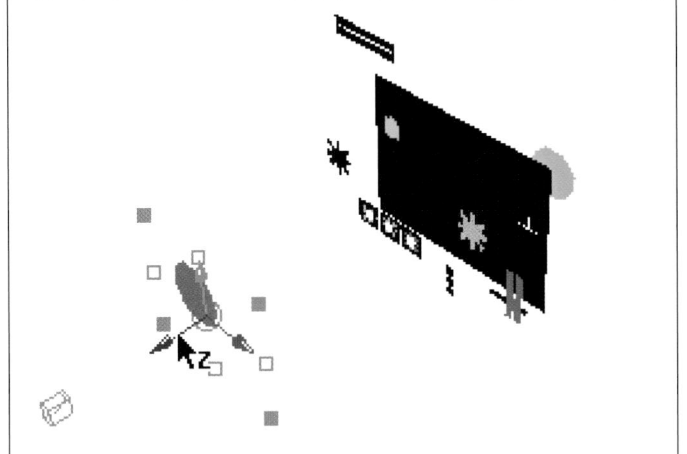

Drag the purple circle by its Z-axis and watch its size change automatically.

7 Set the Z position value back to zero in the Timeline when you are finished.

Note: Because of the way importing from Illustrator works in After Effects, each shape layer's axis is located at the center of the composition, and the outer boundary of each shape layer matches the outer boundary of the composition. The expression you are using relies on this. If you had imported these shapes from Photoshop instead, each layer would have had its anchor located at the center of the shape's geometry instead of at the center of the composition. You would then have had to move the anchor points of each shape to the center of the composition to use the expression. In this case, because the shapes came from Illustrator, you do not have to do this.

Finishing Pasting the Expression to the Other Layers

Now add the expression to the rest of the shape layers. After you have done this, you'll be able to move any shape to any distance from the camera without changing the shape's appearance in the camera view.

The next few steps can be done completely within the Timeline window:

1 Close the left Composition window, then while pressing the Option/Alt modifier key, temporarily close the right Composition window.

This will leave the Timeline window open without its Composition windows.

2 Expand the Timeline window to fill most of the screen.

You might need to scroll up in the Timeline window to reveal all of the layers.

3 Option/Alt + click the Stopwatch switch for the Scale channel of the first shape layer in the Timeline. Paste [Cmd/Ctrl + V] and then press Enter (not Return) to enter the newly pasted expression.

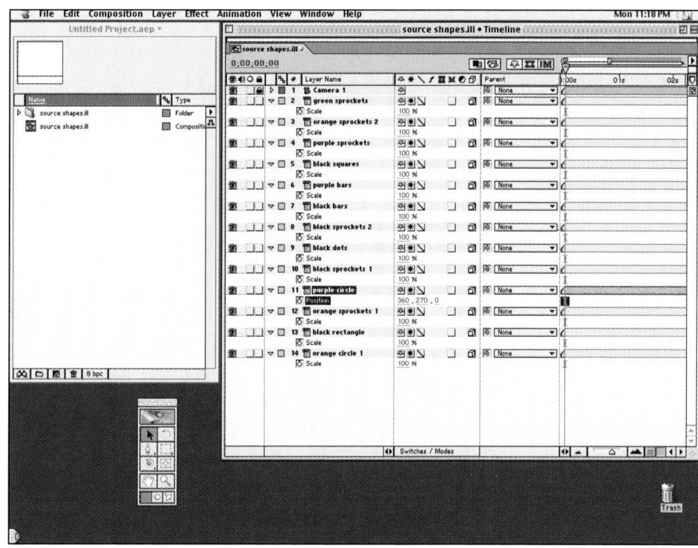

Press the Option/Alt modifier key while closing the Composition window to leave the Timeline window open without the Composition window.

4 Repeat the preceding step for the Scale channels of the rest of the shape layers.

Be careful not to accidentally paste the expression into the position channel of layer 11, purple circle.

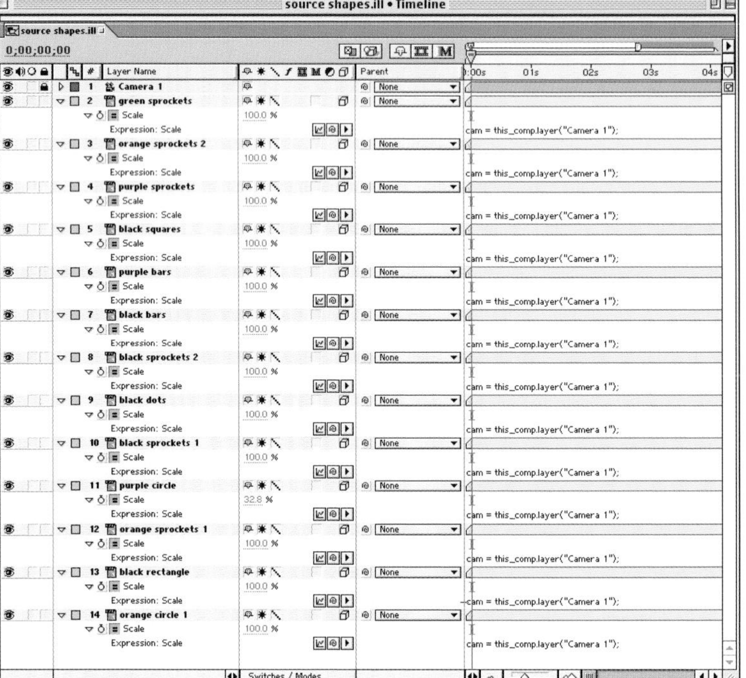

Apply the expression to all shape layers' Scale channels.

Setting the Z Values for the Shapes

To start from this point, you can use the project file **1_expressions_entered.aep** on the accompanying CD-ROM. To do this, copy the project file 1_expressions_entered.aep and the source file **SourceShapes.ai** to the same place on your hard drive. Then open the file 1_expressions_entered.aep. If you're continuing with your own project, now is a good time to save it again.

Now that you have the basic setup done, the real fun begins. In this section, you will place each of the shapes at a different distance from the camera. This will create a three-dimensional arrangement for the camera to move through, in perspective. Thanks to the expression you applied to each layer in the last section, the initial layout will not change when you place the layers at different distances. In the next section, however, when you animate the camera, the three-dimensional arrangement will be revealed.

1 Select all the layers [Cmd/Ctrl + A], type **P** to expose the properties for each in the Timeline, and deselect all the layers [Cmd/Ctrl + Shift + A].

2 Select Window > Workspace > One Comp View to return to the default layout.

You should still be viewing Custom View 3 in the Composition window. (If not, select Custom View 3 from the View pop-up menu at the bottom of the Composition window.)

Choose One Comp View to reset your layout.

3 Set the Z position value of each shape layer in the Timeline window using the accompanying table's values. Do this one shape at a time while arranging the shapes in 3D space.

Note: These are suggested Z values for all the shape layers, but this is not the only possibility. You can enter the values from the table, experiment with your own values, or do a combination of both.

Layer Number	Layer Name	Z Value
2	green sprockets	–250
3	orange sprockets 2	–200
4	purple sprockets	–150
5	black squares	–100
6	purple bars	–300
7	black bars	–150
8	black sprockets 2	–200
9	black dots	–50
10	black sprockets 1	–150
11	purple circle	–100
12	orange sprockets 1	–50
13	black rectangle	100
14	orange circle 1	200

4 Arrange the shapes in layer Z space. Orbit the custom view you are looking through by using the Orbit Camera tool from the toolbox (press C to cycle through the Camera tools).

You can also pan and zoom using the Track XY and Track Z Camera tools. Because you are looking through Custom View 3, this will not affect Camera 1. You are changing the custom view, not the camera settings.

Note: When panning and zooming a 3D view, use the Track XY and Track Z Camera tools instead of using the Pan and Zoom tools.

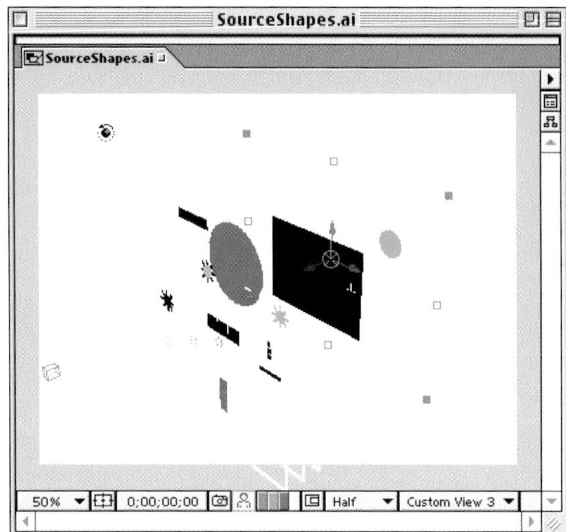

Arrange the shapes in three-dimensional space. The Orbit tool appears at the upper left of the frame.

Animating the Camera

Now that the layers are arranged in 3D, it is time to animate the camera. You will be animating backward, starting the animation with a view that is off center and ending the animation with the exact view that Camera 1 now sees.

To start from this point, you can use the project file **2_z_values_entered.aep** on the accompanying CD-ROM. To do this, copy the project file 2_z_values_entered.aep and the source file **SourceShapes.ai** to the same place on your hard drive. Then open the file 2_z_values_entered.aep.

1 At frame 0:00, create a new null object (Layer > New > Null Object).

A new null object appears in the Timeline and in the composition. Because it is not yet a 3D layer, the new null is unaffected by the fact that you are viewing the scene through Custom View 3. It simply appears in the center of the Composition window, as any new 2D layer would.

Note that, by default, null objects have the Opacity value set to 0%, so all you see is their outline unless you change the Opacity value.

Note: You use a null object in this section to achieve the kind of camera motion you want. Null objects are never rendered in final output; they are used as reference objects for the purposes of animation, like invisible markers in 3D space. Because null objects are visible in the Composition window but do not show in the final render, they are very useful as parent objects with After Effect's Parental Hierarchy feature.

2 Turn on the 3D Layer switch for the null object layer by clicking on the switch that looks like a cube to the right of the null layer in the Timeline.

This places the null in the center of the 3D composition, which happens to be exactly where you want it.

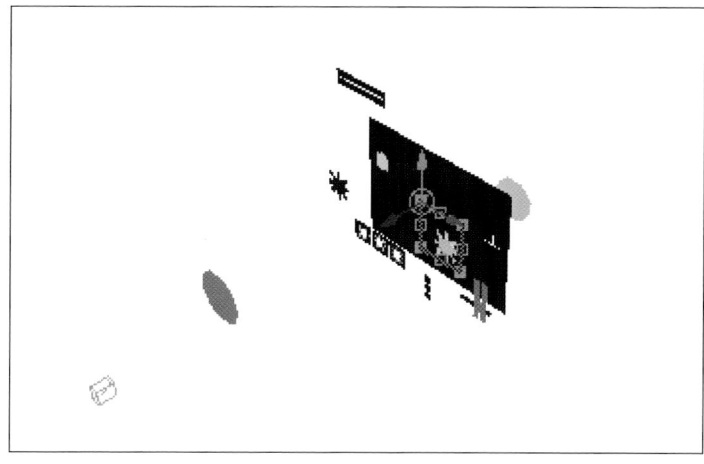

Create and place the null in the center of the 3D composition.

Note: Naming nulls according to their purpose makes it a lot easier to keep track of what you're doing, especially when you come back to the same project months later.

3 Click the null in the Timeline to select it. Press the Return key to edit the name, type **Camera Null**, and press the Return key again to enter the new name. (Be sure to use the Return key in this case, not the Enter key.)

4 Lock all layers [Cmd/Ctrl + A and then Cmd/Ctrl + L] and then unlock Camera 1 and Camera Null.

5 Parent Camera 1 to Camera Null. In the Parent pop-up to the right of Camera 1, select 1.Camera Null.

Camera 1 is now a "child" of Camera Null.

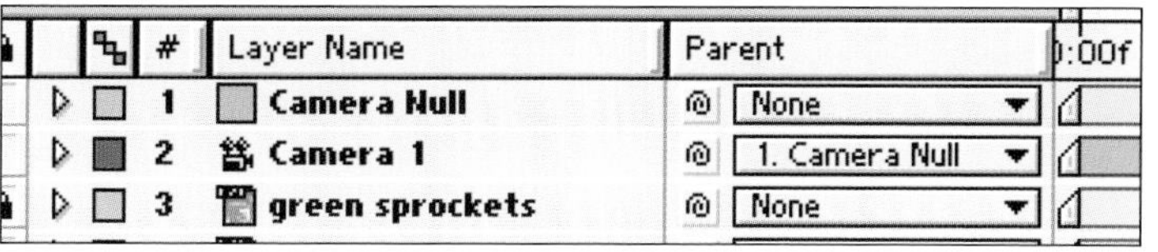

Parent Camera 1 to Camera Null. Alternatively, you can use the Camera's parent pickwhip. To do this, click Camera 1's parent pickwhip and drag it to Camera Null.

6 From the View pop-up at the bottom of the Composition window, select Active Camera instead of Custom View 3.

Camera 1, the only camera, is the Active Camera. If there were more than one camera, the uppermost camera layer would be the Active Camera. The view through Camera 1 should still look exactly the same as the default view did when you first imported the shapes at the beginning of this tutorial.

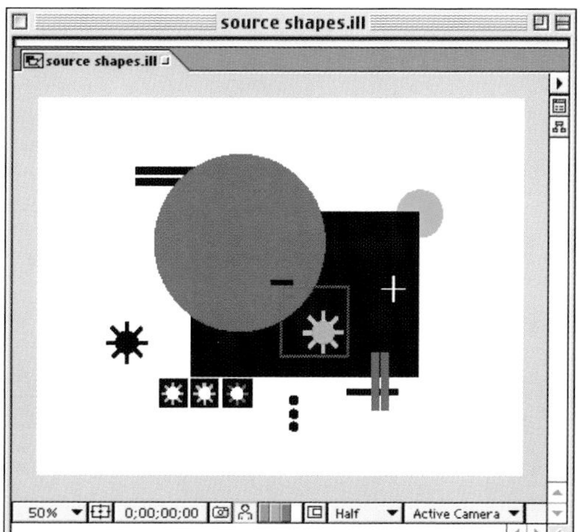

Select Active Camera view.

Note: In After Effects' Parental Hierarchy feature, a child layer will inherit any animation characteristics of its parent object. This means that Camera 1 is attached to Camera Null, and whenever Camera Null moves, rotates, or scales, Camera 1 will move, rotate, or scale right along with it.

7 This means that your Camera Position should have moved to X = 0.0, Y = 0.0 (with Z remaining at –617.1) when you parented Camera 1 to Camera Null. Check it out: With the layer highlighted, press P for the numbers.

8 Move the current-time marker to the last frame of the composition by clicking on the Last Frame button in the Time Controls palette or by pressing the End key.

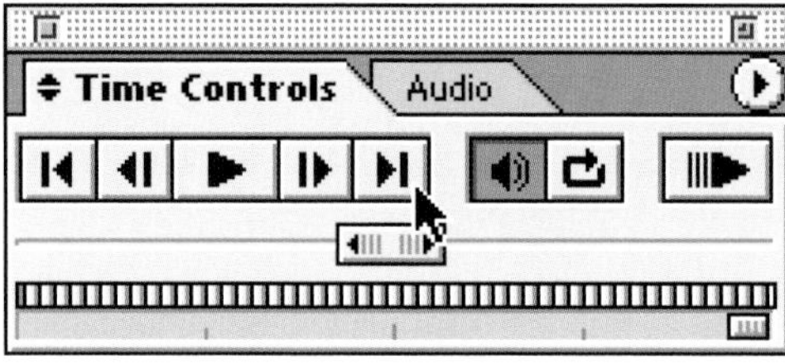

The pointer is over the Last Frame button of the Time Controls.

9 Open the Position and Rotation properties for Camera Null in the Timeline [press P and then Shift+R]. Create a keyframe for Position and Y Rotation at the last frame of the composition by clicking the stopwatch on the channel for each property.

10 Open the Transform and Options properties for Camera 1 in the Timeline. Create a keyframe for Z Rotation at the last frame of the composition by clicking the stopwatch.

11 Select both the Camera Null layer and Camera 1 in the Timeline. Then press the U key on the keyboard.

This limits the display for the selected item's layers to only properties being animated. If the layers instead close, press U again—it's a toggle. If you press "UU" (U twice in quick succession) you will see all of the properties that have been in any way altered for that layer.

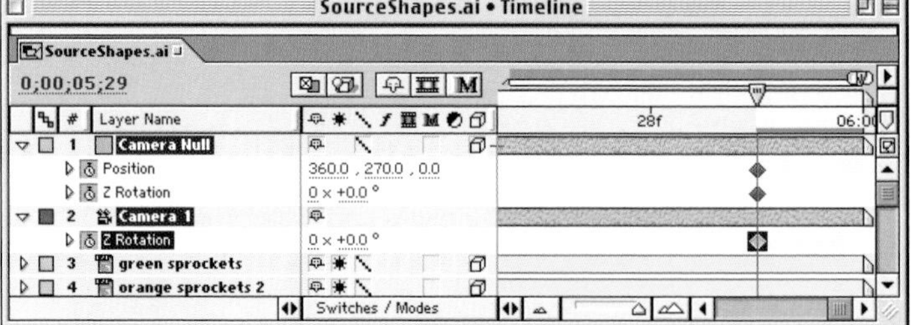

Limit the display for selected layers to only properties being animated by pressing U (aka the überkey).

12 In the Timeline, move the current-time marker to 0:00:02:00. (You can click the current time, enter **200**, and then click OK to do this quickly.) Then set the Camera Null layer Y Rotation to –35.

> **Note:** The first field in a rotation channel is for the number of complete rotations; the second field is for rotation in degrees. Enter the degree values specified here into the *second* field of the rotation channel.

13 Move the current-time marker to time 0:00:00:00.

This is easily done by clicking on the First Frame button in the Time Controls palette or by pressing the Home key.

14 Enter the following values at time 0:00:

For Camera Null: **Z position** = **300**
For Camera 1: **Z Rotation** = **–60**

You now have keyframes at time 0:00 and time 2:00.

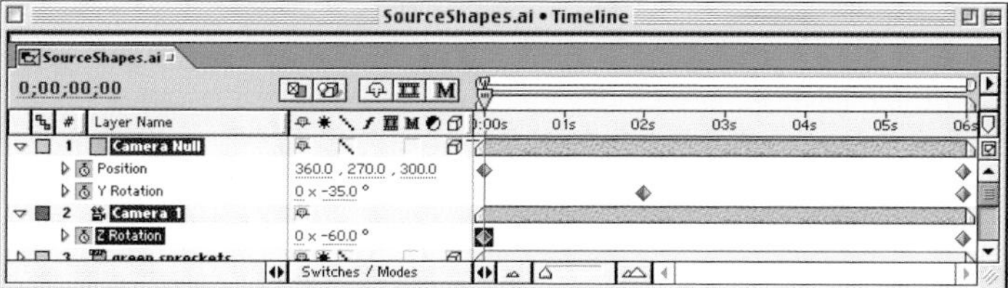

Create keyframes at time 0:00:00 and time 0:02:00.

15 Drag the current-time marker from the beginning of the composition to the end to sample the move. Then do a RAM preview by clicking on the RAM Preview button in the Time Controls palette or by pressing 0 on the numeric keypad.

Save your project and you're ready for the next set of steps.

Adding Velocity Control

This animation is a good start, but it stops suddenly at the end, and there is an abrupt change in motion at time 2:00. It would look a lot better with a nice, gradual ease-out at the end of the animation and an ease-in for the keyframe at time 2:00. Rather than easing out the Camera Null's Position property over the course of the entire animation, you want the ease-out for that property to occur only during the last 2 seconds of the animation. During the first 4 seconds, the Camera Null's Position channel will have a constant speed, called the "cruising speed."

Because an ease-out starts at the cruising speed and ends at zero speed, the average speed during an ease-out is half the cruising speed. So the first step is to create linear keyframes that create the places in the composition where the two speeds occur.

1. Go to time 4:23 in the Timeline. Create a keyframe for the Camera Null's Position channel at the current frame by clicking on that channel's keyframe check box in the Timeline.

2. Click on the triangle next to the Camera Null's Position property to view its velocity graph.

   As you can see, your velocity is approximately 50 pixels/second.

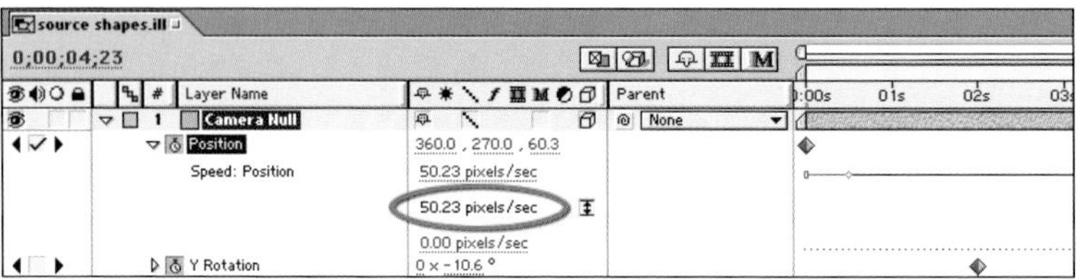

View the Camera Null's velocity graph.

3. Move (click and drag) the keyframe you just made from time 4:23 to time 4:00 in the Timeline.

   Notice that the velocity during the first 4 seconds of the animation is now approximately 60 (which will be our cruising speed) and the velocity during the last 2 seconds is now approximately 30 (half the cruising speed). You can see the velocity at any given time by moving the current-time marker head to that time and looking at the current velocity value in the Timeline.

4. With the keyframe still selected, open the Keyframe Velocity dialog box (Animation > Keyframe > Velocity) [Cmd/Ctrl + Shift + K]. Click the Continuous check box, forcing the Outgoing Velocity to match the incoming Cruising Speed. Set the Outgoing Velocity Influence to 50%. (Incoming Velocity Influence should be set to 0%.) Click OK to accept the changes.

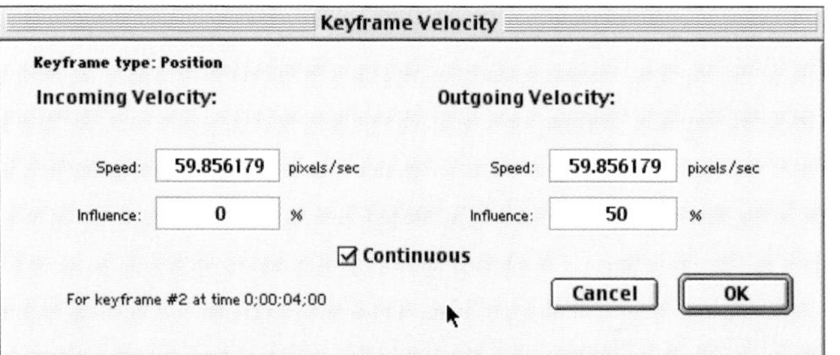

Set Keyframe Velocity for Camera Null position channel at time 4:00.

5. Select Camera Null's last position keyframe at time 5:29. (You can use the K key to skip to the next visible keyframe.) Open the Keyframe Velocity dialog box [Cmd/Ctrl + Shift + K]. Set the Incoming Velocity Speed value to 0 and set the Incoming Velocity Influence value to 50%. Outgoing Velocity Speed and Influence should both be set to 0. Click OK to accept the changes.

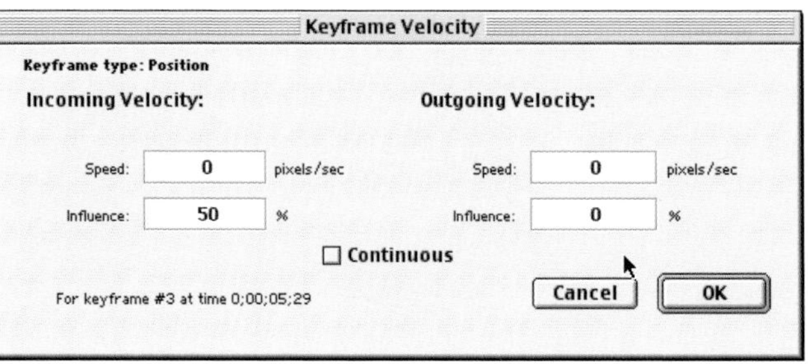

Set Keyframe Velocity for Camera Null's position channel at time 5:29.

The Camera Null's Position property now has a constant cruising speed during the first 4 seconds of the animation and an ease-out during the last 2 seconds of the animation.

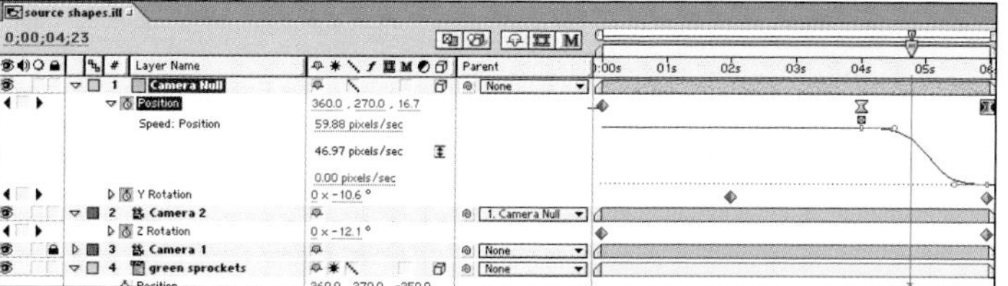

Create an ease-out for Camera Null during the last 2 seconds of the animation.

Now create the eases for the other properties.

6 Click on the text label for Camera Null's Y Rotation properties to select both of its keyframes.

7 Open the Keyframe Velocity dialog box [Cmd/Ctrl + Shift + K]. Click the Continuous check box and set the Incoming and Outgoing Velocity Speed values to 0. Set the Incoming and Outgoing Velocity Influence values to 50%. Click OK to accept the changes.

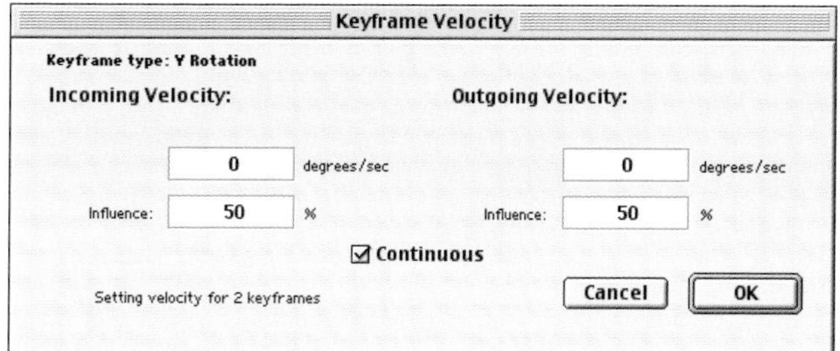

Set Keyframe Velocity for both of Camera Null's Y Rotation keyframes.

8 At 4:23 on the Timeline, create a keyframe for Camera 1's Z Position channel at the current frame. Click the Keyframe check box for Camera Null's Position channel in the Timeline.

9 Drag the keyframe you just made from time 4:23 to time 4:00 in the Timeline.

10 With the keyframe still selected, open the Keyframe Velocity dialog box [Cmd/Ctrl + Shift + K]. Click the Continuous check box, forcing the Outgoing Velocity to match the Incoming Cruising Speed. Set the Outgoing Velocity Influence value to 50%. Click OK to accept the changes.

11 Select Camera 2's last Z Rotation keyframe at time 5:29 (the last frame). Open the Keyframe Velocity dialog box [Cmd/Ctrl + Shift + K]. Set the Incoming Velocity value to 0 and set the Incoming Velocity Influence value to 50%. Click OK to accept the changes.

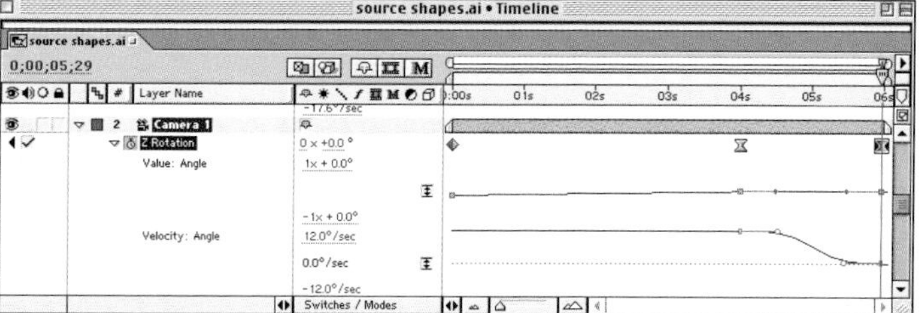

Here is how your speed position curve should look.

12 Do a RAM preview to see the animation. (Click the RAM Preview button in the Time Controls palette.)

Save your project before continuing.

Anchoring the Sprockets

This animation now needs some motion in the shape elements themselves. You will rotate the sprockets, but you need to move the anchor point of each sprocket layer to the center of each shape.

To start from this point, you can use the project file **3_camera_move_completed.aep** on the accompanying CD-ROM. To do this, copy the project file 3_camera_move_completed.aep and the source file **SourceShapes.ai** to the same place on your hard drive. Then open the file 3_camera_move_completed.aep.

Before you get started, use the Shy Layers feature to hide the layers you are not going to be working with in the Timeline.

1. Unlock all layers [Cmd/Ctrl + Shift + L]. Select all [Cmd/Ctrl + A]. Click the Shy switch for any layer to make all layers shy. Lock all layers [Cmd/Ctrl + L].

Make all selected layers shy by clicking the Shy switch.

2. Unlock the following six sprocket layers by clicking on each sprocket layer's padlock icon:

   layer 3, green sprockets
   layer 4, orange sprockets 2
   layer 5, purple sprockets
   layer 9, black sprockets 2
   layer 11, black sprockets 1
   layer 13, orange sprockets 1

3. Select all [Cmd/Ctrl + A]. All six sprocket layers are now selected. Click the Shy switch of any sprocket layer. All sprocket layers are now not shy.

4. Click the Hide Shy Layers button at the top of the Timeline window.

   This hides all shy layers, leaving only the six sprocket layers visible in the Timeline window. You might need to scroll up in the Timeline window to see them.

5. Lock the remaining layers [Cmd/Ctrl + L].

   Now it's time to move the anchor points.

Hide shy layers.

6 In the Composition window, select the Front view from the Views pop-up menu at the bottom of the window.

This gives us a view of the scene directly from the front.

7 In the Timeline, unlock and select layer 3, green sprockets.

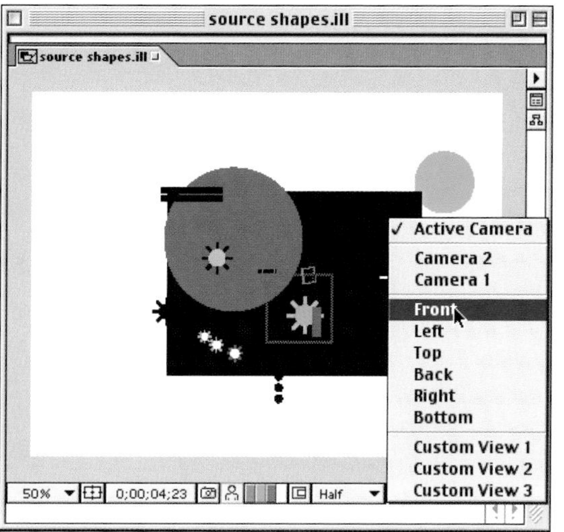

Select the Front view from the Views pop-up menu.

8 Use the Track Z and Track XY Camera tools to zoom in and pan the view so that both the green sprockets layer and its anchor point are just within the view.

Do not use the regular zoom or pan tools.

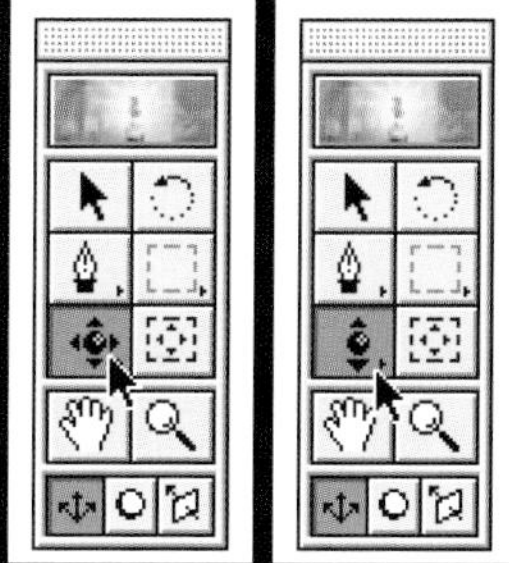

Shown highlighted here are the Track XY and Track Z Camera tools, respectively. To toggle between them and the Orbit Camera tool, Press C repeatedly.

Note: You might need to turn off and on the visibility switch for the layer to figure out which pixels belong to it in the view.

9 Use the Pan Behind tool [the Y key] to move the anchor point over the sprockets.

10 Use the Track XY Camera tool to center the green sprockets in the center of the view.

To more easily see where the center of the view is, click the Action/Title Safe button in the lower-left corner of the Composition window. This places a plus sign (+) at the exact center of the view.

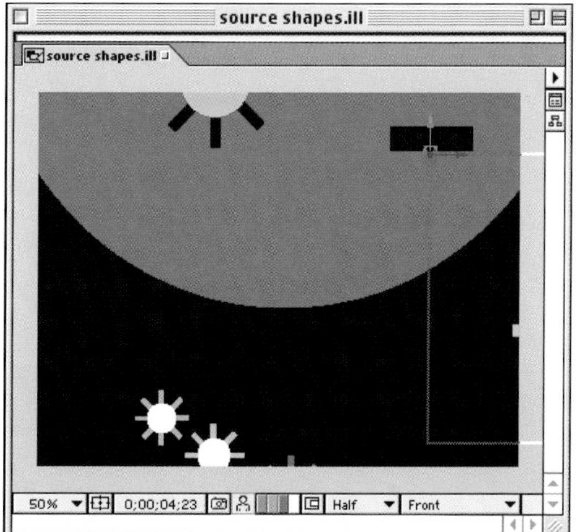

Resize the screen so that the "green sprockets" layer and its anchor point are just within the view. The green sprockets appear at the lower left, the anchor point at the upper right (with the green and red arrows protruding from it).

11 Once the green sprockets are centered, use the Track Z Camera tool to zoom in all the way on the sprockets so that they fill the view.

Note: The Track Z Camera tool gets a bit touchy once you get zoomed in all the way on something. When this happens, hold the Cmd/Ctrl key down *after* you begin to drag; this enables you to zoom in one-tenth as fast.

12 With the green sprockets filling the view, use the Pan Behind tool again to move the anchor point as close to the exact middle of the green sprockets as you can.

13 Lock the layer. Use the Track Z Camera tool to zoom out so that you can see the entire scene again.

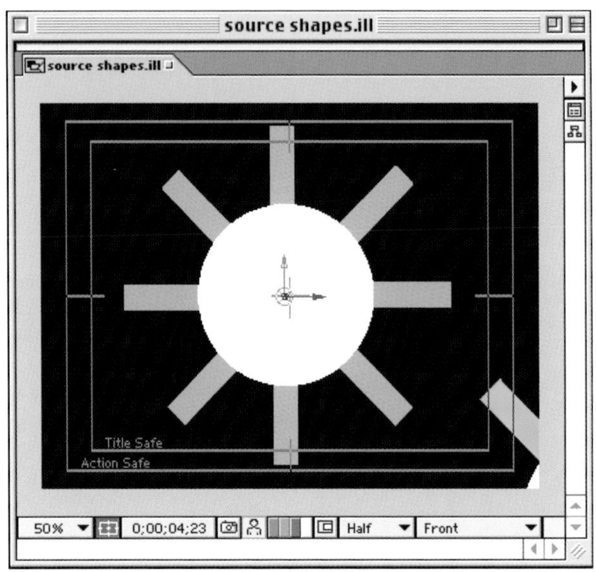

Move the anchor point as close to the exact middle of the green sprockets as you can.

14 Repeat the preceding steps for each of the other sprocket layers until all sprocket layers have their anchor points at the center of their sprockets.

If you'd prefer to just enter values for the Anchor Points, they are as shown in the table.

Layer Number	Layer Name	X Value	Y Value
3	green sprockets	199.8	423.9
4	orange sprockets 2	247.1	424
5	purple sprockets	295.6	423.8
9	black sprockets 2	132.5	350.5
11	black sprockets 1	258.9	238.3
12	orange sprockets 1	422.6	335.3

Note: As you create centered anchor points, you might find it necessary to turn off the visibility of one or more shy layers to clearly see the sprockets you are trying to center on. If so, simply click on the Hide Shy Layers button at the top of the Timeline window again to reveal the shy layers and temporarily turn off the video switch for any layers you need to. Click the Hide Shy Layers button again to hide the shy layers on the Timeline again.

When all sprocket layers have their anchor points at the center of their sprockets, make sure visibility is turned back on again for any layers for which you might have temporarily turned it off.

15 Save your project and get ready to bring it on home.

Animating the Sprockets

Now that each sprocket layer has its anchor point centered on its pixels, you can easily animate the sprockets so that they rotate. To do this, simply create rotation keyframes for them.

1 In the Composition window, return to the Active Camera view. (Select Active Camera from the View pop-up menu at the bottom of the Composition window.)

Tip: You can use function keys to access and change your main camera views. By default, F10 activates the Front view, F11 activates Custom View 1, and F12 activates the Active Camera view. Try it—you'll like it.

2 Unlock all of the sprocket layers one at a time, or even better, "zip click" the lock switches by clicking and dragging the point down the entire column of visible sprocket layers. Then select all [Cmd/Ctrl + A] to select all of the sprocket layers.

Do not use Cmd/Ctrl + L to unlock all layers; otherwise, you'll unlock the shy layers, too. You don't want that.

3 With all six sprocket layers selected, type the **R** key to reveal the rotation properties.

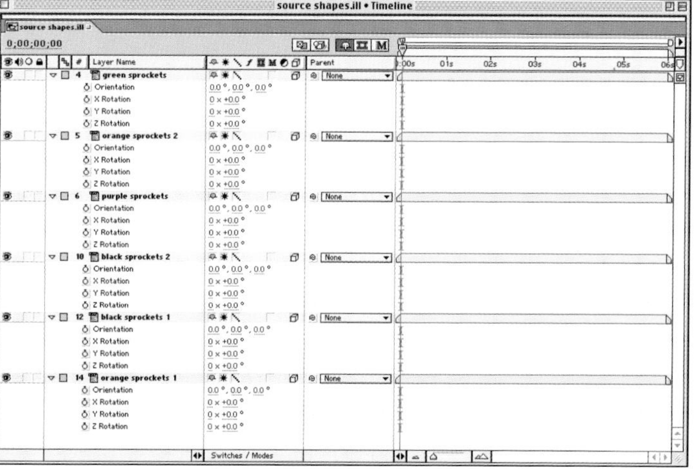

Reveal all six selected layers' rotation channels.

4 Deselect all [Cmd/Ctrl + Shift + A].

To save time, create a keyframe animation for one sprocket layer and then make the other sprocket layers mimic the first one using an expression.

5 Make sure the current-time marker is at 0:00 in the Timeline (if not, press Home). Click the stopwatch for Z Rotation for layer 3, green sprockets, to create a keyframe at time 0:00.

6 Move the current-time marker to the last frame of the animation by pressing End.

7 Set the first field of the Z Rotation value for layer 3, green sprockets, to 3 full revolutions. Note that the first field of the Rotation property is the number of revolutions (360-degree rotations).

Now make the other sprocket layers mimic the first one using an expression.

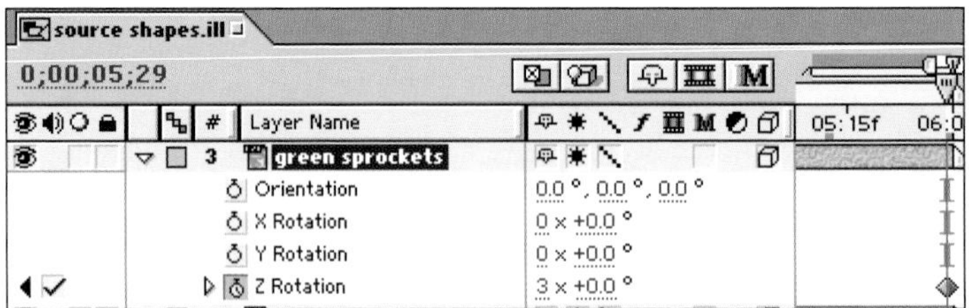

Animate the green sprockets layer so that it makes three full rotations.

8 Option/Alt+click the stopwatch for the Z Rotation channel for layer 4, orange sprockets 2.

This creates a new expression for the channel.

Note: Three buttons are revealed next to the expression in the Switches column of the Timeline when the expression is created. The middle button of these three is called a "pickwhip" (the spiral icon).

9 Click and drag the pickwhip to the right of the Z Rotation property (for layer 4) to the Z Rotation property for layer 4, green sprockets.

This creates an expression that causes layer 4's Z Rotation to mimic layer 3's Z Rotation (so that when layer 3 rotates, layer 4 will rotate, too).

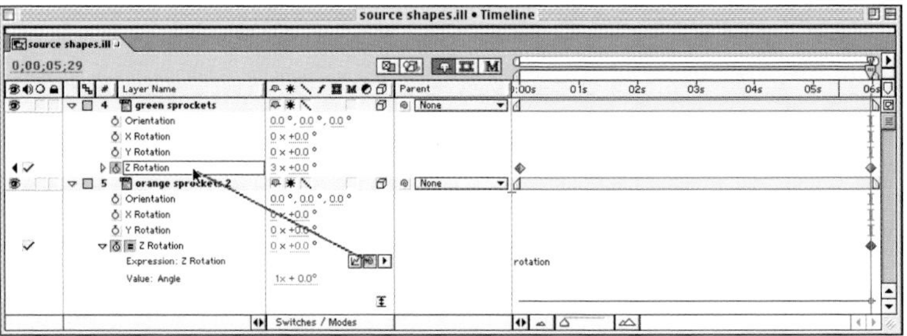

Drag the expression pickwhip for layer 4's Z Rotation channel to layer 3's Z Rotation channel.

10 Press the Enter key to officially enter the new expression. Be sure to use the Enter key, not the Return key.

11 Repeat these last three steps for the other four sprocket layers' Z Rotation properties so that all sprocket layers' Z Rotation properties mimic layer 4's Z Rotation property.

You might want to expand the Timeline window to fill your screen to be able to do this more easily.

12 Create another RAM preview to view the results.

Your animation should look similar to the QuickTime movie **3D_motion_graphics.mov** on the accompanying CD-ROM. If you'd like to render it out after seeing the full RAM preview, you have the option of selecting Save RAM Preview under the Composition menu. Note, however, that the resolution and quality settings will be as they were set for the RAM Preview.

Modifications

For those of you who are feeling more adventurous with expressions, try adding a scale factor to some of the expressions to make different sprockets turn at different speeds or in opposite directions.

For example, simply add -2* to the beginning of any expression to make it go backwards at twice the speed. Try using other values to create your own results. For even more dynamic 3D rendering, try adding lights and shadows to the scene.

3D Match Moves Using 2D Tracking

"Even if you're on the right track, you'll get run over if you just sit there."

—ARTHUR GODFREY

Using the After Effects Tracker to Smooth the Match Move of 3D Rendered Elements Composited with a Moving Background

Ever wonder how to get a 3D match move to track even better than what you could get from a 3D match move package or by match moving by eye? With After Effects and a spreadsheet program such as Microsoft Excel, you have all the tools you need to do just that. The procedures described here will teach you the technique of smoothing the match move between a moving background and a 3D rendered animation. The following pages will go over the fundamentals of this process. By the end of this project, you will understand how this procedure can be used for more complex situations.

Project 11

3D Match Moves Using 2D Tracking

by Eric Chauvin

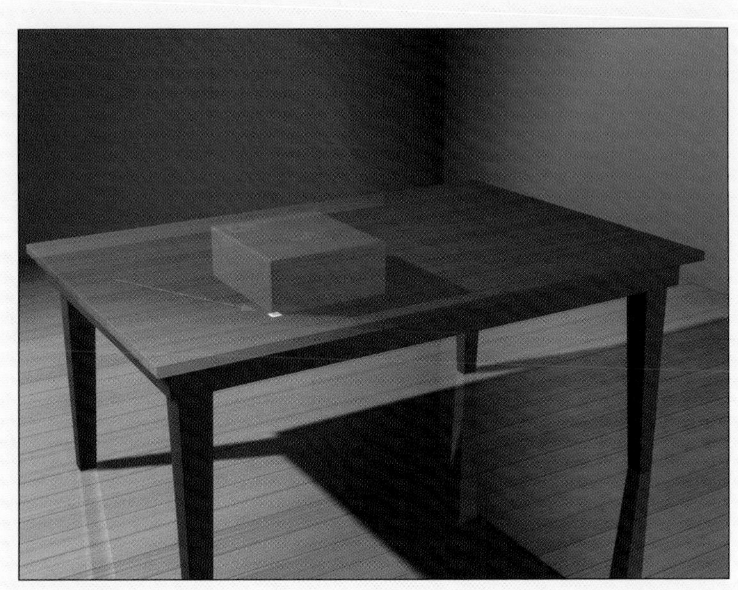

How It Works

How do 2D and 3D tracking work? Quite simply, a 2D tracker is a pixel analyzer. You give it a pattern of pixels to analyze and a search region for it to find that pattern. It will then track where that pattern goes from one frame to the next, plotting a course as it goes. When it reaches the end of the sequence, it will then assign the tracking information to an element in your composite.

In After Effects, the tracker data can be assigned to any of the layers you have in a particular composition by using a pull-down menu in the Motion Tracker Options box before you begin the tracking process. The quality of the tracking is defined by specifying the degree of subpixel matching using the Subpixel menu. The smaller the fraction of a pixel defined, the greater precision the track will have.

A 3D tracker works just like a 2D tracker except it analyzes several patterns and then calculates depth by how fast those patterns move through the frame. If you define a search area on an object in the frame that is close to the camera and define another area that is on an object farther away from the camera, the pattern on the closer object will travel through the frame faster than that of the farther pattern. This is accomplished by establishing a relative scale: The closer an object is to your eye, the faster it will appear to move relative to a similar object farther away from you.

The 3D tracker takes the data from all these different track points in the scene and creates a virtual version of the scene in 3D space. That data is then imported into a 3D rendering program where the elements to be composited can be animated and rendered to match the movement of the tracked plate. In the best-case scenario, the 3D tracking data works perfectly, and the shot goes together without a hitch. What usually happens, however, is that although the match move is very, very close, it isn't close enough. A secondary 2D match move is required to lock the movement of the plate and rendered elements together perfectly.

Getting Started

As digital compositing tools get ever more sophisticated, the types of effects seen in television shows and movies are becoming increasingly more complex. It was not too long ago that a matte painting shot had to have the plate element shot with a steadied, locked-off camera. This was necessary to ensure that there wouldn't be any noticeable weave (that is, subtle but mismatched motion) between the plate and the composited elements when viewed after the two were composited together. Nowadays, plates are routinely shot without steadied cameras. More and more, plates are being shot with a moving camera—on a dolly, a crane, a steadicam, or even hand held. This opens up more creative possibilities for the filmmaker and makes for more exciting cinema, but it creates much more work for the visual effects artist doing the effects compositing.

> **Note:** The portion of an effect shot that is photographed on the set is referred to as a "plate."

The effects compositor can take one of three approaches to solve this issue: digitally steady the plate (removing the movement of the camera altogether), perform a 2D match move (moving the composited elements on just the X- and Y-axes), or do a 3D match move (further moving the composited elements on the Z-axis as well). Usually, these types of composites require a combination of all three techniques to some degree, depending on what kind of movement the camera did while it shot the plate. If the only movement the camera did was tilting, panning, or rolling, the matchmoving could be accomplished with a 2D tracker. However, if the camera actually moved three-dimensionally (moving along the Z-axis) through the environment it was shooting, the match move would need to be done with a 3D tracker. In some instances in which the camera is moving dimensionally, you could also use just a 2D tracker. An example would be when the effects element to be composited is so far away from the camera that it wouldn't appear to have depth (for instance, adding distant buildings at the horizon in a scene shot out the window of a moving car).

> **Note:** A steadied, 35mm motion-picture camera is usually a camera that utilizes a pin-registered movement and that has been steady tested before being used to shoot the plate.

Here's the problem: 2D trackers are designed to add motion data to a still image. An example would be adding a purse (a still image) to a woman swinging her arm back and forth as she walks (moving footage). What is needed is a way to track both the rendered animated element and the background plate and then figure out the offset between the two tracks. It's that little bit of jiggle between the two tracks that you need to get rid of. After talking with people much smarter about these things than I am, I was taught how to solve this problem.

> **Note:** Matching an effects element to a moving plate element is, naturally, called a "match move."

First of all, use a 3D tracker or do a 3D track by eye. Take the rendered footage into a 2D program such as After Effects or Commotion and do a 2D track of the rendered footage and also the plate footage. Copy and paste this data into a spreadsheet program such as Microsoft Excel. Create a formula that simply subtracts the data of one track from the data of the other and paste the result into the appropriate channel in After Effects. That's it. To illustrate how to actually do this, look at the accompanying figure.

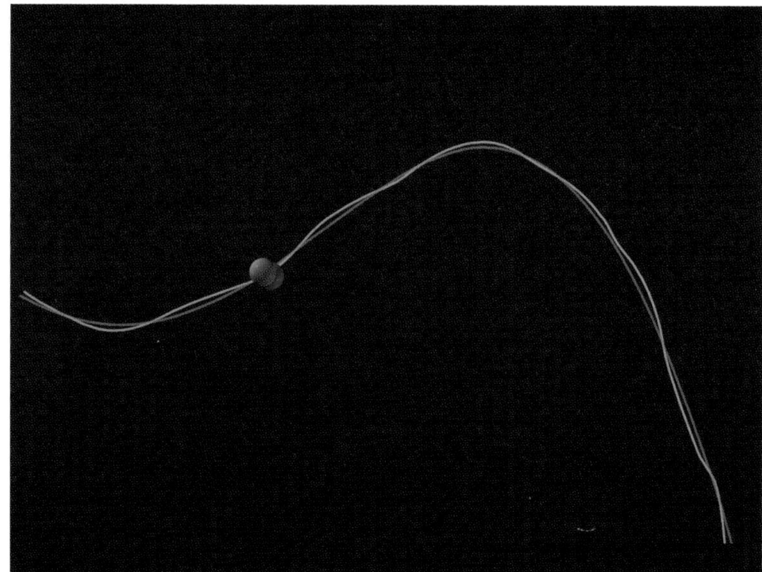

Blue ball and red ball moving across the frame.

In the figure, you see a blue ball and a red ball with a motion path showing how they will move across the frame. The blue ball represents the plate element, and the red ball represents the 3D animated element you want to track to the plate. If you look at the motion path for each ball, you'll notice that they move pretty much the same way, except that the blue ball has more of an organic quality to it whereas the red ball seems smoother by comparison.

Setting Up for Motion Tracking

You will usually want to track a rendered element to a plate element. However, there are times when you will want to or need to track the plate element to the rendered element. This is the case when the plate makes up a smaller portion of the frame than the rendered element does. Normally, it is the other way around. The plate takes up most the frame, and the rendered element is smaller. The reason for tracking the smaller element to the larger is to minimize the amount of frame edge that might be visible during the track. For instance, if you hypothetically had two elements that were 720×486 pixels and you wanted to track one element to the other, you would likely see the edge of the element to which the track was applied as it moved through the shot. Now, if the element receiving the tracker data was 300×300 pixels, it probably wouldn't have any noticeable frame edge showing up during the shot.

Note: What if you are doing a shot that requires 3D tracking and you don't have access to a 3D tracker? Well, you could do the 3D tracking by eye in a 3D rendering program. I have done this several times in the past, and let me say this: It's doable but very painful. The objective isn't to get a perfect match move but to get something really close. More specifically, replicating the general move of the camera without worrying about the more subtle "organic" parts of the move. By that I mean the little bumps, wobbles, and general deviations evident in the move, caused by the fact the camera was operated by a human and not a machine. People are so used to experiencing these organic imperfections in cinematography that they subconsciously notice when they aren't there. Elements shot with a motion-control camera or animated and rendered in a computer usually lack this organic quality. If you are going to attempt the 3D track manually, you can get this last bit of movement automatically using a 2D tracker.

1 Make a new composition and set the size to 640×480 and the length to 120 frames at 24fps. Import the files called **Movie_red_ball.img** and **Movie_blue_ball.img** from the accompanying CD-ROM. Drag both movies to the composition. Click the RAM Preview button.

See how the two balls slide against each other as they move across the frame.

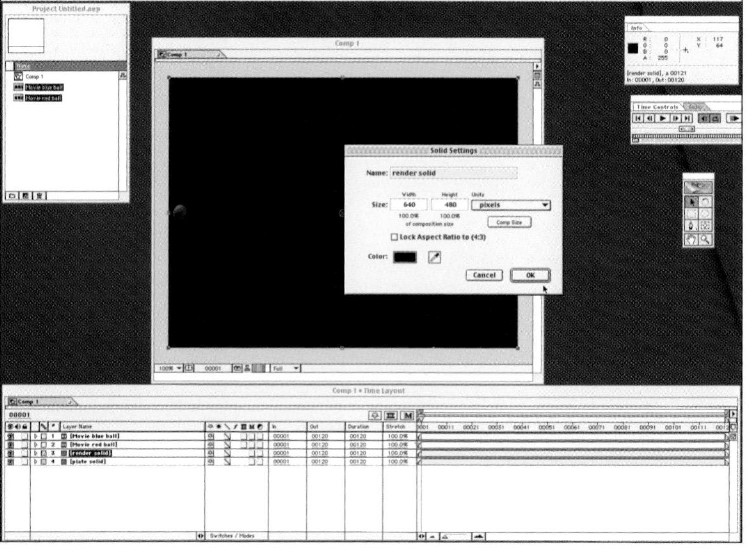

Create two solid layers called plate solid and render solid.

2 Make two solid layers by going to the Layer menu and selecting New Solid. Make the solids the same size as the composition. Name the first solid **plate solid** and the second one **render solid**.

These solids are simply going to be placeholders for the tracker data. They won't be used in the final composite.

3 Select Movie blue ball in the composition and select the Motion Tracker under Layer > Keyframe Assistant > Motion Tracker. Click Options and select plate solid as the layer to which to apply the motion. Click OK.

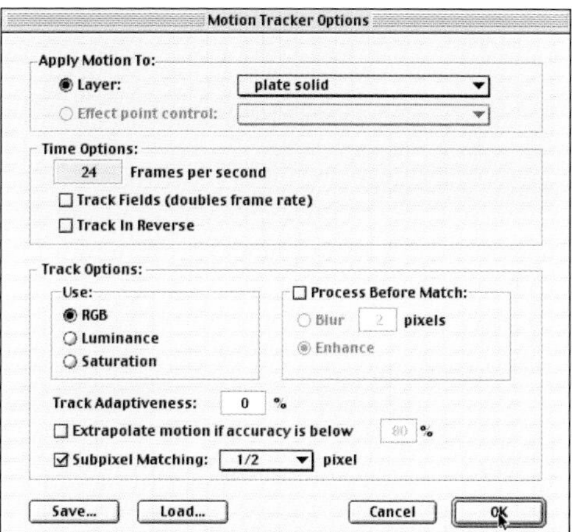

Modify the Motion Tracker options.

Leave the Subpixel Matching at the default level of 1/2. This is the least accurate setting, but it will do the fastest track. For a more accurate track, set the Subpixel Matching to a smaller fraction. You are now ready to do the 2D track. If you haven't used the tracker in After Effects before, it might be a good idea to read up on it in the After Effects manual.

Note: The tracker is only available in the Production Bundle of After Effects. For the purposes of this project, it is assumed you have a reasonable understanding of how to use the tracker.

Note: This project will be using Microsoft Excel as the spreadsheet application.

4 Make sure you are at frame 1 and set the tracking target over the ball, ensuring that the search region is big enough for the tracker to work properly. Now click Track. When it's finished, click the Apply button.

If you select the plate solid layer in your Composition window and twirl down to the Position channel, you'll notice that there are now keyframes for every frame under Position.

5 Repeat the preceding steps for Movie red ball. Be sure to select render solid as the layer to which to apply motion.

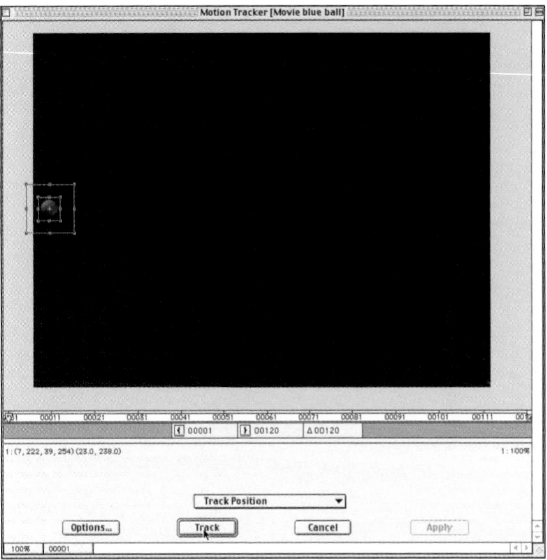

Click the Track button to add keyframes to the plate solid layer.

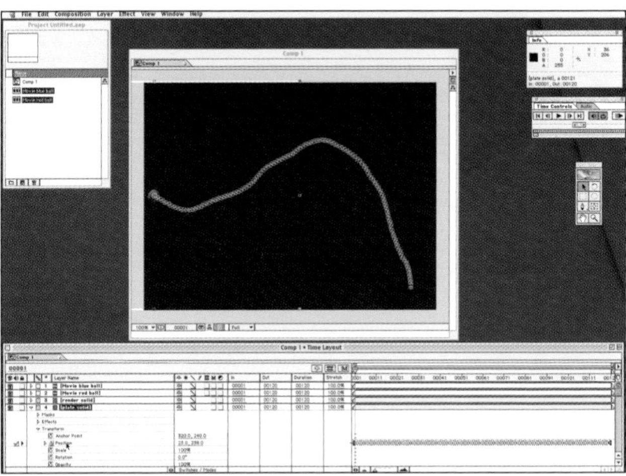

Exporting Tracking Data to Excel

Most of what you are doing in Excel is copying and pasting data. You're simply copying keyframe information from After Effects and pasting it into Microsoft Excel. From there, you write some very simple formulas to manipulate that data and then paste the result back into After Effects. By doing this, you will smooth the match move in your composite.

1. Once you have tracked Movie red ball, go back to the Position channel for plate solid and click on the word Position.

   This selects all your keyframes.

2. Go to the Edit menu and select Copy.

   This will copy the keyframe information to the clipboard in the After Effects format.

3. Open your spreadsheet program, select cell A4, and paste the data from the clipboard to your spreadsheet.

4. Go back to After Effects and select the Position keyframes for render solid. Copy these keyframes to the clipboard.

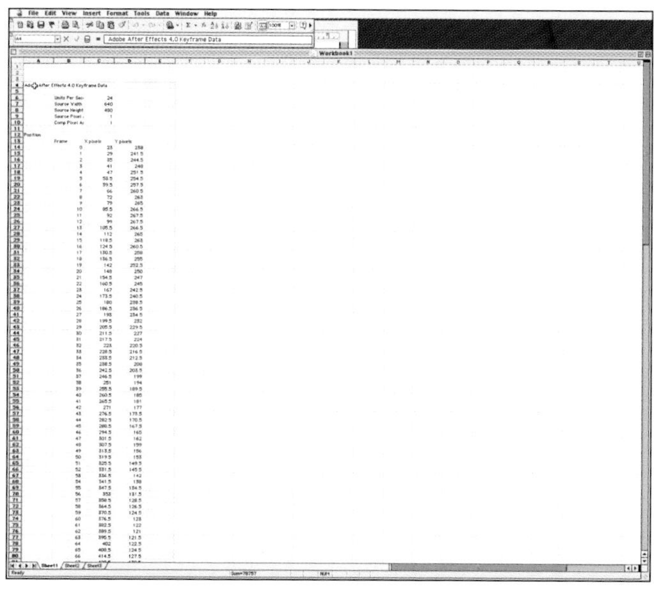

Copy your data from After Effects into Excel.

5. In Excel, select cell G4 and paste the data from the clipboard. So that you will know which group of data belongs to which layer, go to cell A1 and type **Plate tracker**. In cell G1, type **Render tracker**. The data from After Effects should still be on the clipboard, so go to cell L4 and click Paste and then go to cell Q4 and hit paste.

   You are simply making templates that you will ultimately use back in After Effects. It doesn't matter what data you're currently copying; you just want to preserve the After Effects formatting for the data.

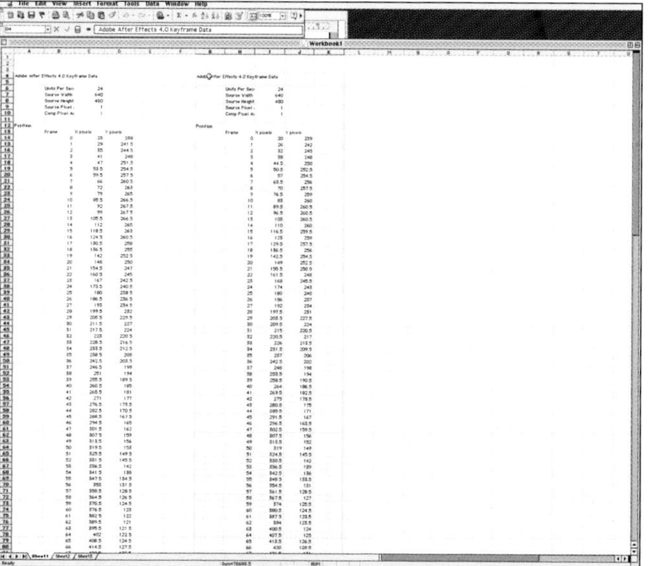

Paste the render solid keyframes into Excel.

6 Go to cell L1 and type **Reset**. In cell Q1, type **Result**.

7 To be on the safe side, save the spreadsheet.

Let's review what you just did: You brought the two ball movies into a new composition in After Effects, made two solid layers, tracked the balls in each movie and assigned the tracker data to its corresponding solid, copied and pasted the Position keyframes from After Effects into Excel, and labeled the different columns of data to keep them straight.

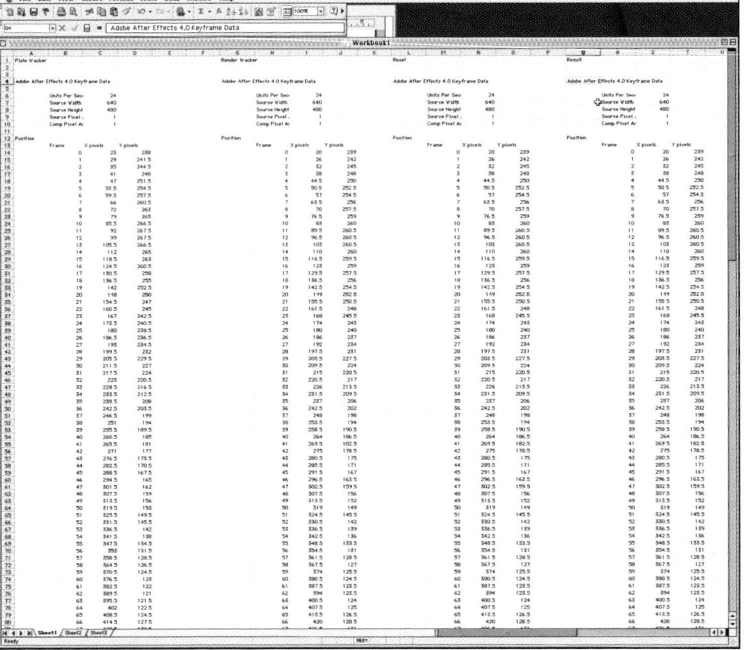

Type Reset in cell L1 and Result in cell Q1.

TRANSFORMING THE TRACKING DATA

At this point, you are probably wondering what Reset and Result mean. If you look at the number in cell C14 and compare it to the number in I14, you'll notice that the two numbers are close but not the same. For this technique to work, you have to make the number in I14 match the number in C14. To do this, simply subtract the number in I14 from the number in C14.

1 Select cell L14 and then type in this formula: **+c14-i14**. This formula subtracts the number in I14 from the number in C14 and gives you a result.

2 Repeat this for the numbers in D14 and J14. Go to cell L15 and type in **+d14-j14**.

You now have the difference for the X-axis and the Y-axis for the first pixel in the series. What you now want to do is reset the corresponding pixels for the first frame in the Reset column using this difference amount.

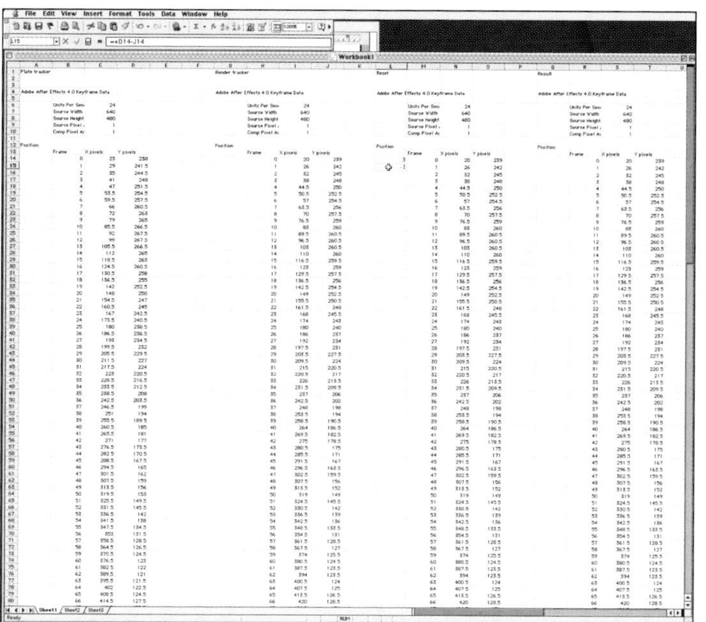

Apply this formula to cell L15.

Note: Because everyone doing this tutorial will get a different result from his or her track in After Effects, I can't give you a hard number to use as a variable for the difference amount. You need to use the numbers you see in L14 and L15.

3 Go to cell N14 and type **+I14-x** (x represents what number you see in L14; instead of typing x, put in the number from L14). After you press Enter, the number you see in that cell should equal the number in cell C14. If it doesn't, then instead of **+I14-x** try **+I14+x**.

The important thing is the that result has to match the number in C14.

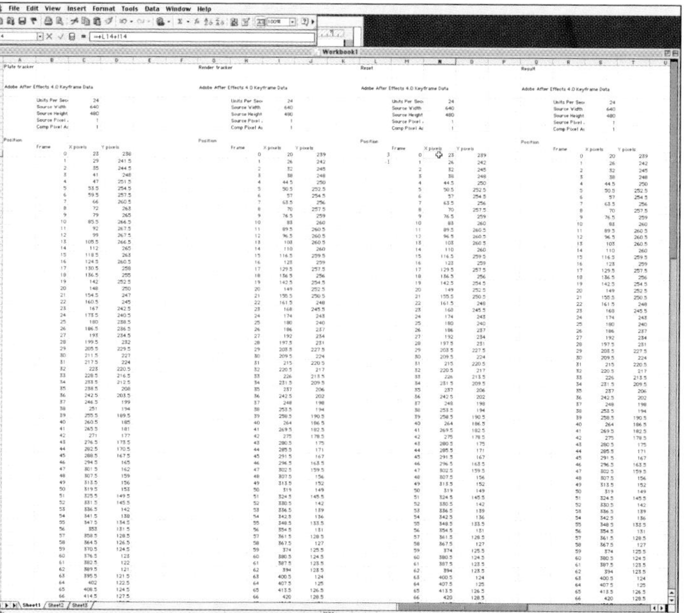

Your result for number C14 should equal the number in N14.

4 Do the same for O14. Type **+J14-x**. (Now x represents the number in L15.)

The result should equal the number in D14.

5 Select cells N14 and O14 and copy. Select N15 through O133 and select paste.

You have now reset the rest of the rows to correspond with the data for the plate.

This might seem a little confusing, but think of it this way: Because what you ultimately want to do is figure out the difference between the tracks for the plate and the rendered element, you need to establish a baseline from which to start. By resetting the numbers in the reset columns, you have made the first row zero, and the numbers that follow are just the offset between the plate and the rendered element only.

The last step in Excel is to subtract the numbers in the Reset columns from the Plate Tracker column.

6 Go to cell S14 and type **+c14-n14**. You'll notice that the result is zero. Now go to cell T14 and type **+d14-o14**. You get the same result—zero.

7 Copy and paste these formulas to the rest of the rows in columns S and T. Save your worksheet.

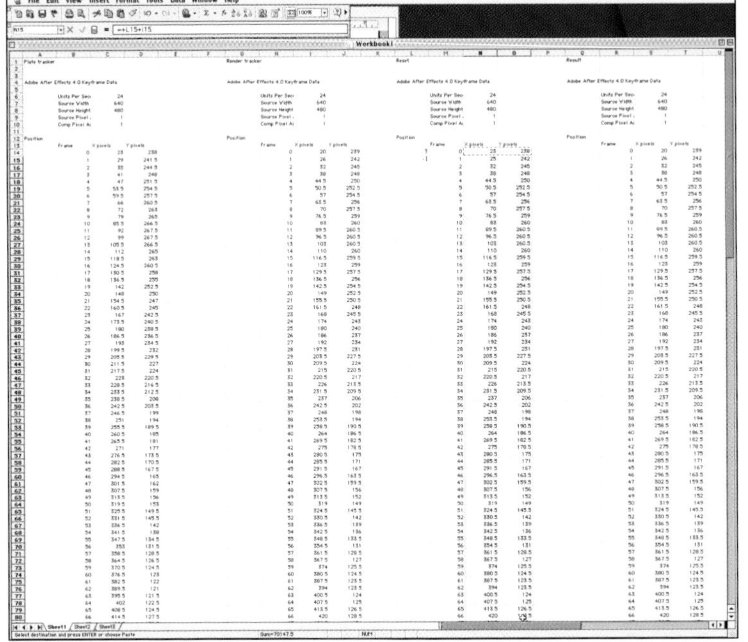

Paste N14 and O14 into N15 through O133.

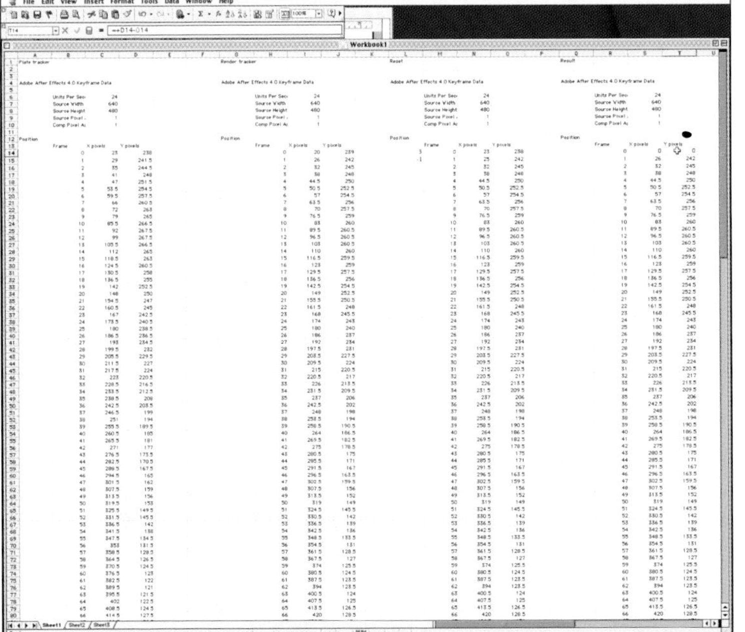

Your results for cells S14 and T14 should both be zero.

APPLYING THE TRANSFORMED DATA

The only thing left to do in Excel is copy and paste the result into After Effects.

1 Go to cell Q4 and click+drag to T136. Copy this selection to the clipboard.

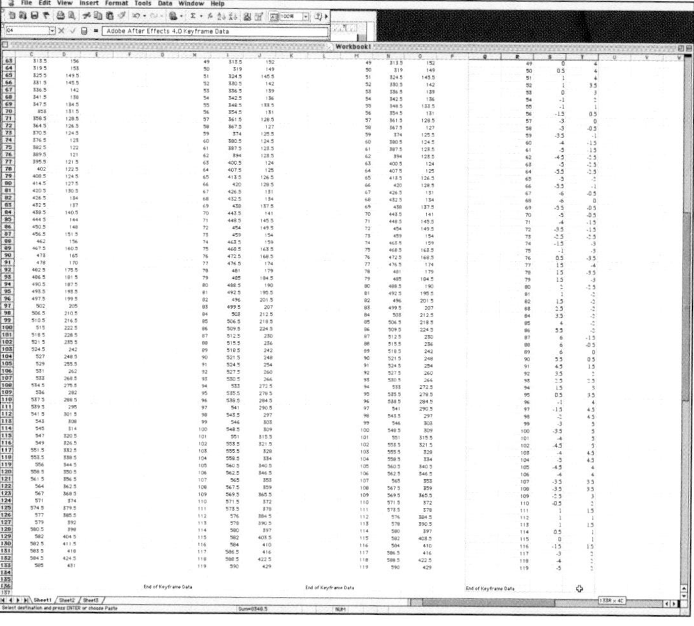

Drag the contents of cell Q4 to T136 and copy T136 to the clipboard.

2 In After Effects, select the layer Movie red ball and select Paste.

If you twirl down to the Position channel for Movie red ball, you'll notice that there are now keyframes for every frame. If you look at the Composition window, you will see that the anchor point is now in the top-left corner of the frame.

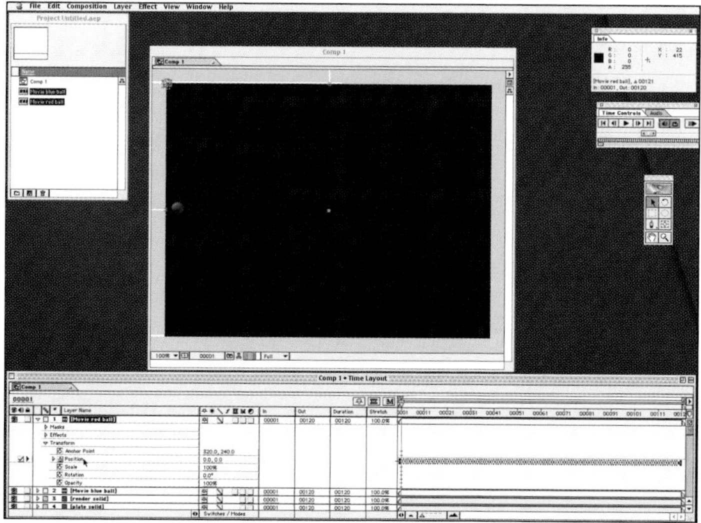

Paste the data back into After Effects on the Movie red ball layer.

3 Making sure that all keyframes are still selected, move the Movie red ball layer in the Composition window while holding down the Shift and Option keys.

This will snap the layer to the center of the frame as you move the layer close to the center. You can now delete the solid layers you were using as placeholders.

4 That's it! Click the RAM Preview button and see what happens.

Whereas before the red and blue balls were visibly sliding back and forth against each other, they now move in perfect unison. If you were to go back to the beginning of this tutorial and try retracking at a more accurate subpixel level, the resulting track will be even better.

You might be wondering why, when you pasted the Result data into the red ball movie, the layer jumped up into the upper-left corner. After Effects calculates Position information based on a layer's anchor point. Because by default the anchor point is in the very center of the layer and the numbers you were pasting into the layer from Excel started from pixel number 0, it moved the layer up and over so that the center of the layer started at pixel 0. I had you move the composition so that it snapped back to the center because, in this particular case, both movies were the same size, 640×480. By snapping it back to the center, it lined up to where both balls began in the first place. However, you can move the layer to anywhere you want. Just remember that all your keyframes have to be selected before you move the layer; otherwise, you will ruin the track.

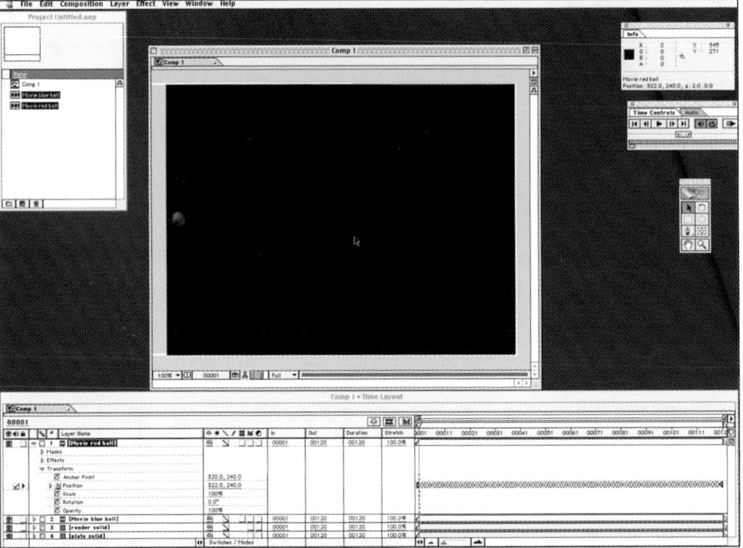

Hold down Shift+Option and move the Movie red ball layer. Then delete your placeholder layers.

Comparative Tracking

In the preceding example, you practiced how to go through the procedure of doing a 2D track to a 3D moving object. In this tutorial, you will see what happens when you track a point that isn't in close proximity to where the composited object will go and track a point that is close to the composited object.

1. Open **Project_tutorial_2.aep** from the accompanying CD-ROM and select the tab in the Time Layout window labeled nontracked comp. Click the RAM Preview button.

   After the frames load into memory, take a look at how the package on the table appears to bounce around in relation to the rest of the frame. To help you see this, I've included a layer that is simply a grid laid over the tabletop (called Movie table top grid).

2. Launch Excel and open the **tutorial 2 spreadsheet.xls** file.

   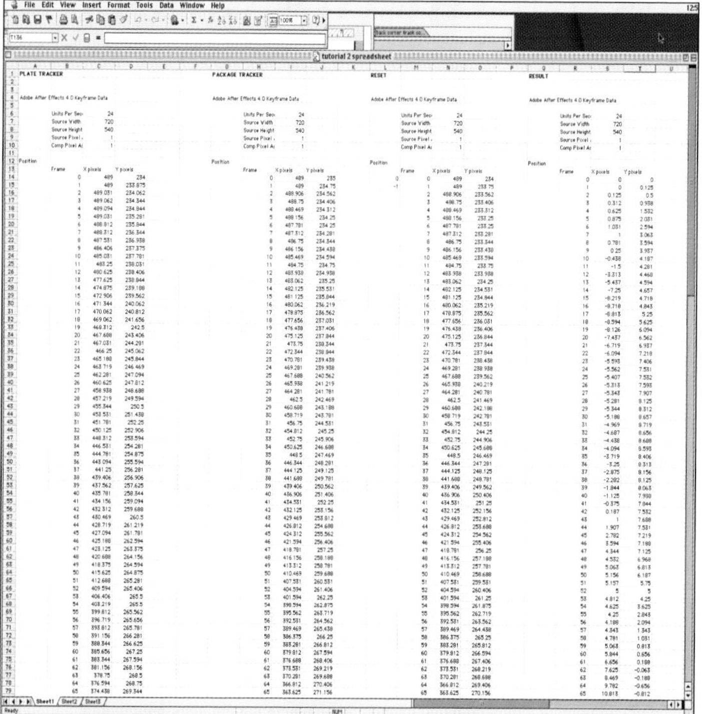

   Open tutorial 2 spreadsheet.xls from the accompanying CD-ROM.

   This spreadsheet has everything laid out for you already, so all you need to do is track the various points, copy and paste the data into this spreadsheet, make some small revisions, and paste the results back to the appropriate layer in After Effects. For those of you who don't want to go through the trouble of retracking points and fussing with the spreadsheet data, I've included in the After Effects project some other compositions, which you can click on and see the results. These compositions are called back corner track comp, front corner track comp, and proper track comp.

   What you are going to discover is the importance of having a track point close to the composited object, in this case the package on the table.

3. Click the tab for the composition labeled Practice comp and select the layer marked Movie package tracker.

4 Open the tracker. Under Options, name the layer to receive the track **Package tracker solid** and make the subpixel matching 1/32.

5 Set up your target over the white ball and begin the track.

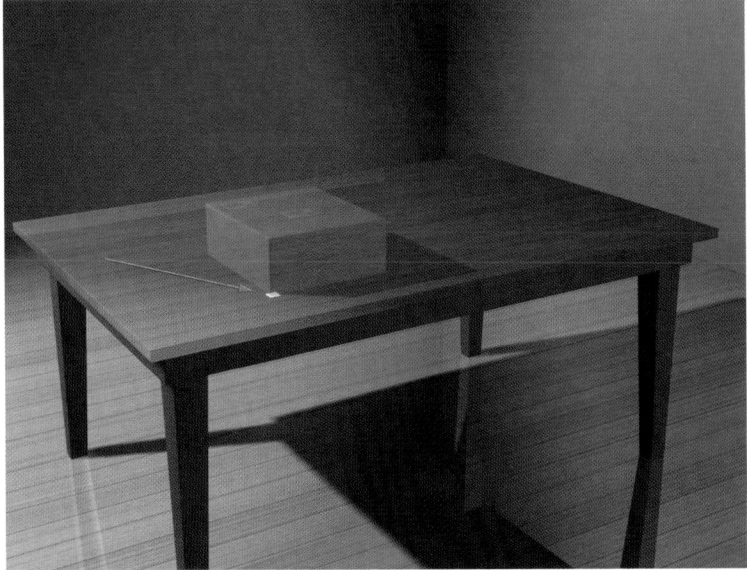

A box sitting on a table.

Note: Keep in mind that you want to pick tracking targets that are close to where the rendered element (or plate element) is going to go. If you look at the example of a box sitting on a table (an example used in this chapter), you will see that there is a track target on the table underneath where the box will go. Remember what I mentioned earlier about relative scale: Things closer to the camera appear to move faster than things farther away from the camera. If you track a target too close or too far away from where you want to place your rendered object, the object won't behave the way you need it to work in the shot.

6 After the track is finished, select the layer marked Package tracker solid and copy the keyframes for Position to the clipboard.

7 Go to Excel, select cell G4, and paste the data from the clipboard.

8 Go back to After Effects and do a track on the layer marked Movie back corner tracker.

9 Change the layer to receive the track to back corner tracker solid and, again, be sure to make the subpixel matching sample 1/32. Do the track and copy and paste the Position information to cell A4 in Excel.

10 Go to cell N14 and modify the formula so that it reads **+I14+x** (remember that x represents the number in cell L14). The result should equal the number in cell C14. If it doesn't, try **+I14-x**.

11 Do the same for the formula in O14, only make it **+J14+x** (x being the number in cell L15).

12 After you have done this, copy and paste these formulas into the rest of the cells below.

13 Copy the result (cells Q4 through T136) to the clipboard.

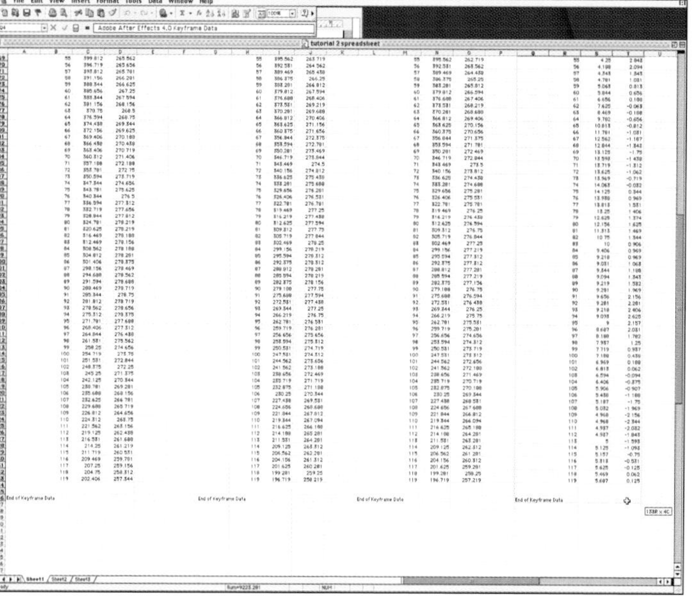

Copy the results of your formulas.

14 In After Effects, click the tab for the composition labeled back corner track comp and select the layer marked Movie package render (tracked).

15 Paste the data from the clipboard and reposition the layer so that it is centered in the Composition window.

16 Click the RAM Preview button and watch what happens.

The layer with the package has incorporated the bumps from the background plate movement, but it is also sliding off the table.

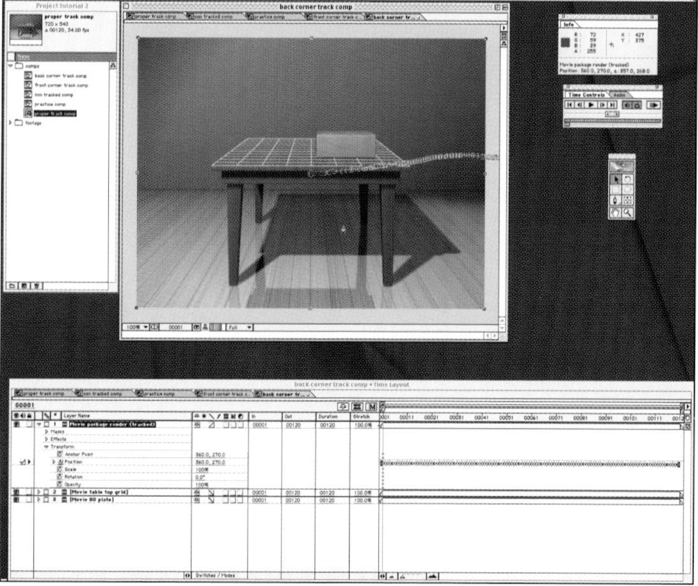

Paste your Excel data into the Movie package render layer.

TRYING OTHER TRACK POINTS

Now that you have seen what happens when you track a point too far away from the rendered element, try tracking a point that is too close and a point that is in the correct position.

1. Repeat the preceding steps in practice comp with the layer marked front corner tracker solid.
2. Apply the track to the solid marked front corner tracker solid and paste its Position information into Excel like you did before.
3. When you have made the proper modifications, paste the result into the layer marked Movie package render (tracked) in the front corner track comp.

   If you watch the RAM preview, you will notice that the package now slides in the opposite direction from when you tracked the point on the back corner.

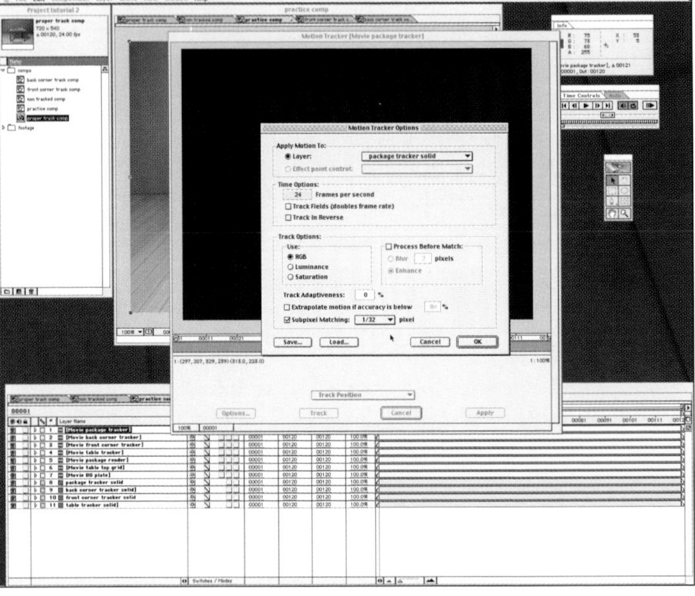

Paste the front corner tracker solid info into Excel.

4. Repeat the preceding steps with the layer marked Movie table tracker in practice comp.
5. Select table tracker solid as the receiver of the track. After you have exported the data to Excel and imported the result, click the RAM Preview button.

   Violá! The track works perfectly.

Repeat the preceding steps with the Movie table tracker layer.

Modifications

There are a few little steps in using this technique correctly, but the overall procedure is pretty simple. The examples used in these tutorials were very basic so that you could get a better idea of the technique. In real life, you will most likely have more complicated scenarios. However, now that you understand the process, you can adapt this technique to suite your future 2D tracking needs.

Remember that when working with tracking and match moves, there are always tradeoffs. For example, let's say you're doing a 3D composite in which you need to add a second story to a row of buildings. In the move in the plate, the camera starts close to the buildings, looking down the row obliquely as if it were looking down the street. As the shot progresses, the camera moves away from the buildings but stays pointed at them. The effect is that the horizontal lines of the buildings appear to converge to a point at the beginning of the shot but then tend to be parallel by the end of the move. If you wanted to smooth out a 3D track to this type of shot, you would be faced with a dilemma. Do you track from a point closer to the camera, farther from the camera, or halfway in between? If it's too close, the background will fall apart. If it's too far, the foreground won't track right. If you pick the middle, neither the foreground nor the background will look right. What do you do? In this case, you would need to add cornerpinning to the equation, but that is a topic for another day. The point I'm making is that, depending on the type of shot you are working on, you need to be aware that the track might work beautifully in one area at the cost of it falling apart in another.

I've actually used this technique in a couple of television shows. The first was in an episode of *Star Trek: Voyager*. The plate was of one of the cast members standing in front of a blue screen as the camera dollied back and away from the actress. My job was to create an environment for her to stand in and to add a camera move to the background environment that matched the move of the camera that shot the actress. I didn't have access to a 3D match move application, so I did the match move by eye. As expected, I got the majority of the move to work well, but I couldn't get the little bumps and imperfections that were in the real camera move. By using this technique, everything locked right into place.

Another place where I used this method was in a show in which the camera was following an actor walking past a wall. In the wall was a window, and beyond the window was a green screen. My job was to track another plate element into the window where the green screen was. The camera was moving pretty smoothly, but the cameraman was using a really wide-angle lens that was causing a lot of lens distortion on the edge of the frame. Because of this, I couldn't just 2D track the second plate to the first because it wouldn't distort the same way. To solve this problem, I keyframe-animated the distortion to the second plate. In doing this, however, it tended to jump around when viewed composited in with the first plate. By once again using this technique, I was able to eliminate the wobble between the two elements.

ELEMENTARY EXPRESSIONS

"It was my understanding that there would be no math."

—CHEVY CHASE (AS GERALD FORD)

Introducing Expressions

Who's afraid of big bad expressions? This powerful set of features was added to After Effects 5 not to intimidate visual artists but to offer animators more powerful ways to translate animation or to create it from scratch. You might not even realize the times when expressions can save you a lot of repetitive effort or lead to a more elegant solution, but they exist everywhere. Just because you've gotten along this long without expressions doesn't mean you can't (or shouldn't) be won over to them, right?

Why, you ask? Beyond reducing tedious tasks, expressions will broaden the way you're able to animate. When you become used to the idea that properties can easily be linked together or even scaled with simple math, you might start wanting to try it everywhere. Linking two disparate properties together, scaling or offsetting the result when needed, constitutes the majority of what most people will initially do with expressions, and that's what you'll start doing in this project. After you've learned to do this effortlessly, you'll never want to live without this feature because it leads to many elegant solutions that would otherwise be somewhat tedious and repetitive.

Project 12

Elementary Expressions

by Mark Christiansen

How It Works

The first few animations of our "Question Authority" motion graphics sequence make exclusive use of the pickwhip, an automated tool used to create an expression by linking one After Effects property to another. The pickwhip is the easiest way to get started with expressions because the syntax it creates is guaranteed to be correct, and it remains a useful tool to support more complex expressions.

Of course, like most automated solutions, the pickwhip doesn't always give you the output you're looking for by default; often you have to do simple math (yes, math), but by "simple" I mean addition, subtraction, multiplication, and division. Sound okay? Let's give it a try.

You'll start by linking the rotation and scale of a single layer so that, as you animate the rotation, you see the scale move up and down along with it, following its keyframe eases, stops, and starts. You'll experience the difference between controlling parameters separately and linking them, gaining the power of expressions.

Then you'll look at cases in which you need to use elementary school math (most often multiplication and/or division for scaling, with a little addition and subtraction thrown in for offsets) to make these links more useful. For example, you'll link a second layer's scale and rotation together but then "slow down" the rate of rotation by making it happen only at a one third proportion of scale. This kind of control is essential to getting the results you want out of expressions, and it's not difficult. Working with two linked properties in real time might, by itself, set off the proverbial light bulb over your head.

Soon you'll start to recognize other situations in which you can avoid tedious tasks and open new possibilities by linking together properties. Have you ever tried repeating the same animation with several layers and then wanted to change that same animation across all of them? With expressions, changing one could change them all in one step, as you'll see.

Getting Started

This project and the ones that follow create a lot from relatively little. There is an Adobe Illustrator file called **question_mark_centered.ai** on the accompanying CD-ROM that you should copy to your local drive. If you want, you can move the entire Projects 12–15 folder over to your drive and open the file called **CH12_INITIAL.aep** to start these exercises. To exactly reproduce the project as I originally created it and precisely match the look of the images in projects 12–15, you'll need the Dogma font from Emigré. The main project files, however, use the font Comic Sans MS Bold, which is standard on Mac and Windows. The look is very similar, but not identical. If you own the Dogma font, you can complete this project using the files in the Dogma Projects folder in this project's folder on the CD-ROM. Note that you must load the font before starting After Effects.

Note: The Dogma font is available for purchase from Emigré's web site (**www.emigre.com**).

Using the Pickwhip for Single Properties

Let's start with a simple use of the pickwhip: to tie one set of animation values to another. You'll immediately start to see why using expressions can give you more control as an animator.

1 Create a new project and begin by importing the **question_mark_centered.ai** file that you moved to your local drive. Go ahead and save the project (with whatever name you like) in the same folder as the question_mark_centered.ai file.

This is an Adobe Illustrator 9 file that consists only of a large question mark and a set of crop marks drawn around its periphery.

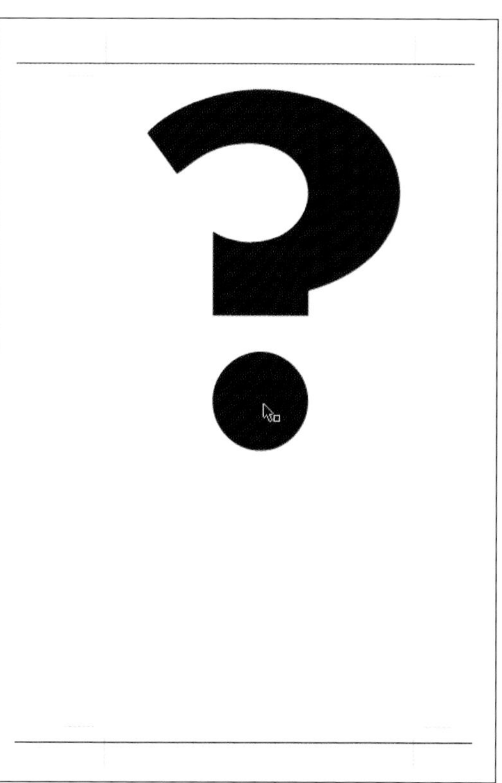

Use crop marks in Adobe Illustrator to define a boundary for After Effects. Here, the pointer shows the center defined by the crop marks, top and bottom.

Note: Crop marks are a useful feature to know about if you use Adobe Illustrator to create graphics for After Effects. Whenever you create a shape (or set of shapes) within Illustrator and save it for use within After Effects, it's a good practice to also draw a rectangle that bounds all of your shapes and then choose Object > Crop Marks > Make to convert the rectangle into crop marks. Then, when you bring the shapes into After Effects, it constrains the boundary of the file to your crop marks. In this case, I've set the crop marks so that the center of the rectangle falls right at the center of the dot in the question mark, which will be your rotation center.

2 Create a new composition by clicking on the little Create Composition icon at the bottom of the Project window (the third one from the left) or press Cmd/Ctrl + N. In the dialog box that opens, name the composition **Question Authority FOREGROUND** and under Preset choose the NTSC DV: 720×480 setting. Be careful not to select NTSC DV Widescreen 720×480, or your footage will look very odd, compressed to a 16:9 aspect ratio.

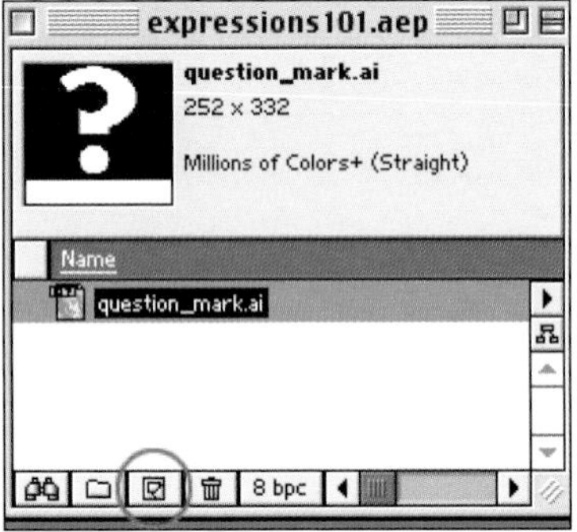

Circled here is the Create Composition icon at the bottom of the Project window.

3 Set the Resolution to Half and the duration to 12 seconds (the length of the final animation that continues in Projects 12 through 15). Click the Advanced tab at the top and set the shutter angle to 360 for a nice, generous motion blur. Click OK.

Setting the resolution to half will give you faster previews.

Note: Those of you in countries that use the PAL format are welcome to choose the PAL D1/DV setting, but some of the pixel dimensions I specify in this exercise will be incorrect.

4 Drag the question mark logo into the composition by dragging the question_mark.ai footage item and dropping it onto the Question Authority FOREGROUND Composition icon in the Project window. In the Switches panel, turn on Collapse Transformations for this layer, as shown in the figure.

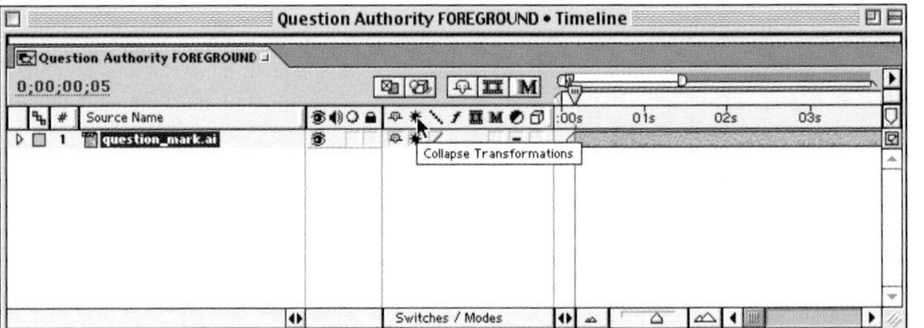

Tool tips show you the location of the Collapse Transformations switch in the Timeline window.

Collapse Transformations enables you to scale the Illustrator layer above 100% without having it look quantized (pixilated at the edges). It forces After Effects to look at the Illustrator source when transforming it, and the source is made up of vectors, which can be scaled infinitely.

Now you're ready to start playing with expressions.

Note: Collapse Transformations is the little black sun icon next to the Layer Quality setting. If you're ever unsure which icon is which, hold your mouse over the icons at the top of the Switches panel (as in the figure) without clicking, and you should see a tool tip that labels the icon—unless, of course, you have Show Tool Tips unchecked under General Preferences.

5 With the question_mark.ai layer highlighted in the Timeline window, press S for Scale and then press Shift+R to add Rotation.

You will see these two properties revealed for the layer. You're going to connect the Rotation values to Scale so that, as you scale the layer up and down, it automatically rotates proportionally.

6 Option/Alt+click the stopwatch icon just to the left of the word "Rotation" (or highlight the word "Rotation" and choose Animation > Add Expression).

You should see the word "Rotation" appear highlighted in blue along a line that reads "Expression: Rotation." Try a very simple expression, a constant value. You won't be using this for your final animation, so you are welcome to skip this step, but it might help you understand how expressions operate.

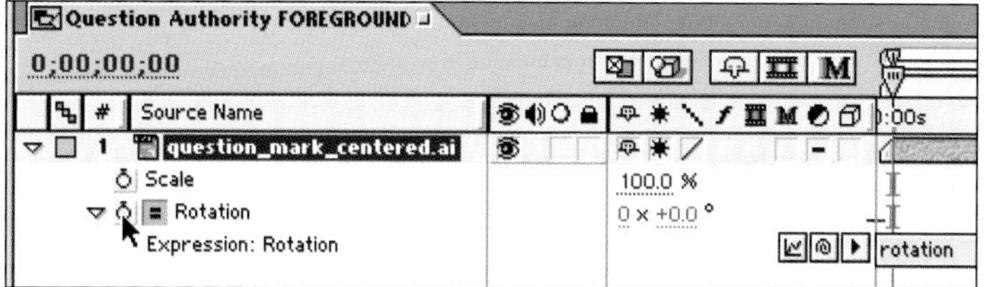

Option/Alt + clicking the stopwatch next to a property sets an expression for that property.

Understanding the Default Expression

This default entry is the simplest expression possible, one that returns the property itself, and it doesn't actually do anything. If you had a series of keyframes for Rotation and then set the expression with the default "Rotation" as its only parameter, you would see no change to your animation. "Rotation," in this case, acts as a placeholder for whatever else you might want to enter. It is necessary because, if the window contains nothing, the expression will be turned off.

To prove this assertion, try this: Create a keyframe for Rotation by clicking the stopwatch (no Option/Alt key this time) and then go to a different time and change the values. After Effects will ask you if you want to turn off the expression for this stream. You will have to turn off expressions to change the value; once you have set your keyframes, reactivate expressions by clicking the equal sign with a forward slash through it (≠), and you will see that your keyframes behave the same whether the expression is on or off. The word "Rotation" tells After Effects to look at the Rotation values, including keyframes, just as it would by default.

When you're ready to go on to the next step, delete all the Rotation keyframes.

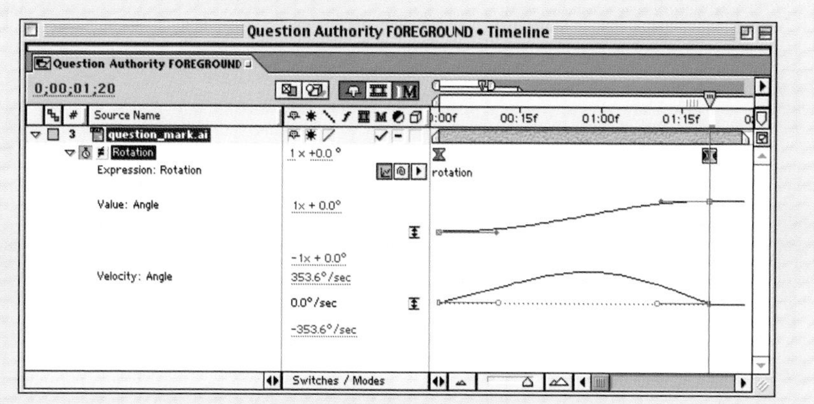

With the default expression entered, keyframes remain active.

7 Highlight the text in the expression area that says "Rotation" by clicking in the text area; you should see the whole area highlighted in color. Now type in any number you want—an integer or a decimal number, positive or negative—replacing the word "Rotation." Press Enter (not Return).

When you press Enter (*not* Return, which indicates a carriage return, adding a line to the expression, but the Enter key on your numeric keypad) or click outside the expression text area, you should see the rotation snap to whatever value you entered, in degrees. If you move the cursor along the Timeline, you will see that this value remains as a constant.

So what you have done here is essentially create a "hold" keyframe on a single value for this property.

Tip: This is a great way to temporarily disable a set of keyframes, replacing them with a static value. Set however many keyframes you like, Option/Alt + click the stopwatch, and replace the text with a number. That number will override all keyframe values.

Note: What's going on here? One of the most confusing things about expressions to a novice is understanding where the value is returned. The end result of an expression always has to stand for a value—a single value in the case of a property like Rotation that only uses one value, or an array of multiple values for properties like Position or RGBA that use more than one number to describe them.

Note on D1 Aspect Ratio: Is the round dot of that question mark looking a little oblong to you? You're working in DV NTSC, which is a standard that uses nonsquare pixels. When the signal is sent to an NTSC monitor, the pixels are only 90% as wide as they are tall to get more information into the horizontal scan line, so when you look at it on your RGB computer monitor (which uses square pixels), it looks a little too wide, and round objects thus look oblong. This is often referred to as *D1 aspect ratio*. If this annoys or distracts you, After Effects gives you the option of working in a corrected view without losing the final output of nonsquare pixels. Click on the small black triangle arrow at the upper right of your Composition window to access the Composition window menu and choose Pixel Aspect Correction. If it's not checked, you can click on it to activate this feature. You might see a warning that items will not appear fully antialiased, which is okay because final output is not affected. Click OK.

Real-World Pickwhip

At last, it's time to use the pickwhip to set an expression for your final animation.

1 Highlight whatever text is entered for the Rotation expression because you want to automatically replace it. Choose the middle of the three buttons, the pickwhip; it's the one that looks like a swirl to the left of your highlighted text. Click and drag from this button up to Scale. You should see a line extend to a black border around Scale or around the number 100%. Either target is okay in this case; the distinction is important only if you're working with a property that has two or more parameters, like Scale or Position.

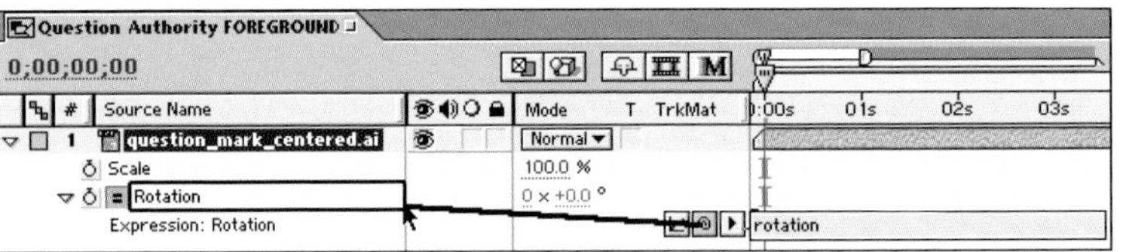

Clicking and dragging from the middle Expressions icon to a property reveals the pickwhip, which automatically sets a link between the two properties. Here, you are replacing Rotation with the Scale value.

As soon as you let go, you should see the little whip icon crack, and the following will appear in the Rotation expression text area:

scale[0]

2 Click outside the text area or press Enter. The question mark symbol snaps around to 100 degrees because the scale value is set at 100.

Note: You know that the word "Scale" is telling After Effects to look at the Scale channel for Rotation values. Why do you need [0] after scale? Scale is a property with two parameters. In After Effects, you can scale an object separately along the X- or Y-axis, although by default you only see one value for Scale because, in most cases, you want a layer to scale proportionally. [0] is telling After Effects to use the first parameter (because parameters are numbered starting from zero) of Scale, but because you are leaving your scaling proportional, you could change [0] to [1] in this case, and it would still work. It would be referring to the Y value instead of the X. In this case, the distinction is not important because the values are the same for X and Y; it will be important later, however.

3 Test that the two properties are joined together by "scrubbing" the Scale value up and down. (Click and drag where you see 100% next to Scale.)

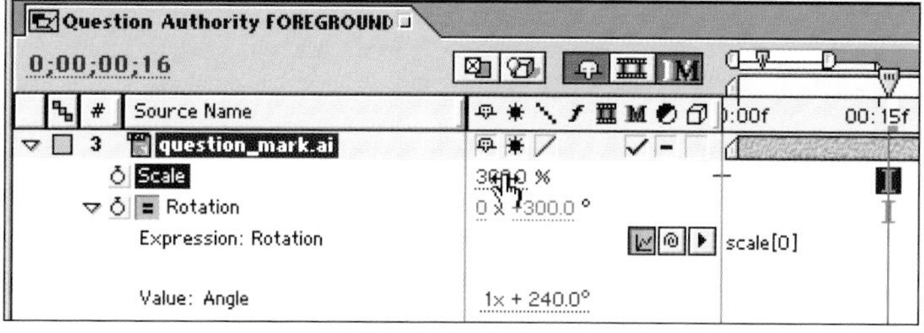

Scrubbing the Scale value with Rotation pickwhipped to it gives an immediate sense of something new and different happening.

You will see both the Scale and Rotation values change together in real time. Welcome to the power of expressions. You could, of course, set keyframes to make the values of each property the same, but you wouldn't have this kind of interactivity with the result. Expressions get you thinking about how to link things together.

Note: Expressions are not a two-way street. If you try changing the value for Rotation, which is now shown in red because it has an expression applied, you will be asked to turn off the expression. Rotation is now dependent on Scale for its value.

For your animation, you want to scale down from a huge dot to the point where the question mark just about disappears. The effect you're going for is as if the question mark were the propeller on a rubber-band-propelled airplane, and you were winding it up and then letting it go. To achieve this effect, you're going to add a few frames of what a traditional animator would call "anticipation." First, let's set up the straight scale.

4 At Frame 0, set Scale to 300% and create a keyframe by clicking on the stopwatch to the left of Scale. Then, at 1:25, change the value to 0.5%, which will automatically set another keyframe.

5 Preview this using RAM Preview. This is a good time to save your project.

You'll see that it's not too interesting yet, and the scaling starts too slowly and finishes as if it's spinning quickly down a drain. Let's improve it by adding a little anticipation.

6 Go to frame 0:12 and scale the layer up to 600%. Preview this.

You'll see that it's less like anticipation and more like a "bounce" at the top. You can fix your remaining problems by tweaking the animation curves.

7 Click on the white triangle to the left of Scale to twirl down the animation curves.

Depending on how you have your view scaled, you'll see something like what's shown in the figure. The Value keyframes will look like a lopsided pyramid, while the Velocity keyframes will be two flat lines connected by a diagonal. Even on the graph, it's a boring-looking animation.

8 You only need to make two changes: You need eases into the second and third keyframes. Select the second and third keyframes so that they are highlighted. Now select the Velocity handle to the left of the second keyframe and move it downward just a little.

You will immediately see Bezier handles spring out along the Value curve, just where you want them.

9 With the second and third keyframes still highlighted, select one of these Bezier handles and then hold down the Shift key to constrain it to the X-axis and move it as far as you can to the left. The other will follow suit. If you want to double-check that you did this right, with both frames highlighted, press Cmd/Ctrl + Shift + K to bring up the Keyframe

Note: If you have a limited amount of memory, you can do several things to get a better RAM Preview. You can set the endpoint of the composition at 2:00 (go to this frame and press the N shortcut), you can reduce the view to 50% and the resolution to half [Cmd/Ctrl + Shift + J], and you can Shift+click on the RAM Preview Play button to skip frames and play at a lower frame rate.

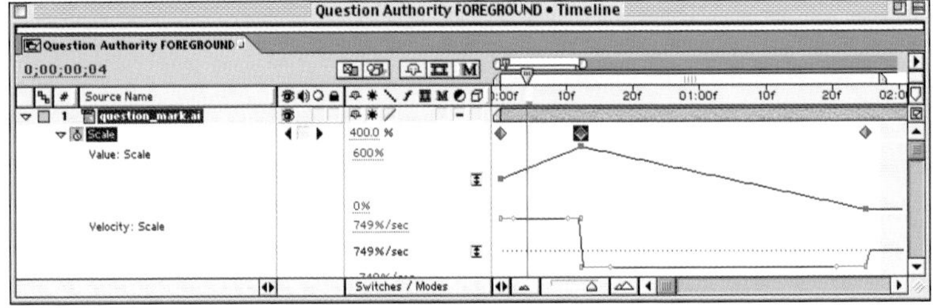

Value and Velocity curves are seen by twirling down the arrow next to the property. They are your best friends when animating with keyframes.

Velocity dialog box. Under Incoming Velocity, both the X and Y Influence settings should read 100%. All other settings (Incoming and Outgoing Dimension, Outgoing Velocity) should be at zero. If this isn't what you see, you can make the changes here.

10 Now activate Motion Blur by clicking the check box under the M icon for the layer, as well as the bigger matching M icon at the top that turns on Motion Blur for the whole composition.

The result should look something like what you see in the figure, and when you play back the animation, you should see some nice hesitation, a sudden snap, and a realistic scale into the distance.

Note in the figure that I've also clicked the little graph button among the Rotation expression controls. This reveals that the Rotation graph (in red) matches the Scale graph.

11 Twirl the white arrow at the left of the layer to close the graphs. Save your project.

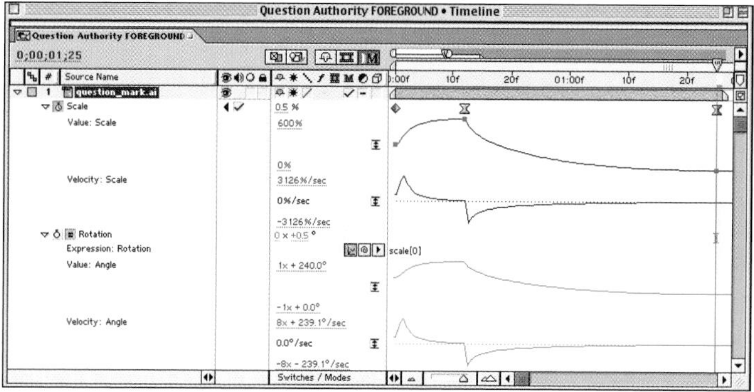

This is a much healthier looking set of curves; note that Motion Blur is checked for the layer and the composition (look for the M symbols).

Note: You could highlight these two frames and Ctrl+right-click to choose Keyframe Assistant > Easy Ease In, but that's too mild and automated a result for what you're looking for here. Similarly, with the Production Bundle, you could make the scale look more natural by highlighting the second and third frames and choosing Keyframe Assistant > Exponential Scale, but then you're stuck with a keyframe on every frame, so you can no longer manipulate it. It's better to get comfortable with doing this stuff manually; once you get a feel for it, it's nearly as simple and much more powerful.

Scaling Single Properties

Now let's go beyond what the pickwhip gives you by default by using simple multiplication to modify the values.

1 Go to 1:25 and, with the question_mark.ai layer highlighted, press Option/Alt+] to trim the layer's out point.

2 Still at 1:25, use Cmd/Ctrl+Y to create a new solid. Name it **QUESTION** and click on Make Comp Size. Click OK to close the Solid Settings dialog box.

The color doesn't matter because you're going to be replacing this solid with text.

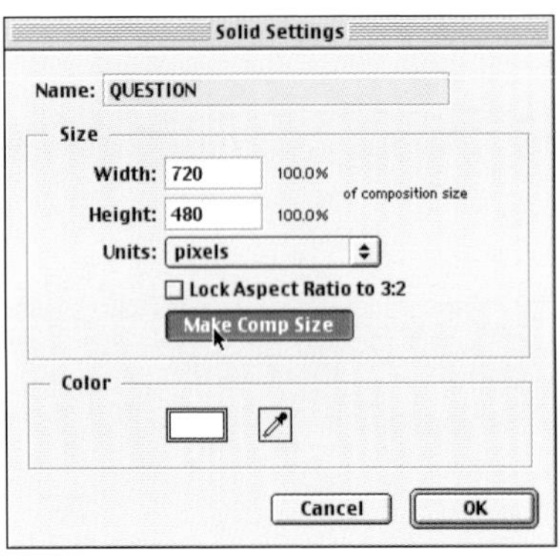

Setting a solid to match your composition.

3 Now choose the Apply Favorite option under the Effect menu to add a preset text effect. The file **PathText_ Question.ffx** is in your Projects 12–15 folder, which you should have copied to your local drive. Choose it using the dialog box that appears and click OK. If you have the Dogma font installed on your machine, go to the Dogma Projects folder inside Projects 12–15 and use that version of PathText_Question.ffx for a result that identically matches what you see in the figures.

Note: For anyone who wants to do this the hard way, if for some reason you don't want to use Apply Favorite, the settings are as follows: Choose Effect > Text > Path Text (or choose Path Text from the Effects palette). In the option window that appears, choose your font and style (Comic Sans MS Bold or Dogma Bold) and then type (in all capitals) **QUESTION** in the text box. Click OK. It's an unfortunate fact about Path Text that the default settings always look gnarly. Somewhere in Seattle there must be an engineer who loves red curvy text. Let's fix the settings. In the Effect Controls window, under Path Options, click the pull-down menu under Shape Type and choose Line. Under Fill and Stroke, click the Eyedropper for Fill Color and then click in the white box just below it to sample the white color reserved for Stroke (which isn't active). Whew—that gets the red out! Under Character, choose a Size of 60. Under Paragraph, make the Alignment setting Center.

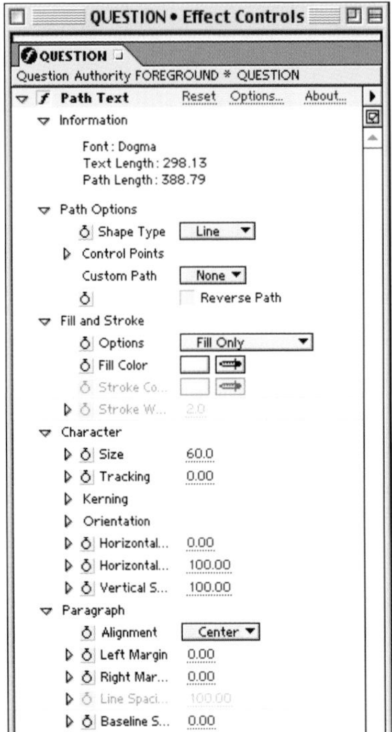

These are the correct Path Text settings.

4 Back under Character, you're going to add an expression to Tracking, so Ctrl+right-click on it and choose Reveal in Timeline from the context menu. Now, in the Timeline window, next to Tracking (which has just appeared) Option/Alt+click the stopwatch to add an expression.

The effect you're going for is this: Out of the question mark you just scaled down, you want to scale up the word "question." But rather than just do a boring old scale up, let's tie the Scale value to both the Rotation and the Text Tracking value.

5 With the QUESTION layer highlighted, press EE (press the E key twice) to reveal just the property containing the expression and then press Shift+S to add the Scale property. Click on the pickwhip for Tracking, drag it to Scale, and then let go. The whip cracks and scale[0] is entered in the text window. Click outside the highlighted text, and you'll see that tracking is now set to 100.

Now set some keyframes for scale.

6 At 2:15, click the stopwatch icon for Scale to add a keyframe with Scale at 100%. Then, at 3:03, set Scale to 250%. Now go back to 1:25 and set Scale to 1%. Highlight the first two Scale keyframes (at 1:25 and 2:15) by selecting one and Shift+selecting the other. Now Ctrl+right-click one of these highlighted frames to bring up the context menu and choose Keyframe Assistant > Easy Ease. Preview this either by dragging the time cursor along the Timeline or with a RAM Preview.

7 Save your project before moving on.

The basic effect is there, but the text is tracking so much at 100 that it goes right off the layer. You'll fix this by scaling it proportionally.

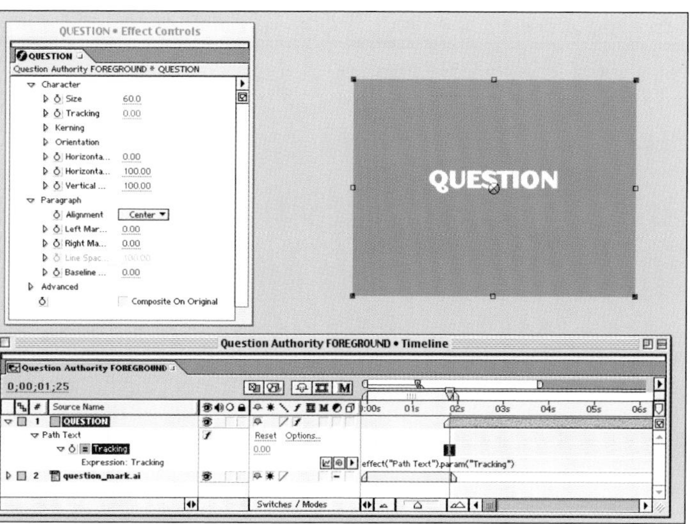

Note: The text that appears by default, effect("Path Text").param(21), is really no more complicated than a web address. In the first part, the effect is named inside quotation marks so that expressions know to look for that literal text. Then, just as with a web site, there is a dot, which tells expressions to look inside the Path Text effect, and param(21), which is an accurate if slightly obscure way to name the Tracking control.

You can replace the digits 21 with the word "Tracking" (including quotation marks and still surrounded by parentheses) in cases in which the clarity is helpful. Try it if you like and then click outside the text area or press Enter before moving on.

param("Tracking") is a parameter within effect("Path Text"), separated by a single dot.

8 Highlight the expressions text for Tracking and click at the very end of the line. Type ***.3** to make the line read scale[0]*.3. Note that * means "times" (multiply) and that you don't have to put a zero before .3. Press Enter to activate the expression.

You're telling Tracking to take 3/10 (.3) of the value of Scale. There is a [0] after "scale" because Scale is an effect with two parameters, X and Y scale, and the [0] tells expressions to use the first (X) value. (You'll look more closely at parameters in the next project.)

This is cool, but you need some rotation to get the effect of the text spinning out of the question mark.

10 Press Shift+R to reveal Rotation. Highlight it and Option/Alt + Shift + = to add another expression. With the text still highlighted, drag the pickwhip to Scale to get scale[0] again. Click at the end of the line and type in ***-3.6** to get a more dramatic spin (one full 360-degree revolution counterclockwise for 100 degrees of scaling). Press Enter to activate the expression.

The negative number puts it in the direction you want (counterclockwise), matching the direction of the previous layer. Okay, but you're probably wondering why you're using expressions to do this, besides as a pedagogical device. The key thing you've done here is link three properties to a single ease curve so that the text animates as one organic whole. Any change you made to your single set of keyframes (or by rubbing the text of that Scale value) is picked up proportionally by the properties linked to Scale. This not only simplifies making any changes, it leads to a graceful result.

Note: You could get nearly the same result by adding **/3.333** to the line (dividing by 3 1/3). For whatever reason, probably simplicity, it is more normal to multiply by a decimal than to divide, but as you'll recall from those early math days, multiplication and division are interchangeable.

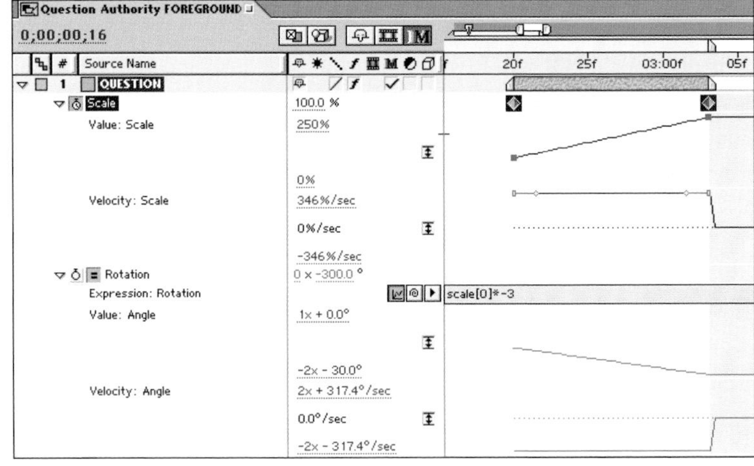

Activating the expressions graphs clearly shows the result of inverted scaling of a value.

11 Go ahead and activate the graphs for the two properties with expressions (by clicking on the Graph button next to the pickwhip). You'll see that Tracking looks like a more subdued version of Scale, while Rotation shows the inverse graph (as shown).

12 Preview the animation.

If you turn on Motion Blur (as noted earlier), it looks pretty slick.

13 Save the project here.

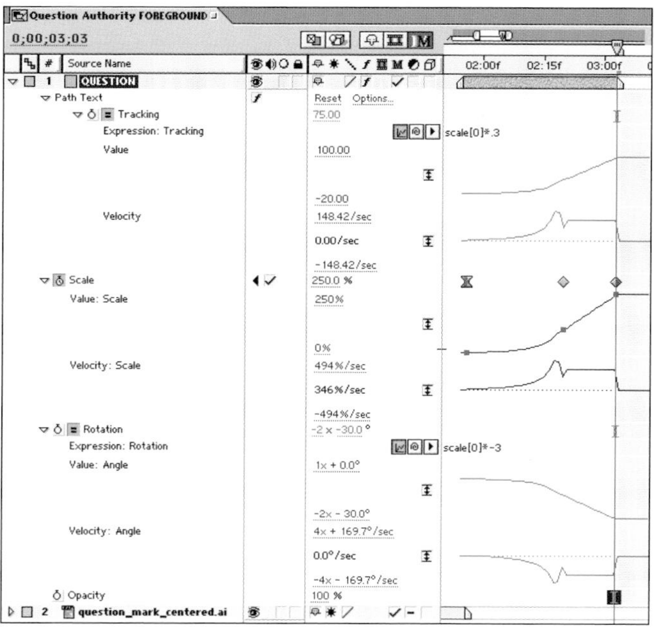

Scale, Rotation, and Tracking all animate together dynamically.

Creating the Exploding Text Effect

You have one more effect to add: that of the text flying apart as you scale up from 100%.

1 Go to that keyframe (at 2:20) and, in your Effect Controls window, find Baseline Jitter Max under Advanced > Jitter Settings. Click on the stopwatch by Baseline Jitter Max to set a keyframe of 0 here at 2:20.

2 Now, if your Scale keyframes are still revealed in the Timeline window, use the K key to skip ahead to the final Scale keyframe at 3:03. The J and K keys enable you to skip back and forth between any keyframes or markers that are revealed on the Timeline. Set the Baseline Jitter Max value at 3:03 to 1500. This sets a keyframe and makes each individual character fly far off its initial position over time.

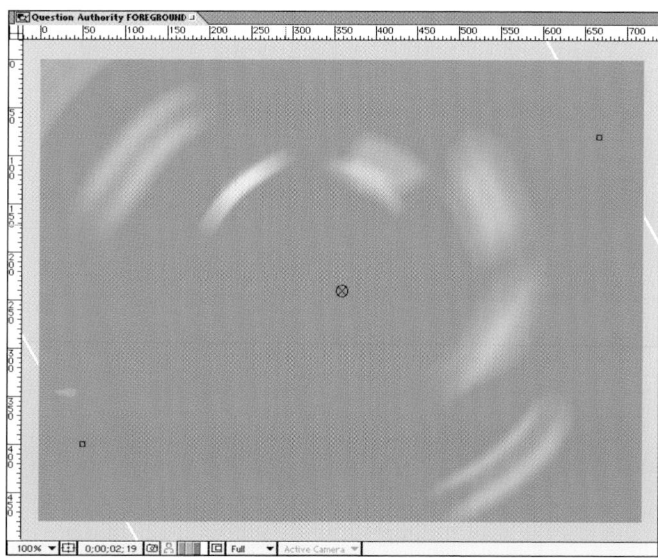

Our QUESTION flies apart.

3. RAM Preview from 0:00 to 3:02 to see your full animation in action. (For more on RAM Preview, see the Note in the "Real-World Pickwhip" section earlier in this project.)

4. After it's imported, highlight the clip in the Project window and press Cmd/Ctrl+F to bring up the Interpret Footage dialog box. At the bottom, you'll see Loop 1 Times. Change the 1 to a 4 to span the 12-second clip (although, at this point, you're only previewing the first 3 seconds of it). Click OK.

5. Drag the LIL124.mov clip to the bottom layer of the composition, also starting at 0:00.

6. Now be sure to extend the Layer Duration bar so that it spans the length of the composition (or at least the length of your work area for what you've animated so far) to 3:02.

7. Do you want sound, too? Import the file **Question_Authority.mp3** from the Footage folder and drop it in at 0:00. It has been designed by Dave Levison (**www.h-machine.com**) to fit this animation, the first quarter of which you have completed. You'll have to complete the next three projects to make full use of the audio.

8. Save the project. You can render it out by pressing Cmd/Ctrl+M, or you can wait until you've completed this four-project grouping. (You'll be continuing it in the next three projects.)

There you have it. You now know how to set expressions and make them work for animation tasks. If this has whetted your appetite for more, read on. You'll expand greatly on what you've seen here in the next few projects.

Note: If you'd like a preview of how this section of the animation will look at the end of Project 15, "Animating Without Keyframes" (and how it looks in the opening figure of this project), move the **LIL124.mov** file from the Footage folder of this project on the accompanying CD-ROM to your drive (the same folder as this project) and import it into After Effects.

Modifications

You've now become comfortable with dragging the pickwhip from one Transform value to another, as well as to and from Effect values. You even know how to use simple multiplication to offset or scale the relationship. This is the primary use of expressions.

Now let's explore the range of values you can link in this manner. Start a new composition, add a single solid to it, twirl down the white arrow next to the layer name in the Timeline window, and then twirl down the white arrow next to Transform. These are basic properties you can try linking together. Use the +, -, and * operators to do simple scaling or offset of values.

Notice that some Transform properties have two values but others have one. This project touched on parameters, and you'll look at them more closely in the next project. For now, notice that if you set an expression for Rotation and pickwhip to Position, After Effects will add a [0] after "position" to take its first (X position) value, as you did in the preceding exercises. But note that if you instead drag to the second value of Position, After Effects will add a [1] because you've chosen the Y value.

Now try setting the expression on Anchor Point and linking to Rotation. After Effects will automatically enter [rotation, rotation] because Anchor Point is a two-dimensional property; brackets are used in expressions script to enclose multiple parameters of a single property. Turn on 3D for that layer and the fun increases. Now certain properties actually have three dimensions, which would be numbered by expressions (in order) [0], [1], and [2], corresponding to X, Y, and Z values.

One error that you might encounter as you edit your expressions reads, "expression result must be of dimension 2, not 1," or conversely, "expression result must be of dimension 1, not 2."

After Effects warning: expression result must be of dimension 1, not 2.
Error occured at line 1.
Expression disabled.
OK
After Effects warning: expression result must be of dimension 2, not 1.
Error occured at line 1.
Expression disabled.
OK

Two variations on a very common expressions error.

In the first case, After Effects is looking for the result to be two values, typically contained in brackets and separated by a comma, like [360, 240] or [rotation, rotation] or even "scale," a property that refers back to two values.

The second case is the opposite. After Effects is getting two values but wants just one. This one number could be 16 or rotation*5/3.6 or position[1], all of which denote a single value. You'll also have trouble if you simply try to say position*2. Try it and you'll get an error saying "invalid numeric result (divide by zero?)" This is because JavaScript—and thus After Effects—won't use ordinary math operators (+, -, *, /) on a vector, which is the name for any property with two values. You'll deal with this in the next project.

Finally, here's an experiment with linking properties from different layers, or even from different compositions, using the pickwhip. A typical expression resulting from such an arrangement would look like this:

```
this_comp.layer("Solid 1").opacity
```

Although the preceding appears more unwieldy than the following:

```
opacity
```

It's really just saying "look for the value of opacity of Solid 1 in this composition," with dots separating the composition, the layer, and the property in order from most global (composition) to most local (property). Try a few of these and look at each component separated by dots. You'll soon be able to identify these as easily as web addresses or file locations.

USING ARRAYS, MATH, AND LOOPS IN EXPRESSIONS

"And once again, where does it rain?"

"On the plain, on the plain."

"And where the devil is that soggy plain?"

"In Spain, in Spain."

—HENRY HIGGINS AND ELIZA DOOLITTLE, *MY FAIR LADY*

Extending Expressions

In the preceding project, you worked on getting more comfortable with expressions in After Effects and how they work at a basic level—using expressions to link a single property to another. Now you're going to try some more advanced uses for expressions that you'll use a lot of the time: linking vectors and arrays (which are properties with two or more values together), using built-in methods (commands that do something automatically like generate a random value), using simple math in more creative ways, and looping a set of keyframes (which in version 5.5 is easily possible with expressions).

Project 13

Using Arrays, Math, and Loops in Expressions

by Mark Christiansen

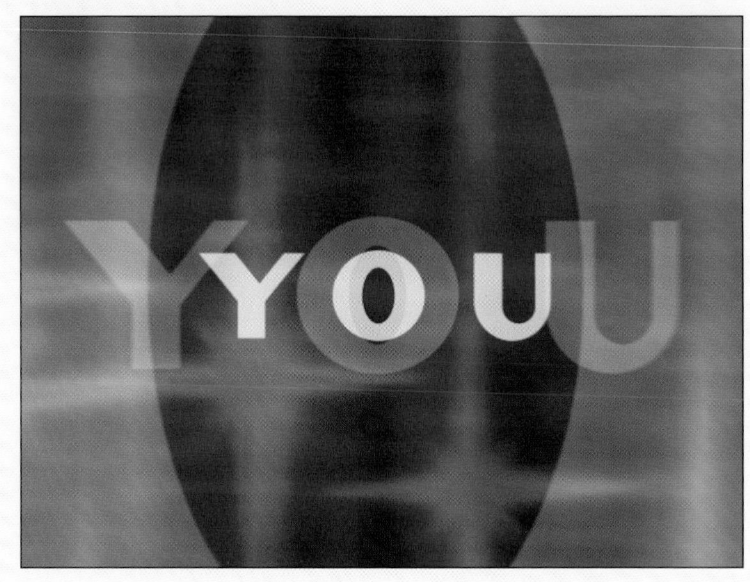

How It Works

To complete the next few seconds of foreground text animation for the Question Authority piece, you'll still use the pickwhip for setup, but you will rely on it less and less for the final result as you become more comfortable adding your own variations to expressions. Every animation that you add will have at least one expression applied to it.

Getting Started

You can continue with the project file from the preceding project, or you can copy the Projects 12–15 folder to your hard drive and open **CH13_INITIAL.aep**, which contains all of the Illustrator source files you'll be using for this project as well as the animation you did in Project 12, "Elementary Expressions." If you are continuing with your previous animation file, copy **question.ai** and **you.ai** from the Footage folder within the Projects 12–15 source files folder, import them into your project, and then save. Also, you should probably turn off the **LIL124.mov** clip, if you added it to your composition at the end of the last project, to speed previews and have your work look like what you see in this project's figures.

If you own the font Dogma from Emigré, you can install that font (if you haven't done so already), which was originally used to do all of the type in Chapters 12–15. You can find the project files that use this font in the Dogma Projects folder within the Projects 12–15 main folder. If you don't have the font, don't worry, the main project files use the Comic Sans MS font found on most Macs and PCs.

STARTING THE PROJECT

In previous versions of After Effects, the only way to generate random values for an animation was to apply The Wiggler, an effect that is based on a particular algorithm and that generates many extra keyframes (one per frame, thus you can't rework the original animation very easily after it's applied). With expressions, you not only have more than one type of random value generation available, there is no need for keyframes, making the whole process much more flexible. You can change your mind about overall timing as much as you like.

1. Save your newly prepared project (with whatever name you like) on your local drive (preferably in the same folder as the other source files).

2. With the Question Authority FOREGROUND composition open, go to 3:10 and add the you.ai footage item to the composition beginning at that frame. Activate High Quality and then the Collapse Transformations switch for that layer. Trim the layer's out point to make its duration just 10 frames, from 3:10 to 3:20, by pressing Option/Alt+] at 3:20.

   Note: You're using an Illustrator file here because you're going to be scaling this text above its initial size, and the continuous rasterization of Illustrator vectors provided by the Collapse Transformations feature will keep the text looking clean.

3. With this new layer highlighted, press S to bring up the Scale property. Option/Alt+click its stopwatch to add a Scale expression.

4. With the Expression window highlighted, type in **random** to replace the scale text. Press Enter (not Return) to enter the expression.

   What happened? You just generated an error, which reads, "Object of type Function found where a Number, Array, or Property is needed."

   You're going to delve into this a little before moving on because generating errors and understanding them is part of creating more advanced expressions. Why did you get this error, when it seems like just saying "random" should be enough to generate some random values?

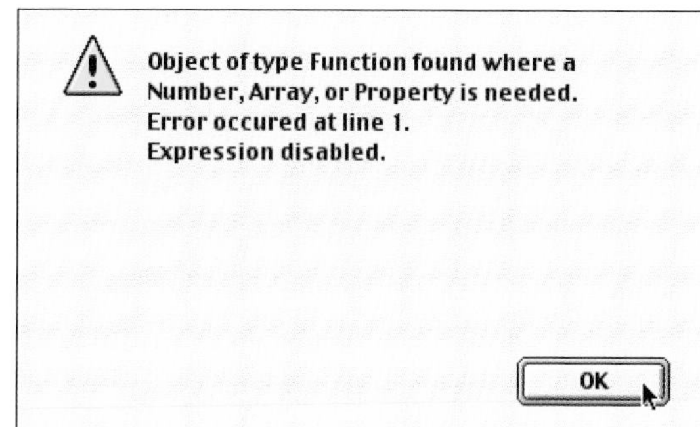

The key line of this error is "Number, Array, or Property is needed."

5 Click OK to close the error message. Highlight the text and click on the black triangular arrow just to the left of the expressions text area.

This is a pop-up window showing expressions keywords organized hierarchically. (For a better understanding of how they're organized, see Appendix D, "Expressions Explained.")

6 In the pop-up, choose random Numbers. Under that submenu, you will see one clue: "random" is listed three times, and in each case, it is followed by parentheses, which means that random is a method, a function that wants to be followed by arguments. *Method* is the correct term for a function that is built-in and predefined with a keyword in After Effects.

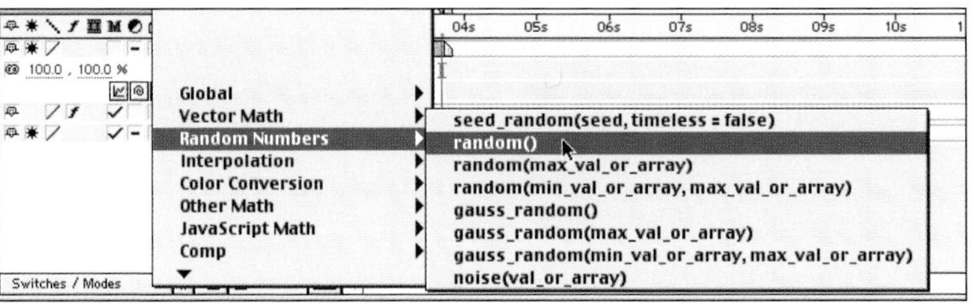

All of the method names under Random Numbers are followed by parentheses containing hints as to which arguments to use.

So now you add arguments. You probably think of "arguments" as something to avoid in life. I know I do. In the case of expressions, an argument is a parameter to a method like random().

A Note on Terminology: There are two types of keywords in the expressions pop-up menus: methods and attributes. Think of them like verbs and nouns: Methods *do* things (using whatever follows them in parentheses), whereas attributes *are* things.

That's all you need to know, but here's an added bonus: Look through the menus and you'll see that the majority of keywords are attributes (the ones with no arguments in parentheses at the end). This means they only can represent a number; they don't *do* anything. So if you've ever looked at those menus and worried that you'll never understand what all those words do, remember that only the methods *do* anything; the attributes only stand in for some value.

So how do you know what arguments to add? When you're starting out, the best way is to look in the manual or the online documentation under the section titled "After Effects Expression Language Guide." However, in After Effects 5.5, hints have been added to the method defaults regarding what belongs in the parentheses, and these might be enough to get you started. Let's take a look at the three options that random gives you and what the User Guide has to say about them:

- **Menu item: random()**
  The User Guide says: "***Number*** **random()**. The resulting value is a random number between 0 and 1."
- **Menu item: random(max_val_or_array)**
  The User Guide says: "***Number*** **random(max)** {max is a number}. The resulting value is a number between 0 and max, and is the same dimension as max."
- **Menu item: random(min_val_or_array, max_val_or_array)**
  The User Guide says: "***Number*** **random(min, max)** {min and max are numbers}. The resulting value is a number between min and max."

This isn't too hard to understand. You can do the following:

- Leave the argument space (between parentheses) empty, and it will be assumed that you want a random number between 0 and 1.
- Use one argument (a number), and the minimum will still default to zero, but the maximum will be whatever you set.
- Use two numbers, separated by a comma, to set both the minimum and maximum numbers.

The last option is the one you want in this case. Choose it from the menu.

7 Highlight the stand-in text between the parentheses, *min_val_or_array, max_val_or_array*, with values of 100 and 400, as follows:

Random(100, 400)

8 Press Enter (not Return) to activate the expression.

Now what error did you get?

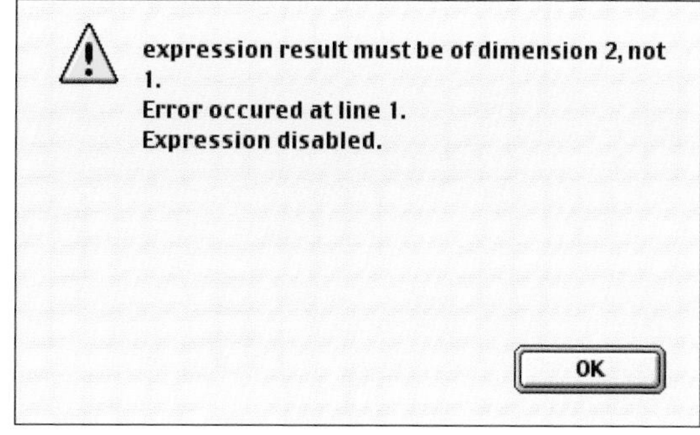
expression result must be of dimension 2, not 1.
Error occured at line 1.
Expression disabled.
OK

The expression typed has generated the error seen in the dialog box.

"Expression result must be of dimension 2, not 1" is an error you might see often, so I'm having you generate it here so that you can get comfortable with it. It reminds you that Scale is a two-dimensional property (containing both X and Y values), which means your final result must appear in expressions as an array.

As you saw in the last project, an array in expressions is a series of numbers (two or more) enclosed by brackets ([ ]) and separated by commas. So [100, 100] would describe a layer's default scale at 100%, just as [360, 240, 0] would describe its default 3D position (in this composition, because it's 720×480) and [0, 0, 255, 128] would describe a pure blue color with a 50% alpha channel (the values corresponding to

RGBA or red, green, blue, and alpha). Even though in this case you want to scale your text uniformly, with the same value for X and Y, you have to return your numbers as an array within the expression text.

To correct this error, it becomes useful to use a variable; I'll explain why after you're done.

9 Place your expressions cursor at the very beginning of the line and type **xy** = before random(100, 400), as follows:

xy = random(100, 400)

With this expression, you still get the same error when clicking outside the text area because you're not quite done yet. You've set your expression but haven't applied it to anything.

10 At the end of the line, add a semicolon (;) because you want to start a statement in a new line, separate from the variable. Press the Return key (or the Enter key with the carriage return symbol under it in Windows) to create a new line and then type in **[xy, xy]**, which is an array (because it appears in brackets) telling Scale to use xy for both of its values.

If you didn't use a variable, the single line expression would read as follows:

[random(100,400), random(100,400)]

The result would be separate, individually randomized numbers for x and y, leading to disproportionate scaling. The variable exists, in this case, to ensure that the aspect ratio is maintained as the layer is randomly scaled.

11 Set a work area and preview this short animation.

You'll see that the text scales up and down in a jittery, random manner but uses the same values for x and y, maintaining the aspect ratio of the layer. It also generates only values between 100 and 400, as determined by the argument used.

Note: xy is a variable. What does that mean? Think back to high school Algebra class (assuming you're not there now). You're 14 years old, and you encounter a problem like this:

You have a lemonade stand. Each pitcher contains 8 glasses of lemonade. How many pitchers of lemonade will you need to serve 40 glasses? 56 glasses? 104 glasses?

Now, you realize that you solve this problem by dividing the number of glasses by 8, which is always the number of glasses in a pitcher, but the problem gives you three different total numbers of glasses resulting in three different numbers of pitchers. That means the number of glasses and the number of pitchers are both variables in the language of expressions logic.

If you wanted to make a formula to solve this problem in plain English, you would write it like this:

Pitchers needed = number of glasses × 8

This is essentially how you would write it in After Effects, with a couple of syntactical changes: You use * rather than × to do multiplication, and you cannot have spaces within variable names like "Pitchers needed." "Syntax" just means "the way you say (and spell) it."

In the following expression:

xy = random(100, 400)

I have spaces around the = sign and after the comma, but After Effects ignores these. However, it is imperative *not* to have a space between x and y because it is a variable name, and a variable name cannot have spaces.

12 Turn on Motion Blur by checking the Motion Blur switch for this layer as well as the Enable Motion Blur switch at the top of the Timeline window for a nice effect.

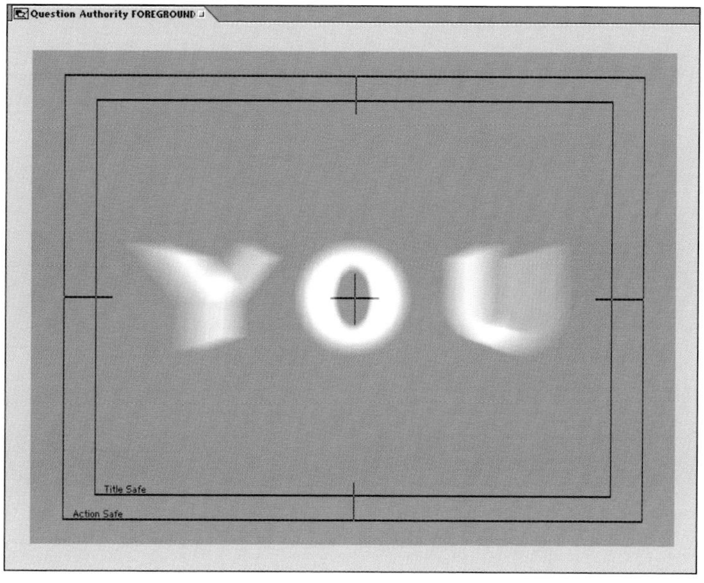

With Motion Blur active, the jitteriness of the scaling becomes quite nice to look at.

Note: Each time you set up this project and choose Random, you will get a different set of values, but after you have set this expression, the values won't change each time you open and close the project or preview the animation. The same random values will appear for this layer at a given time until you change its arguments. But try duplicating the layer and you'll see different results in the duplicate because the random seed varies with the layer number.

You'll revisit randomization and its many flavors more thoroughly in the next project.

Multiple Layer Offset

Now you're going to see what happens when you link the values of multiple layers with expressions. You'll even play around with some math methods in a very amateurish, undisciplined way (just to comfort those of you who shudder at learning any actual math).

1 Add another layer of the you.ai footage to the composition at 3:26. Set the end of this layer to 5:20 by going to that frame and pressing Option/Alt+]. Turn on Best Quality and Collapse Transformations for the layer. Once again, you'll be scaling above 100%.

2 Set two keyframes for Scale: On the first frame (3:26), set scale to 50% and create a keyframe (by clicking the stopwatch next to Scale). On the last frame of the layer (5:20), set scale to 200% (which automatically adds a keyframe).

This time you're going to make the end animation look like the rebel fleet zooming out of hyperspace in *Return of the Jedi*. (Trust me on this if you have no idea what I'm talking about.)

Tip: To skip quickly to a layer's in point, select the layer and press I; press O for the out point.

3 Once again, the fastest way to get the Bezier curve you want is to twirl down the arrow next to Scale, select the keyframe at 5:20, and below it "disrupt" (my term) the Velocity: Scale handle associated with that keyframe (on the lower of the two graphs). By "disrupt" I mean move it up or down a little, and a Bezier handle appears above, along the Value: Scale graph.

4 Click the Value: Scale handle, hold down Shift, and drag the handle to the left as far as it will go (while still holding Shift to force it to align with the end value).

Your curve should look roughly like the figure when the Timeline view is zoomed out all the way (so that you see the entire duration of the composition on the Timeline).

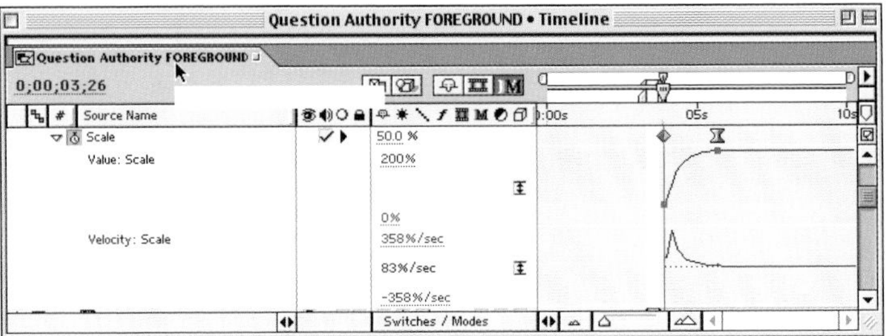

The velocity curve spikes early and then eases.

5 Highlight the name of this layer by clicking on it in the Timeline, press Return, and rename the layer **youscale**. Change its Opacity value to 33%.

You want it to seem like an "echo" of the source. You're going to create two duplicates of this layer that scale geometrically relative to the source. In other words, by using the square and square root of the existing keyframe values, you'll get two other layers to scale to a related but nonproportional amount. The end effect is sort of like time-lapse footage of a flower opening. (Again, I did not ingest illicit substances while writing this project; trust me on this.)

6 Make one duplicate of the youscale layer you animated above. With the youscale layer highlighted, press Cmd/Ctrl+D to duplicate it and then press Return to highlight the name field of the duplicate. Rename it **youroot** and press Return again.

7 Highlight both youscale and youroot and press S to bring up Scale keyframes for both.

You have both open because you're going to use the pickwhip in a moment to link the two.

Note: Pressing U for "überkey" would have worked here, too, because the überkey brings up all properties with a keyframe or expression, and the only keyframes you have on these layers are for Scale.

8 With Scale highlighted under the youroot layer option, click the Scale stopwatch to add an expression.

The text in the Expression window is now highlighted.

9 Replace the text in the Expression window with a variable; call it **xyscale**.

Now you need to define the variable.

10 After xyscale, type in = , as follows:

xyscale =

This tells After Effects that this is a variable. Note that the spaces around the = sign are optional, but it can be good practice to put them in if it avoids a jumble of text.

11 With the cursor still blinking at the end of the line that now reads **xyscale =**, click on the black triangle next to the pickwhip to bring up a menu of expressions keywords. Under JavaScript Math, choose Math.sqrt(val).

This is a method that calculates the square root of the value described within its parentheses. Remember that (val) is there as a placeholder to remind you that you have to assign arguments to this method.

12 Highlight just the placeholder val and then click and drag the pickwhip down to the X value Scale line under youscale to use those keyframes as source. You'll know you've hit X scale when you see a highlight line around the first number 200%.

Note: If you got an error here, it's probably because you pickwhipped to Scale instead of just its X value, which gives you both X and Y scale parameters when square root can only handle one at a time. You could just as easily use the Y scale—the two values are identical—but for consistency in a case like this, you use the first value.

Isn't that more pleasant than trying to type in the path to that layer and property and forgetting the odd period or bracket?

13 Add a semicolon to end that line and then press Return to add a new line to your expression. Here's what you have at this point:

xy = this_comp.layer("youscale").scale[0];

If you click outside the text window, you're going to get an error stating that "the result must be of dimension 2, not 1" because all you've done is define a variable. Let's fix that.

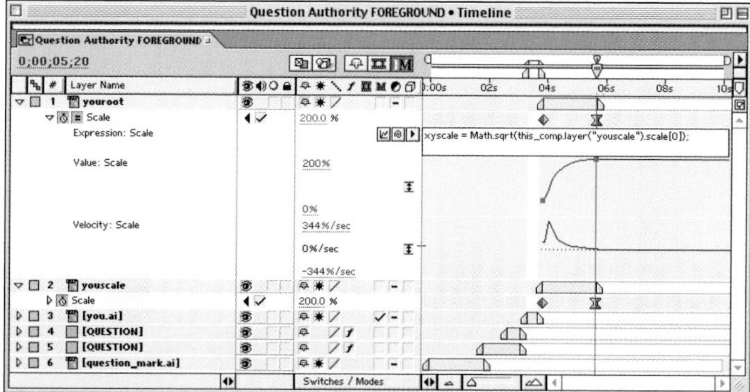

The layer youroot contains scale keyframes, but they'll be ignored as soon as you've completed your expression.

14 On the new line, type the following:

[xyscale, xyscale]

On the new line then press the Enter key or click outside the expressions text on the new line.

Where's the layer?

15 Go to frame 5:20 and look at the Scale value (in red, because the expression is applied) for Scale of youroot.

This highest end value is only 14.1, the square root of 200. Whoops! Luckily, because you've set a variable, all you have to do is increase this to an acceptable value. I don't know much about math, so I say let's multiply the square root and the source together to get a result that scales more than the source but that scales in geometric proportion.

16 Click twice at the beginning of the expression text and press Return to add a new line at the top. On this line, type the following:

xy =

Then drag the pickwhip to the X Scale value under the yousource layer again, followed by a semicolon, giving you the following:

xy = this_comp.layer("youscale").scale[0];

Now just add ***xy** at the end of your final line and you're set.

Note: Click the black triangle next to the pickwhip again; under Vector Math, you'll see **mul(** along with other math commands that apply to a vector, which in this case means the same as an array (as previously defined). Keep these commands firmly in mind when you need to scale any kind of array (and you will) and remember the format: contained within parenthesis, the components separated by commas—the standard format of a method as you learned earlier.

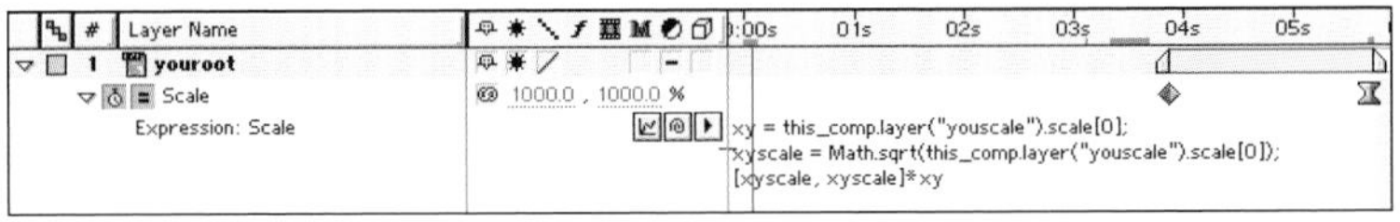

The Scale expression is complete.

Note to 5.0 Users: If you try this final step, you'll get an error about an "invalid numerical result."

In JavaScript 1.2—and therefore in After Effects 5.0 (which adheres more strictly to the rules of JavaScript 1.2)—the * symbol can be used for single values only, something that was changed for 5.5. To multiply an array in 5.0, you need to use mul and phrase the expression differently, as follows:

mul([xyscale, xyscale], xy)

The full expression for 5.0 users now looks like this:

xy = this_comp.layer("youscale").scale[0]

xyscale = Math.sqrt(xy);

mul([xyscale, xyscale], xy)

17 Duplicate your youroot layer (Cmd/Ctrl+D again) and rename it **youmul**. Opacity should still be set at 33% (having been copied from a layer with that setting). You can check this by pressing T (or UU—the U key twice) to reveal all changed properties.

You're going to change the expression so that it multiplies the source value by one-hundredth of itself. Again, your goal is to have a geometric (rather than a linear) relationship between the values, and using the square, like using the square root, is a prime way to do this.

You might already have an idea of how to do this by changing one line of the expression. Feel free to try this before doing the following; with expressions, you can learn from mistakes.

18 With the layer highlighted, press S to reveal Scale (if it's not already revealed) and twirl down the white left arrow to view the expression that copied over with the layer. Change the second line by removing **Math.sqrt** and adding **/100** at the end of that line, followed by the semicolon.

```
xy = this_comp.layer("youscale").scale[0]
xyscale = xy/100;
mul([xyscale, xyscale], xy)
```

The graphs look like they do in the accompanying image: similar in shape, very different in scale.

Note: Let me stress again that I'm no mathematician (just in case that's not clear from these crude equations). I knew that using the square of the source and then scaling it to the proper range would give me the result I was after.

One final bit of housekeeping before you move on to the next animation: I want all of these "you" layers to fade out together.

Note: Can you see a way to simplify this further? How about using the first variable in the square root method of the second, like this:

```
xy = this_comp.layer("youscale").scale[0];
xyscale = Math.sqrt(xy);
mul([xyscale, xyscale], xy)
```

This is easier to look at and understand than the alternative of using no variables or line breaks, as in the following mess:

```
mul([Math.sqrt(this_comp.layer("youscale").scale[0]),
➥Math.sqrt(this_comp.layer("youscale").scale[0])],
➥this_comp.layer("youscale").scale[0])
```

Painful to look at, isn't it? Strictly speaking, the variables you set are in fact literals, which are the opposite of variables in that they don't vary; "variable" is often used as a generic term for symbols that stand for a value. You are never obligated to use literals to make an expression work, but they help keep things tidy, economical, and easy to decipher.

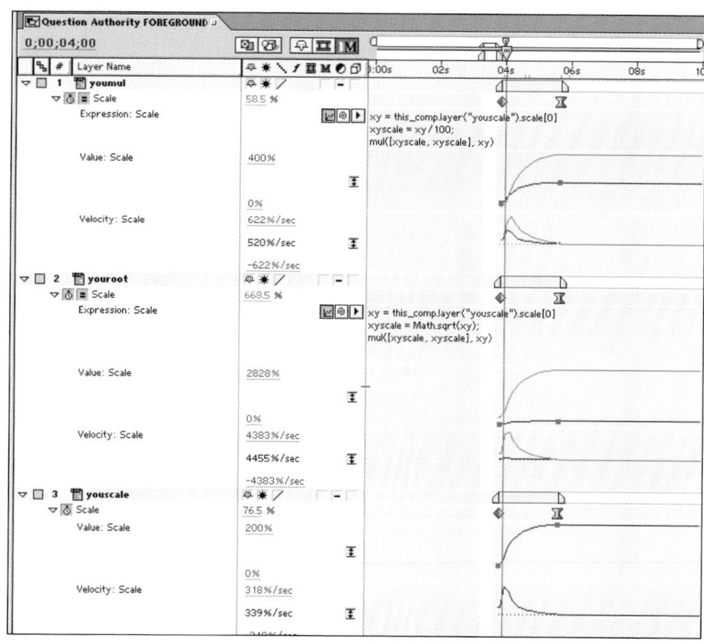

In red, you see the bottom curves replicated in the upper two layers; in black, you see that they've been scaled down in each.

19 Select all three layers and precompose them by pressing Cmd/Ctrl + Shift + C. Name the new composition **You x 3** in the Precompose dialog box and click OK to close. Keyframe this layer's Opacity to fade from 100% at 4:10 to 0% at 5:00. Changing the Opacity will enhance the feeling of echoing.

20 Activate the Collapse Transformations switch for this new composition layer so that all of your scaling stays clean and continuously rasterized.

21 To keep your layers tidy, at 5:00, you can trim the layer's out point by pressing Option/Alt+] at that frame.

Looping

One thing that's always been a challenge in After Effects is getting an animation to loop; until version 5.5, there's been no automated way to loop keyframes in a composition. Thanks to expressions, it doesn't have to be like this.

1 At 5:10, drag the question_mark_centered.ai footage item into the Timeline window, creating a new layer that you can rename **question loop** to distinguish it from the initial layer. Place this layer at the top of the layer stack. You're going to make this layer rotate endlessly.

You want the question mark to ease into its top and bottom positions. Let's start by setting up the basic, three-keyframe animation, which you'll then loop.

Note: If you just wanted this question mark to rotate around and around, you'd have a few different options. You could just set a start and end rotation keyframe for the layer with a difference of several revolutions between them, or you could set an expression that would tie the rotation values to time. For example, time*360 would cause the layer to rotate once per second.

2 At the first frame of the layer, 5:10, with the layer highlighted, press R and then click the stopwatch by Rotation to set a Rotation keyframe to the default value, 0 rotations plus 0.0 degrees.

3 Skip ahead 10 frames by pressing Shift+PgDn. Change the value to 180 degrees, which automatically sets a keyframe. Go another 10 frames forward and set another keyframe by changing the value to 360 degrees, which After Effects will translate to 1 revolution and 0.0 degrees.

4 Now add an ease into the second and third by highlighting them, Option/right-clicking, and then choosing Keyframe Assistant > Easy Ease from the context menu.

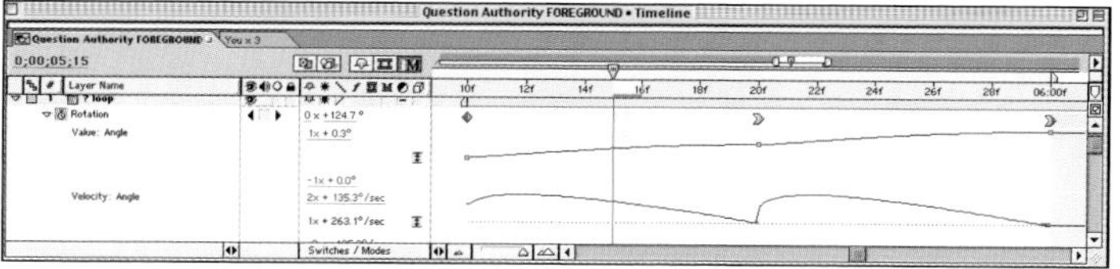

A set of eases.

5 Highlight Rotation for this layer and Option+click the stopwatch to add an expression. From the Expressions menu, choose Property > loop_out(type = cycle", num_keyframes = 0) to replace the default rotation expression. Now highlight the number 0 that currently defines num_keyframes and change it to a 3. The final expression reads as follows:

loop_out(type = "cycle", num_keyframes = 3)

This expression is pretty simple to understand. You have chosen to cycle the three keyframes from the last of these keyframes to the out point of the layer.

Roll past your final keyframe and you'll see that these keyframes keep looping. Magic? Why yes, the magic of expressions.

6 To complete this layer's animation, fade Opacity from 50% at 6:20 (making all previous frames play at 50% Opacity) to 0% 10 frames later at 7:00.

Note to 5.0 Users: You've just found a major reason to upgrade to 5.5, as looping in 5.0 has to be done with a rather complicated three-line expression, as follows. Replace the highlighted expression "rotation" with the following:

looplength = 20;

startframe = 5.33;

rotation.value_at_time((time % (this_comp.frame_duration ➥*looplength)) + startframe)

This text is saved on the accompanying CD-ROM as **5.0_loop.txt** in the _AEv5_projects folder within the Projects 12–15 folder; it includes comments (after the // symbol on each line) for easier reuse.

There's a full explanation of this expression in the "Modifications" section later in this project. For now, I consider this expression fairly advanced and don't want to confuse you by dissecting it in the interest of time. You're in the home stretch of this project.

7 To complete this project, you'll set some more loops to overlay a text effect on the question mark loop. Go to frame 5:10 (the in point of your question loop layer) and create two solids at composition size (color doesn't matter). Name one **do** and the other **you** and set the end of both layers at 6:20 (to match the end of the question loop layer).

8 Setting the Path Text effect is tedious, so just like Julia Child, you'll pull a prebaked effect out of the oven for each layer. Choose the do layer, choose Effect > Apply Favorite, and then choose **text_do_5.5.ffx** from the Projects 12–15 folder on the accompanying CD-ROM or your local drive. Now choose the you layer and apply the text_you_5.5.ffx favorite. If you have Dogma installed, use the favorites with the same names from the Dogma Projects folder.

If you highlight these two layers and press U, you'll see that there are keyframes and your loop effect applied to text tracking; the text tracks in and out from a 15 to a –50 value and back every 1/3 of a second, with eases. Now you'll animate the position along the X-axis so that the two words appear to bounce in and out in tandem.

9 With the do layer highlighted, press P to reveal the Position controls. At 5:10, set the Position value to 160, 280 and click the stopwatch to set a keyframe there. Highlight this keyframe, go to 6:00, and copy and paste it into place at that frame. Now go back 10 frames to 5:20 and set the position value to 560, 280 (moving it right on the X-axis).

10 Highlight all the Position keyframes of the do layer by clicking on the word "Position." Now Ctrl/right-click on one of the highlighted keyframes to bring up the context menu and choose Keyframe Assistant > Easy Ease (which is applied to all three keyframes).

11 With the you layer highlighted, you'll undertake the same steps but with different settings. Press P to reveal the Position controls. At 5:10, set the Position value to 520, 280 and click the stopwatch to set a keyframe there. Highlight this keyframe, go to 6:00, and copy and paste it into place at that frame. Now go back 10 frames to 5:20 and set the position value to 200, 280 (moving it left on the X-axis).

12 Highlight all the Position keyframes for the you layer by clicking on the word "Position." Now Ctrl/right-click on one of the highlighted keyframes to bring up the context menu and choose Keyframe Assistant > Easy Ease (which is again applied to all three keyframes).

13 Now you'll apply your loop function to each of these keyframes series. The same expression that you used for Rotation within question loop will work, so highlight that layer and press EE (the E key twice in succession) to reveal that expression and then Cmd/Ctrl+C to copy it. Option-click the Position keyframes of the do and you layers, and paste the expression into each, replacing the default.

14 At 6:20, set an end point for the do and you layers by highlighting them and pressing Option/Alt+].

15 If you'd like a preview of how this section of the animation will look at the end of Project 15, "Animating Without Keyframes" (and how it looks in the opening figure of this project), move the LIL124.mov file from the accompanying CD-ROM onto your drive (in the same folder as this project) and import it into After Effects.

16 Once it's imported, highlight the clip in the Project window and press Cmd/Ctrl+F to bring up the Interpret Footage dialog box. At the bottom, you'll see "Loop 1 Times." Change the 1 to a 4 to span the 12-second clip (although at this point you're only previewing the first 3 seconds of it). Click OK.

17 Drag the LIL124.mov clip to the bottom layer of the composition, also starting at 0:00.

18 Want sound, too? Import **Question_Authority.mp3** from the Footage folder of Projects 12–15 and drop it in at 0:00. It has been designed by Dave Levison (**www.h-machine.com**) to fit this animation, the first half of which you have now completed. You'll have to complete the next couple of projects to make full use of the audio.

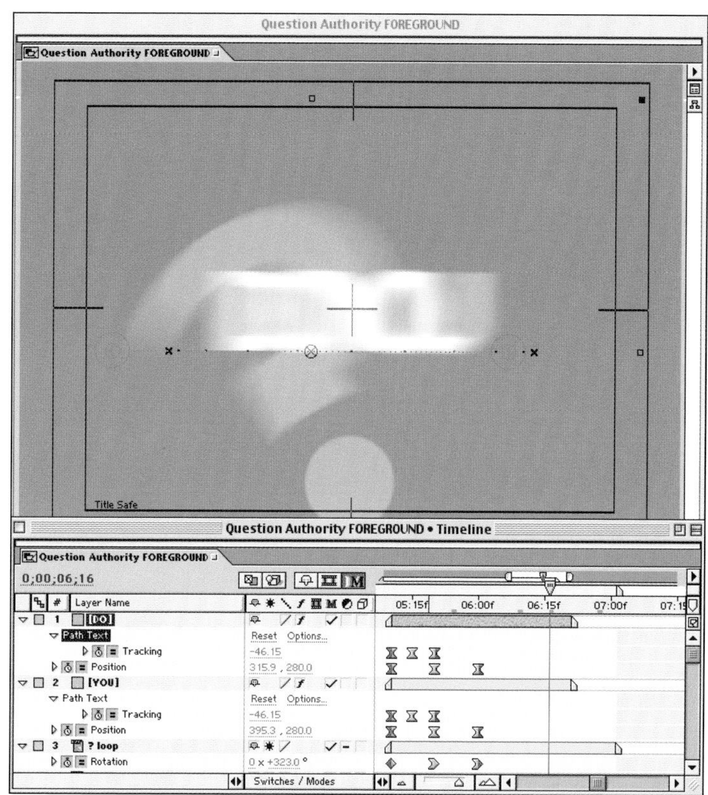

Long after the final keyframe, the animation loops on.

Note to 5.0 Users: You can also apply the expression for Rotation from the question loop layer, with one change. Highlight that layer and press EE (the E key two times in a row) to reveal the expression for that layer. Click once in the expression text field to highlight all text and then press Cmd/Ctrl+C to copy it.

Now Option-click Position for do and press Cmd/Ctrl+V to replace the default "position" text with your four-line expression. You're almost done, but on the top line, you must replace the word "rotation" with the word "position." Everything else is fine as is because this keyframe loop has the same start and length as the one you copied.

Highlight the full text for this Position loop, press Cmd/Ctrl+C to copy it all, and Option-click "position" for you; now press Cmd/Ctrl+V to replace the default with the same expression you used for do.

19 Now be sure to extend the layer duration bar so that it spans the length of the composition, or at least the length of your work area for what you've animated so far, to 6:20.

20 Save the project. You can render it out by pressing Cmd/Ctrl+M, or you can wait until you've completed this four-project section. (You'll be continuing with it in the next two projects.)

Wow, you've moved way beyond just the pickwhip in this chapter. You've now dealt with most of the more advanced concepts that come into play with expressions: using methods (which are predefined keywords that do something), working with variables to make your work easier to read and for cases in which values change over time, and looping.

Modifications

There are a couple of new concepts in this project that you would do well to try out further so that you can more easily put them to use later.

You learned how to use the random() method in this project with two arguments, but you learned that it also works with one argument or even no arguments (just open and closed parentheses after random). In the next project, you'll revisit random and look at the other ways to generate random numbers in expressions, but for now, you could try other variations on using random() as it was previously explained.

Again, any time you want to know more about the arguments associated with any method, it's best to look them up in the User Guide or in the online help, reading for clues as you did in the first section of this project.

You'll get more practice with methods as well as variables in the following three projects.

You've also learned to use the loop expression, although you've only used one version of it. You can try looping keyframes that start somewhere besides the beginning of the composition from the beginning to the first keyframe using the loop_in command. You can also try the loop_in_duration and loop_out_duration expressions that use time, in seconds, rather than keyframes to determine the length of the loop section.

Note to 5.0 Users: For those of you who are brave enough to undertake an explanation of the loop expression, let's take a look at it. If this remains obscure after reading through it, don't worry. I myself only understand it when I concentrate really, really hard. Here's the expression with the initial values plugged in:

```
loop = rotation //use whatever property initially appears in your
➥expression window

looplength = 20; //enter the total number of frames to be looped

startframe = 5.33; //the time, in seconds, of the first loop frame. For partial
➥seconds, use decimals

loop.value_at_time((time % (this_comp.frame_duration * looplength)) +
➥startframe)
```

First of all, this expression could theoretically be written on one long line. In this case, I have defined variables for two of the values to make the expression easier to reuse: information about the length of the loop, or looplength (which is 20 frames in this case), and about where the loop starts, or startframe (5 seconds and 10 frames). Expressions look at time in whole seconds, so you would write this as 5.33.

Note: For those of you who are willing to geek out a bit, the keys to this expression are the value_at_time() method, which returns the value of Rotation at whatever time number is returned between the parentheses, and the symbol %, which does not mean "percentage" in this case but "modulo," a mathematical method that returns only values to the right of the decimal point.

In plain English, the final line

```
rotation.value_at_time((time % (this_comp.frame_duration *
➥looplength)) + startframe)
```

is saying: "For Rotation, change the value over time as follows: First, multiply the duration of the composition, in seconds, by the number of keyframes we're looping. Now give me the 'modulo,' the remainder when I divide the current time by this number. This will give me a continuous ascending loop that returns to zero every 20 frames, the length of my loop. Finally, offset this loop so that it starts at the first frame of our loop."

RANDOMIZATION WITH EXPRESSIONS

"When thou at the random grim forge,

powerful amidst peers,

Didst fettle for the great gray drayhorse

his bright and battering sandal!"

—GERARD MANLEY HOPKINS

Adding Randomness with Expressions

This project focuses on how to use the various flavors of "randomness" that you can access using expressions. This will complete the Question Authority foreground type animation. Random number generation and "wiggle" are methods that all animators need at one time or another; this project will familiarize you with your options for animating with these methods.

In some cases, you want truly random values that fall within a certain range; in others, you want some control over how much the keyframes differ from one another. You want the animation to have a more organic quality that comes from numbers that are somewhat random but that have a relationship to one another. Both of these uses are possible with After Effects expressions, and this project will show you how to access each one.

Project 14

Randomization with Expressions

by Mark Christiansen

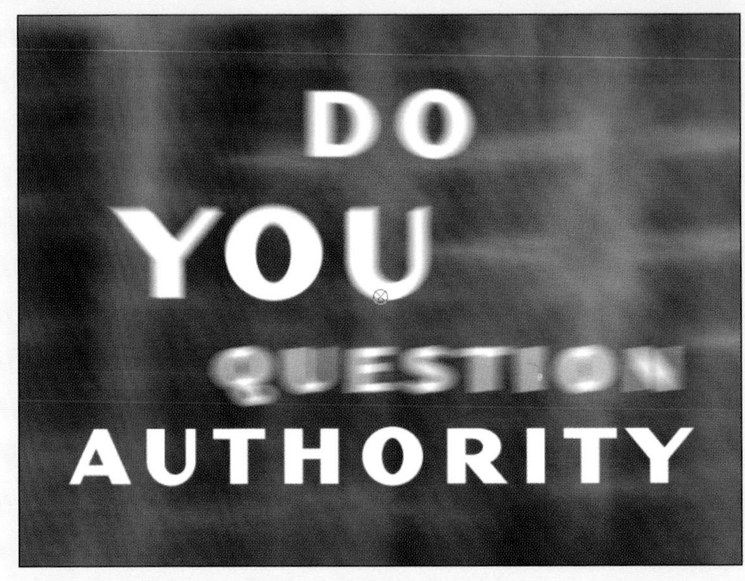

How It Works

Expressions in After Effects include lots of powerful ways to generate numerical data, which is to computer animation what DNA is to the body. There are fundamentally two sets of methods for randomizing data in After Effects: One is pure randomization (evoked with the random and gauss_random methods); the other uses a noise algorithm to derive a more "organic" effect by preserving more continuity between frames (as is used by the wiggle and noise methods). You'll use methods of both sets.

Getting Started

You can continue with your After Effects file from the preceding project (saving a new version with whatever name you choose if you want to preserve each project separately), or you can copy the Projects 12–15 folder to your drive and open **CH14_INITIAL.aep**, which contains all of the source files you'll be using for this project. If you are continuing with your previous After Effects project file, you should already have everything you need.

Randomizing Options

At the beginning of the last project, you tried using the random expression method on the Scale value of a layer. Now you're going to try the other options for randomizing values using expressions: gauss random, seed random, wiggle, and noise.

1 At 7:00, create a new solid by pressing Cmd/Ctrl+Y. Make it the size of the composition. Name it **DO gauss** to distinguish it from your existing DO layer. Click OK.

Note: You don't always have to be this careful about keeping your names distinct from one another for expressions, only when you're calling values from a layer that needs a unique name. However, it's a good habit to get into because expressions will automatically choose the lowest-number layer to associate with a given name if multiple layers have that name.

2 Choose Basic Text within Text in the Effect menu or from the Effects palette. Type **DO** in capital letters again, set the Type to Comic Sans MS Bold (or Dogma Bold if you have it), click OK for Options, and then set the Fill Color to white, the Size to 80 (90 for Dogma), and the Tracking to 15. Set the Position (at the top of the Basic Text controls, not of the layer itself) to 360, 80. If the text looks jaggy, go ahead and set layer quality to Best.

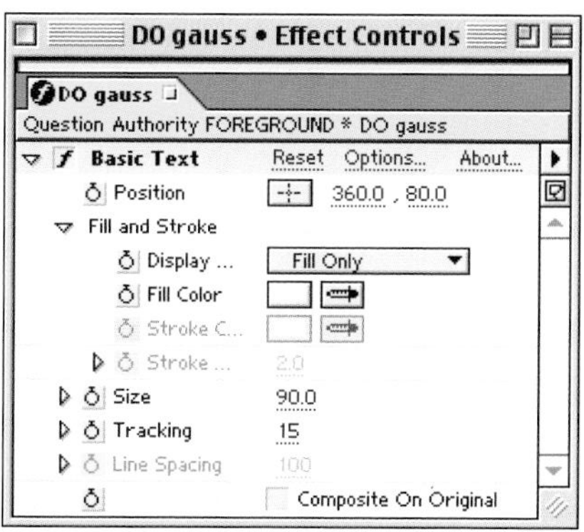

Basic Text settings for the DO gauss layer.

3 With this new layer highlighted, press P to bring up the Position property. Highlight Position and press Option/Alt + Shift + = to add a Position expression.

4 With the Expression window highlighted, choose Random Numbers > gauss_random (min_val_or_array, max_val_or_array).

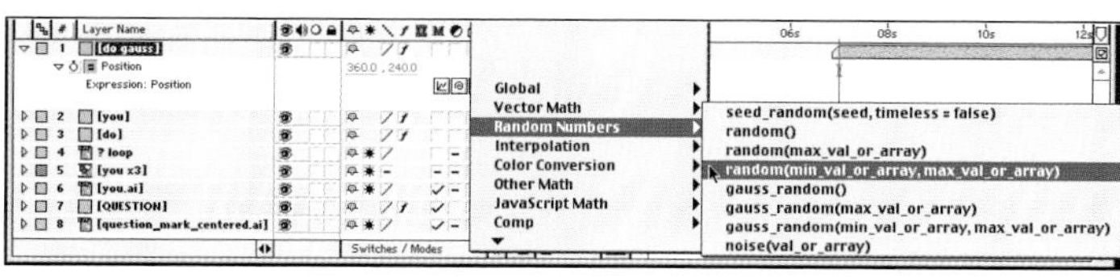

gauss_random(min_val_or_array, max_val_or_array) can be selected from the Expressions menu.

Once again, you see parentheses containing stand-ins for arguments. If you were to choose gauss_random(), you would get the default argument, a number between 0 and 1. If you enter a single number as an argument (between the parentheses), it will set the maximum value at that number, but the low number will still be zero.

In this case, you want to randomize your position around its current point, so you're best served by a minimum and maximum array for the X and Y position (no Z because this is a two-dimensional layer). Let's keep the random numbers within a 30-pixel square around the initial position.

5 Replace min_val_or_array with an array containing the minimum values for X and Y. Subtracting 15 from the current positions, you get [345, 225], which is the first thing to type following the open parenthesis. Next, leave the comma to separate this first set of values from the second, which will be the maximum value array. Adding 15 to the current position, you replace max_val_or_array with [375, 255], leaving your close parenthesis to end the line so that it looks like this:

```
gauss_random([345, 225], [375, 255])
```

6 Save the project, set a work area if necessary, and preview the animation. Note that if you're having trouble seeing the animation run smoothly, you not only can reduce size and resolution and Shift-click the Preview Play button to use a lower frame rate, you can also select a Region of Interest to only preview part of your frame—a great option in this case because you're only animating over a small area of the frame.

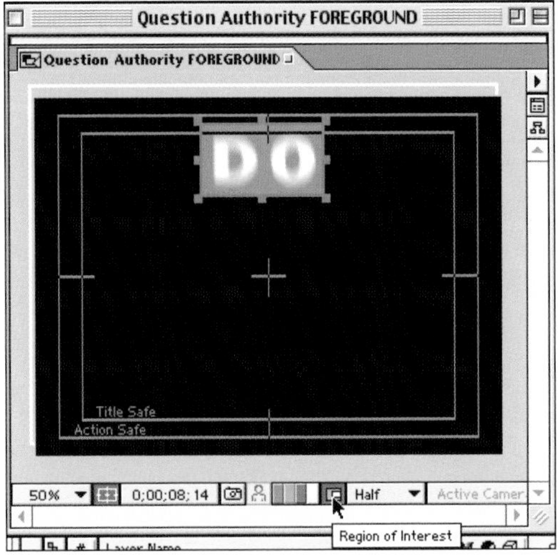

A Region of Interest (highlighted) reduces your RAM Preview area to a manageable size.

You'll see the random movement; turn on Motion Blur to get a more realistic-looking jitter (see the figure).

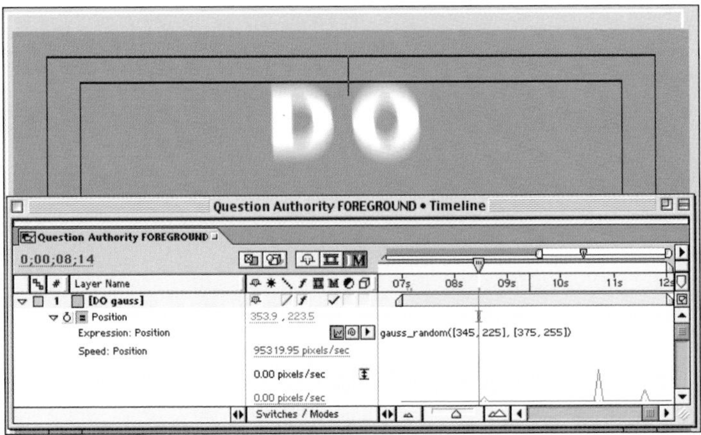

With Motion Blur on, you see "DO" look good jumping and jiving without the use of a single keyframe.

GAUSS_RANDOM VERSUS RANDOM

gauss_random differs from random in the way it distributes random information. Whereas random creates completely random numbers, all of which fall between the specified minimum and maximum values, gauss_random creates a "bell curve" distribution of random values, meaning the values are more likely to fall in the center of the range than at its edges. An additional feature of gauss_random is that a few values will fall slightly beyond the minimum and maximum limits, so in this case here you will find X and Y values that are lower or higher than the limits at certain keyframes.

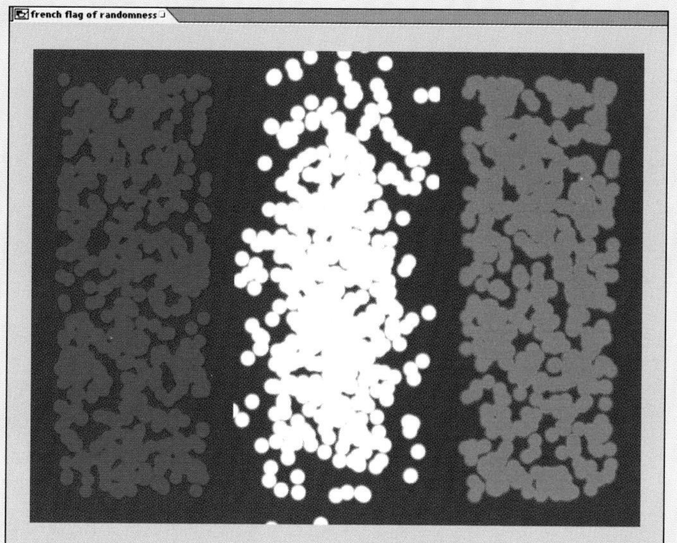

"Vive l'hasard!" The center white area uses a gauss random function, while the blue and red use a random function. All three use the same numerical settings.

For a pictorial representation of the difference between random and gauss random, look at the accompanying figure, called the "French Flag of Randomness." The blue and red dots have been generated by assigning random values to the Write-on brush, while the white dots use gauss_random with the same range. If you want to study this project and its resulting animation further, both are included in the folder for this project: **French_Randomness.aep** and **french_flag_of_randomness.mov**.

Under the Random Numbers menu, you might have also noticed seed_random(seed, timeless = false), a method you can add on a line prior to random or gauss_random to change the seed, which will change all of your random values to a different set of random values with the same parameters. You need it only if for some reason you don't like the default result. It cannot be used on its own; it merely changes the seed for other random effects. You would set it on the line before another random effect with a single argument, the "seed" number.

Noise Methods: Wiggle

Now let's try the next layer with wiggle, a completely different kind of random effect. If you're a Production Bundle user of After Effects, you might have used The Wiggler, a keyframe assistant (or motion tool) based on a similar algorithm. However, not only do you not need this tool for the most part thanks to expressions, you're going to use it in a situation in which The Wiggler would not work.

1 Go to 7:10 on the Timeline, create a new solid [Cmd/Ctrl+Y] the size of the composition, and name it **YOU wiggle**. Don't worry about the color. You can copy the Basic Text effect from DO gauss and, in the Options window that pops up when you paste it, type in **YOU** as the text and then press Enter. To avoid overlapping the previous layer, set Basic Text Position to 260, 200.

2 In the Timeline window, highlight the layer and press E to bring up the Basic Text effect. Twirl down using the triangular arrow next to Basic Text to reveal the character Size property. Set a keyframe here at 7:10 and change the Size value to 0. Go to 7:20 and set the value to 108 (120 for Dogma), which automatically adds a keyframe. Select the first keyframe, right/Ctrl-click and hold to choose Keyframe Assistant > Easy Ease Out as in the figure.

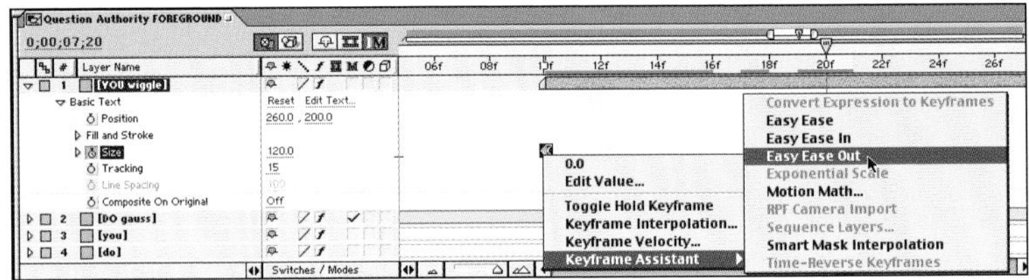

Easy Ease Out of the first keyframe.

3 Option-click this same Basic Text Size stopwatch to add an expression. Replace the text that appears by choosing wiggle(freq, amp, octaves = 1, amp_mult = .5, t = time) under Property in the Expression menu. According to these defaults, wiggle has five arguments, but the last three (octaves, amplitude multiplier, and time) are shown to have defaults (hence the = signs after these). You're going to keep those defaults and only enter the first two arguments, with values of 10 for Frequency and 20 for Amplitude. The line now reads as follows:

wiggle(10, 20)

Note to 5.0 Users: Replace step 3 as follows: After adding the default expression, click at the end of the expression text that appears to put your cursor at the end of the line because wiggle is a local method and thus follows the property. Enter a period (.) to separate the property from the method wiggle, followed by the parameters for wiggle, which you'll make (10, 20). So the full line reads as follows:

effect("Path Text").param(20).wiggle(10, 20)

4 Save the project and preview the animation. Set a work area if necessary.

You'll see a bounce to the scaling of the letters that is less jittery than if you had used random or gauss_random. This is because wiggle is not random; it is based on a more organic noise calculation that creates values, each with a relationship to its neighbors, based on the difference between keyframe values. The parameters you set specify the frequency (the number of wiggles per second) and amplitude (the maximum amount) of the wiggle; at a minimum, you must specify these two parameters.

You can use expressions to set a temporal wiggle as well, where appropriate. Let's try that next.

5 At 8:00, create a new solid layer called **QUESTION temporal** with the same settings as before, and again, paste in the Basic Text effect. Enter the word **QUESTION** in the Options window, click OK, and then enter 440, 320 for Basic Text Position. Make the Character Size 54 (60 for Dogma).

6 Now create a position keyframe for this layer (not Basic Text) at 8:20. This will be your end position. Go to 8:00 and set the start position to 660, 248, which is to the right and down slightly from the final. This is a pretty boring entry so far; let's add a little overshoot by going to 8:17 and setting position to 330, 235, which automatically adds a keyframe.

Overshoot is great fodder for wiggling time, as you'll see. Rather than fix the timing, let's leave it as it is (because our wiggle expression will change the timing anyhow) and make one change to the spatial data of our current keyframe, at 8:17.

Note: Why couldn't you have used The Wiggler from the Production Bundle for this? If you apply The Wiggler to these keyframes, After Effects will give you only the option of a temporal wiggle because it doesn't understand text size as a spatial property. Temporal wiggle doesn't help you here because your final keyframe acts like a "hold" keyframe, and you want the wiggle to continue after that keyframe. Try it and see for yourself.

7 Click on the little black arrow in the upper-right corner of the Composition window to access the Composition View Options, and make sure that Layer Motion Paths, Layer Keyframes, and Layer Motion Path Tangents are all activated with a check next to the respective names.

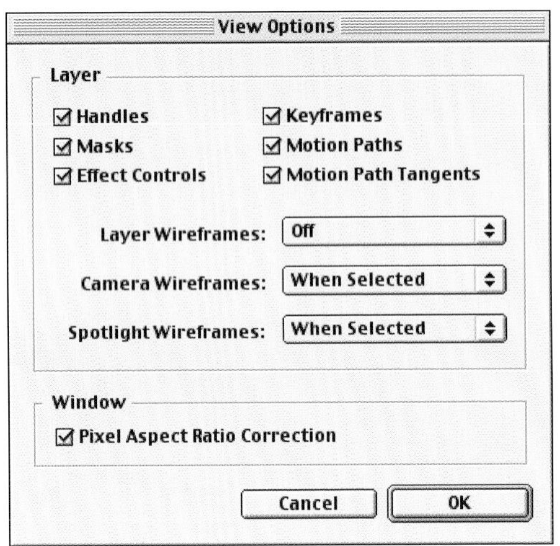

Layer Paths, Keyframes, and Tangents are all active in the View Options menu, allowing you to see the motion path.

8 Highlight the keyframe you just created at 8:17 in the Timeline. With your Tools palette open, press the G key repeatedly and watch the Pen tool.

The Pen tool will cycle through its four modes. You want the one that looks not like a pen but like a small carat.

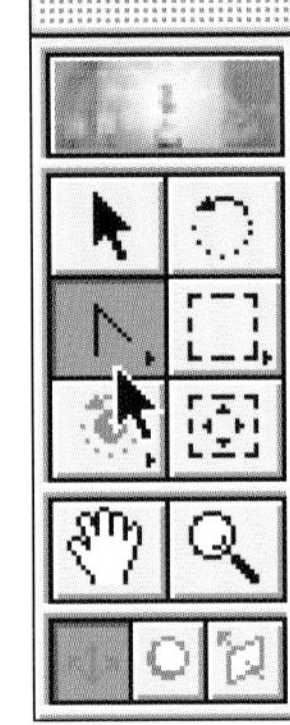

The fourth Pen mode is a carat-shaped tool used to toggle Bezier handles.

9 With this Convert Point tool highlighted, go to the Composition window and click on the spatial keyframe for this frame, the one that has a circle around it. Click and drag downward about 10 pixels or so, pulling out the Bezier handles attached to this keyframe to change the path shape from a straight line to a hairpin turn.

Check the accompanying figure for a detail of what I'm talking about.

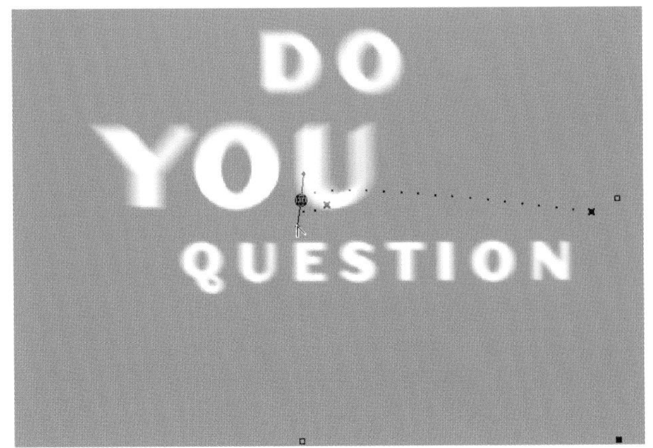

The Convert Point tool makes a hairpin turn at the second keyframe of your motion path.

10 Back in the Timeline, click the Position property (or press P so that it appears, highlighted). Option/Alt-click the stopwatch to add an expression for Position. Then in the window that appears, you will see the word "position." From the pull-down Expressions menu, choose Property > temporal_wiggle(freq, amp, octaves = 1, amp_mult = .5, t = time), as shown in the accompanying figure.

Once again, you have defaults indicating that temporal_wiggle requires between two and five arguments. You're going to set the first three and leave the last two at the default settings.

11 Set the first two values, Frequency and Amplitude, to 5 and 1, respectively; change the default octave value (the third value) to 2 so that the final line reads as follows:

```
position.temporal_wiggle(5, 1, 2)
```

Press Enter and your expression will be activated.

12 Check Motion Blur for the layer and enable it for the composition. Then go ahead and set a work area and Region of Interest as needed to get a good RAM Preview.

The result is pretty much what you're looking for, but let's add something unexpected because the word "question" is exactly what is expected here. Save the project and you're ready to complete it.

13 Still at 8:17, highlight the QUESTION temporal layer and split it (Edit > Split Layer) [Cmd/Ctrl + Shift + D]. The new layer runs from 8:00 to 8:16 and is highlighted. Use Cmd/Ctrl + Shift + T or press the F3 key (if enabled, in the case of Mac users) to bring up the Effect Control window. Click on Options at the top of Path Text and replace the QUESTION text with eight question marks (????????). Click OK.

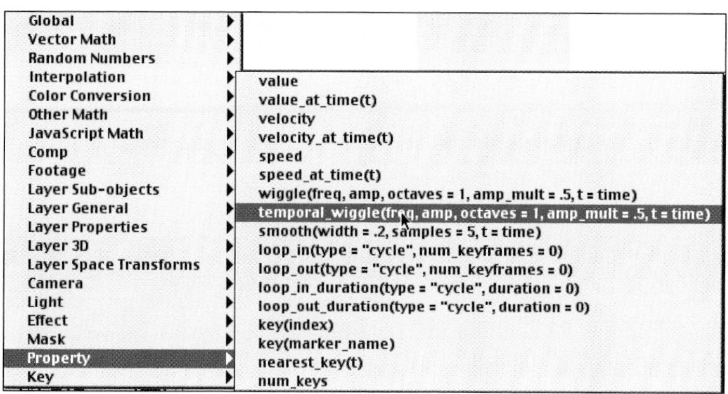

temporal_wiggle is a method with five arguments, the final three of which have defaults.

14 Make sure Motion Blur is checked on for this layer.

Finally, your subject needs a predicate. You'll use the final method for generating random numbers, the noise method, to give it a quick, randomized scale up into a static position.

15 Create a new solid at 9:10. Make it the composition size, name it **AUTHORITY**, and then click OK. Paste in the text effect, enter the text as **AUTHORITY** under Options, and click OK. Change the Text Size to 64 (75 for Dogma). Now reset Basic Text Position (by Ctrl/right-clicking on the Property and choosing Reset from the contextual menu that appears) and set Position for the whole layer (by highlighting it in the Timeline window and pressing P) to 360, 400.

16 At 9:20, press S to reveal the Scale property and click the stopwatch to set a keyframe with the Scale value at 100%. Now roll back 10 frames to 9:10 (Shift+PgUp or just I) and change the value to 65% (X and Y), which creates a second keyframe automatically.

17 Now Option/Alt-click the stopwatch to set an expression and replace the default text that appears, "scale," with the following:

```
n=scale[0]+noise(scale[0])*20;
[n,n]
```

Here's what you just did. Scale is a property with two values that you want to keep proportional even as you randomize them, so you set a variable to stand for the X and Y Scale values. You called it "n." You took the X Scale value, scale[0], and added your noise effect to it. The noise effect consists of applying the method noise to the same scale[0] value. As long as this value changes from one frame to the next (that is, between your keyframes), the noise value changes as well. Noise can only generate values between –1 and 1, so you multiplied the noise value by 20 so that a number between –20 and 20 would be added to your Scale value.

On the final line, you called "n" twice in an array so that the same value would stand for the X and Y Scale values.

At the final keyframe, the noise value holds along with the Scale value itself, so your layer stops varying its Scale at that point.

18 Again, preview the animation (setting your work area as needed) and save the project.

You've now been introduced to the main methods for generating random values using expressions: random, gauss_random, and wiggle (plus the seed_random effect as needed).

19 If you'd like a preview of how this section of the animation will look at the end of Project 15 (and how it looks in the opening figure of this project), move the **LIL124.mov** file from the accompanying CD-ROM onto your drive (in the same folder as this project) and import it into After Effects.

20 Once it's imported, highlight the clip in the Project window and press Cmd/Ctrl+F to bring up the Interpret Footage dialog box. At the bottom, you'll see Loop 1 Times. Change the 1 to a 4 to span the 12-second clip (although at this point you're only previewing the first 3 seconds of it). Click OK.

21 Drag the LIL124.mov clip to the bottom layer of the composition, also starting at 0:00.

22 Want sound, too? Import **Question_Authority.mp3** from the Footage folder of Projects 12–15 and drop it in at 0:00. It has been designed by Dave Levison (**www.h-machine.com**) to fit this animation. You still have one project to go to add the background effects that also go with the sound.

23 Now be sure to extend the Layer Duration bar so that it spans the length of the composition.

MODIFICATIONS

Practice using random, wiggle, and noise on other keyframe animations until you're so used to the syntax and the variations that you're comfortable dropping it in wherever you see fit. Keep in mind that wiggle methods, in particular, can be useful to simulate camera shake (either using an After Effects 3D camera or by faking it and shaking the entire composition with Motion Blur active). Noise generates a result more similar to wiggle than to random. The values have some relationship to one another and are based on Perlin noise, which is a computer graphics standard.

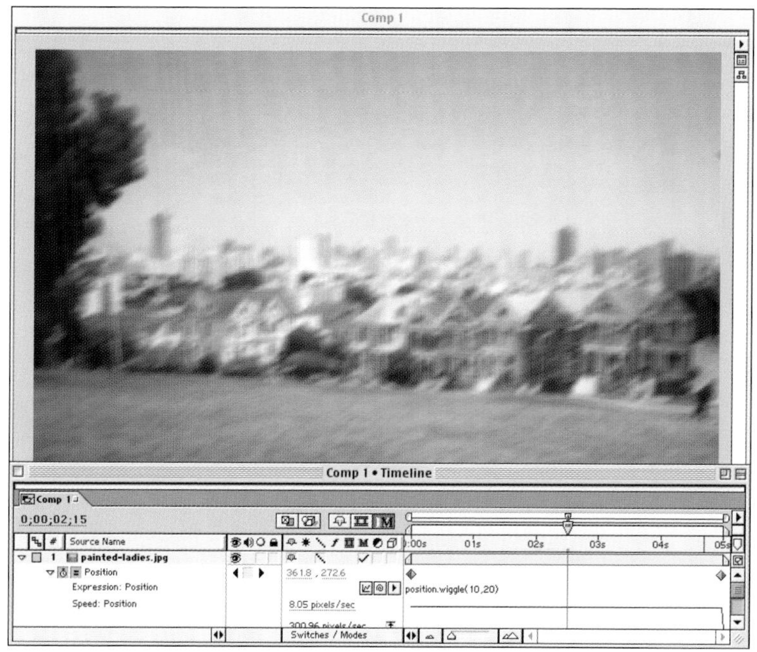

Nothing to see here folks, just another California earthquake. Move along, move along.

"I'm very well acquainted too with matters mathematical,

I understand equations, both the simple and quadratical,

About binomial theorem I'm teeming with a lot 'o news,

With many cheerful facts about the square of the hypotenuse."

—"I AM THE VERY MODEL OF A MODERN MAJOR GENERAL"
FROM GILBERT AND SULLIVAN'S *PIRATES OF PENZANCE*

ANIMATING WITHOUT KEYFRAMES

Animating with Expressions

In this project, you're going to complete the Question Authority animation using some advanced techniques that you might want to learn in order to reuse them. This project is called "Animating Without Keyframes" because these are techniques that enable you to add motion using only expressions.

To create a keyframe-free animated background, you'll make use of trigonometry and its capability to describe curves using sine and cosine methods. If you've never been that hot on trig, working with it in After Effects could change your mind. You'll also use time to offset values and layers and to create interpolations, a powerful technique that you'll want to learn even if you never think about trigonometry again. You'll also make several objects follow one another in a manner that you control by using time to offset them.

Project 15

Animating Without Keyframes

by Mark Christiansen

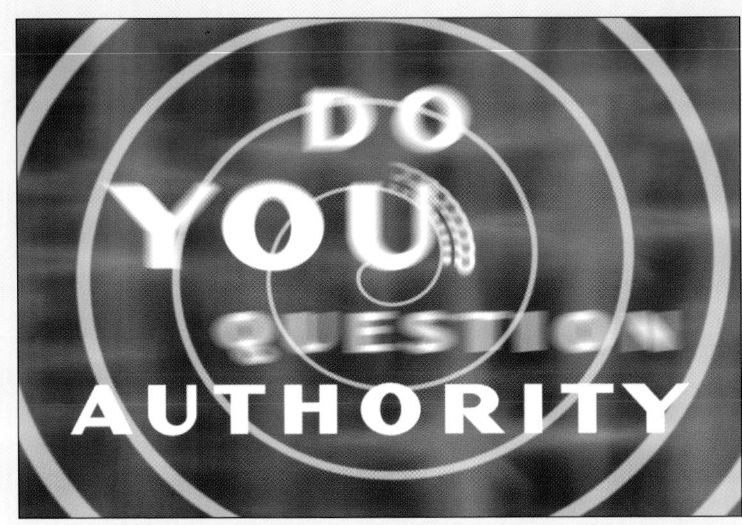

How It Works

It's beyond the scope of the book to explain how trigonometry works, other than in the broadest terms. This is partly because it would take a much better mathematician than I am to do this. Tied to expressions, however, are clever ways of changing or offsetting data over time that use the Timeline itself to generate animation.

Interpolation works in a subtle but powerful manner; it enables you to set a start and end value and interpolate between these two values over time. This sounds just like keyframes, but there is a key difference: The start and end values can both change over time, enabling you to keyframe between a pair of moving targets. These can even be formulas that change over time. You also have control over whether the interpolation is linear or includes any eases.

Creating a leader layer and having other layers follow it, with some amount of offset, is just the kind of thing that is really a pain other than with expressions. Offsetting an animation several times by copying and scaling keyframes is bad enough, but then let's suppose you make a simple change to the animation of the leader—you have to update each of your follower layers by hand.

Getting Started

In this project, you're going to create a 12-second background animation to accompany the foreground animation you created in the last three projects. If you are continuing with your previous animation file, you only need to import the Artbeats stock footage that you'll be using in the background (if you haven't done so already). The file **LIL124.mov** comes compliments of **www.artbeats.com** (a great source for stock and background footage) and is found in the Footage folder, but you should move it to your local drive for optimum performance. Alternatively, you can move the Projects 12–15 folder to your local drive and open the **CH15_INITIAL.aep** file from inside it. This file already contains this clip and all previous animations.

Swirl

The first animation was created using only expressions. It will draw a swirling shape over time using the Write-on effect (an effect that is also essential in Project 16, "How to Draw with Spirograph™").

1. Create a new composition called **Question Authority BACKGROUND** and choose the NTSC D1 Square Pix preset from the Preset pull-down (which automatically sets the frame rate to 29.97). Set the duration to 12 seconds by entering 1200 in the Duration area. Click OK.

Note: This time you're using the larger, square-pixel format because you're going to be animating circular patterns, and this is far less complicated with uniform, square pixels. This composition setting is good for anyone working in NTSC who prefers not to work with nonsquare pixels in After Effects. You can always render to a lower resolution (such as the standard DV aspect of 720×480, nonsquare pixels).

2. In this composition, at 0:00, create an oversized solid called **Swirl** by pressing Cmd/Ctrl+Y and setting the size to 900×900. You'll need this extra area on the layer a little later. There's no need to worry about the color of this solid, so click OK.

3. Choose Effect > Stylize > Write-on (or double-click Write-on in the Effects palette) for this layer. Leave the brush color as the default white, but change the Paint Style setting to On Transparent using the pull-down. Leave all other settings at their default values.

4. In the Timeline window, highlight the Swirl layer and press E to show the effect controls below the layer. Twirl down the arrow next to Write-on to show all of its properties. Highlight Brush Position and set an expression [Option/Alt + Shift + =]. Replace the text in the Expressions window with the following:

```
r = linear(time, 0, out_point, 0, width/2);
s =  3;
x = Math.sin(time * s) * r + width / 2.0;
y =  Math.cos(time * s) * r + height / 2.0;
[x,y]
```

Roll forward in the Timeline a few seconds, and you'll see a spiral drawing itself over time, as shown in the figure.

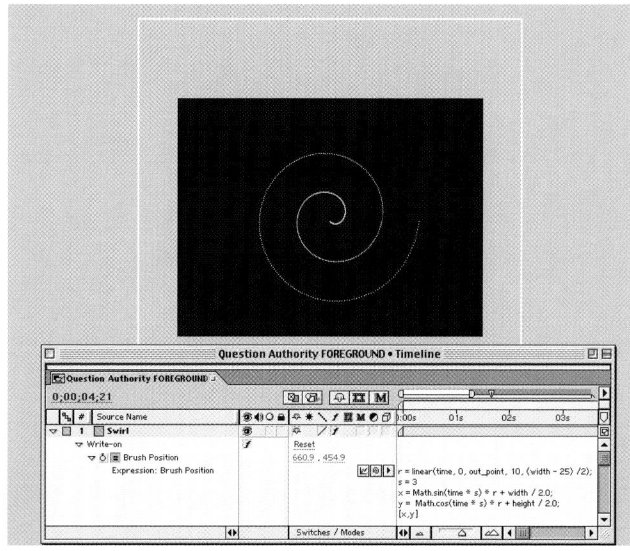

Like the earliest photos of distant planets, the first signs of a swirl appear against the blackness.

Having taken care of the complicated part of this animation, you have some tweaking to do, for which you'll use a couple more expressions. First, the default brush size isn't quite working here; the dots are spaced apart and grow to be even more spaced apart as the spiral grows. Let's try to make this look more like a continuous curve.

5 In the Effect Controls window, set the Brush Spacing (secs) to 0.006. This makes things look better in the center, but you're still seeing individual dots toward the edges by the end of the animation. Preview the animation or move the current-time marker a few seconds ahead on the Timeline to see this. Note: It's easier to see if you set the layer's quality switch to Best.

6 Now set an expression for Brush Size under Write-on and replace the text that appears with the following single line:

```
(time * time/3 + 5)/2
```

Note: If your swirl is difficult to see, change Resolution to Full to see it as it appears in the figure.

What It All Means

Here is an explanation of what is happening in step 4:

The first line sets a radius, which will be used by sine and cosine on the third and fourth lines to draw a curve. The curve does not draw a circle but a spiral because the radius is set to grow from the center of the composition over time using **linear**, which is an interpolation method.

The second line, **s**, sets a variable that inversely affects the distance covered over time. The higher the number you set for it, the tighter the coils of the spiral will be, although you'll find that the results get a lot stranger when you get into double-digit values (or greater). Feel free to play with different settings for **s** and then set it back to **3**. It doesn't matter that I call it **s**. You could call it **grover** if you want, as long as there are no spaces or illegal characters (like an ampersand) in the name. In choosing **s**, I had "spiral" or "scale" in mind.

Let's dissect the **linear** method for a moment. In this case, I'm using **linear** with five arguments, separated by commas within the parentheses that follow the method name. According to the manual, these arguments refer to the following (in order): t, tmin, tmax, var1, var2. Here's how you decode them:

- The letter "t" refers to "time," so I've entered **time** because I want the expression to look at the current time. (Later, you will offset this on a different layer.)
- "tmin" and "tmax" are merely the start and end values for time, which I want to be the start (or **0**) and end (or **out_point**, a term that expressions use to find this automatically).
- "var1" and "var2" are the values for the radius length that correspond to the start and end time values, so at "tmin" the value is "var1," and at "tmax" the value is "var2"—simple as that. I'm setting it to start with a value of 0 and expand to a value half the width of the layer, which means the radius ends up reaching from the center to the edge.

The only complicated part left to explain in this expression is, of course, the trigonometry, but even that's not so complicated if you realize that sine and cosine are doing their basic job of describing values along a curve. In fact, the formulas for X and Y are the standard formulas for calculating a circle, with the exception that the radius is changing over time. Don't believe me? Change the first line of the expression to **r = 200**, and you'll see that a perfect circle is drawn over time with a radius of 200 pixels.

7 Click outside the box or press Enter, and you'll see the spiral line become immediately much thicker. Go to the Brush Time Properties and set the pull-down to Size to take advantage of the way you just wrote your expression, causing the spiral to thicken proportionally as it expands, as in the figure.

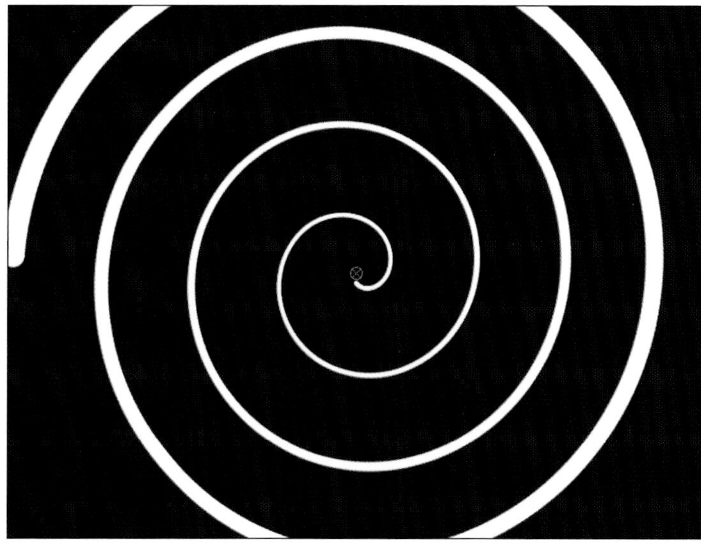

Your spiral begins to look more like a continuous shape.

Note: The expression, and the manner in which it was derived, is less complicated than it appears. Essentially, you want the value to scale exponentially over time, so you multiply time by itself to derive it. That results in too great a change over time, so you divide and offset it to get what you're looking for.

So to get to this result, I might have started with the following:

time * time

I might have realized that the line was too thin at the center and too thick at the edges (as in the figure).

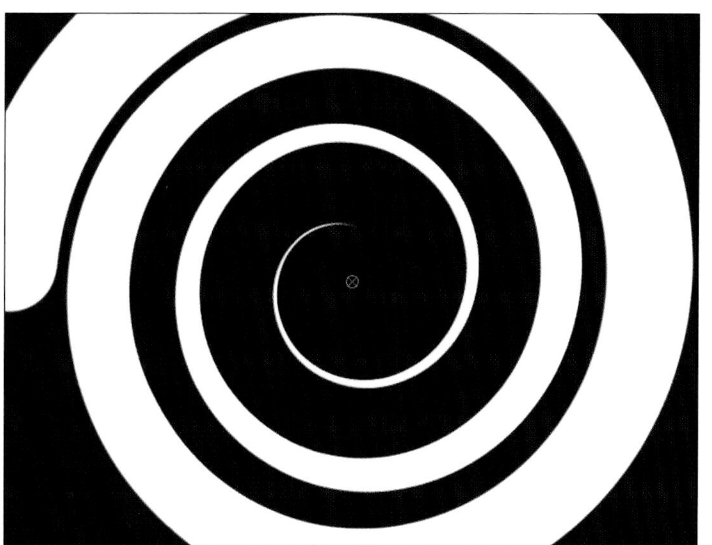

Whoops! Too thick!

From this result, I would see that I need a higher starting value and a diminished increment over time, which would lead me to use division to lower the increment and addition to add the offset. So I might try this:

time * time/3 + 5

The **+5** guarantees a higher start value, and the **/3** diminishes the exponential scale. The result (shown in the figure) is better, but it's too thick overall, so I divide the whole thing in half, giving me the final expression you previously entered:

```
(time*(time/3) + 5)/2
```

This is looking good. One final design decision is that it would be nice to have the brush soften proportionally to its growth.

8 In either the Effect Controls window or the Timeline window, set Brush Hardness to 100. Then set an expression for Brush Hardness [Option/Alt + Shift + =], which automatically enters the following in the expression text area:

```
effect("Write-on").param(4)
```

Right now, this points the effect to itself to derive a value of 100. To soften the brush over time, you want to subtract an increasing amount as time progresses.

9 Add a minus sign after the default text, as follows:

```
effect("Write-on").param(4) –
```

You want the softening of the brush to relate to its increase in size.

10 Take the pickwhip next to Brush Hardness and drag it up to Brush Size, which makes your line appear as follows:

```
effect("Write-on").param(4) - effect
➥("Write-on").param("Brush Size")
```

This is fine except that it only gets you back to about your default value of 79% by the final frame, whereas you'd actually like things to soften down closer to 60% by the end frame. Well, that's not too hard. It just means doubling the amount that you've subtracted, like this:

```
effect("Write-on").param(4) - effect
➥("Write-on").param("Brush Size") * 2
```

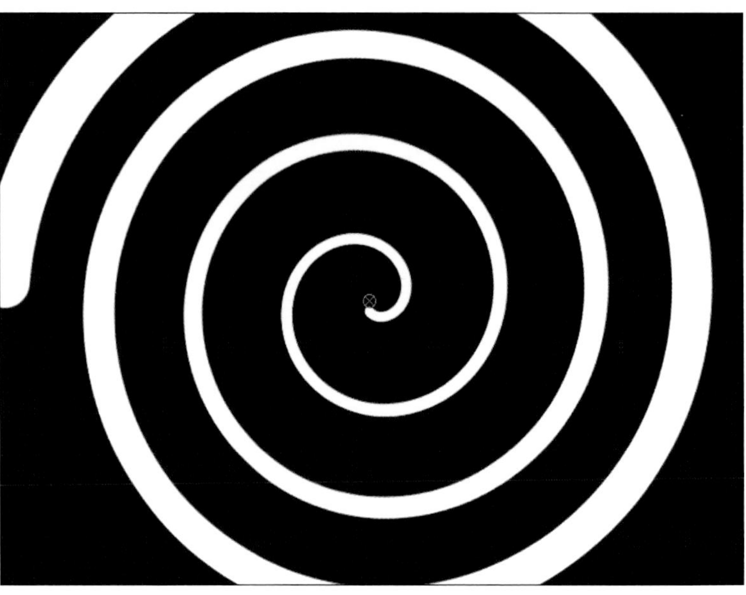

That's better; there is a closer proportion between the inner and outer thickness.

A Note on Syntax: You might be wondering how you know where to put parentheses to get the result you want when using addition, subtraction, multiplication, and division. Try entering the expression without parentheses, and you'll get a somewhat different result.

Here is the rule you must remember: After Effects does not simply read the line from left to right; it does multiplication and division before it does addition and subtraction. However, it will do calculations within parentheses before using the total to complete calculations outside of parentheses.

This is a good thing. You need to be able to tell the expressions the difference between 2 + 2 / 2 (which equals 3 because 2 is divided by 2 before being added to 2) and (2 + 2) / 2 (which equals 2 because 2 and 2 are added and then divided by 2).

This gives you the slightly softened result shown in the figure. There's one more thing to make your swirl look swirlier.

11 Highlight the layer and press R to bring up the Rotation control.

You made the layer oversized so that you could rotate it around to add to the effect. You could do this with keyframes, but if you do it with an expression, you can later change the length of the composition and have this rotation continue as a constant. Expressions are useful for setting constants for this reason.

12 Set an expression for Rotation and replace the text "rotation" with the following:

```
time * 50.
```

Using **time** means you'll get a regular increment, and multiplying it by 50 scales it to about the right value.

13 Set the Opacity of Swirl to 60%.

It is a background effect, so you don't want it quite so prominent for the final mix, which you'll see after you complete the following section.

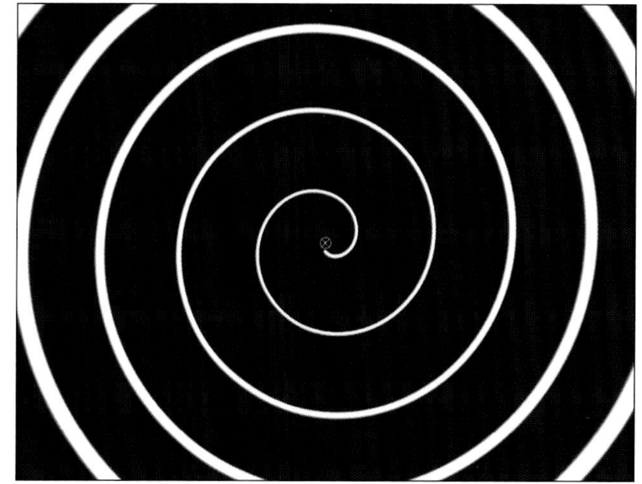

It's subtle, but your curve is now softer at its edge.

Cleaning Up the Expression

There's nothing technically wrong with the expression you've just written, but anyone, whether a novice or an experienced programmer, would probably find it quicker and easier to decipher if the final line looked like this:

```
100 – (brush_size  * 2)
```

This is how you could write it if you set a variable on the previous line and replaced the default parameter with its value, 100:

```
brush_size = effect("Write-on").param("Brush Size")
```

The other unnecessary extra information here is the parentheses around **brush_size * 2** because you know that an expression will do multiplication and division before it does addition and subtraction. However, if this were high school geometry, you would need the parentheses to make it clear that you wanted multiplication to happen before subtraction, so it's sometimes helpful to add in the parentheses for your own sake. It's up to you.

And if you *really* wanted everything to be clear, you could add a comment line:

```
//brush hardness decreases in inverse proportion to brush size
brush_size = effect("Write-on").param("Brush Size");
100 – (brush_size * 2)
```

With such a small amount of code, though, commenting is kind of overkill. However, it's up to you and where you are on your learning curve, as well as who else will have to decipher your work, as you decide how much extra commenting, partitioning with parentheses, and adding variables to do.

Followers and Controllers

Now you're really going to have some fun; you'll invert your previous animation into a set of question marks that follow one another into your existing layer's snail shape. You'll also create a "dummy" invisible layer whose effect sliders will let you control the follow distance and Opacity falloff in real time or easily animate these values over time.

You'll start by animating your leader. You want a little question mark to travel along a path similar to the spiral, but you want it to offset so that it travels inside the gap formed by the spiral. It also should travel in the opposite direction, from the outermost point clockwise to the innermost point.

Before you look at the expression, let's just think through what you're doing in plain English. You want to use the Brush Position value of Spiral but in inverse time, so that at frame 0:00 you use the value at 11:29 and vice versa, including all of the points in between. You need to offset the values so that they start from the center of the layer (because you're translating Brush Position data to Position, and they have different center points). Finally, you want to offset your layer so that it travels just to the outside of Spiral.

There are several ways to solve this problem. I'll start with the one that I think is most elegant.

1. Drag **question_mark_centered.ai** into your composition and make it the top layer, starting at 0:00. Press the Return key to rename the layer and type **Leader** to give it a distinct name; you'll need that later.

2. Press S to reveal Scale properties for this layer and drag your mouse across the blue number 100%, toward the left, to rub the text down to 10%. You can also click the number once to highlight it as a number field and then type in **10**.

3. Now press P to open the Position property for the Leader layer, highlight the property, and press Alt/Option + Shift + = to add an expression. Highlight the text in the expression text area and replace it with this expression:

```
t = out_point - time;
sub(this_comp.layer("Swirl").effect("Write-on").param("Brush Position")
➥.value_at_time(t), [90,180])
```

   This represents the first two of your "plain English" steps from earlier. Before you solve the third, preview the animation and let's look at what you just did.

First, you set a variable to invert time by subtracting **time** (the current time on the Timeline) from **out_point**, which is the value of the final frame of the composition. On the next line, you called the value of Brush Position (using the pickwhip), modified it with **.value_at_time(** to use your inverted time value **t**, and then subtracted the difference between the center point of Brush Position and the center of Position. To do this, you had to use the vector math method **sub(** because, as you learned a couple of projects back, this is the correct way to subtract one array from another.

You're good except that your question mark overlaps the path of the spiral. Let's fix that. Happily, you don't have to mess with the expression; all you have to do is offset the anchor point of the Leader layer.

4 With the layer highlighted, press A to bring up the Anchor Point values. Set them to 110, 600 and the layer will pop off of the path and into a position between spirals.

Great. But wouldn't it be cool if the question mark would orient itself around the spiral so that its bottom always pointed to the center and its top always pointed outward? Luckily, this doesn't require an expression at all.

5 With the Leader layer highlighted, choose Layer > Transform > Auto-Orient or press Option/Alt + Cmd/Ctrl + O. In the pop-up that appears, choose Orient Along Path and click OK. Magic!

Now it's time to set up your follower layers, a set of seven question marks that will trail behind the leader in equivalent distances and fade slightly in Opacity the further they are from the leader, as if they were mere echoes. You're going to do one other cool thing, which is to add a control layer that will remain turned off. The layer's effect sliders will control the distance and fade of your followers so that you can adjust them in real time or keyframe them if you want to.

You'll start by creating your control layer.

Note: The terms **time** and **out_point** are keywords that represent specific values to expressions; to see all of the keywords that exist in After Effects, look through the terms that appear in the pop-up menu when you click the black triangle next to the pickwhip. The ones without an open parenthesis after them are all keywords. The words that *are* followed by an open parenthesis are considered methods. Once you're done you can close this menu without selecting anything; you were only browsing.

Note: There is something very cool that you've just inadvertently discovered about expressions in After Effects: You can refer to values that come from them as if they were actual keyframe data. In step 1, you pointed to an expression but inverted its time, so you needed the last value first. Here, you need data from a curve that is being described with that expression, so you're now effectively two expressions away from "real" data (if you want to think of it that way), yet After Effects is still able to calculate the orientation. Pretty cool.

6 Create a new Adjustment layer and name it **Follow Controls**. No other settings matter. This layer's in point should be at 0:00. Add Effect > Expression Controls > Slider Control (or just choose Slider Control from the Effects palette). With the effect highlighted in the Effect Control window (which happens automatically), press Return to make the effect name active and type in **Follow Distance**.

7 Duplicate this effect and rename the duplicate **Follow Fade**.

8 Duplicate the Leader layer and rename the duplicate **Follower** for clarity. Move Follower up to the top layer, number 1.

You'll see why moving the layer to the top is important after you're done with setup.

9 Press P to bring up the Position property for the Follower layer. Position still has Leader's expression on it, so twirl down the arrow next to Position to reveal the expression text and highlight it. Start by replacing it with **offset** =, which will Follow Settings.

10 Select the Follower Controls layer and press E. Then twirl down the white arrows next to Follow Distance and Follow Fade.

Expressions gave you an error that you can ignore; you're not done yet.

11 On the Follower layer, place your cursor at the end of the expression text line (after **offset** =) and pickwhip to the Slider Control under Follow Distance that you just revealed. Then type **/100;** and return to complete the line.

12 On the next line, type **t** = **time - offset * index;** and press Return. On the final line, pickwhip to Position within Leader (revealing it in the Timeline if necessary beforehand) and then type **.value_at_time(t)** to complete the expression. You can select value_at_time(from the expressions pull-down under Property, but make sure to put a period (**.**) beforehand and **t**) to set an argument for value at time.

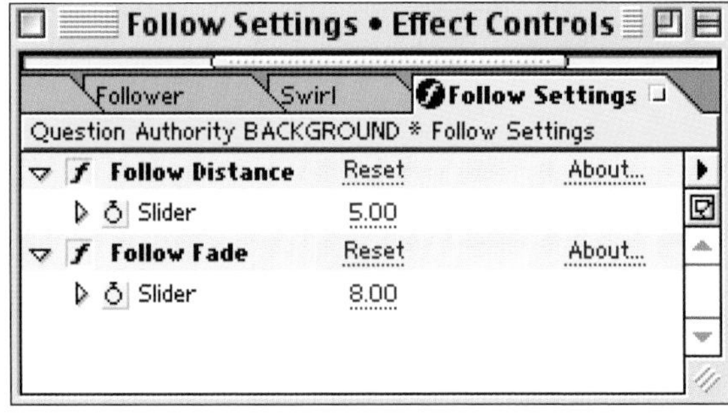

The Expressions sliders don't do anything until you link an expression to them.

13 Go to the Follow Distance slider in your Effect Control window. (If you can't see it, highlight the Follow Controls layer and press either Cmd/Ctrl + Shift + T or, more simply, the F3 key to reveal the effect.) Twirl down the arrow next to Slider to reveal the slider. Slide the value up and down, and you'll see your Follower offset from your leader. (It's easier to see it somewhere in the middle of the animation, like around 5:00.) Go to a different time to see that the follow distance remains constant. Set Follow Distance to 5.

Now you'll offset the Opacity as well.

14 Hold down Shift and press T with the Follower layer highlighted to reveal the Opacity control and set an expression for it. Replace the default text "opacity" with **100 – index *** and then pickwhip the Follow Fade Slider Control property (either in the Effect Controls window or under the Follower Controls layer in the Timeline window). Slide Follow Fade up from zero, and you'll see the Opacity of Follower decrease. Set Follow Fade to 8.

15 Highlight the Follower layer and press Cmd/Ctrl+D seven times to make seven duplicates of Follower.

Ta-da! You now have a series of question marks that fade as they become more distant from the leader. The distance and the amount of the fade are still controlled by sliders within Follow Settings.

The row of question marks is aligned along a path that falls within the gaps of the spiral.

Note: The secret ingredient to both expressions is "index," which uses the actual layer number as a factor for Offset and Opacity. That's why it's crucial for the Follower layers to all be at the top in layer positions 1 through 8; the actual numbers 1 through 8 are being used to determine how they relate to one another. If you add another layer amidst these layers or drag one of the bottom layers up between 1 and 8, you'll see a gap open up in your nice, tidy follow animtion. If you really want to ensure that this won't happen, precompose layers 1 through 8 by highlighting them and pressing Cmd/Ctrl + Shift + C and then locking the resulting composition by activating the lock switch for this layer.

16 Check Motion Blur switches for the Leader and all Follower layers. You can "zip click" by dragging down the column of check boxes. You'll need to also check the Enable Motion Blur switch at the top of the Timeline window (if it's not already) to see the Motion Blur applied in the Composition window.

Ready to finish four projects of work?

17 Go to the Project window and drag the Question Authority FOREGROUND composition over the New Composition icon at the bottom of the window to place it as a layer in a new composition. Press Cmd/Ctrl+K to change the resulting composition's name to **Question Authority FINAL** and click OK. If the LIL124.mov background clip is still in Question Authority FOREGROUND, go into that composition and remove it; you need to place it differently in the hierarchy.

18 Add the Question Authority BACKGROUND composition as a layer below the foreground, also starting at 0:00.

Its scale is oversized for this composition.

19 Press S for the Scale control, Ctrl/right-click on the value, and select Edit Value. Then change the Units pulldown to % of Composition, check the box next to Include Pixel Aspect Ratio, set Width to 100, and click OK. Turn on the Collapse Transformations switches for both layers.

20 Drag the LIL124.mov clip to the bottom layer of the composition, also starting at 0:00.

This is great, except that (unless already looped) it's only three and a half seconds long. Luckily for us, the fine folks at Artbeats designed it to loop seamlessly.

21 In the Project window, highlight the clip and press Cmd/Ctrl+F to bring up the Interpret Footage dialog box. At the bottom, where it says Loop, enter **4** in the field (unless it says 4 already) and click OK. Next, be sure to extend the layer duration bar so that it spans the length of the composition. (Press End to go to the last frame of the composition and press Alt/Option+] to extend the layer's out point.)

Let's make this looping background vary in tone over time.

22 For the layer, set Effect > Adjust > Hue & Saturation. You'll start with the layer in a greenish tone; set the Master Hue to −160.

It would be nice to set an expression using time to have the hue change (so that if you changed the duration it would automatically scale itself), but it's not possible to set an expression for Master Hue in After Effects.

23 Set a keyframe at 0:00 for Channel Range and then go to the end (use your End key or go to 11:29) and change the Master Hue value to 90.

24 Now add sound. Import **Question_Authority.mp3** from the Footage folder of Projects 12–15 and drop it in at 0:00. It has been designed by Dave Levison (**www.h-machine.com**) to fit this animation.

25 Preview the animation (with Motion Blur activated, if you have time) or render it out. Don't forget to save your work—and you're all done!

Now, you might think that what you've learned here is rather esoteric and limited to making things move around in a spiral, but upon closer inspection, you'll realize that you've become more comfortable with using trigonometry, which is the gateway to creating animated patterns without keyframes. You've learned how to make a series of layers follow a leader, and you've learned to set a slider control for variables that you want to adjust on the fly, without digging into the expressions text. It's a lot like programming your own plug-in, isn't it? Just wait for the *next* project!

Note: For those of you running with less RAM available, several strategies were discussed in previous projects to optimize your RAM previews. They are as follows: reduce the Composition window size [Cmd/Ctrl +], reduce the resolution [Cmd/Ctrl + Shift + J], reduce the frame rate (Shift-click on the RAM Preview Play button), and set a Region of Interest with the ROI button at the bottom of the Composition window.

Final Note: You'll notice that your render or preview becomes progressively slower the further you go into the animation. This is because you are creating an effect that requires cumulative data. To create the next step of the spiral, the program needs to know the data from all previous frames. At this point, these calculations are slow using expressions.

Modifications

You can use the same basic principles of this project to derive a number of different looks for this animation or other animations that use the same techniques. You should be able to grasp how you might do the following, based on what you've done here:

- Vary the tightness/looseness of the spiral and the leader/follower path by keyframing the effect parameters on the Follower Settings layer.
- Change the spiral's color or opacity as it radiates outward (can also be done with keyframes).
- Make the question mark followers successively smaller as they become more distant from the leader.

You will also find other powerful uses for creating leader/follower animations. For example, in this case, your animation proceeds at a steady rate, set by the expression. But try keyframing the leader to move around the frame more at random or with specific starts and stops, and you'll find the behavior of the followers even more interesting to watch.

Also, now that you're getting more comfortable with linear and how it works, keep in mind that the other interpolation methods (ease, ease_in, and ease_out, all under the Interpolation submenu in Expressions) work exactly the same as linear; they just add eases at each end or at the start or end (respectively). You don't really have a use for eases in this case, but now that you know how linear interpolations work, you can replace linear with these ease functions where appropriate.

Finally, get into the habit of linking expressions whose values you want to tweak to Expressions Controls effects. Adobe supplies all six basic types of effect controls, although most of the time, slider is the one you'll want. Remember, too, that if you want to change the range of the slider from its default of 0 to 100, you can Ctrl-click on the value, choose Edit Value, and then set a new range in the dialog box that pops up.

HOW TO DRAW WITH SPIROGRAPH™

"The true skill of a digital designer is the practiced art of computer programming, or computation…"

—JOHN MAEDA, DIGITAL DESIGNER, IN ***DESIGN BY NUMBERS***

"A simple and fascinating way to DRAW a million marvelous patterns"

—SLOGAN FOR THE ORIGINAL SPIROGRAPH, BY KENNER (NOW HASBRO)

Drawing Patterns with and Without Math

I'm not sure why I'm such a champion of 1970s culture. Maybe it's because that's where I spent my early childhood. (Spirograph and I apparently came into the world in the same year.) Maybe it's because I think of the '70s as the most underrated decade; sure, there's plenty to look back and be embarrassed about, but it was an amazingly creative time when many artists did their most brilliant work. It was the golden age of American filmmaking, the rebirth of Hollywood, from Coppola and Scorcese to Spielberg, Lucas, and Altman. It was a time when artists from David Bowie and Stevie Wonder to Led Zeppelin, James Brown, and Miles Davis reinvented music. What do you think drove the creativity? The drugs? The liberal morals? Synthetic fabrics? The political climate? The drugs?

I have no idea. I was busy with elementary school, and Spirograph was part of that. In this project, you not only will learn how to make your own Spirograph-like patterns draw over time and how to set up controls to easily configure them into "a million marvelous patterns," you'll actually look at two ways to set up these patterns. One will use pure mathematical expressions; the other will use parenting and will require only a single one-line expression. You'll also look at a neat trick using expressions to make one animated object "pick up" and then "drop off" another animation over time.

Project 16

How to Draw with Spirograph™

by Mark Christiansen

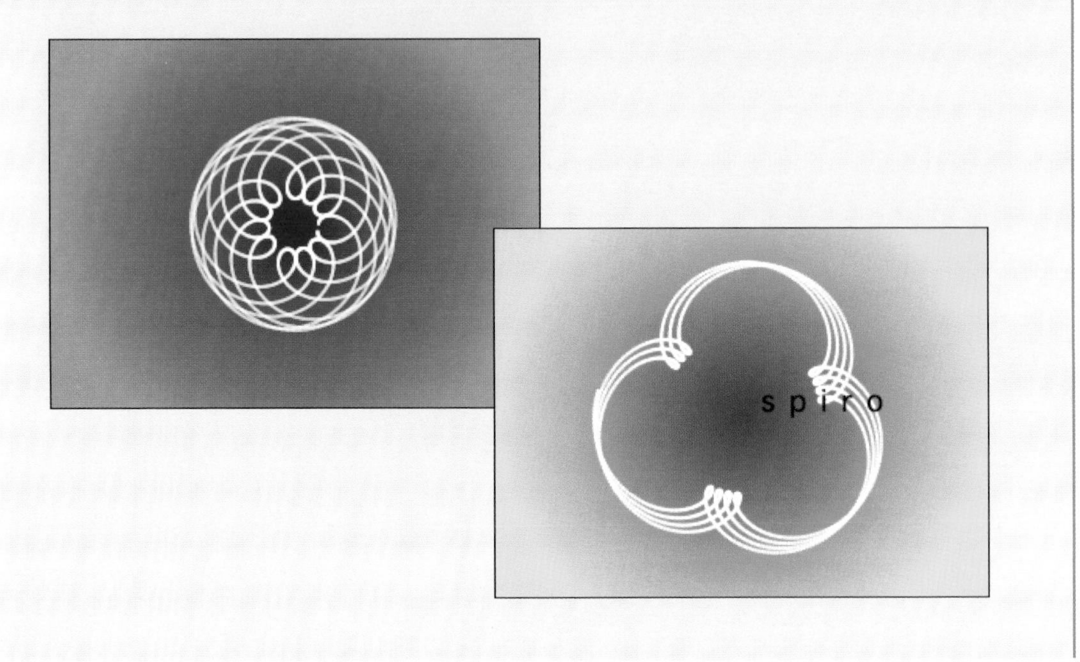

How It Works

This project demonstrates two basic ways to create a Spirograph effect in After Effects; both use the Write-on effect that was also used to draw the spiral in Project 15. This effect is key because it's one of the few ways to trick expressions into affecting pixel data. Expressions have no capability to read pixel data, and in most cases, it is not possible to write pixel data with expressions either. The fact that the Write-on brush can be animated over time provides an exception.

There is a price to pay for this trickery, and it is speed. You are creating the illusion of drawing a continuous pattern, but in fact, expressions and Write-on are only capable of producing a series of dots with intervals between them, and each point has to be calculated separately. The animations get slower as they increase in time because each new frame has to recalculate all of the previous frames to know its position. Hopefully, there will someday be a better way to draw with math.

The way in which an actual Spirograph works is that a pen is inserted into a small hole somewhere inside of a circular gear, offset from its center. This gear is, in turn, placed to the inside or outside of another static gear, and by rolling the circular gear around the static gear with the pen, you create patterns that one would describe as somewhere between "floral" and "psychedelic."

You can use math to re-create one rotation and offset occurring inside another, but if you stop thinking about a Spirograph as literally a circle inside another circle, you'll realize that you can also create the necessary rotation and offset using parenting.

Expressions can be used to set up complex relationships between animations. You'll use interpolation once more to change how two animations—that of the brush drawing the pattern and that of a logo—interact over time.

Getting Started

The beauty of this project's material is that you're going to create everything from scratch, and you will be allowed to modify it however you like. It will make having a copy of After Effects just like having a new Spirograph box from the toy store, still in its shrink wrap and with none of the gears or pens having been chewed by the dog or lost in the couch.

Spirograph— The Mathematical Approach

Let's try animating the pattern with a formula first before examining a less mathematical way to achieve the effect. This section is based on a Java applet that Michael Natkin at Adobe discovered on the web. Java and JavaScript are not the same thing, but making it work was mostly a matter of deciphering and translating the formula. (Check out Appendix D, "Expressions Explained," for more on the difference.) The source can be found (as of this writing) at **www.wordsmith.org/~anu/java/spirograph.html** (or search on "Spirograph" for other sources).

1. Create a new project and go ahead and save it as **spiromania.aep** on your local drive. Create a new composition and choose the Medium option from the Presets pull-down menu to make its size 320×240, 30 fps with square pixels. Set its duration to 15:00 so that you can see how this effect works over time. You can call it **Spirograph (trig)**.

2. At frame 0:00, create a new solid [Cmd/Ctrl+Y] the size of the composition, name it **SpiroScript**, and then click OK.

   I'm tired of looking at gray, black, and white backgrounds, aren't you? Let's make a nice background for this animation.

3 Create a new background (Cmd/Ctrl+Y and composition size once again) and name it **BG**. Using Effect > Render > Ramp (or choosing Ramp from the Effects palette), change the Ramp Shape to Radial Ramp and set the Start of Ramp to 160, 120 and the End of Ramp to 160, 275.

You can set your Start Color and End Color to suit your taste. I've chosen a couple of nice, soothing blues of the same hue, the inner (Start Color) a deeper and more saturated tone and the outer (End Color) more of a cornflower color.

As you did with the follow effect in the preceding project, you're going to set up an invisible control layer with a dummy Slider Control effect so that you can easily control the variables associated with the pattern. This time you need to be able to adjust more than two values, however, so you're going to use multiple instances of Slider Control.

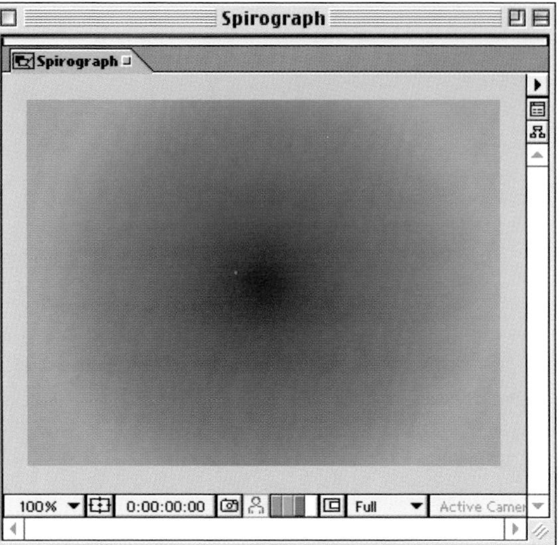

There's no harm in using a circular gradient, but beware if you change its levels in 8-bit color—you might see banding.

4 Create a new Adjustment layer called **Controls** (choose Layer > New > Adjustment Layer). Its settings don't matter.

5 Now choose Effect > Expression Controls > Slider Control. With the effect highlighted in the Effect Controls window, press Return and rename it **Fixed Radius**.

6 Duplicate the effect [Cmd/Ctrl+D], press Return again, and rename this new effect **Moving Radius**. Repeat this duplicate-and-rename process for three more effects, which you should name **Offset**, **Rate**, and **Density**. Your resulting Effect Control window should look like the figure.

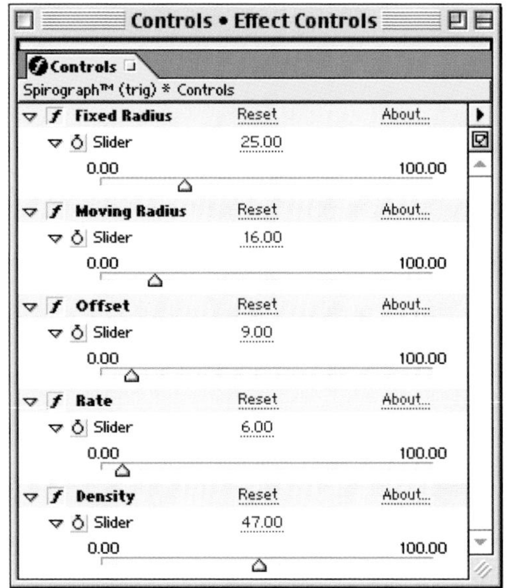

Each effect has been renamed almost as if you had made custom effects.

Now you set up the expression that uses these effect sliders. You're going to pickwhip to each of them.

Note to 5.0 Users: If you don't have the Expressions Controls that ship with After Effects 5.5, you can instead make use of the Sharpen effect (found under Blur & Sharpen in the Effect menu). Pressing Return will still enable you to rename this effect; just substitute Sharpen Amount for each Slider reference in the following steps.

7 Highlight the Controls layer and press E to reveal each effect in the Timeline window. Then twirl down the triangular white arrow next to each to reveal its parameter, to which you'll link your variables.

Your Timeline window should look something like the figure.

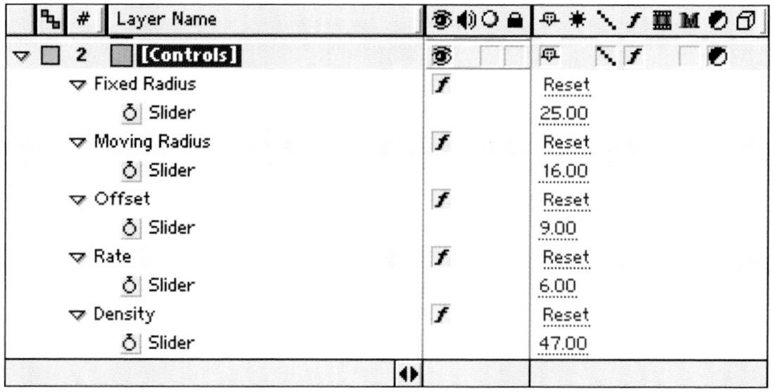

#	Layer Name		
2	[Controls]		
	Fixed Radius	ƒ	Reset
	Slider		25.00
	Moving Radius	ƒ	Reset
	Slider		16.00
	Offset	ƒ	Reset
	Slider		9.00
	Rate	ƒ	Reset
	Slider		6.00
	Density	ƒ	Reset
	Slider		47.00

This is where the individual effect names become helpful.

8 Highlight your SpiroScript layer and choose Effect > Stylize > Write-on. With the layer highlighted, press E and you will see this effect and Ramp revealed. Twirl down the white arrow next to Write-on and highlight the first parameter, Brush Position. Now add an expression by Option/Alt+clicking on the stopwatch for this parameter.

You're going to replace the text that appears for the expression with four variables corresponding to the first four effects in your Controls layer. You'll call these "R" for Fixed Radius, "r" for Moving Radius, "O" for Offset, and "t" for Rate. You've probably already guessed what you need to do; enter each of these on its own line followed by an equal (=) sign and then pickwhip up to the corresponding effect parameter in Controls. End each line with a semi-colon and a carriage return to start a new line. The result looks like the following (comments following double slashes [//] are mine):

```
R = this_comp.layer("Controls").effect("Fixed Radius").param("Slider");
➥//radius of the fixed circle
r = this_comp.layer("Controls").effect("Moving Radius").param("Slider");
➥//radius of the moving circle
O = this_comp.layer("Controls").effect("Offset").param("Slider");
➥//offset of the pen point
t = this_comp.layer("Controls").effect("Rate").param("Slider") * time;
➥//rate at which it is drawn
```

9 Now add your formula on the line below the last variable.

```
x = ((R+r)*Math.cos(t) - (r+O)*Math.cos(((R+r)/r)*t)) + (this_comp.width/2);
y = (R+r)*Math.sin(t) - (r+O)*Math.sin(((R+r)/r)*t) + (this_comp.height/2);
[x,y]
```

This will currently generate an error if you press Enter or click outside of the text window because your sliders are still all set to zero. Feel free to move the time control a few seconds into the animation and try moving the values up a bit, somewhere in the 1 to 30 range for each of them. To get a classic Spirograph image, try entering the largest value for Fixed Radius, a value that is a fraction of that (half or a third and so on) for Moving Radius, a value that is a fraction of Moving Radius for Offset, and something modest for Rate (like a number under 10). Your dots are very spaced apart right now; you'll be setting your final slider to control that next.

Keep trying different values. The best results seem to come from values that have no mathematical relationship to each other. Try cranking some of the values much higher just to see what they do.

Okay, let's set your last effect control, Density, which controls how often Write-on draws a new point. Remember that you're free to set more controls than this if you feel you need them; line thickness, for example, is something you might want to tweak.

10 Below Brush Position among the parameters for Write-on is Brush Spacing (secs). Highlight it and set an expression (Option/Alt + Shift + =; if you've been playing along, you don't need me to remind you). Pickwhip up to the Slider control for Density, which should still be revealed on the Controls layer.

11 Press Enter and—whoops!—your shape disappeared.

That's because the values you want for this parameter are very small. Let's divide to bring your effect control into range.

Note: I tried dissecting this formula into plain English for you, but it gets hard to follow when you are multiplying all of your parameters together combined with cosine. If you want to examine the formula, look at the basic structure of each line, as follows.

First, **(R+r)*Math.cos(t)** sets the maximum extent reachable by adding the two radii together and multiplying them by the cosine of the current time. Remember that cosine always returns a value between 0 and 1, and it translates a linear progression—like the advance of time, in this case—into numbers that describe a curve.

From this, it subtracts the most complicated part of the formula, that which determines the offset from the maximum possible extent, again by multiplying by the cosine of a number that again increments linearly with time.

Finally, all of this is added to the width or height of the composition divided by 2, also known as the center. You'll use this a lot in expressions because the X, Y coordinates (0, 0), which are the mathematical center of any geometric formula, are not the center of the composition—they're the upper-left corner.

12 Place your cursor at the beginning of the line and insert **.1** followed by a forward slash (**/**) symbol (spaces around the / are optional).

This moves the Density slider values down into a range where setting the control to single digits should allow for reasonably fast updates even further down the Timeline, but moving it up into double digits will lead to a much smoother curve.

13 When adjusting for a final look, remember to set your layers to Best quality.

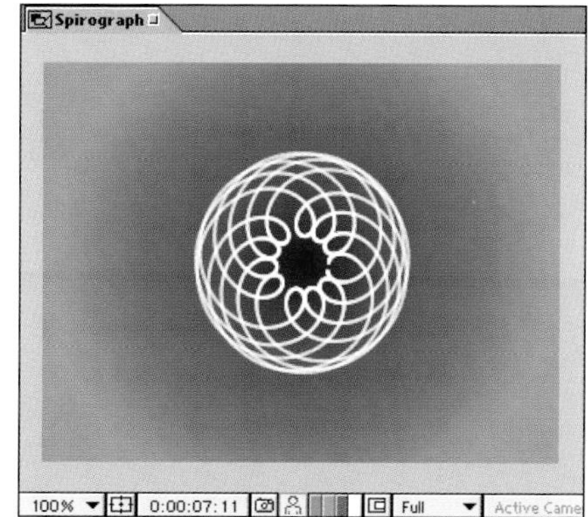

Ah, what a lovely math blossom, don't you agree?

Spirograph—The Parenting Approach

When I was searching around for a formula that would let me do Spirograph-like patterns, I mentioned the problem to Stu Maschwitz at The Orphanage, an independent film and effects studio in San Francisco. He was able to think outside the proverbial box or, in this case, think outside the clear plastic gears. He rapidly came up with a way to draw these patterns without the need for trigonometry, instead using After Effects 5's new parenting controls. By rotating the Brush Position around a couple of nulls, which are themselves in rotation, you can achieve an identical effect. Let's try it. You'll start with the same first three steps as before.

1 Create a new composition and choose the Medium pull-down option to make its size 320×240, 30 fps with square pixels. Set its duration to 15:00 so that you can see how this effect works over time. You can call it **Spirograph (parenting)**.

2 At frame 0:00, create a New Solid [Cmd/Ctrl+Y] the size of the composition, name it **Background & Brush**, and then click OK.

3 Add a background with Effect > Render > Ramp. The settings are as follows: Change Ramp Shape to Radial Ramp and set the Start of Ramp to 160, 120 and the End of Ramp to 160, 275.

Again, choose whichever colors you like; I'm going for a warm red/orange/yellow spectrum this time.

4 Copy your Controls layer from the other composition.

You'll make this version use those same effect controls, which will transfer over when you copy and paste the layer.

5 Press E with the pasted Controls layer highlighted and twirl all five white arrows down to reveal the Slider parameters for each so that you can pickwhip to them.

6 Create a new solid [Cmd/Ctrl+Y], call it **Fixed Radius**, and make its dimensions 2×100. Duplicate it [Cmd/Ctrl+D] and rename the duplicate [Cmd/Ctrl + Shift + Y] **Moving Radius**. Under the Parent column in the Timeline window, set the parent of Moving Radius as Fixed Radius. (If you don't see the Parent column, Ctrl/right-click on one of the gray column labels [like Source Name], choose Panels, and then choose Parent, as in the figure.)

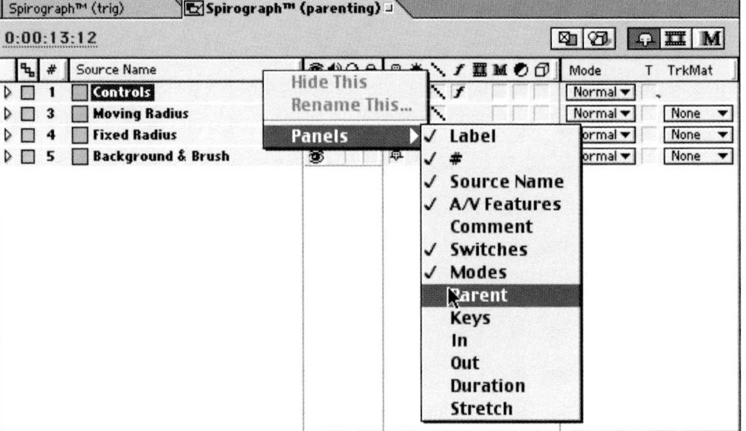

Panels can be turned on and off via their context menu.

7 Create a 2×2 solid called **Offset**.

Its size doesn't matter because you're only interested in its center, which will correspond to the Brush Position. Making it 2×2 is just a reminder that it describes a point. Parent Offset to Moving Radius. You don't need to see any of the solids you just created, so turn off Visibility for all three layers (Moving Radius, Fixed Radius, and Offset). Your Timeline window should look like the figure.

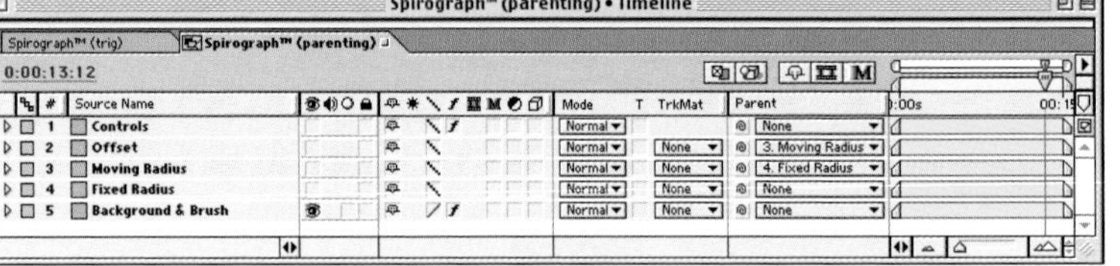

Your second and third layers have been parented in succession.

This doesn't make much sense yet; don't worry, everything will be clearer in a moment. You're going to link the effect controls for Fixed Radius, Moving Radius, and Offset to the Y value of their anchor points.

8 Highlight the Fixed Radius, Moving Radius, and Offset layers and Press A to reveal the Anchor Point control for each.

9 Start with Fixed Radius; highlight Anchor Point and set an expression (Option/Alt+click the stopwatch). Set a variable called **a** to equal (=) the value for the Fixed Radius slider in Controls (use the pickwhip to link to it). Add a semicolon (;) at the end of the line, start a new line and enter the final value **[1, a]**, and then press Enter.

The second Anchor Point value, in red, should equal the value shown on the Fixed Radius slider in Controls.

10 Repeat this process for Moving Radius and Offset, linking each to its respective control but otherwise keeping each expression the same.

Now you're going to set an expression for Rate that will control the rotation of the Fixed Radius, which will in turn control the rotation of the Moving Radius.

11 Highlight the Fixed Radius and Moving Radius layers and press R to reveal the Rotation controls for each. Highlight Rotation under Fixed Radius and set an expression. Set a variable by typing **m** = and then pick-whip to Slider under Rate within Controls. (It should still be visible; if not, reveal it so that you can pickwhip to it.) Add a semicolon (;) to end the line, insert a carriage return, and then on the next line type **m * 100 * time**, which scales your Rate amount by 100 and causes the Rotation value to increase over time.

Note: Parenting these layers and offsetting the Anchor Points is the way you get around using trigonometry. Each layer is parented to the (0, 0) point on the previous layer and rotates around its own anchor point. By changing the location of the anchor point on the Y-axis, you change the radius when, in your next step, you start rotating the layer.

12 Highlight Rotation under Moving Radius and set an expression. This time, type in the following to replace the default text:

```
m = (this_comp.layer("Fixed Radius").anchor_point[1] + anchor_point[1]) /
➥anchor_point[1];
m * this_comp.layer("Fixed Radius").rotation
```

Did you figure out which parts you could enter using the pickwhip? What you're doing here is making the rotation of the Moving Radius behave like the inner ring of a Spirograph. Its rate of rotation moves proportionally to the outer ring, and the proportion can be found by adding the radii of both rings and then dividing by the radius of the inner ring.

The only thing left to do is set the Write-on effect and link the Brush Position to the Offset layer. You'd think this would be very straightforward, wouldn't you? Just set an expression for Brush Position and pickwhip it to the Position value for Offset, right? Try it and see what values you get for Brush Position. It will be a static value of 1 for X and whatever you have set for Offset as Y.

The problem is that Position within Offset is a value local to Offset, which tells you nothing about its position within the composition overall. The position of Offset, as far as that layer's Position control is concerned, is static. The movement occurs as a result of this layer having been parented to two other layers, so you need a way to capture its position in absolute or "world" space as it changes over time.

Fortunately, the Layer Space Transforms methods within expressions are designed for just this type of situation. The only downside is that they are less than straightforward to set up.

13 Let's start by entering the correct expression and then you can analyze it; replace whatever text is in your Brush Position Expression window with the following:

```
offset=this_comp.layer("Offset");
p=offset.anchor_point;
offset.to_world(p)
```

The variables here exist only to make the final line easier to read; you could use a single-line expression instead, which would look like this:

```
this_comp.layer("Offset").to_world(this_comp.layer("Offset").anchor_point)
```

Note: The only case in which you have to consider local versus composition or world coordinates is when you're dealing with Position. The preceding one-line expression is basically saying, "Go to the Offset layer in this composition and send its Anchor Point value to world coordinates." However, there are a couple of keys to doing it right that you should keep in mind.

First, before you use "to_world" or "to_comp," you must call the layer that you're sending to world or comp coordinates; otherwise, you are transforming the layer on which the expression lives.

Also, you used Anchor Point as your tracking point for the brush instead of Position. Why? Because Position is not a local value; in this case, for example, Position is being inherited from the parent layer Moving Radius, which in turn is inheriting Position from its parent, Fixed Radius. Anchor Point and effect coordinate values, on the other hand, also contain positional data, but they are always local coordinates.

As Michael Natkin at Adobe, who helped me work this out, said, "This is super tricky stuff. Even those of us who make a living dealing with transform spaces get confused by it."

THE HANDOFF AND PICK UP AND DROP

Let's do one more nifty little trick before you call it a day with this tutorial. You're going to animate a title in front of your Spirograph pattern and then get it to gradually be picked up by the movement of the pattern itself and then be handed back to the original animation. Ready? First let's do a simple keyframed title animation.

1. Create a new solid the size of the composition, name it **Text Null**, and click OK. Choose Effect > Text > Basic Text. (Some people will tell you never to bother with Basic Text, but in this case, it suits us fine.) Type **Spiro** as the text (or whatever you like), choose a typeface you like (I'm using the default, Geneva), and click OK. Now change the Fill Color to black (you can use the Eyedropper on something black in the interface itself) and set the Size to 18 and the Tracking to 50.

   You are also free to change these options. I'm just trying for something with an acceptable basic look.

2. Set some Position keyframes to bring the text on from out of the frame, hold it at the center for a few seconds, and then exit back out of the frame. I've set an offscreen keyframe of –90, 120 at 0:15 and a hold keyframe of the center position, 160, 120, at 2:00. (Use Cmd/Ctrl + Option + H to highlight a keyframe and toggle it to a hold keyframe.) Set a matching keyframe at 5:00 by clicking the Position check box in the A/V Features column (and use Cmd/Ctrl + Option + H again to toggle off the hold for this keyframe, turning it back to a linear key). Finally, at 8:00, set a keyframe off the opposite side of the composition, at a Position of 410, 120.

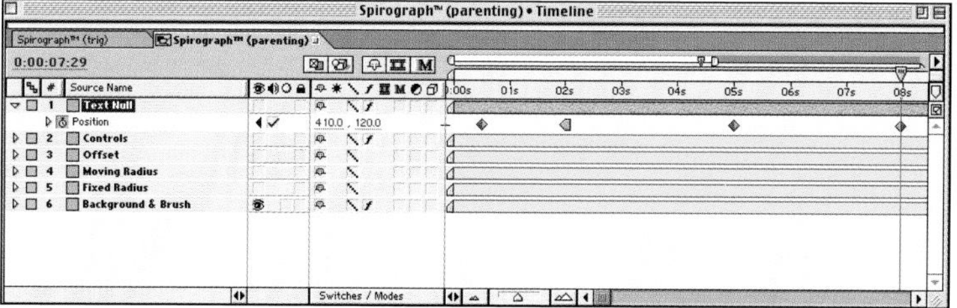

Our basic text animation has been set.

3 Preview the animation.

You'll see that you have the most basic left-to-right text animation the world has ever known. At this point, you might want to turn off your Background & Brush layer or turn Density way down; your preview will go a lot faster without it. However, because the text is black, you should make sure your background is something lighter than black.

4 Use Cmd/Ctrl + Shift + B to change the background color.

I just eyedropped the background of the pop-up window. Okay, you're done with your basic text animation (other than using it as a reference).

5 Turn the animation's Visibility off. Create a new solid called **Spirographic** the size of the composition. Copy the Basic Text from the Effect Control window of Text Null [Cmd/Ctrl+C], highlight Spirographic, and paste it.

Let's start with a handoff, which is dead simple using the "linear" method.

6 With Spirographic still highlighted, press P to reveal the Position controls. Set an expression and, with the text "Position" highlighted, choose **linear(** from under Interpolation in the Expressions pull-down. Click your forward arrow to go to the end of the line.

7 Type **time,** (with a space after it) to set the first parameter, which tells linear to use values at the current time. Next, following a comma and a space after "time," type in **1, 3,** (with a space after it) to have the handoff start at 1:00 and be completed by 3:00.

The fourth parameter is the value from which you're interpolating, the position of Text Null.

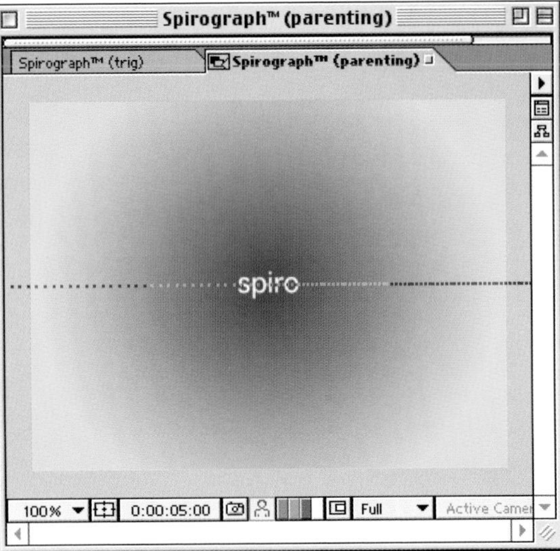

With layer paths turned on, you can see just how flat your animation is.

8 Reveal the Position keyframes of Text Null (if they're not already revealed) by highlighting Text Null and pressing P. Now pickwhip to the word "Position" to add the fourth parameter, followed by a comma and a space.

The fifth and final parameter, the value to which you're interpolating, is the Brush Position of Background & Brush.

9 Reveal the Brush Position of Background & Brush by highlighting that layer and pressing EE. Now pickwhip to the words "Brush Position." End the expression with a close parenthesis to match the open parenthesis after "linear." Your final expression looks like this:

```
linear(time, 1, 3, this_comp.layer("Text Null").position,this_comp.layer
➥("Background & Brush").effect("Write-on").param("Brush Position"))
```

10 Preview the animation. You'll see the text move gradually from its source animation (Text Null) to that of the Spirograph. Pretty cool.

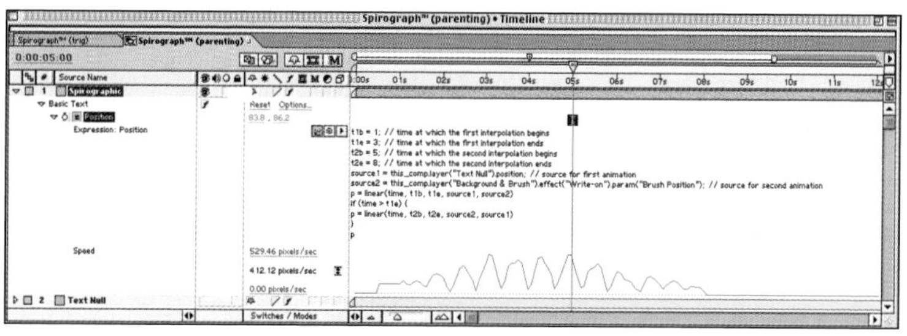

It's a complex expression, but the graph shows the result: A linear animation picks up the variations of the Spirograph pattern between 1:00 and 8:00.

Now let's say you want the animation to transition back to its original linear path from 5:00 to 8:00 where it exits the frame. All you have to do is set a second linear animation, the inverse of the one you just set (and with new start and end frames), and then create an if/else statement that tells After Effects when to perform each interpolation. Here is the expression to do this, which is simpler than it looks:

```
p = linear(time, 1, 3, this_comp.layer("Text Null").position, this_comp.layer
➥("Background & Brush").effect("Write-on").param("Brush Position"));
if (time > 3) {
p = linear(time, 5, 8, this_comp.layer("Background & Brush").effect
➥("Write-on").param("Brush Position"), this_comp.layer("Text Null").position)
}
p
```

Note: All you've done is put **p =** before your previous linear expression to make it a conditional variable, followed by a semicolon. On the following line, you've started your conditional **if(** followed by the condition that time is greater than 3, the end of your first interpolation, and a close parenthesis. If that's the case, then you do what follows between brackets {}, which is the same linear interpolation but from 5 to 8 seconds and with the interpolation values in inverted order. On the final line, the single letter **p** calls the else statement, the interpolation that occurs before the 3:00 point.

The final AEP file for this project contains the expression with extra, commented variables so that it is easier to reuse at a later date. Here it is. Note that the expression itself, contained in the last five lines, should be easier to decipher now.

```
t1b = 1; // time at which the first interpolation begins
t1e = 3; // time at which the first interpolation ends
t2b = 5; // time at which the second interpolation begins
t2e = 8; // time at which the second interpolation ends
source1 = this_comp.layer("Text Null").position; // source for first animation
source2 = this_comp.layer("Background & Brush").effect("Write-on").param
➥("Brush Position"); // source for second animation
p = linear(time, t1b, t1e, source1, source2)
if (time > t1e) {
p = linear(time, t2b, t2e, source2, source1)
}
p
```

MODIFICATIONS

Pattern-form expressions, parenting, and interpolations provide a great base for infinite customizable modifications.

With the sliders, you have the option to easily change to values that affect how your Spirograph pattern looks. You can also parent other items to the Brush Position, such as trailing text (as with the row of question marks in the last project) or even crazier stuff like a 3D camera position or target.

Interpolations, moreover, can unlock a whole new world of translating animations. Try creating some keyframe animations of your own that use the handoff and the pick-up-and-drop capabilities of interpolation. Remember, too, that your interpolation doesn't have to be linear. You can choose to ease in or out of your interpolation. At some point, you will find that a very handy option.

The need for if/else statements doesn't come up all the time, but there are cases in which nothing else will solve your expressions problem. Become comfortable with the syntax for creating if/else statements so that you can create them when you need them.

Finally, just as with a real Spirograph, you can experiment with other shapes along which to animate. For example, a Spirograph set comes not only with torus-shaped outer radius rings but also with long, narrow, linear cogs along which to twirl the moving cog (see the figure). How would you do that?

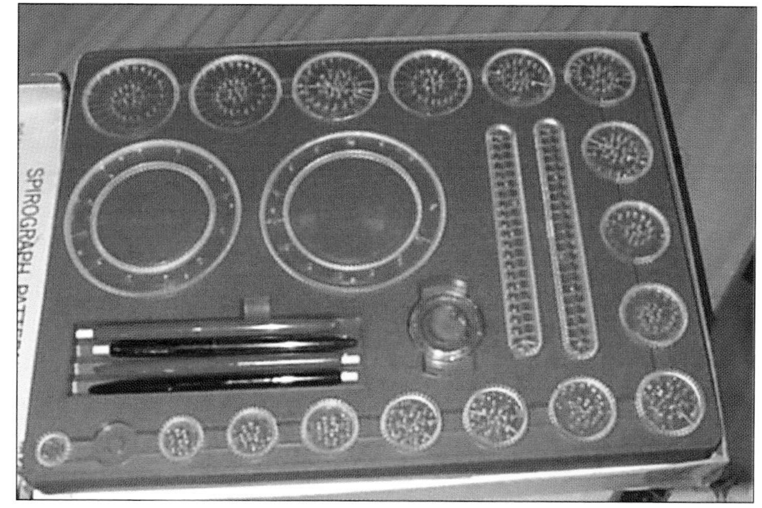

A simple and fascinating way to draw a million marvelous patterns.

SYNCHRONIZING MOTION WITH AUDIO

"You are in another universe where the dominating force is sound!"

—LORD OOK, ***WAVE TWISTERS***

Automatic Synchronization of Motion to Audio Using Motion Math and Time Remap

In this tutorial, you will produce an animation in which a mutant baby (the villain, Lord Ook, from DJ Qbert's *Wave Twisters*) works the fader knob on a mixer console in perfect synchronization with the accompanying audio. The project was constructed so that a minimum of manual animation is required. All you have to do is move the hand of the cartoon baby so that it matches with a single, front-to-back motion of the fader knob. (The knob itself is a QuickTime movie produced in the 3D package Electric Image.) From there, you will allow After Effects to perform the otherwise tedious task of matching the motion of the hand and fader with the audio by using the Layer Audio Motion Math script to set keyframes for the Time Remap property of the composition as a whole.

Project 17

Synchronizing Motion with Audio

by Michael "Syd" Garon and Eric Henry

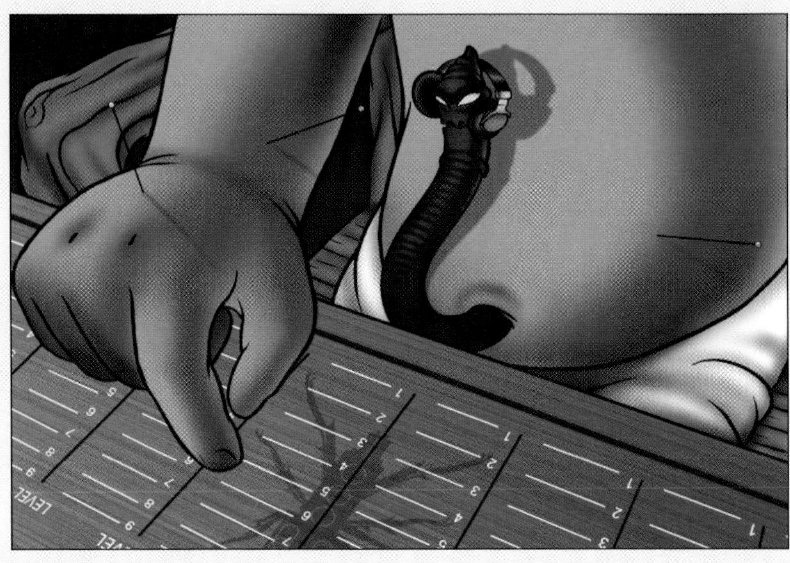

How It Works

Before you get down to business, consider briefly the two parts of this equation, Time Remap and Layer Audio Motion Math. When you enable Time Remapping for a time-based layer (an audio clip, image sequence, QuickTime movie, or composition with motion in it), you can then set keyframes that correspond to *points in time* in the original layer. By default, After Effects automatically sets a keyframe at the beginning of the layer with a value of 0 seconds and one at the end of the layer with a value corresponding to the total duration of the clip or composition. This produces no change whatsoever; you get temporal movement that flows normally from beginning to end.

If, however, you swap the position of the beginning and end keyframes, the clip will start at the end and go to the beginning. In other words, the clip is run in reverse. If you set a bunch of random values for Time Remap keyframes, it will be as if you are scrubbing randomly back and forth over the clip as the Time Remap keyframes force certain frames of the clip to play back at specified points on the timeline. In your case, the back and forth scrubbing will not be random; it will be generated instead by the Layer Audio Motion Math script.

The Layer Audio Motion Math script will assign temporal values for your original composition that correspond to the amplitude or loudness of the audio. As the audio gets louder and softer, values for *earlier* or *later* points in time within your original composition will be recorded as Time Remap keyframes, causing the playback of your composition to scrub back and forth in sync with the audio.

Getting Started

This project has been assembled from Photoshop layers and a QuickTime movie of the fader moving. A quick RAM preview (press the RAM Preview button in the Time Controls palette) will illustrate that, except for the fader movie, there has been no animation applied to this project.

Animating the Hand

Start by creating the initial animation that will be used for the Time Remapping.

1. Copy the entire folder for this project from the CD-ROM to your hard drive.

   This will speed up performance by preventing After Effects from having to access files from the CD-ROM.

2. From the folder you've just copied, open [Cmd/Ctrl+O] the project **AudioSync.aep**. Select File > Save As and save the project under the name **AudioSync1.aep** so that you can keep a "clean" copy of the original to refer back to if necessary.

   Note: The time display for this project is in frames, not timecode. After Effects 5 changed how time display settings are handled, making it a project-based setting rather than a Preference. You can change the time Display Style by selecting File > Project Settings [Cmd+Option+Shift/Ctrl+Alt+Shift + K] or by simply [Cmd/Ctrl] clicking on the timecode numbers in either the Composition or Timeline windows.

3. In the Timeline window, select the hand layer (Layer 3) and press A to inspect its Anchor Point property.

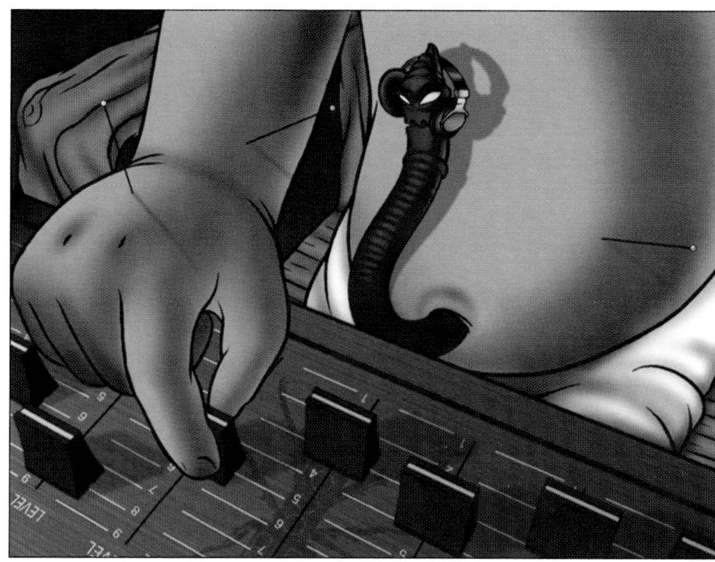

Animate the hand.

4 Click on the Anchor Point property's numerical values and enter **X = 195, Y = 368**.

This will move the Anchor Point for the hand layer to the point where the finger touches the fader. Notice that the layers shift upward after the Anchor Point coordinates are changed.

Note: You can also move the Anchor Point using the Pan Behind tool [Y key] from the Tool palette; this changes the Anchor Point and Position properties simultaneously.

5 With the hand layer still selected, press P to reveal its Position property and enter the same values as in the previous step: **X = 195, Y = 368**.

You'll see that the layer shifts back downward into place after the Position coordinates are changed.

6 Select the finger layer and, from the Parent pop-up menu, select 3. hand.

If you do not see the Parent panel in the Timeline window, go to the Timeline window menu and choose Panels > Parent. This "parents" the finger layer to the hand layer: Wherever the hand layer goes, the finger must follow it, inheriting its movement.

7 Select the hand layer, whose Position property should still be visible. Holding down the Shift key, press R and S individually to reveal this layer's Rotation and Scale properties, respectively. Create Position, Rotation, and Scale keyframes at frame zero by clicking on the stopwatch icon to the left of each property name under the hand layer.

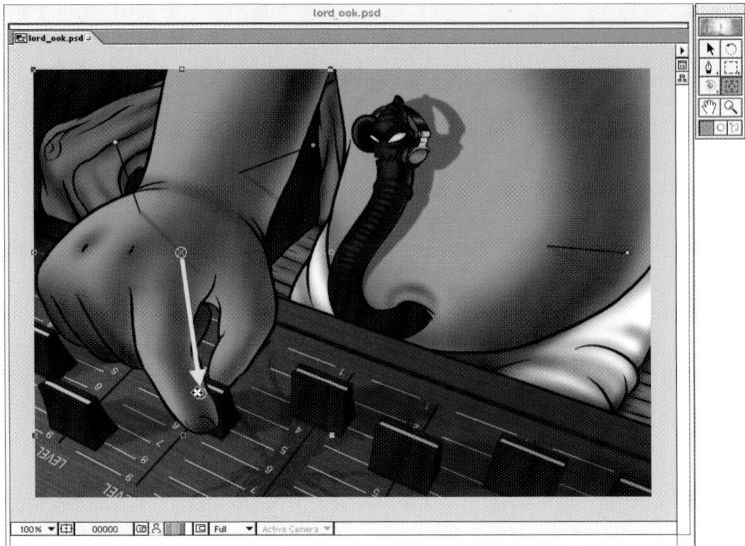

Placing the Anchor Point at the tip of the finger.

Parenting the finger layer to the hand layer.

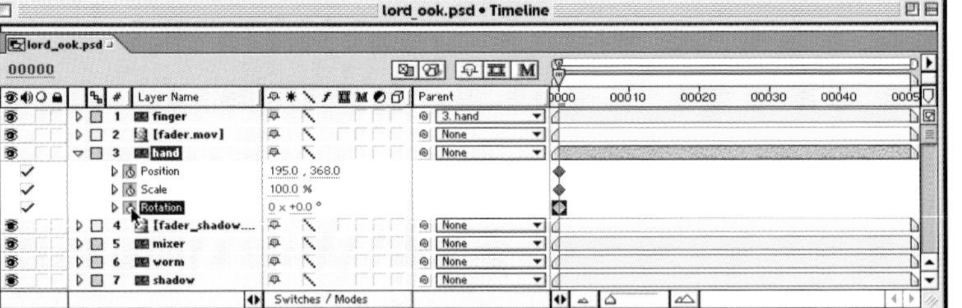

Setting the keyframes.

8 Advance to the end of the composition by pressing the End key (frame 49) and move the hand layer to match the position of the fader that has now moved. After Effects will automatically set a Position keyframe.

9 Stay at frame 49 and Scale the hand to about 99%.

This will simulate depth. The hand is farther away; therefore it would appear smaller to the viewer.

10 Add a little rotation (–4%) for more natural arm movement and to keep the arm from visually crossing the line of the body.

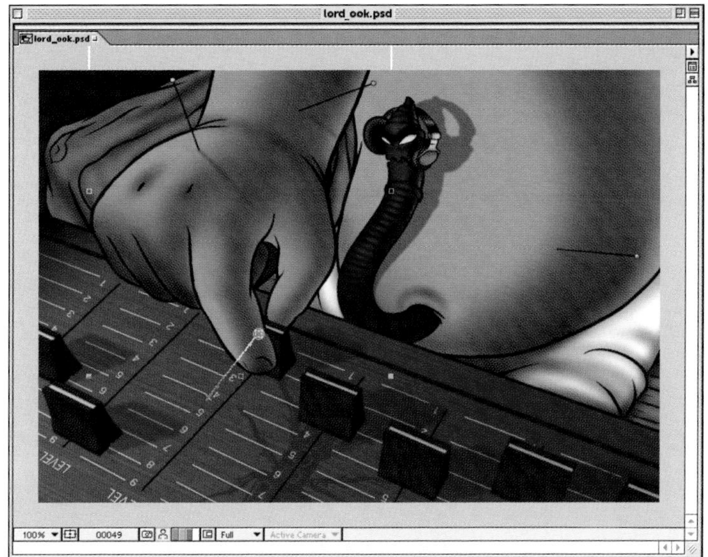

Moving the hand layer to its final position at frame 49.

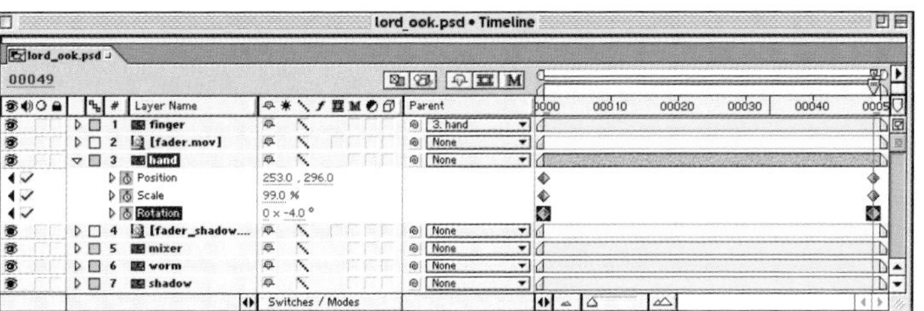

Setting keyframes at the final position.

Remapping Time and Space

Now that you have created a simple downward motion of the fader and hand, you will use this animation as the basis for a more complex, up and down motion synchronized with the audio. This will not require any further animation. To achieve this, you will use Time Remapping to force the temporal movement of your original animation to oscillate back and forth. Furthermore, the Time Remapping keyframes will be automatically generated by the audio itself by applying the Layer Audio Motion Math script.

1 Make a new composition called **Ook time remap**. Choose the Preset NTSC D1, 720×486. For frame rate, enter **29.97**. For duration, enter **240** frames, which is the length of the audio file you'll be using, **anotheruniverse.aif**, located on the accompanying CD-ROM.

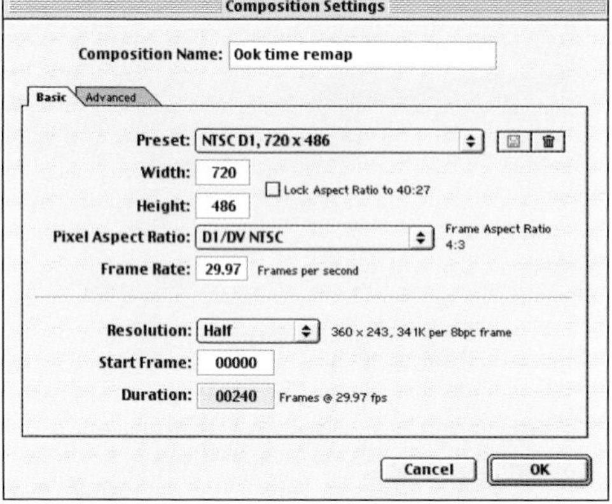

Creating a new composition.

2 Drag the lord_ook.psd composition and the audio file anotheruniverse.aif into this new composition.

Adding the lord_ook.psd composition to the Ook time remap composition.

3 Select the lord_ook.psd composition layer and enable Time Remapping (Layer > Enable Time Remapping) [Cmd+Option/Ctrl+Alt + T].

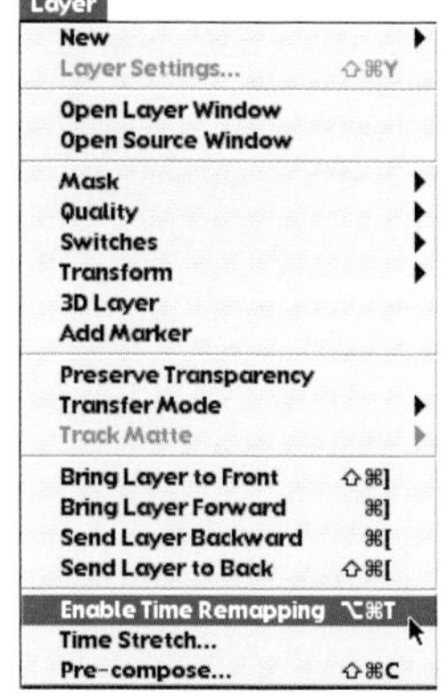

Enabling Time Remapping.

4 Highlight the lord_ook.psd layer and then U on the keyboard. This handy little shortcut displays any properties that have keyframes.

You will notice that Time Remapping has default keyframes when enabled.

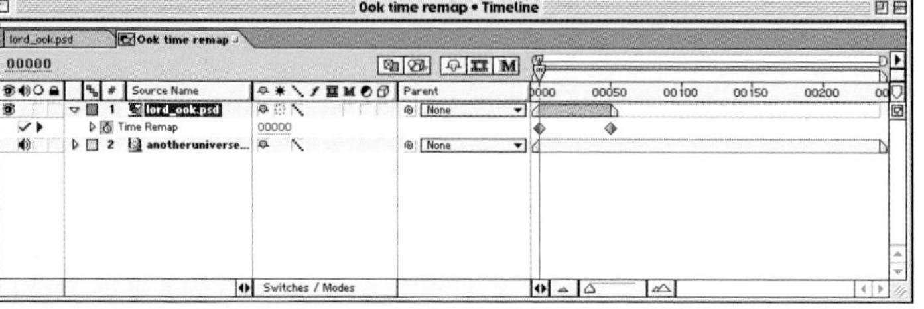

Viewing the Time Remapping keyframes.

5 Drag the layer out point for lord_ook.psd to the end of the composition (frame 239).

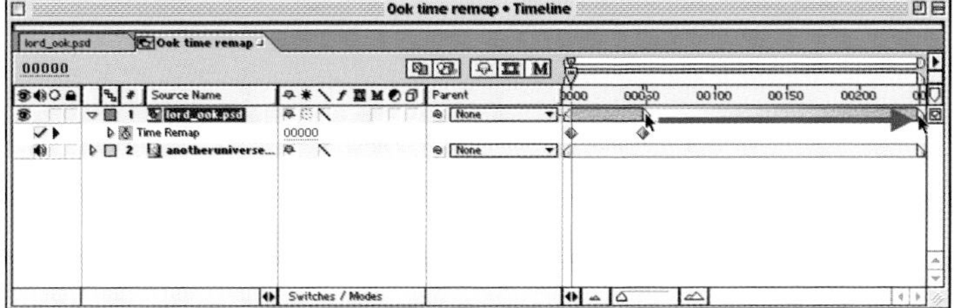

Dragging the layer out point.

Note: Moving the layer out point can also be done by selecting the lord_ook.psd layer, pressing the End key to go to the last frame in the composition, and then pressing Option/Alt+] to pull the layer's out point to the current time indicator.

The Nitty Gritty

In this section, you use Motion Math to generate Time Remapping values.

1 With the lord_ook.psd layer selected, choose Animation > Keyframe Assistant > Motion Math.

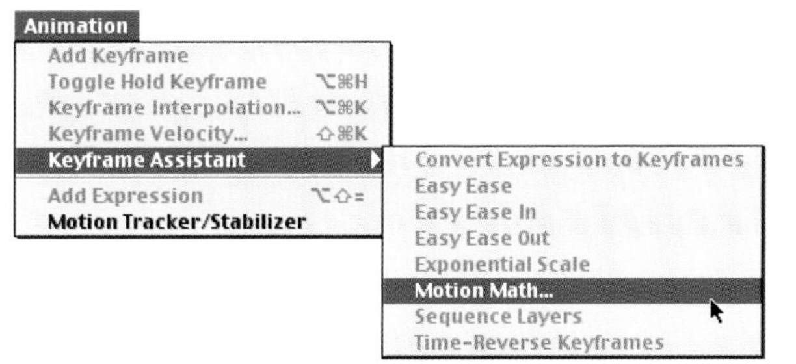

Selecting Motion Math.

Note: When you select a Motion Math script, After Effects frequently doesn't know where it is located on the hard drive. Motion Math scripts are usually kept in the After Effects folder in a subfolder named Motion Math Scripts.

2 Hit the Load button in the Motion Math dialog box, select layeraud.mm in the Motion Math Scripts folder, and click Open.

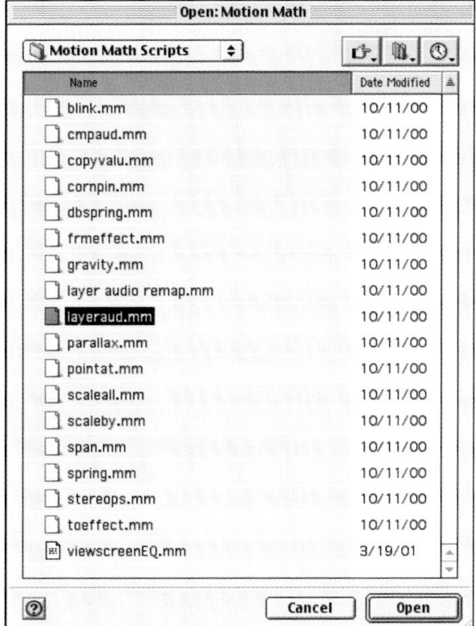

Be sure to select layeraud.mm and *not* layer audio remap.mm.

3 In the Motion Math dialog box, set Layer 1 to lord_ook.psd and set its property to Time Remap. Set Layer 2 to anotheruniverse.aif.

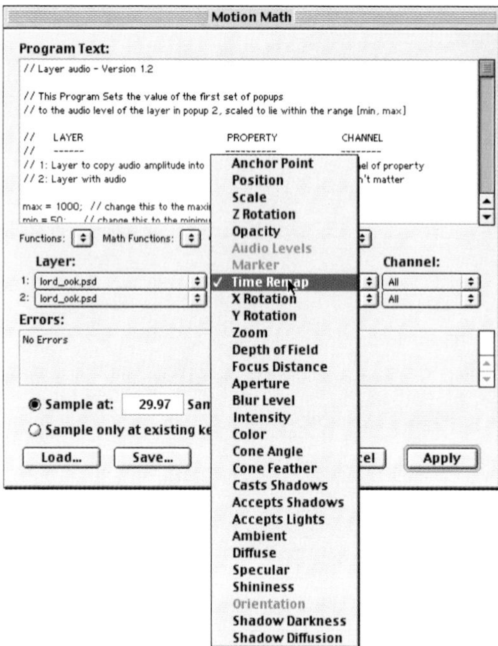

Selecting the Time Remap property.

You might find that Layer 2 is already set correctly because After Effects tries to guess and automatically select a layer with audio. Don't worry about setting the property for Layer 2 because After Effects will automatically set it to Audio Levels. Everything is now properly configured so that Time Remap keyframes for lord_ook.psd will be generated in direct proportion to the audio levels of anotheruniverse.aif. But first, you must set the range within which those Time Remap keyframes can vary.

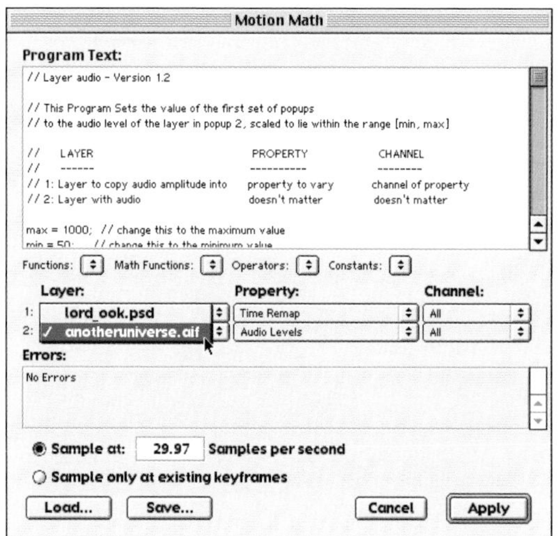

Selecting the layer with audio.

4 Locate the window at the top of the Motion Math dialog box called Program Text.

This window contains the actual programming that enables the script to run, and it includes numerical values that can be changed to achieve different results.

5 Find the text that says "max=" and "min=" (scroll down if necessary).

These numbers represent the latest and earliest points in time (measured in seconds) that you want the time-remapped composition to be forced to display. Given that lord_ook.psd is 50 frames in duration, the maximum value should correspond to the last frame of animation, or frame 49, and the minimum value should be the first frame of animation, or frame 0. Because the script requires values in seconds rather than frames, you need to do a little math to obtain the right numbers. If you divide 49 frames by 29.97 frames per second, you get 1.63 seconds. Zero frames, of course, is equal to zero seconds.

6 Change the max value to **1.63** and the min value to **0**.

Be careful not to disturb any of the syntax in this window when changing the min and max values; otherwise, the script will not work properly.

7 Press the Apply button.

The progress bar lets you know that the script is being applied, and the window closes after it's finished.

8 Notice that 240 keyframes were added to the Time Remap property of the lord_ook.psd layer. Do a RAM preview or render out the shot to take a look at what happened.

Instead of the full range of up and down motion, you will notice that the hand on the mixer console gives only a pathetic little wiggle. This is because the audio levels of anotheruniverse.aif do not go all the way to 100%. If they did, the Time Remap values for lord_ook.psd would have reached the max you set in the Motion Math dialog box, and the hand would have moved all the way to the top of the console when the audio reached its loudest. To compensate, you can input a new max value that is higher, but how much higher? To find out, take a closer look at the keyframe you just generated.

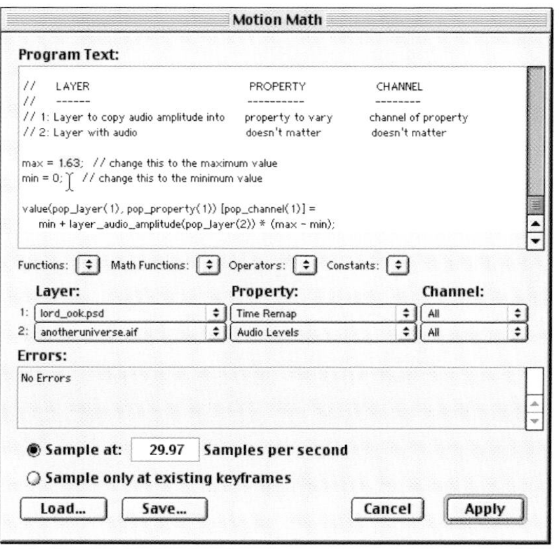

Changing the max value to 1.63.

9 Expand the Time Remap property for the lord_ook.psd layer by clicking the triangle to the left of Time Remap.

You will see a graph of the Time Remap values. (Beneath that is another graph displaying the velocity—or rate of change—of these values, which you can ignore.) Although the graph is very flat, notice that there are a few discernable peaks that correspond to the largest, or latest, Time Remap values.

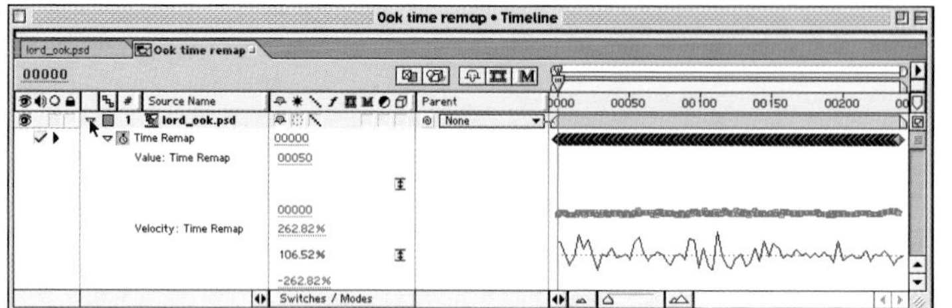

Examining the Time Remap values.

10 Zoom in slightly on your timeline [+ on the main keyboard] and locate the tallest peak on the graph, around frame 56.

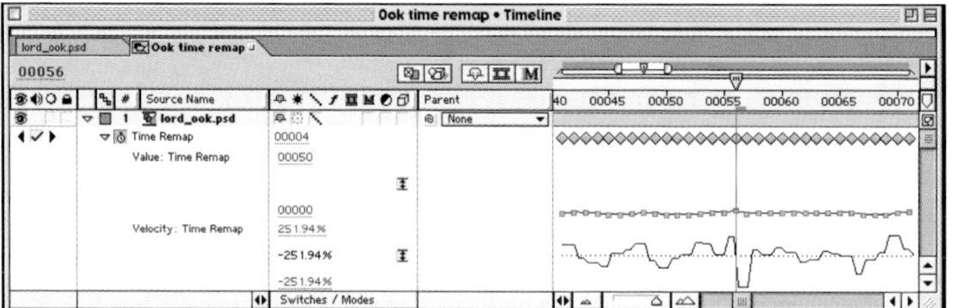

The maximum value is at frame 56.

11 Double-click on the Time Remap keyframe at frame 56. A dialog box appears, revealing that the value at this point in time is 4. Click Cancel.

So instead of peaking at frame 49, as you had planned, your Time Remap keyframes fall short by a factor of approximately 12.25 (49 divided by 4). Now you have a good idea of how much higher you need to set the max value in the Motion Math dialog to reach your target.

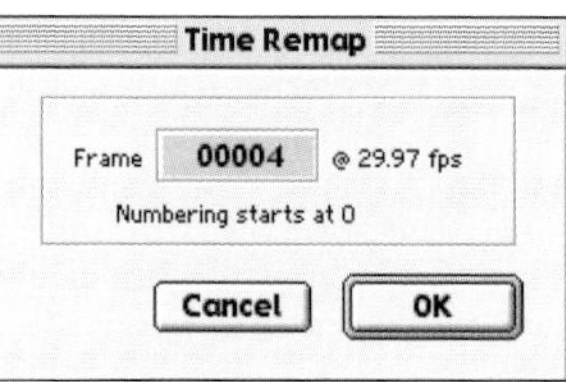

The "latest" keyframe is 4 frames.

12 Go back into Motion Math and enter a new max value of **19.97**. Click Apply.

In step 5, you arrived at a value of 1.63. This would have worked fine had the audio been ideal (that is, 0 to 100% volume). However, real-world audio is rarely this perfect. Take the 1.63 value and multiply it by your new scale factor of 12.25; you get 19.97 ($1.63 \times 12.25 = 19.97$).

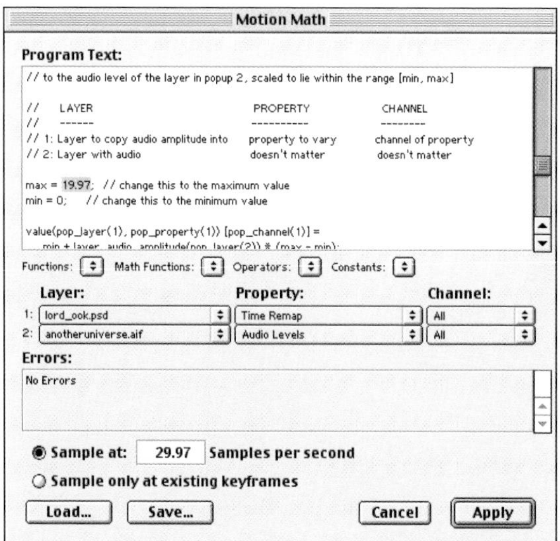

Setting a new maximum value of 19.97.

13 Preview the animation.

Notice that the animation has become much more dynamic. The hand now moves all the way up and down the mixer console. You can confirm that the Time Remap keyframes are peaking at your target value of 49 by double-clicking again on the keyframe at frame 56. A dialog box reveals that the Time Remap value at this point—and hence the frame that lord_ook.psd composition is being forced to display—is 49. Perfect!

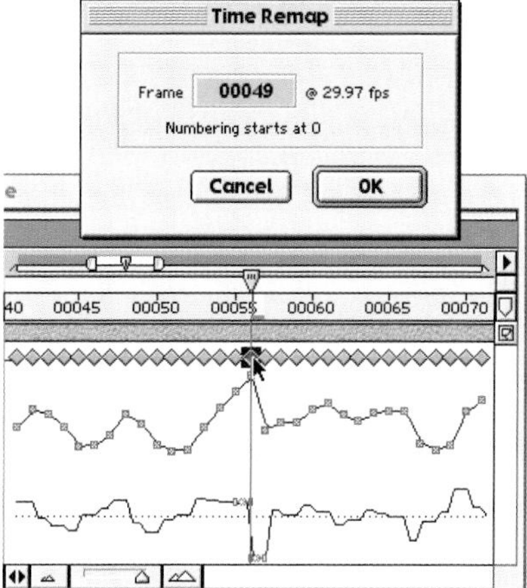

Right on target!

14 Click Cancel.

This process is not always an exact science. It can be difficult to accurately locate the peaks in the graph of Time Remap values. As a result, you might end up with a new max value that is either too low or too high. You should be prepared to engage in some trial and error, incrementally increasing or decreasing the max value until the animation peaks as close as possible to the final frame of the Time Remapped layer without going over. If you do go over, you might notice that the Time Remapped layer is forced to display a black frame because no information exists for points in time later than the end of the composition.

15 Open the nested composition lord_ook.psd and click the Enable Motion Blur button. Next, turn on Motion Blur for the finger and hand layers. You will not see the result of applying the Motion Blur in this composition. Rather, you will see the result of the applied Motion Blur in the Ook time remap composition. Return to the Ook time remap composition and click the Enable Motion Blur button. Preview the results.

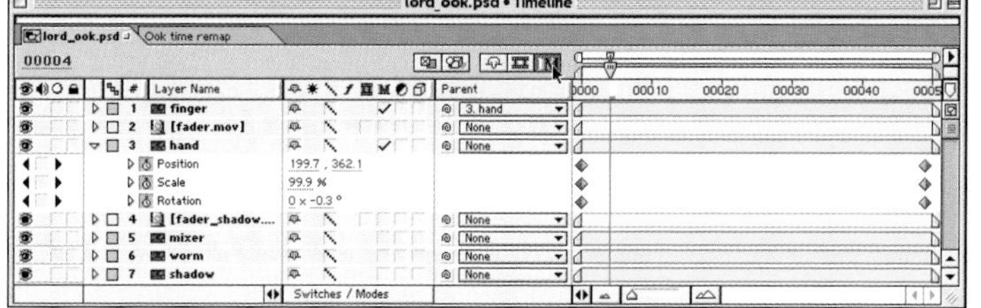

Enabling Motion Blur for the composition and selected layers.

Motion Blur gives the animation a more realistic look—if, in fact, you can call anything with a DJ Voodoo baby and a parasitic worm "realistic." If you are a total perfectionist, you will notice that sometimes the hand and the fader do not line up perfectly. Although both the hand and the fader are now being animated and displayed for the 240 frames of the Ook time remap composition, the fader is a QuickTime movie with 50 distinct frames (and therefore 50 distinct positions), while the hand is a still image that can be rendered in an infinite number of new positions. For the fader to match up with the hand, you need to create new in-between frames for the fader movie using Frame Blending.

16 Open the nested composition lord_ook.psd. Click the Enable Frame Blending button and turn on Frame Blending for the fader.mov and fader_shadow.mov layers. Return to the Ook time remap composition and click the Enable Time Remapping button. Preview the results.

Enabling Frame Blending for the composition and selected Layers.

Note: Turning off Enable Frame Blending and Motion Blur happens by default when you choose the Render Settings preset Best Settings.

Notice that the hand and fader now line up perfectly. Instead of jumping abruptly from one frame of the fader QuickTime movie to the next, Frame Blending tells After Effects to create new in-between frames by inserting a series of dissolves. In this way, both the hand layer and the fader are displayed and animated smoothly over the 240 frames of the Ook time remap composition. At this point, you might want to turn off Enable Frame Blending and Enable Motion Blur, as these options tend to slow performance. You can re-enable them at render time by choosing Enable Frame Blending and Enable Motion Blur for checked layers in the Render Settings dialog box.

MODIFICATIONS

This process is easy to apply to all kinds of animation. For example, you could also use these techniques to make the worm "dance" to the audio. Open the lord_ook.psd composition and use the Pan Behind tool to move the anchor point of the worm and shadow layers to near where the worm meets the torso. Set Rotation keyframes with a value of zero degrees for the layers at frame 0. At frame 49, set the Rotation of the worm layer to –5 degrees and the shadow layer to +3 degrees. Open the Ook time remap composition and watch the worm dance!

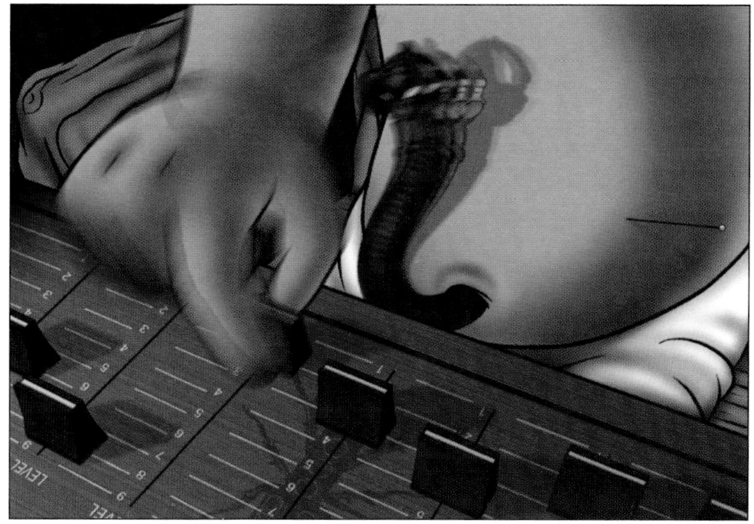

Making the worm dance.

Note: The *Wave Twisters* DVD (available at music/DVD stores everywhere and on Amazon.com) contains many images and scene files from the film as well as permission to use them. The projects are in After Effects, LightWave, and 3ds max formats. For more information on *Wave Twisters*, visit **www.wavetwisters-themovie.com**.

Appendix A

WHAT'S ON THE CD

The accompanying CD-ROM is packed with everything you need to work with this book and with After Effects 5.0 and 5.5. The following sections contain detailed descriptions of the CD-ROM's contents.

For more information about the use of this CD-ROM, review the ReadMe.txt file in the root directory. This file includes important disclaimer information as well as information about installation, system requirements, troubleshooting, and technical support.

> **Technical Support Issues:** If you have any difficulties with this CD, you can access our web site at **www.newriders.com**.

System Requirements

This CD-ROM was configured for use on systems running any version of Windows or the Mac OS. Your machine will need to meet the following system requirements for this CD-ROM to operate properly:

- 2x CD-ROM drive (or faster)
- 24-bit display running at 1024×768 or higher
- QuickTime 5.0.2 or later

Loading the CD Files

To load the files from the CD-ROM, insert the disc into your CD-ROM drive. If autoplay is enabled on your machine, the CD-ROM interface starts automatically the first time you insert the disc. You can copy the files to your hard drive or use them right off the disc.

> **Note:** This CD-ROM uses long and mixed-case filenames, requiring the use of a protected-mode CD-ROM driver.

Exercise Files

This CD-ROM contains all the project and footage files you'll need to complete the exercises in *After Effects 5.5 Magic*, as well as prerendered movies of the projects' final output. These files can be found under Book Examples in the main menu. Each project has its own directory, with the exception of Projects 12 through 15, whose project files are all contained within a single directory. To access the files for Project 2, "Algorithmic Video Distortion," for example, click the Book Examples button from the main menu, click Browse Examples, and open the Project02 folder.

> **Note:** If you are using After Effects 5.0 (instead of 5.5), 5.0-compatible files are stored within each chapter's directory in a folder called _AEv5_projects.

Bonus Appendixes

The CD contains five additional appendixes that cover a range of topics related to the book's main projects. Learn everything from basic expressions to setting up a design studio to building a homemade green screen.

- Appendix B, "The Digital Motion Design Studio."

  Nathan Moody relates the essentials of conceptualizing and building your own motion design studio.

- Appendix C, "The NTSC DV Video Standard and QuickTime."

  Mark Christiansen covers some important points to remember when working with NTSC DV format footage in After Effects.

- Appendix D, "Expressions Explained."

  Mark Christiansen walks you through the basics of using expressions and answers the questions most beginners have about expressions.

- Appendix E, "Difference Mattes."

  Sherry Hitch shows you how to pull a difference matte when you don't have time to use a green screen.

- Appendix F, "No Budget? Build a Do-It-Yourself Green Screen!"

  Sherry Hitch demonstrates how you can create your own green screen from readily available and inexpensive materials.

Read This Before Opening the Software

By opening the CD-ROM package, you agree to be bound by the following agreement:

You may not copy or redistribute the entire CD-ROM as a whole. Copying and redistribution of individual software programs on the CD-ROM is governed by terms set by individual copyright holders.

The installer, code, and images from the authors are copyrighted by the publisher and the authors.

This software is sold as-is, without warranty of any kind, either expressed or implied, including but not limited to the implied warranties of merchantability and fitness for a particular purpose. Neither the publisher nor its dealers or distributors assume any liability for any alleged or actual damages arising from the use of this program. (Some states do not allow for the exclusion of implied warranties, so the exclusion may not apply to you.)

INDEX

B

C

D

E

F

G-H

I

J-K

L

M

N-O

P

Q-R

S

T

U-V

W-Z

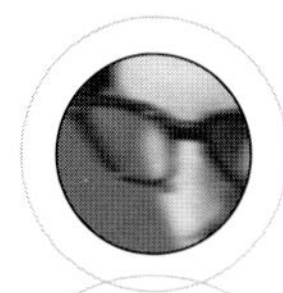
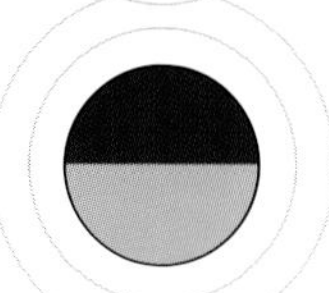

VISIT OUR WEB SITE

WWW.NEWRIDERS.COM

On our web site, you'll find information about our other books, authors, tables of contents, and book errata. You will also find information about book registration and how to purchase our books, both domestically and internationally.

EMAIL US

Contact us at: **nrfeedback@newriders.com**

- If you have comments or questions about this book
- To report errors that you have found in this book
- If you have a book proposal to submit or are interested in writing for New Riders
- If you are an expert in a computer topic or technology and are interested in being a technical editor who reviews manuscripts for technical accuracy

Contact us at: **nreducation@newriders.com**

- If you are an instructor from an educational institution who wants to preview New Riders books for classroom use. Email should include your name, title, school, department, address, phone number, office days/hours, text in use, and enrollment, along with your request for desk/examination copies and/or additional information.

Contact us at: **nrmedia@newriders.com**

- If you are a member of the media who is interested in reviewing copies of New Riders books. Send your name, mailing address, and email address, along with the name of the publication or web site you work for.

BULK PURCHASES/CORPORATE SALES

If you are interested in buying 10 or more copies of a title or want to set up an account for your company to purchase directly from the publisher at a substantial discount, contact us at 800-382-3419 or email your contact information to `corpsales@pearsontechgroup.com`. A sales representative will contact you with more information.

WRITE TO US

New Riders Publishing
201 W. 103rd St.
Indianapolis, IN 46290-1097

CALL/FAX US

Toll-free (800) 571-5840
If outside U.S. (317) 581-3500
Ask for New Riders
FAX: (317) 581-4663

WWW.NEWRIDERS.COM